Advance Praise

Aman bears the awesome Hingorani—Kapila and Nirmal—legacy of the great humanism permeating penology from Hussainara Khatoon onwards. In respecting the rule of law, the book is replete with Hingorani's impress. Aman's present work is an excellent addition to the continuing Kashmir debate.

—**M.N. Venkatachaliah**
Former Chief Justice of India, former Chairman of the National Human Rights Commission and of the National Commission to Review the Working of the Constitution

The book makes fascinating and compelling reading about the trauma and the running sore of partition of the Indian subcontinent. The author has thoroughly researched and covered every aspect of the subject so as to suggest the possible way forward. It will be interesting to see if the suggestions made are prophetic.

—**Ruma Pal**
Former Judge, Supreme Court of India

This book offers fresh insight from a legal, historical and practical perspective on the persistent and at times violent dispute between nuclear India and nuclear Pakistan over Kashmir. Hailing from a prominent family of human rights lawyers, A. Hingorani spares no criticism for the bungling line of leaders in both countries, along with Great Britain, for their failure to find a path to peace. As both countries face larger issues for their citizens' future, this gaping failure is ever more urgent given India's rising struggle with China for regional dominance and Pakistan's internal fight over the true meaning of Islam. Hingorani's book moves that debate in the right direction.

—**George Charles Bruno**
Former US Ambassador

Aman Hingorani's riveting, absorbing and thought-provoking explorations of the Kashmir issue are both broad and deep. Beyond the trodden paths, his historically rich and analytically focused approach is illuminating in every respect. All serious students of international relations and all practitioners of foreign policy will want to come to terms with this penetrating analysis. It will be a much discussed volume in the continuing debate over one of the most prolonged conflicts in world affairs.

—**Dr Victor Mauer**
International Security and Strategic Studies expert, Zurich

Unravelling the
KASHMIR KNOT

Unravelling the
KASHMIR KNOT

Aman M. Hingorani

Los Angeles | London | New Delhi
Singapore | Washington DC | Melbourne

First published in 2016 by

 SAGE Publications India Pvt Ltd
B1/I-1 Mohan Cooperative Industrial Area
Mathura Road, New Delhi 110 044, India
www.sagepub.in

SAGE Publications Inc
2455 Teller Road
Thousand Oaks, California 91320, USA

SAGE Publications Ltd
1 Oliver's Yard, 55 City Road
London EC1Y 1SP, United Kingdom

SAGE Publications Asia-Pacific Pte Ltd
3 Church Street
#10-04 Samsung Hub
Singapore 049483

Published by Vivek Mehra for SAGE Publications India Pvt Ltd, typeset in Adobe Garamond 10/12 pts by Zaza Eunice, Hosur, Tamil Nadu and printed at Sai Print-o-Pack, New Delhi.

Library of Congress Cataloging-in-Publication Data Available

ISBN: 978-93-515-0971-4 (HB)

The SAGE Team: Supriya Das, Alekha Chandra Jena and Ritu Chopra

In loving memory of my parents
who proudly stood by me during the writing of this book
and whose respect for human values
struggle for truth and justice and
belief in the rule of law
continue to drive me

Thank you for choosing a SAGE product!
If you have any comment, observation or feedback,
I would like to personally hear from you.
Please write to me at **contactceo@sagepub.in**

Vivek Mehra, Managing Director and CEO, SAGE India.

Bulk Sales

SAGE India offers special discounts
for purchase of books in bulk.
We also make available special imprints
and excerpts from our books on demand.

For orders and enquiries, write to us at

Marketing Department
SAGE Publications India Pvt Ltd
B1/I-1, Mohan Cooperative Industrial Area
Mathura Road, Post Bag 7
New Delhi 110044, India

E-mail us at **marketing@sagepub.in**

Get to know more about SAGE

Be invited to SAGE events, get on our mailing list.
Write today to **marketing@sagepub.in**

This book is also available as an e-book.

To
Manni
for her thoughtfulness and understanding
in letting this book be a
constant companion during our marriage

Contents

Foreword

This lucid, lively and thought-provoking work rather successfully conceals the fact that writing on Kashmir is a difficult and even dangerous affair in India. Ralph Waldo Emerson once said that it was a luxury to be understood; nowhere in India is this dictum true as in the writing of, and about, Kashmir, or rather the erstwhile princely Indian state of Jammu and Kashmir (referred to as the PIS of J&K in the book).

Despite some notable initiatives over the past 67 years of the Indian Republic, even an elusive 'solution' has failed to engage all parties (state and non-state). To generalize, '… Kashmir has too many paradoxes to display too much patriotic horror …' (M.J. Akbar, *Kashmir: Behind the Vale*, Viking Penguin India, 2002, p. 154). State-sponsored and cross-border infiltration and terrorism constitute a real threat to India's sovereignty, integrity and unity. However, it is also a global fact that any 'solution' has to be based on a dialogue with all the stakeholders inside and outside the borders. It is a small consolation to learn that colonial boundaries and borders continue to be disrupted everywhere, and a considerable slice of humanity lives under the reign of terror and human rightlessness, and also that a dialogue is even more difficult when it has to be conducted thus in the shadow of insecurity and the lawlessness of terror (that victimizes and revictimizes the communities of suffering). India inaugurated a new constitutional device of state accession to the new Republic; the device has largely worked but not without Kashmir's 'frozen turbulence' (as Jagmohan names this) or even a state of civil war. It is difficult, and some consider impossible, to write analytically about Kashmir with the aim of producing a common dialogue. Conditions of such a dialogue between nations and peoples require a commitment to an emerging human right to peace.

Aman Hingorani (notwithstanding citizens who consider themselves super-patriots and are easily offended by any analysis of which they disapprove) faces this aporia or paradox bravely and provides a lucid but wide-ranging historical and contemporary analysis of the subject. This is one of the few books written on constitutional and legal aspects of the continuing problem, although it is also unsparing of 'New Delhi', a metonymy that stands not just for the ruling regime but also signifies the political elite as such. Clearly, while social facts rarely speak to us univocally, the learned author is no ideologue of the Left or Right; this helps to attain a balance in a difficult summation of acts and trends. Even though at times deeply provocative, the purpose of this work is not to offend or incite but to enable us to think afresh; the method is largely one of juristic analysis. If the problems are rather well known, it is the responses that interest the author and should also concern the reader. Pandit Kumarilla Bhatt's notion of *sahriday ipathak* (a reader with heartfelt or soulful engagement) stands summoned by this work.

Touching faith in law, both national and international, animates much of the analysis which also resolutely faces contemporary peace process and governmental as well as resistance policy and politics. How far the law leads the nation when politics and the political system fail has been thematically well considered in this work. If there are limits to effective legal action, there are also opportunities for judicial action as well illustrated by Justice Gita Mittal of the High Court of Delhi in a 2010 decision, which bemoaned 'the admitted failure of the respondents to protect the constitutional rights of the petitioners' (internally displaced persons, in this case the Kashmiri Pandits) and the 'arbitrary and wrongful failure to exercise the discretion' by the Union Government officials; and the 'drastic violation of the fundamental and basic human rights: that result upon such implementation of the statutory provisions'. Justice Mittal had no hesitation in staying the administrative action, thus 'completely misdirected and unwarranted'. This decision is a cameo example of the difference between adjudicative cultures that take human rights seriously and political/administrative cultures that accentuate only the 'hyper-technical'.

Aman Hingorani is deferential to all colleagues, past as well as contemporary, but he charts his own narrative path in this painstaking work; his writing here is sober and constructive, as all good writing is. As a human rights analyst, the learned author critiques all those involved in violations of human rights and the right to be, and to remain, human, which underlies all human rights. He lays bare the handling of diverse political activity or opinion by 'coercive laws' which are plentifully used and abused; even justices and courts uphold the security of state over gross violations of core or fundamental human rights claims.

Hingorani also remains critical of regime styles that are excessively state-centric rather than tilted towards victim or violated individuals and groups. To take an example, the mass exodus of Kashmiri Pandits and their 'trauma and misery' are of little concern to the regime or the wider civil society. So are the agonies of citizens who constitute the common people of Kashmir even today. 'The minds got scarred in Kashmir, with people not knowing whether they would be alive by the evening, young girls being taken to the police station against the law, and graveyards springing up and a whole host of sinister evils created by the overhanging geographies of injustice and human rightlessness. Of particular importance is the author's observation that the fundamental rights guaranteed by the Constitution of India constitute the core values of the Constitution and 'one of the essential pillars of the vibrant Indian democracy'; in this context, the uneasy existence of Article 35(c) (the best kept constitutional secret in India, a constitutional amendment made by the President, which still did not follow the procedure of amendment under Article 368 nor was published as such in the official text of the Constitution) is noted, with the observation that it 'deprived the residents of the state of constitutional guarantees available to other citizens of India'. Despite many a justification that might be validly offered, the learned author displays, rightly, a degree of constitutional unease at this happening. Furthermore, as the author notes, the tendency for 'subversion from within' fuelled by systemic governance corruption and 'lack of governance' aggravates citizens' helplessness and humiliation.

The author is equally critical of the 'political role' of the army (and paramilitary forces) while appreciative of the 'felt insecurity' of security forces, confronted by 'faceless and nameless enemies enjoying popular support' conducting a 'proxy war'; this has taken 'its toll ...' on the Indian security forces and the state police, with the uncertainty and insecurity stemming from the sudden attacks by militants reported to have had an adverse psychological effect on them'. However understandable the reports of the 'growing tendency amongst the security personnel to overreact to the slightest provocation' (a phenomenon termed 'decompensation' by psychoanalysts), the learned author does not think that violations of core human rights are ever justified or justifiable. He notes that the common refrain of the security forces has been that '[w]e are unwilling, led by the unqualified, doing the unnecessary for the ungrateful'. This, according to the author, however, does not justify human rights violation, immunity or impunity.

Despite the 'failings of the Indian State [which] rule out the ability of New Delhi to formulate, and give effect to, a cohesive policy towards the PIS of J&K', the learned author offers some indicators for the way ahead. The suggestions for resolving the dispute are many, but the strength of this work, in my estimate, lies in the suggestion that the Simla Agreement does not rule out a limited reference to the International Court of Justice at The Hague. Looking at the Court's precedents, Aman Hingorani maintains that a favourable ruling by the Court would mean that the 'very presence of Pakistani and Chinese troops in the territory of the PIS of J&K would constitute "aggression"' and that the world community has 'no option but to put an end to that illegal situation'. He maintains that this is a 'first step to unravel the Kashmir knot' and a favourable verdict is bound to 'change the national and international political discourse on the Kashmir issue'. Any further unravelling, to which the learned author devotes three chapters of this work, however, would depend on 'New Delhi' winning the 'faith and confidence of the people of the PIS of J&K so that it can legitimately claim moral authority to be in the state'.

Writing contemporary history and offering solutions to a knotty situation is always subject to many a hazard of disagreement and disputation. The road to peace and *aman* (well-being) is always paved by conflict, insurrection and repression. Aman Hingorani's conclusions on ways to attain an enduring peace may well be debated and contested; indeed, there are many aspects where the analysis may be further problematized. But this studious work cannot be ignored.

It also needs saying that the author, like all citizens of India, is bound by a fundamental duty (under Article 51A(h) of the Constitution of India) to develop 'scientific temper, humanism, and the spirit of enquiry and reform'. I have written this merely descriptive Foreword in the same spirit, reciprocating and reinforcing a just solution to a vexed problem. Some will consider such activities akin to publicly confronting the nation with its failings, but how can a responsible discharge of one's fundamental constitutional duty be otherwise? One has, at the end of the day, to read this work as speaking to alternatives of peace and prosperity in the state of Jammu and Kashmir as distinct from narratives justifying 'transgenerational massacres, bloodshed, trauma, misery and pain of innocents…'.

The principal message of the book in your hands is worth pondering, and we should all recall (in the wise words of Professor Julius Stone): 'It is not given to any generation of men to complete the tasks of human improvement and redemption but no generation is free to desist from them.'

Upendra Baxi
Emeritus Professor of Law
University of Warwick and Delhi

Acknowledgements

Along with my professional law practice, I take keen interest in studying challenging issues. After having written on varied subjects ranging from the grant of intellectual property protection to bioengineered life forms to the dynamics of missile proliferation globally, I was in search of a topic in 1995 for my doctoral research. I chose the Kashmir problem because discussions with my father, Nirmal Hingorani, gave me an insight into how every conceivable principle of law had been turned on its head to create and sustain this issue.

My father had a standing of nearly 70 years as a constitutional lawyer and was the senior most lawyer in the Indian Supreme Court at the time of his demise on 21 July 2015. Enrolled as a lawyer on 27 March 1946 in Sind in undivided India (now in Pakistan), he was fully conversant with the legal principles underlying the partition about 18 months later, on 15 August 1947, of the Indian subcontinent and also of the accession of the 560-odd princely Indian states to India or Pakistan. Indeed, the paternal lineage of Nirmal Hingorani can be traced to the royal family of the then princely Indian state of Jaisalmer. His paternal grandfather, Diwan Banasing, was a renowned judge in Tharoo Shah, Sind, while his maternal grandfather was Diwan Man Singh of the then princely Indian state of Khairpur (Khayrpur). Nirmal Hingorani's father, Harsadmal Banasing Hingorani, also a judge, was awarded the civilian honour of *Tamgha* by the then Pakistan President Mohammad Ayub Khan for his service as the Chairman of the Sind and West Pakistan Public Service Commission. Nirmal Hingorani was, thus, familiar with the affairs of the state. Before coming to New Delhi to start his legal practice in the newly formed Indian Supreme Court, Nirmal Hingorani, among other things, assisted the Government of Sind in resolving issues pertaining to the distribution of water of the Indus River, and was appointed by the Governor of Sind under the Sind Special Court of Inquiry Ordinance of 1948 as Special Counsel in the conduct of the first ever Commonwealth inquiry against a sitting Chief Minister—M.A. Khuhro, the then Chief Minister of Sind—over misconduct and corruption charges. On migrating to India in 1952, Nirmal Hingorani was enrolled in the Indian Supreme

Court, of which he was later designated as Senior Advocate. During his years of practice, Nirmal Hingorani oversaw the evolution and development of constitutional law in independent India, having appeared in landmark cases before the Supreme Court that contributed to the growth of constitutional jurisprudence and to a humane approach to law.

Following discussions on the Kashmir issue with my father, who had witnessed the horrors of partition, and with the benefit of his knowledge, his clarity and novelty of thought, I set upon my doctoral research on Kashmir in the year 1995. This book builds on my doctoral thesis completed in the year 2001, and in particular, the proposals made at that time for the resolution of the Kashmir issue. It would, therefore, be fitting that I first acknowledge my father's contribution to the very conception of this work. My father's guidance continued during the writing of the book over our frequent and interesting discussions around the areas covered in the book.

My mother, Kapila Hingorani, a leading lawyer of the Indian Supreme Court, an eminent Barrister from Lincoln's Inn, London, and Honorary Fellow of the Cardiff University, was, until her passing away on 30 December 2013, the senior most woman lawyer enrolled with the Indian Supreme Court. Having been born and brought up in Nairobi, Kenya, studied in the UK and then worked and lived in India, she had a world view that had few parallels and a concern for humanity, which has greatly influenced my outlook. My mother wholeheartedly encouraged me to take on this trying subject, never forgetting to draw my attention to any material that could add to the research. She took the utmost care that I be able to write undisturbed. I am truly indebted to her for being part of everything that went into writing this book.

Nirmal Hingorani and Kapila Hingorani conceived and initiated the remedial jurisprudence of public interest litigation in 1979 in India with the *Undertrial Prisoners'* case. The case, filed pro bono before the Indian Supreme Court, sought and secured the release of thousands of prisoners languishing in jail awaiting trial for cruelly long periods, at times exceeding the period they would have been in jail had they been tried, convicted and given maximum sentence and such sentence was to run consecutively. It was primarily through my parents' work that I learnt firsthand about the extent of state lawlessness, custodial torture and the terrible prison conditions in the country, which assume grave significance in the context of persons apprehended under anti-terrorism or preventive detention laws on suspicion of terrorist links. My approach to these aspects in the book has been shaped by the exposure to their work for the preservation of human life and dignity.

I appreciate the unflinching support of my wife, Dr Manni Hingorani, who, being well-versed in current affairs, has always been glad to hear out the legal and political dimensions of the Kashmir issue. I have had to take weeks off, often at the cost of family life, to work on the book. My wife has willingly taken on the increased responsibility of taking care of the home, along with her busy practice as an ENT surgeon. Our son, Aryaman, has been most patient about my preoccupation with the book.

I am grateful to my sisters, both lawyers having their independent standing, for their steadfast enthusiasm and assistance. Priya Hingorani has, over the years, often cheerfully filled in for my professional commitments as a lawyer so that I could free up time to write this book. Typical of an elder sister, she has been excited about my writing this book and has taken a deep interest in its progress. Dr Shweta Hingorani, my younger sister, has an extraordinary eye for detail, and has readily and painstakingly read the voluminous texts, till early hours of the morning, not only of this book but also of my doctoral thesis. I have enjoyed the brainstorming sessions with her on the ticklish issues that arise in the context of Kashmir. She has been extremely generous both with her time and with her invaluable and incisive inputs. She deserves special mention for having been involved at every step, from the several rounds of review of the manuscript to the engagement with the publishers.

I deeply value the backing of Susan Anand, Professor B.B. Pande, Reema Bhandari, Rakesh Chatterjee, Kunika and Swati Sumbly for this book, the administrative support facilitated by Yashpalji, D.P. Singh and Amit Kumar, and the immense interest shown by the many people who have been with me over the course of the years that this book has taken.

I am thankful to Professor Upendra Baxi for accepting my request to write the Foreword so warmly and instantaneously. The distinguished professor is known around the world not only for his passionate and erudite oration and scholarship, but also for his sensitivity to causes that matter. I consider myself fortunate that Professor Baxi has penned the Foreword to this book.

SAGE Publishers has extended full cooperation in the publication of the book. I express my gratitude to Vivek Mehra, Dr Sunanda Ghosh, Rajan Dhameja, Sharmila Abraham, Elina Mazumdar, Savitha Kumar, Supriya Das, Shreya Chakraborti and Alekha Chandra Jena, in particular, for making the process so seamless.

Aman M. Hingorani

Introduction

Kashmir, the word evokes a bundle of thoughts. A place endowed with natural beauty, blue skies, snow-capped peaks, crystal-clear lakes, waterfalls, green meadows. A place brutalized by never-ending violence, gunshots, bombs, unmarked graves, missing children, wailing mothers and agonizing fear for the safety of loved ones. The violence in the erstwhile princely Indian state of Jammu and Kashmir (hereafter referred to as 'PIS of J&K' for the sake of brevity) has killed tens of thousands of innocents, rendered millions homeless and led to trans-generational trauma, misery and destruction.

The violence in the territory of the PIS of J&K with India (the other part being occupied by Pakistan and China) has reportedly been sponsored in no small measure by Pakistan, which feels that it has been unjustly denied Kashmir by India. I have written elsewhere about terrorism-related incidents in the territory of the PIS of J&K with India as also the technological sophistication through which the terror outfits operate.[1] These outfits thrive on their nexus with international narcotics traffickers and counterfeiters. Fighting the supposed jihad or freedom struggle in the territory of the PIS of J&K with India are foreign mercenaries recruited from almost every Islamic country, as also from countries like the UK. They include well-educated youth with highly technical education, such as commercial pilots and medical students. Terrorism from the territory of the PIS of J&K with India has spilled over to other parts of India and has included attacks on the Indian Parliament and the historic Red Fort at Delhi, bomb blasts in trains and crowded places, the 26/11 sea-borne multiple attacks in Mumbai and the hijacking of airplanes.

The situation is compounded by the alienation of the Kashmiri populace from the Indian Union and its sullen approach towards the world's largest democracy, which has been skilfully exploited by terrorist outfits and Pakistan to sustain violence in the territory of the PIS of J&K with India. A search into the cause for such alienation and approach would raise bothersome questions that concern, or at least should concern, every individual subscribing to the rule of law. These questions refuse to go away by merely condemning Pakistan for waging an untiring proxy war or denouncing the

Kashmiri people as an 'ungrateful, treacherous lot' having not so hidden loyalties with Pakistan. Nothing can absolve the Indian leadership of blame for following a patently flawed approach towards the PIS of J&K from 1947 onwards. It was New Delhi's incredible stand before the United Nations (UN) and the world at large on the question of accession of the PIS of J&K to India that conferred the 'disputed territory' status on the state, internationalized the Kashmir issue and altered the political discourse on the Kashmir problem. Further, it was New Delhi's actions that sustained popular discontentment within the territory of the PIS of J&K with India. New Delhi responded to such popular discontentment by encroaching upon the autonomy of the PIS of J&K—an autonomy guaranteed by the Constitution of India itself. Such encroachment was accompanied by draconian and coercive laws enacted by New Delhi, which conferred extraordinary powers on the Indian security forces to maintain 'law and order'. Indian security personnel, who had neither created the Kashmir issue nor had the solution for it, were simply instructed to contain the violence. Needless to say, this response seriously infringed upon the constitutional rights of the citizens. What could be more grotesque than scores of parents being reduced to helplessly pleading with apathetic authorities to at least confirm whether their children picked up by the security forces were, in fact, dead. Indeed, the flawed policies pursued by New Delhi stoked the fire of terrorism and human rights violations in the territory of the PIS of J&K with India. It did not take much for Pakistan to hijack the popular disillusionment of the Kashmiri populace with the Indian establishment and give it the colour of a jihad.

The PIS of J&K has been characterized as a nuclear flashpoint on the Indian subcontinent, having the potential to disrupt international peace and stability. India and Pakistan have, in the past, gone to war over the PIS of J&K. The Kashmir problem has dictated political developments in the rest of the Indian subcontinent, with wide repercussions throughout the world. The reckless strategies adopted by Pakistan to wrestle the territory of the PIS of J&K from India is said to have resulted in Pakistan becoming a breeding ground for international terrorism. Indeed, the festering Kashmir issue between India and Pakistan has contributed immensely to the rise in international terrorism.

The Kashmir issue touches a raw nerve, both in India and Pakistan. The leadership of both countries share a love–hate relationship, with the people of the PIS of J&K becoming the casualties when that relationship goes awry. Several efforts have been made to resolve the Kashmir issue between India and Pakistan, with and without the intervention of the international community.

There are a series of broken peace accords between the countries. The primary reason for this sad state of affairs is that the affected parties—India, Pakistan and the people of the PIS of J&K—do not even share the same view of what precisely constitutes the Kashmir issue. As in the past, the governments will continue to talk to each other but in a different language. The question, therefore, is not whether the countries should talk. The question is what they should talk about. This book suggests what that conversation ought to be.

Having researched on the Kashmir issue since 1995, I believe that it has been rather simplistically painted as a tussle for territory between India and Pakistan, following the partition of the Indian subcontinent in 1947 into the dominions of India and Pakistan. The genesis of the Kashmir problem runs much deeper. I believe that the Kashmir issue was the inevitable result of the ruthless policies followed by Britain, the colonial power, to satisfy its political, defence and strategic interests in the Indian subcontinent and of the utter ineptitude and political naivety of eminent Indian leaders of undivided India in rising to the challenge. The Kashmir problem was deliberately created by the British, sustained by the British and intended by the British to remain the end product of the British Raj (rule) in the Indian subcontinent to serve their interests. The Kashmir issue later assumed its present dimensions due to Pakistan's persistent efforts, India's habitual bungling as also the political expediency of the international community. In the process, it is the people across the Indian subcontinent—whether in India, Pakistan or Bangladesh—who continue to be taken for a ride.

The book analyses the genesis of the Kashmir problem and the inadequacies of the solutions often proposed to resolve it. The book offers a solution to the Kashmir issue that appears to have so far escaped consideration. However, in order to appreciate such solution, it is imperative to first depoliticize the Kashmir issue and an appropriate way to depoliticize any issue is to subject it to a legal analysis.

An examination of the legal underpinnings of the Kashmir issue would not only reveal how misdirected the approach of each of the affected parties has been towards the PIS of J&K since 1947 till date, but it could form the basis for forward movement on the Kashmir problem. It will be readily agreed that the law merely reflects the political decision taken with regard to a matter. However, once that political decision has been taken and crystallized into law, all actions taken by those in power in respect of that matter must invariably be in consonance with such law. Any solution for the Kashmir issue must be consistent with principles of law governing the matter. It is true that law alone would not resolve the Kashmir issue. However, the legality of the stands adopted by the affected parties would influence the national and international political discourse on the Kashmir problem, as also mobilize public opinion, so necessary for a just resolution of the Kashmir issue.

Having depoliticized the Kashmir issue, the book then deals with the ground realities in the state, and whether and how the roots of disaffection can be addressed so as to restore faith in the rule of law and to give effect to the solution for the Kashmir issue proposed in this book.

This book is being written at a time when India and Pakistan have intermittently resumed the process of dialogue as also their trade and cricket. Circumstances have never looked so favourable for a resolution of the Kashmir issue between the two countries, with Pakistan claiming itself to be 'a victim of terrorism' after having to distance itself from the Taliban and outfits such as the Al Qaida and having been put on the mat by the international community for the 26/11 Mumbai attacks. India has also been engaging with the Hurriyat and militant outfits active in the Kashmir valley. Pakistan and the international community, especially the US and the UK, have never before been so alive to the price to be paid for premising foreign policy on terror. The 'global war on terror', post 9/11, 26/11 and 13/11, has reaped good dividends for India. It has put India and Pakistan, even if only ostensibly, on the same side.

In view of the emotive and volatile response that the Kashmir issue evokes, at least in this part of the world, the literature on the subject is replete with distortions, prejudices and assumptions tailored to suit the interests of those concerned. In this book, therefore, an attempt has been made to reconcile varying perspectives culled from UN documents, judicial decisions, official publications, authoritative writings and articles.

The fact that New Delhi has bungled the Kashmir issue is evidenced by no less than the judicial authority of the Indian Supreme Court, which has, in a series of decisions, negated several premises underlying New Delhi's stand since 1947 on the PIS of J&K. The book, therefore, refers to the decisions of the Indian Supreme Court in particular, since these decisions bind New Delhi under the Constitution of India. The book takes note of Indian press reports indicting the Indian State and its instrumentalities, as such reports would necessarily have an element of truth. The book also relies on declassified British archives relating to the partition of the Indian subcontinent, which have been reproduced by several authors referred to in the book, notably Wali Khan, President of Pakistan's National Awami Party and a widely respected Pashtun leader, and Narendra Singh Sarila, who was the *aide-de-camp* to Louis Francis Albert Victor Nicholas Battenberg, or simply Louis Mountbatten, the last Viceroy of India. Other useful sources are the books authored by Henry Vincent Hodson, or H.V. Hodson, the British economist, who was the editor of *The Round Table* from 1934 to 1939, the Director of the Empire Division of the Ministry of Information from 1939 to 1941 and the Constitutional Advisor to the Viceroy (1941–1942), and by Rao Bahadur Vappala Pangunni Menon, or V.P. Menon, who was the Constitutional Advisor to the last three Viceroys and member of the Indian Civil Service.

I write this book as a lawyer, rather than as an academician. The approach, accordingly, is to draw on the facts of the Kashmir case taken from various sources, and then to present my evaluation of such facts and the possible solution to unravel the Kashmir knot. Though I write as an Indian and suggest the way forward to New Delhi on the Kashmir issue, my analysis of the Kashmir case would have remained the same had I belonged to any other nationality.

Introductions invariably give the chapterization scheme together with an outline of the contents of the chapters of the book. But then, cold facts and circumstances surrounding the Kashmir issue have to be divorced from the subjective feelings towards them. It has, indeed, become necessary to first rediscover bare facts about the Kashmir problem, which have been unceremoniously buried due to political expediency. The chapterization or outline of chapters would run the risk of prejudging the possible solution for, or for that matter, overlooking the subtleties of, the Kashmir issue. This introduction, therefore, stops here.

Note and Reference

1. Hingorani, Aman. 2007. 'The Kashmir Issue: Differing Perceptions', *The International Relations and Security Network*, 10 January, Zurich. Available online at http://www.isn.ethz.ch/Digital-Library/Publications/Detail/?id=27333 (downloaded on 30 August 2015).

conditions... that New Delhi should allot... to the international... the Kashmiri people from the mainstream. He opines that it is the responsibility of the elite: residents, teachers, lawyers, social workers and political activists to persuade alienated youth to return to the mainstream. Such persons must also interact with the state government in a determined manner, to create the conditions necessary to convince the people about the sincerity of the government. The state should then hold a dialogue, dismantle the security apparatus and provide for the safe return of migrants. Sharma feels that the administrative structure needs to be substantially overhauled and that the deployment of local administrators of proven merit and integrity would create the necessary goodwill.

Baltar Puri argues that human rights should form the basis of any policy in the state, and that the human rights movement in the area

I

The Indian Subcontinent under the British Colonial Rule

The mass struggle for independence throughout the Indian subcontinent has been well documented. The persistent demand of the Indian leadership was that the British should withdraw from the subcontinent, leaving India to govern itself as a sovereign republic having no relations with the British Commonwealth. The British did transfer power on 15 August 1947, but only after partitioning India into the dominions[1] of India and Pakistan within the British Commonwealth. The Kashmir issue, as will be evident shortly, stems from the British politics behind the partition of the Indian subcontinent. It is, therefore, imperative to place the Kashmir issue in the context of the British colonial rule. Let us, accordingly, start with an overview of the British colonial rule in the Indian subcontinent as it existed prior to 15 August 1947.

Indian Territory under the British Colonial Rule

The British rule in the Indian subcontinent commenced with the arrival of the British East India Company, a trading corporation which had received the royal charter on 31 December 1600 from Elizabeth I, the Queen of England. The company established a trade transit point at Surat in Gujarat by 1608. The character of the company ceased, by the middle of the 18th century, to be merely that of a trader and, instead, became that of a territorial power. Over the years, the company acquired de facto sovereignty over huge territories exercised through the Governor General appointed by its Court of Directors. The powers of the company were regulated initially by the British Crown and then by legislation enacted by the British Parliament.

The first battle for Indian independence in 1857, or the 'Mutiny' as the British viewed it, ended the role of the company in the governance of the Indian subcontinent. The Government of India Act of 1858 contemplated the appointment of the Governor General by the British Crown, later referred to as the Viceroy and Governor General of India or simply as the Viceroy of India. The Viceroy was to be instructed in the exercise of his powers by the British Secretary of State, a member of the British cabinet. The Secretary of State headed the India Office in London, which was a British government department set up in 1858 for this purpose.

There were two kinds of territory in the Indian subcontinent under the British colonial rule. One was the British-annexed territory, known as British India, which was divided into provinces. The Governor General appointed Governors to head each province. The administration was unitary and highly centralized.

The other territory under the British colonial rule was that of 560-odd princely Indian states. These states covered an area of 715,964 square miles out of the total area of 1,581,410 square miles under British rule.[2] Reversing its earlier policy of annexation, London decided, at least from 1858 onwards, not to annex such territory, but to maintain 'a territorial and constitutional standstill'.[3] Alexandrina Victoria, the Queen of the United Kingdom of Great Britain and Ireland, declared in 1858 that the British desired 'no extension' of their 'present territorial possessions' and that they 'shall respect the rights, dignity and honour of the Native Princes'.[4]

The British did not generally interfere with the internal affairs of the princely Indian states, which continued to be governed by their respective monarchical rulers, who, in turn, owed allegiance to the British Crown. The princely Indian states under British paramountcy (or sovereignty) had no international personality and the British Crown had exclusive authority to make peace or war and to negotiate or communicate with foreign states.[5]

By 1876, the territory, which includes modern India, Pakistan, Bangladesh and parts of Burma, had become the 'British Raj'. Alexandrina Victoria, the British monarch, was proclaimed as 'Empress of India' at the Delhi Durbar (Court of Delhi) on 1 January 1877.

Communalization of the Indian Polity

Until the year 1857, the year of the 'Mutiny' against the British colonial rule, the British perceived the Muslims to be their primary enemy in the Indian subcontinent, having deposed Bahadur Shah Zafar, the last Mughal Emperor of India. Sarila asserts that thereafter, 'the British identified a new enemy, namely, the growing Indian middle class, who were imbibing Western ideas of democracy, and a majority of whom happened to be educated Hindus'.[6] The Muslim leaders, however, were 'anxious to unite with the Hindus and with other communities to present a unified front against British imperialism'.[7] Wali Khan gives the instance of Syed Ahmad Khan, a highly respected Muslim leader, who declared at a function in Gurdaspur on 27 January 1884 that:[8]

> We [i.e. Hindus and Mohammadans] should try to become one heart and soul, and act in union. In old historical books and traditions you will have read and heard, we see it even now, that all the people inhabiting one country are designated by the term One Nation. The different tribes of Afghanistan are termed One Nation and so the miscellaneous hordes of people in Iran, distinguished by the term Persians, though abounding in variety of thoughts and religions, are still known as members of One Nation.... Remember that the words Hindu and Mohammadan are only means for religious distinction—otherwise all persons whether Hindus or Mohammadans, even the Christians who reside in the country, are all in this particular respect belonging to one and the same Nation.

Wali Khan quotes Syed Ahmad Khan as again stating at a gathering of the Indian Association at Lahore later that year that:[9]

> I heartily wished to serve my country and my nation faithfully. In the word Nation I include both Hindus and Mohammadans, because that is the only meaning I can attach to it.... I call both those races which inhabit India by one word, i.e. Hindu, meaning to say that they are the inhabitants of Hindustan.

The British were wary of such Hindu–Muslim unity and offered influential Muslim leaders their hand of friendship to wean them away from the Hindus. Sarila writes that the idea of 'divide and rule' came rather naturally to the British; 'a British Member of Parliament, John Bright, had, as early as 1858, suggested the break-up of the Indian Empire and placing of some parts under Muslim control'.[10]

The Indian National Congress (the Congress) was formed in 1885 and included amongst its founders Allan Octavian Hume of the Theosophical Society and Dadabhai Naoroji. The membership of the Congress was open to all, and included persons of all faiths. When the Congress started spear-heading the movement for responsible self-government, the British strategy was to 'support other movements in the country with a view to loosening the Congress grip'.[11] The British took deliberate steps to paint the Congress as a 'Hindu' party, though 'the Congress had as members a large number of Muslims on its rolls, often a Muslim as its President and routinely Muslims as members of its executive'.[12] The idea was to pit the Muslims against the Congress so as to keep the latter in check. The reasoning was simple: first, the British would offer to transfer power to Indian hands but on the condition that the Hindus and Muslims should resolve their differences before such transfer, and commit to the 'protection of the minorities'. After all, according to the British, theirs was a responsible government—responsible to the British Crown and the British Parliament—and it was their duty to provide for the protection of the minorities. Having put such a condition, the British would ensure that the differences between the Hindus and Muslims were played up and, as will be seen subsequently, give those Muslim leaders they had won over (and not all Muslim leaders) the ability to veto any possible consensus between the Hindus and Muslims. The British would consequently get to retain power indefinitely.

And so, the British effort now was to win over Muslim leaders, several of whom did choose to align themselves with the British. Jaswant Singh records that Syed Ahmad Khan went on to condemn 'the Congress movement as seditious' in an article published on 23 November 1886 in the *Aligarh Institute Gazette* and came into open conflict with the Congress in the year 1887.[13] With more and more Muslims being drawn to the Congress, Syed Ahmad Khan felt compelled to assert for the first time that 'Muslims were a separate "people", a separate "nation"'.[14] Sarila documents that Syed Ahmad Khan, who 'exhorted the Muslims to ally themselves with their old enemy and distance themselves from the majority community', was knighted by Victoria, the British monarch.[15]

George Frederick Ernest Albert, or simply George V, who was then the Prince of Wales and later the King of the United Kingdom, visited India in 1905–1906. The then Secretary of State, John Morley, in his letter of 11 May 1906, to the then Viceroy Gilbert Elliot, the fourth Earl of Minto, referred to a conversation he had had with the Prince of Wales, during which the Prince of Wales had 'talked of the National Congress rapidly becoming a great power.... There it is, whether we like it or not'.[16]

Jaswant Singh has provided a detailed account of Syed Mohammad Zauqi, editor of the paper *Al-haq*, who had accompanied the Prince of Wales as a local press representative during his India visit in 1905–1906.[17] Zauqi refers to Syed Hussain Bilgrami, an influential Muslim leader, disclosing that Walter Lawrence, the Chief of Staff of the Prince of Wales, had told him that he should not let Muslim youth seeking a political identity join the Congress.[18] Zauqi narrates that Bilgrami, who held the Governor's position in the princely Indian state of Hyderabad (Nawab Imad-ul-Mulk), went on to say that Lawrence had warned:[19]

> 'They will suffer if they do that. Let them start a political organization of their own and fight out their battle independent of the Congress. You keep control of that organization.' I said that the Nizam Government Rules precluded me from taking part in politics. He said, 'let a big man, e.g. the Agha Khan, be its President merely for show. It is the Secretary who does the main work, controls and guides. You be the Secretary; and if your State Rules do not allow you, then let a nominal Secretary take that office and you do the real work behind the scenes. If you do not do that, Muslims will be crushed between two mill-stones....'

Zauqi details the secret deliberations that took place during the India visit of the Prince of Wales, which led to the Agha Khan, who had 'leanings towards the Congress', being won over to set up a kind of 'Muslim Congress', the Muslim League.[20] The news of the impending Minto-Morley Reforms led to a Muslim deputation being organized to call upon Minto. Sarila writes that:[21]

> .... After Sir Syed, the Agha Khan donned the mantle of Anglo-Muslim cooperation.... It was the Agha Khan, who, in 1883, first put forward the idea of separate electorates for Muslims, i.e., that a certain number of seats in every election should be reserved for Muslim candidates and the Muslim electorate should vote exclusively for these Muslim candidates.... Under such a system Muslim candidates would not be required to seek support from people belonging to other religions or to pay heed to the interests of their non-Muslim compatriots ... a sure way to tear people politically apart. The Muslim League was launched by the Agha Khan and some landlords of Bengal in 1906.

On 10 August 1906, William J. Archibold, the Principal of the Mahommedan Anglo-Oriental College that had been set up near Delhi by Syed Ahmad Khan with British help, conveyed Minto's acceptance to receive a Muslim deputation. Minto, who met the deputation on 1 October 1906, was not only encouraging but went on to declare that the Muslims should be represented 'as a community' in 'any system of representation whether it affects a Municipality, a District Board or a Legislative Council'.[22] Minto's wife, in her diary, made an entry dated 1 October 1906 as 'a very eventful day, and epoch in Indian history' stating '... a very big thing has happened today, a work of statesmanship that will affect India and Indian history for many a long year. It is nothing less than the pulling back of 62 million of people from joining the ranks of the seditious opposition'.[23]

This British statesmanship was to govern the Indian subcontinent by communal politics. The Minto-Morley Reforms of 1909, contained in the Indian Councils Act of 1909, predictably provided for separate electorates for elections to local and municipal committees. It may be stated here that these committees had no real power, as no British representative was responsible to them. Jaswant Singh documents Morley as stating before the House of Lords that:[24]

'If it could be said that this chapter of reforms led directly or necessarily to the establishment of a parliamentary system in India, I for one would have nothing to do with it.' There could be no analogy, he said, between Ireland and India or between Canada or India. He derided the idea that 'whatever is good for self government for Canada must be good for India' as a 'gross and dangerous sophism'. It was like arguing, he said, that, because a fur coat is needed in the Canadian winter, it is needed in the Deccan.

The freedom struggle across the Indian subcontinent, however, picked up momentum, notwithstanding coercive penal British laws like the Defence of India Act of 1915 and the Rowlatt Act of 1919 conferring draconian powers on the British machinery in the subcontinent. Furthermore, the Muslim League and the Congress entered into the Lucknow Pact in 1916 to form a united front against the British for self-government in India.

The British, thereafter, intensified their policy of communal electorates in order to hinder the growth of the self-governing principle and to check Indian nationalism. The then Secretary of State Edwin Montagu and the then Viceroy Frederic John Napier Thesiger, First Viscount Chelmsford, put together the Montagu–Chelmsford Reforms in July 1918, which led to the enactment of the Government of India Act of 1919. This Act reaffirmed the principle of communal representation, with seats being reserved for Muslims, Sikhs, Indian Christians, Anglo-Indians, and domiciled Europeans, in both provincial and central legislative councils. Montagu and Chelmsford candidly acknowledged:[25]

Divisions by creeds and classes means the creation of political camps organized against each other, and teaches men to think as partisans and not as citizens.... We regard any system of communal electorates, therefore, as a very serious hindrance to the development of the self-governing principle.... That the principle works so well that once it has been fully established, it so entrenches communalism that one could hardly then abandon the principle even if one wished to do so.

Over the years, the British succeeded in polarizing the Indian polity by playing with religion. Indeed, the then Viceroy Rufus Daniel Isaacs, First Marquess of Reading, or simply Reading, wrote to the then Secretary of State William Robert Wellesley Peel, on 21 September 1922, as under:[26]

> I have just sent you a telegram, which will show you, how near we have been to a complete break between Muslims and Hindus. I have been giving the greatest attention to this possibility, and I have had the greatest assistance from Shafi on my council, who is a highly respectable Mohammadan.

Shafi, referred to by Reading, was Mohammad Shafi, a member of the Viceroy's Executive Council, who had, on 2 November 1921, emphasized that it would be in the interests of the British Empire to lure the Muslims away from the Hindus and to form an Anglo-Mohammadan Union.[27]

The British realized that the more irreconcilable the differences between the Hindus and Muslims could be made, the more the British would become indispensable. The then Secretary of State Birkenhead cabled to Reading in March 1925 that, 'I have always placed my highest and most permanent hopes upon the eternity of the communal situation'.[28] Wali Khan quotes Birkenhead as saying that '[t]he more it is made obvious that these antagonisms are profound, and affect an immense and irreconcilable section of the population, the more conspicuously is the fact illustrated that we and we alone can play the part of the composers'.[29] Wali Khan writes that:[30]

> The British had to adopt several underhand tactics to reach their goals. But reach they did. On 1 January 1925, the Viceroy [had] announced to the Secretary of State, 'The bridge Gandhiji had built to span the gulf between the Hindus and Mohammadans has not only broken down, but, I think, it has completely disappeared.' ... In the same letter, the Viceroy wrote that although the Muslims were united in their support of the British Government but, 'there is no outstanding man to compose the differences and head them'.

The British search for a dependable Muslim leader ended with Mohammad Ali Jinnah, a politically ambitious barrister but enjoying little or no support amongst the Indian Muslims. The Viceroy recorded on 20 May 1929 that:[31]

> I had a long talk with Jinnah a few days ago, which made it very clear to my mind that he and all the Bombay people, who are not disposed to Congress, are disposed to swing towards our direction if we can give them help later.

Wali Khan refers to the British archives to highlight the steps taken by the British to organize the Muslim League into a well funded and strong party, with funds being raised often from compliant rulers of the princely Indian states.[32] He records the then Viceroy Irwin, as stating on 9 February 1931 that:[33]

> I told him [Sir Mohammad Shafi] that I thought they would all have to fight hard and that it was no good supposing that a few packed meetings or news-papers articles would do the job. They must go out as wholetime missionaries and carry the flaming torch throughout the length and breadth of India. They must be prepared to build up a great organisation which might focus all constructive efforts to fight the Congress ... and they proposed to get to work, vigorous and comprehensive. This is encouraging and I only hope their good resolutions do not fade away. The League prepared a scheme, the financial aspect of which was the responsibility of the Princely States.

Wali Khan details the British plan to set the Muslims and Hindus against each other and then to 'tell the world that they were unable to relinquish power because of the hostility between the Hindus and the Muslims'.[34] He records that:[35]

> During the First Round Table Conference the British took maximum advantage of the communal differences.... Although Gandhiji was present at the Second Round Table Conference, the British continued their power-play. In this regard Sir Samuel Hoare, Secretary of State, wrote on 2 October 1931, 'The delegates are much further off with each other than they were last year and I don't believe that there is a least chance of a communal settlement in the minorities committees'.... On 31 October 1932, the Viceroy wrote: The Hindus, Sikhs and Muslims are to meet on 3 November at Allahabad to endeavour to arrive at an agreement which will do away with the communal accord. I am assured by those who know that no agreement will ever be reached.... It was said that in comparison with the Second Round Table Conference there were a lot more differences between the Hindus and the Muslims during the Third Round Table Conference. The British were delighted to invite the various Indian lead-ers to London and allow them to wrangle in full public view. They hoped that whenever the parties reached an impasse, they could triumphantly announce to the world that theirs was not the blame!

The communalization of the Indian polity had its impact, with a section of the Indian Muslims demanding the amalgamation of the Muslim-majority provinces in the Indian subcontinent into one prov-ince, 'a pure land' where the *sharia* would be practiced. However, such demand at that point of time did not contemplate or seek partition of the Indian subcontinent but the consolidation of a Muslim-majority area within India. The Punjabi leader and Urdu poet, Mohammad Iqbal, later viewed as one of the founders of Pakistan, formulated this position in his presidential address at the annual session of the All-India Muslim League in 1930 as under:[36]

> [T]he Indian Muslim is entitled to full and free development on the lines of his culture and tradition in his own Indian homelands.... The Muslim demand for the creation of a Muslim India within India.... I would like to see the Punjab, North West Frontier Province, Sind and Baluchistan amalgamated into a single State.... The formation of a consolidated North West Muslim State....

Hodson writes that:[37]

> [I]t is clear from the context of Sir Mohammad Iqbal's speech that he was thinking not of total partition but of the structure of a confederal India. He spoke of the needs of other 'autonomous states' in India, obviously not all Muslim, based on language, race, history, religion and identity of economic interests, and he declared

> A unitary form of government is simply unthinkable in a self-governing India. Residuary powers must be left entirely to self-governing States, the Central Federal Government only exercising those powers which are expressly vested in it by the free consent of the Federal States.

> Clearly this was neither the two-nation theory nor the true idea of Pakistan.

Yuvraj Krishan writes that Iqbal's state 'did not envisage partition of India but only a reorganisation of the Muslim-majority provinces of North Western India', a model 'Muslim land demonstrating the practice of the *Sharia* ... a *millat* of Imam'.[38] Indeed, one of Iqbal's poems hummed by millions of Indians today contain the lines '*mazhab nahin sikhata apas mein bair rakhna, Hindi hai ham watan hai Hindustan hamara*', which can be translated as 'religion does not teach us to begrudge each other, we are Hindi and our nation is Hindustan (India)'. These lines confirm that Iqbal viewed India as one nation.

British–Muslim League Affinity

The British, on their part, continued their policy to build up Jinnah to oppose the Congress and, indeed, to make prominent Muslims not belonging to the Muslim League, irrelevant. Such a policy did not, however, initially meet with much success even in Muslim-majority provinces.

Nineteen thirty-seven marked a year of elections in the British provinces in the Indian subcontinent. The Congress formed the government in eight out of eleven provinces of British India, including Muslim-majority provinces, and exercised authority over three-fourths of the population of British India. The British now began to apprehend that elections to the federal legislature could result in the Congress coming to dominate the federal government too. The British apprehension was not lost on Jinnah, whose Muslim League was routed in the 1937 elections having 'won only 109 of the total 482 seats allotted to the Muslims, securing only 4.8 per cent of the total Muslim vote'.[39] Wali Khan records that:[40]

[T]he Muslim League did not emerge as the sole representative of the Muslims in the four Muslim dominated provinces; not a single member of the Muslim League was elected to the Provincial Assembly of Sind and NWFP (North-West Frontier Province), and only one out of 84 Muslim members in the Legislative Assembly of Punjab was a League member. In the above provinces, (non League) Muslims had formed governments; Sir Sikander Hayat Khan was the undisputed leader of Punjab, Maulvi Fazlul Haq of Bengal, Khan Bahadur Allah Baksh Somru of Sind and Sir Sahibzada Abdul Qayum of NWFP.

The Congress, on its part, refused to let the Muslim League join the government as a coalition partner. Such refusal cemented the policy of mutual support between the British and Jinnah. The then acting Viceroy Fifth Baron Brabourne is said to have reported to the then Secretary of State Lawrence John Lumley Dundas of Zetland on 18 August 1938 that Jinnah had proposed that the British 'should keep the Centre as it was now … and make friends with the Muslims by protecting them in the Congress Provinces' and that if the British did that, 'the Muslims would protect' the British 'at the Centre'.[41]

On 3 September 1939, the then Viceroy Victor Alexander John Hope Linlithgow proclaimed that war had broken out between Britain and Germany and that a state of war emergency existed in India.[42] The British government, without any consultation with the Indians or their elected representatives, declared India as a belligerent country at war with Germany. The Congress sought clarity on Britain's war aims before it would agree to cooperate in its war efforts.[43] On not getting a response, the Congress declared that the issue of war and peace for India had to be decided only by the Indian people and, in protest, resigned from the governments in the British provinces less than two months after the outbreak of the Second

World War. While India was, in the words of the then influential leader of the Congress and later India's first Prime Minister, Jawaharlal Nehru, 'completely opposed to the idea of the triumph of Nazism, it is no good asking her to come to the rescue of a tottering imperialism'.[44] It has been suggested that such step by the Congress created doubts in the mind of the British about the commitment of the Congress to join the fight against Adolf Hitler and prejudiced the British public opinion against it.[45] With the resignation of the Congress from the provincial governments, the Muslim League positioned itself to fill the political vacuum and assured the British of its cooperation in the war. Jaswant Singh notes that:[46]

> In order then to offset Congress hostility, and perhaps mindful of the dangers of Congress and the Muslims combining in their hostility against the British, as they had done during the Khilafat movement at the end of the First World War … the viceroy sought support elsewhere. The obvious and only choice was Jinnah and his Muslim League. Linlithgow found it expedient to befriend the Muslim League and to become a rival to the Congress on the all India scene. In the process the government used the existence of 'internecine conflicts' between Hindus and Muslims to consolidate its own position.

However, a war-weary Britain, who faced an intensifying freedom struggle across the Indian subcontinent against colonial rule, by now knew that it would eventually have to transfer power to Indian hands.

But then, losing control over the Indian subcontinent would have had far-reaching consequences for the entire British Empire. Sarila refers to the 'Great Game', or the 'Tournament of the Shadows' as the Russians called it, being played between Britain and the then Soviet Union to dominate Central Asia.[47] It was later that the Great Game translated into the Cold War, with the US relying on London's political and strategic support as also its extensive experience. Sarila writes that British strategists apprehended the extension of Russian influence into the Persian Gulf region with its oil fields, popularly referred to as the 'wells of power'.[48] Since this region was of vital interest to Britain, it was necessary for the British to have a Middle-Eastern sphere of influence. Besides, Britain could not afford to lose control over the entire Indian subcontinent that had served as its military base in dominating the Indian Ocean area and which had also been the never-ending source of manpower for the Imperial Army.[49] Indeed, the then Iranian Prime Minister Mohammad Mossadeq had noted in the 1950s that the strategic movements of the Allies in Iraq and Persia during the Second World War had only been possible due to the existence of such an Indian base.[50]

Yuvraj Krishan describes the reasons for Britain's desire to establish military bases in the North-West Frontier of colonial India as follows:[51]

.... The British military experts and imperial strategists felt alarmed by Germany's 'Drive towards the East', and the Soviet extension of power and acquisition of control over critically important raw materials like coal and oil in Central and South Asia. The British ruling classes and their military experts and strategists were unanimous that the German and Russian expansionism and export of Marxist ideology constituted threats to their political dominance in South Asia and South East Asia. These experts and strategists considered the establishment of the British military bases in the North West Frontier essential so as to ensure that the political control of the territories in Central Asia or of the Persian littoral was in friendly hands.

Thus, the way out for the British was to partition the Indian subcontinent in order to create an accommodating and reliable sovereign state in the crucial northwest region of the Indian subcontinent, 'Pakistan'. Menon records that:[52]

[T]he British were bent upon the division of the country; that they wanted to create a Middle-Eastern sphere of influence and in the pursuance of that policy wished to bring about the creation of a separate Pakistan ... was in accord with their policy of protecting the Straits of Hormuz on the Persian Gulf and the Suez Canal from Russian influence, and with their new but overwhelming interest in the oils of Iran, Iraq and Arabia.

Wali Khan adds that:[53]

[T]here was the matter of India's strategic natural location. Surrounded on three sides by vast oceans, its north was protected by the ramparts of the Himalayan range; a few natural passes were the only means of entering the country by land. The fact that those passes linked the country with the USSR posed the only real danger and threat.... During the Russian revolution of 1917 when the world witnessed its first ideological state, the British Government devised various strategies to curb its growth....

[The British] considered the (north west) Frontier their horizon because here they were pitted against a well-matched enemy. It bordered on Russia, where the Czarist empire extended to the river Amu in Afghanistan. After the Soviet Revolution of 1917.... River Amu, which until now was a geographical boundary, became an ideological boundary as well. In order to protect themselves from this ideological revolution, the British felt the need to create a counter ideology....

.... The Secretary ... wrote to the Viceroy that while the Hindus were only confined to India, Muslims were spread from the China border, all the way to Turkey....

.... [The British] wanted to use Islam as a military crescent which stretched from Turkey to the Chinese border, and which could be strung around the neck of the USSR.... To strengthen and complete the crescent an Islamic stronghold had to be created from Turkey and Iran right up to the China border. To achieve this, it was essential to separate, in the name of Islam, the northern part of India which bordered on the Russian territory....

[T]he English proposed to use Islam against Russia. In (colonial) India the Muslims were ruled by a *Kafir* race, the Christians. So to make a distinction between *Kafir* and *Munafiq*, they started calling the Russians anti-God. This was a clever use of semantics to create a Muslim aversion for Russia.

The British 'conjectured' that just as they could use Islam as an idealistic force against Russia ... [i]t could become a communal tool for creating hatred between the Hindus and the Muslims.

The poor relations between the British and the Congress had made the British realize that the Congress, which would rule India after its independence, would deny them military cooperation. The British settled for the Muslim League, which it had so far propped up to counter the political threat of the Congress to their colonial rule. The idea was to tempt the politically ambitious Jinnah, who led the Muslim League, with the plan to detach the predominantly Muslim northwest region of colonial India and to establish a separate state there—'Pakistan'—ostensibly on the basis of the two-nation theory. To put it simply, the theory asserted that Hindus and Muslims could not live peacefully together in one country and were to be considered as two separate nations in every respect.[54] Hence, a separate state should be carved out for the Muslims, namely, 'Pakistan'. The Indian subcontinent would, thus, be partitioned into the dominions of Hindu India and Islamic Pakistan.[55] The proposition became a realizable one following the working relationship established between the British and Jinnah during the Second World War.[56] Menon records that:[57]

[T]he Congress opposition to the war effort and the Muslim League's de facto support for it had convinced the British that Hindus generally were their enemies and the Muslims their friends, and that this consideration must have added force to the silent but effective official support for the policy of partition.

Wali Khan documents that it was at the instance of the then Viceroy Linlithgow that Chaudhry Muhammad Zafarullah Khan, a member of the Viceroy's Executive Council, was asked to submit a map of the two dominions.[58] Linlithgow wrote to the Secretary of State on 12 March 1940 that:[59]

Upon my instruction Zafarullah wrote a memorandum on the subject. Two Dominion States. I have already sent it to your attention.... Copies have been passed on to Jinnah.... While he, Zafarullah, cannot admit its authorship, his document has been prepared for adoption by the Muslim League with a view to giving it the fullest publicity.

Ten days later, Jinnah presented the two-nation theory at the All-India Muslim League session held from 22 March 1940 to 24 March 1940 at Minto Park, Lahore, as under:[60]

Hindus and Muslims belong to two different religions, philosophies, social customs and literature. They neither inter-marry nor inter-dine and, indeed, belong to two different civilizations that are based mainly on conflicting ideas and conceptions. Their concepts on life and of life are different. It is quite clear that Hindus and Muslims derive their inspiration from different sources of history. They have different epics, different heroes and different episodes. Very often the hero of one is the foe of the other, and likewise, their victories and defeats overlap. To yoke together two such nations under a single state, one as a numerical minority and the other as a majority, must lead to growing discontent and final destruction of any fabric that may be so built up for the government of such a state....

The Lahore Resolution of 1940 adopted by the Muslim League accordingly declared that:[61]

No constitutional plan would be workable or acceptable to the Muslims unless geographically contiguous units are demarcated into regions which should so be constituted with such territorial readjustments as may be necessary... the areas in which the Muslims are numerically in a majority as in the North-Western and Eastern zones of India should be grouped together to constitute independent states in which the constituent units shall be autonomous and sovereign.

The idea behind the Lahore Resolution of 1940 was clearly that of the British. Sarila writes that, at that time, neither Jinnah nor the Muslim League in fact represented all the Indian Muslims and that even within the Muslim League there was serious opposition to Jinnah's views.[62] He points out that 'Sikandar Hayat Khan and Fazal-ul-Haq, the Muslim League premiers of the Punjab and Bengal—the major provinces claimed by Jinnah for Pakistan—were totally opposed to the concept of a Muslim nation', with Sikandar Hayat Khan calling it 'Jinnahstan'.[63]

Given that it was the British who had chosen Jinnah to mouth the two-nation theory, the British did everything in their power to convey that Jinnah alone was the representative of 'all' Indian Muslims. Wali Khan documents that:[64]

.... In his letter dated 4 December 1939 the Viceroy wrote to the Secretary of State for India: I am fully alive, as my letter to you about Jinnah's questions will have shown, to the objection to allowing the Muslim minority to turn itself into a majority with the right of veto and that does seem to appear to be a position that we can accept.

This letter is written to explain his stand on the Muslim League Working Committee's proposal that the British Government should give it assurances that 'no declaration of constitutional accord for India should be made without the consent and approval of the All India Muslim League.'

.... During this time Jinnah made the following demand: The Muslim League should be taken into full and equal partnership with His Majesty's Government in the ruling of this country, and authority shared with them. [Viceroy's letter, dated 5 September 1940].

.... During those days, a large representative gathering of nationalist Muslims was held in Delhi. The Assembly was chaired by the Chief Minister of Sind, Allah Baksh Somru. The Secretary of State, Lord Zetland, asked the Viceroy to report on this gathering. On 14 May 1940, the Viceroy wrote:

I attach no particular importance to the Delhi Conference of the Muslims which took place a few days ago. It has been well organised and the Congress press machine has written it up admirably.... We both are, of course, aware that there is a *not unimportant* Muslim element outside the Muslim League.... Indeed, I am sure that Jinnah remains the man to deal with on the Muslim side.

The British deliberately ignored those Muslims, who, along with the Congress, were struggling for freedom. Their very faith was called 'questionable'. More than 1000 representatives, who had gathered together under the leadership of an elected Chief Minister, were totally disregarded. The Viceroy did not mince his words when he wrote to the Secretary of State that 'Jinnah is our man and we accept him as a representative of all Muslims.'

Wali Khan emphasizes that the British 'spared no effort to make it clear to all Muslims that unless they paid homage to Jinnah, they would remain non-entities for them', and to then turn the Muslim minority represented by Jinnah into a majority and accord it the power of veto.[65] Once Jinnah realized that the British needed him for their own interests, he demanded his pound of flesh to eliminate any other Muslim power centre. For instance, the British endorsed Jinnah's demand to dismiss Allah Bakhsh Somru's Sind government, with the Viceroy writing to the Secretary of State on 21 April 1940 that '[a]ll I can say is that if Congress are set on having a fight here, they are going to have a fight not only with us, but also with the Muslims'.[66] Jinnah chose to keep even the British guessing as to the territorial boundaries of 'Pakistan'. Indeed, the Viceroy wrote to the Secretary of State on 4 May 1943 that:[67]

> [F]rom (Jinnah's) own point of view half of the strength of his position is that he has refused to define (Pakistan). Thus I have no doubt that the famous corridor by which he proposes to link North West Pakistan with North East Pakistan, a corridor which would presumably run via Delhi, Lucknow, Allahabad and Patna, cutting off the area north of the corridor from the Hindu majority in the south of it, would almost inevitably figure....

Hodson asserts that 'a certain vagueness and lack of clarity were present by design' and that:[68]

> Mr. Jinnah had no intention of offering a focus of opposition, either within the Muslim ranks or beyond, by spelling out the details of the 'Pakistan' idea, details which were bound to expose both its general difficulties and its particular effects on areas or interests, but was content to leave it as a broad aspiration to which it was politically easier to adhere in principle than to object in application.

Jinnah and the Two-Nation Theory

Ironically, Jinnah, the individual chosen by the British to give effect to the two-nation theory, had worked for Hindu–Muslim unity for about the first 30 years of his political career. Jinnah, already a member of the Congress, had reacted strongly against the Muslim League's demand for separate electorates for Muslims, describing it 'as a poisonous dose to divide the nation against itself'.[69]

Jinnah apparently took a different view of the desirability of separate electorates on joining the Muslim League. Hodson describes this change as under:[70]

.... Jinnah... made his first excursion into politics as private secretary to the Hindu veteran Dadabhai Naoroji at the 1906 session of the Indian National Congress in Calcutta. He became the devoted discipline of another great Hindu and Congress leader, Gopal Krishna Gokhale, with whom he travelled to England in 1913. He identified himself with the Congress, and for long held back from the Muslim League, because its purpose was too sectarian. When he formally joined it, in 1913, he required his two sponsors 'to make a solemn preliminary covenant that loyalty to the Muslim League and the Muslim interest would in no way and no time imply even the shadow of disloyalty to the larger national cause, to which his life was dedicated'. It was this unswerving nationalist who said about separate electorates, in a speech at Ahmedabad in October 1916:

As far as I understand the demand for separate electorates is not a matter of policy but a matter of necessity to the Muslims, who are required to be roused from the coma and stupor into which they have fallen for so long. I would appeal to my Hindu brethren that in the present state of position they should try and win the confidence and trust of the Muslims, who are, after all, in the minority in the country. If they are determined to have separate electorates, no resistance should be shown to their demand.

Jinnah, as President of the Muslim League and member of the Congress, 'engineered the simultaneous meetings of both parties at Lucknow to further their unity in a common cause' of self-government.[71] This led to the Lucknow Pact of 1916 between both parties, which contemplated representation of Muslims through separate electorates in the provinces and the Imperial legislative council. Jinnah had advised the Muslims not to be 'scared away' by 'your enemies' from cooperation with the Hindus, 'which is essential for the establishment of self-government'.[72] Indeed, the *Bombay Chronicle* of 1 January 1916 noted that the Lucknow Pact of 1916 was 'made possible by the "signal service of Jinnah to the cause of Hindu–Muslim unity"'.[73] Sarojini Naidu, a prominent freedom fighter who later in 1925 became the first woman President of the Congress, gave Jinnah the title of 'the Ambassador of Hindu–Muslim Unity'.[74] K.K. Munshi writes that:[75]

In a sense Jinnah dominated the Congress and the League (both) at that same time. He had played a key role in preparing a draft constitution for India and getting it adopted by the sessions both of the Congress and the League. The historical Lucknow Pact was an integral part of this constitution. Under it, the Muslims led by the League promised to work with the Hindus to achieve freedom in return for the Congress conceding to the Muslims separate electorates with weightage far in excess of their numerical strength.

Yuvraj Krishan documents that Jinnah had, in his evidence in 1919 before the Parliamentary Select Committee, stated that 'nothing would please me more than when the day comes when the distinction in political life between Muhammedan and Hindu was done away with' and further had, in 1920, opposed the Khilafat movement spearheaded by orthodox Muslims to restore the institution of the Khalifa that had been abolished after the defeat of Turkey in the First World War (1914–1918).[76]

The Indian Statutory Commission, which had been set up by the British government in the 1920s to suggest constitutional reform in colonial India, comprised seven British Members of Parliament led by John Simon, to the exclusion of any Indian representative. Jaswant Singh records that Jinnah, on his return from England in October 1928 after lobbying with the British Labour Party and the India Office for inclusion of Indian representatives in the Simon Commission, stated in an 'interview to *The Times of India* on 26 October 1928 that it would be a folly to expect any substantial help from any one party in England and that the "one hope for India" was "unity between Hindus and Muslims"'.[77] He documents the anguish of Jinnah at the continuing failure of the parties concerned to achieve Hindu–Muslim unity over the next 10 years,[78] with his even telling Linlithgow, the then Viceroy, in 1938 that he preferred his own ideas of how to maintain a recognizable equipoise between the communities to 'any carving up of the country'.[79]

Linlithgow wrote to the Secretary of State on 5 September 1939 that 'I feel it wiser to be patient with Jinnah and endeavour to lead him into the direction which we desire'.[80] Jaswant Singh details how, in late 1939, Linlithgow used Jinnah to shift the focus from the anti-British freedom movement to Hindu–Muslim rivalry[81] and the steps that the British took to propound that 'the right of self-determination of Muslims as a community should be recognised' to thus provide a 'constitutional garb' to the two-nation theory.[82] These steps were taken by the British despite being aware that the creation of 'Pakistan' would keep the Indian subcontinent in turmoil perpetually, as is evident from the letter of the then Secretary of State Leopold Charles Maurice Stennett Amery to Linlithgow as early as the summer of 1940 in the following terms:[83]

> Now India has a very natural frontier at present. On the other hand, within herself she has no natural or geographic or racial or communal frontiers—the northwestern piece of Pakistan would include a formidable Sikh minority. The northwestern part has a Muslim minority in the United Provinces, the position of Muslim princes with Hindu subjects and vice versa. In fact, an all-out Pakistan scheme seems to me to be the prelude to continuous internal warfare in India.

For Jinnah, 'Pakistan' was more a means of grasping power, than stemming from any conviction of creating an Islamic state. Jinnah himself was not a practicing Muslim. It is well recorded that Jinnah never read the Quran nor performed the Haj; he did not follow the Quranic precepts of prayer; he did not abstain from drinking alcohol or eating pork.[84] Jinnah prided himself on being a 'modern, secular man', and 'moved mostly in the company of rich Parsis who were more Europeanized than other Indians'.[85] Jinnah did not speak 'Urdu nor Hindi and addressed public meetings in English, even if the crowd did not understand a word of what he was saying'.[86] Soon after the passage of the Indian Independence Act of 1947 by the British Parliament, on 18 July 1947, contemplating the formation of 'Pakistan' and prior to the establishment of 'Pakistan' on 14 August 1947, Jinnah himself rejected the two-nation theory in his speech in Karachi on 11 August 1947 in the Constituent Assembly set up for the future 'Pakistan' as under:[87]

.... Now, if we want to make this great State of Pakistan happy and prosperous, we should wholly and solely concentrate on the well-being of the people, and especially of the masses and the poor. If you will work in co-operation, forgetting the past, burying the hatchet, you are bound to succeed. If you change your past and work together in the spirit that everyone of you, no matter what community he belongs, no matter what relations he had with you in the past, no matter what is his colour, caste or creed, is first, second and last a citizen of this State with equal rights, privileges and obligations, there will be no end to the progress you will make.

I cannot emphasize it too much. We should begin to work in that spirit and in the course of time all these angularities of the majority and minority communities, the Hindu community and the Muslim community, because even as regards Muslims you have Pathans, Punjabis, Shias, Sunnis and so on, and among the Hindus, you have Brahmins, Vashnavas, Khatris, also Bengalis, Madrasis and so on, will vanish.... You are free; you are free to go to your temples, you are free to go to your mosques or to any other place of worship in this State of Pakistan. You may belong to any religion or caste or creed that has nothing to do with the business of the State.... We are starting in the days where there is no discrimination, no distinction between one community and another, no discrimination between one caste or creed and another. We are starting with this fundamental principle that we all are citizens and equal citizens of one State....

Now I think we should keep that in front of us as our ideal and you will find that in course of time Hindus would cease to be Hindus and Muslims would cease to be Muslims, not in the religious sense because that is the personal faith of each individual, but in the political sense as citizens of the State....

It will be noticed that Jinnah now referred to Hindus and Muslims in his speech as being different 'communities', and not 'two nations'. And when the first central government of Pakistan was formed, Jinnah gave Joginder Nath Mandal, a Hindu, the Ministry of Islamic Law![88] According to Pakistan's former Foreign Minister Khurshid Mahmud Kasuri, Jinnah 'expected a "multi-religious Pakistan to be counterpoised against a predominantly Hindu India, with both possessing significant minorities"'.[89] Sarila records that:[90]

> To the end of his life, Jinnah showed no respect for Quranic principles and tenets. In his will, he bequeathed certain monies on the basis of interest that would accrue and willed the whole of his property, instead of one-third, the maximum permitted under the Shariat. Jinnah was indifferent to the importance of the holy month of Ramzan for Muslims. For example, to welcome Lord and Lady Mountbatten during their visit to Karachi upon the establishment of Pakistan on 14 August 1947, he ordered an official luncheon. Since he did not practice the Islamic faith, he forgot that the luncheon had fallen in the month of Ramzan, during which Muslims fast from dawn to sunset. The luncheon had to be changed to a dinner party at the last minute.

Jinnah had mouthed the two-nation theory at the instance of the British, after having failed for about 30 years to politically dominate the Congress as a secularist. He had been slighted within the Congress and had serious differences with Mohandas Karamchand Gandhi, later known as Mahatma Gandhi, over the latter's method to achieve independence from the British. The Congress, on its part, had rejected many of the suggestions made by the secularist Jinnah, which he felt could have given more political space to Muslims within undivided India, making him nurse a feeling of having been let down. It was this dissatisfaction that the British exploited and propped up Jinnah to demand a separate Islamic state, 'Pakistan'. Jaswant Singh quotes M.R.A. Baig, who was for some years Jinnah's secretary, as saying that Islam came very little into Jinnah's thinking and that his opposition was not to Hindus or Hinduism but to the Congress leadership.[91] Jaswant Singh writes that:[92]

> The Muslim community for Jinnah became an electoral body; his call for a Muslim nation his political platform; the battles he fought were entirely political—between the Muslim League and the Congress; Pakistan was his political demand over which he and his Muslim League could rule. Religion in all this was entirely incidental....

Gandhi was dismissive of the two-nation theory. As early as 1908, Gandhi had written in the *Hind Swaraj* that[93] 'India cannot cease to be one nation, because people belonging to different religions live in it…. In no part of the world are one nationality and one religion synonymous terms; nor has it ever been so in India'.

Gandhi questioned in the *Harijan* on 28 October 1939 that:[94]

Why is India not one nation. Was it not one during, say, the Moghul period? Is India composed of two nations? If it is, why only two? Are not Christians a third, Parsis a fourth, and so on? Are the Muslims of China a nation separate from the other Chinese? Are the Muslims of England a different nation from the other English?

How are the Muslims of the Punjab different from the Hindus and the Sikhs? Are they not all Punjabis, drinking the same water, breathing the same air and deriving sustenance from the same soil? What is there to prevent them from following their respective religious practices? Are Muslims all over the world a separate nation? Or are the Muslims of India only to be a separate nation distinct from the others?

Gandhi, in his writings in 1940, asserted that:[95]

The 'two nations' theory is an untruth. The vast majority of Muslims of India are converts to Islam or are descendants of converts. They did not become a separate nation as soon as they became converts…. A Bengali Muslim speaks the same tongue that a Bengali Hindu does, eats the same food, has the same amusements as his Hindu neighbor. They dress alike…. When I first met (Jinnah), I did not know he was a Muslim. I came to know his religion when I had his full name given to me. His nationality was written on his face and manner….

…. It is worse than anarchy to partition a poor country like India whose every corner is populated by Hindus and Muslims living side by side. It is like cutting up a living body into pieces.

Jaswant Singh documents the conversation between Gandhi and Jinnah in 1944, during which Jinnah admits that the word 'Pakistan' did not occur in the Lahore Resolution of 1940 but that:[96]

[t]he word now has become synonymous with the Lahore resolution…. We maintain and hold that Muslims and Hindus are two major nations by any definition or test of a nation…. Muslims were a separate nation by virtue of their 'distinctive culture and civilisation, language and literature, art and architecture, names and nomenclature, sense of value and proportion, legal

laws and moral codes, customs and calendar, history and tradition', and, therefore, they were entitled to a separate, sovereign existence in a homeland of their own.

In an open letter to Jinnah on 15 September 1944, Gandhi reiterated that:[97]

> I find no parallel in history for a body of converts and their descendants claiming to be a nation apart from their parent stock.... If India was one nation before the advent of Islam, it must remain one in spite of the change of faith of a very large body of her children.... You seem to have introduced a new test of nationhood....

Muslims in the Indian Subcontinent and the Two-Nation Theory

It is important to emphasize here that since a friendly state, 'Pakistan', in the northwest region of the Indian subcontinent sufficed for Britain's Great Game with Russia, the two-nation theory was made applicable by the British only to partition the provinces of British India in order to create 'Pakistan'. The British were ambiguous about the status of the princely Indian states right upto 1946. As will be noted shortly, it was in the rulers of these states that the sovereignty vested and who were eventually given the option by the British to accede to either dominion or to retain their independence. The two-nation theory was, therefore, made inapplicable by the British to the princely Indian states. Religion had no role to play in determining the future of these states and the religious complexion of their populace was made completely irrelevant by the British for such purpose.

As regards British India, it has been well documented that the 'Pakistan movement' was stronger in provinces like UP, Bihar, Central Provinces and Berar, Bombay, where the Muslims were in a minority, rather than in provinces where the Muslims were in the majority and that eventually became 'Pakistan'.[98] Pakistan's former Foreign Minister Khurshid Mahmud Kasuri acknowledges that it was the Mahommedan Anglo-Oriental College (later renamed as the Aligarh Muslim University) near Delhi that 'produced the core leadership of the Pakistan Movement'.[99] It is ironical that the Muslims in the Muslim-minority provinces, who had called for the formation of 'Pakistan', were excluded from the 'Pakistan scheme', and in fact, were told by Jinnah in his 11 August 1947 speech at Karachi in the Constituent Assembly set up for the future 'Pakistan', that now that the Indian subcontinent had been partitioned, they should remain loyal citizens of India. This is how Jinnah put it:[100]

> I know there are people who do not quite agree with the division of India.... Much has been said against it, but now that it has been accepted, it is the duty of everyone of us to loyally abide by it and honourably act according to the agreement which is now final and binding on all.... Any idea of a united India would not have worked.... All the same, in this division it was impossible to avoid the question of minorities being in one Dominion or the other. Now that was unavoidable. There is no other solution....

The partition of India has, therefore, been said to have been a partition of Muslims. Sarila reasons that the Indian Muslims were not enamoured by the 'Pakistan' scheme because it meant foisting 'Pakistan' on Muslim majority provinces that did not fear 'Hindu domination under a democratic constitution', while excluding 25 to 30 million Muslims living in Muslim minority provinces who might welcome such 'Pakistan'.[101] Further, the Muslim sentiment was not to confine Muslim power to the west and east corners of the Indian subcontinent, as that would mean 'abandoning the heartlands of India such as Delhi, Agra and Lucknow, from where Muslim rulers had held sway over many parts of the country for more than 600 years' and 'where most famous and magnificent symbols of past Muslim power and glory, both secular and religious, such as the great forts of Delhi and Agra, the Taj Mahal, the Jama Masjid, amongst others, were situated'.[102] In fact, the 'Pakistan' scheme appeared 'unnecessarily defeatist to many Muslims', since the Muslim community, though a minority, was a substantial minority and could hold its own against the non-Muslims, who were divided into various faiths, such as Christianity, Zoroastrianism, Sikhism, Jainism, Buddhism and Hinduism.[103] Moreover, there were segments of the Muslim population, like weavers, that were opposed to 'Pakistan' due to fear of 'being uprooted and losing their long-developed and assured markets'.[104] Similarly, Shia Muslims felt that in 'an overwhelmingly Sunni Pakistan they would face more pressure exerted by that sect than in the large polyglot and multireligious India', and 'participated in the Muslims' protest against Jinnah's scheme'.[105] Sarila writes further that:[106]

> ... the Muslim fundamentalist groups were particularly opposed to Pakistan, however anomalous that may sound. The leading Sunni thinker and preacher of this time was Abdul Al Mawdudi of Hyderabad. In 1941, it was he who

formed the Jamaat-i-Islami, an organization whose influence during the last fifty years has spread far and wide over the Muslim world…. Mawdudi was against the type of sovereign authority on the Western model that Jinnah proposed to install in Pakistan…. Mawdudi's views were pan-Islamic and not India-centric. He foresaw a clash between the Muslims and the non-Muslims of the world—'a clash of civilizations'. Mawdudi's ideas have inspired ideologues and jihadis such as Omar Abdullah, the leader of the Taliban, and Osama bin Laden himself.

Several Muslims groups indeed held a meeting in Delhi after Jinnah gave his call for the partition of India to denounce his proposal. There was a long tradition of opposition by the Ulema—Muslim religious scholars—and their followers to British Christian rule. These religious scholars were influenced, among other Islamic religious movements, by the tenets of the Wahhabi creed (founded by Mohammad ibn Abd al Wahhal of Najad in Saudi Arabia). The Jamaat-ul-Ulema (the Congress of the Learned), founded in the 1920s, was a byproduct of such thinking. In the same decade, the Jamaat leader Maulana Shoam Noamani of Azamgarh established the Deoband and the Nadwain Tul Ulema seminaries in the United Provinces…. Many Ulemas felt a certain affinity for the Indian nationalists of the Congress Party because they were also fighting British domination…. Another Muslim group, the Ahrars, was influenced by the teachings of the Persia-born Maulana Afghani. Under his inspiration they worked to create a bridge between the Pathans of the North West Frontier Province and the Pathans of Afghanistan on the one hand and the Indian National Congress Party on the other. The objective was to jointly oppose the dethroning of the Ottoman Sultan, the Khalifa or the spiritual leader of the Muslims, by the British after the First World War. The movements they launched came to be known as the Khilafat Movement. Even after Mustafa Ataturk became the president of Turkey in 1923, and formally abolished the caliphate in 1924, the Pathans of the NWFP and Ahrars retained their links with the Congress Party.

The two-nation theory, which sought to define nationhood solely on the basis of religion, overlooked that Islamic rule over the centuries in the Indian subcontinent had resulted in a blend of Indo-Muslim culture and affinity among its people that touched almost every aspect of an individual's life. Maulana Abdul Kalam Azad, in his presidential address at the Congress session of 1940—the year Jinnah proclaimed the Lahore Resolution announcing the two-nation theory—had asserted that:[107]

> It was India's historic destiny that many human races and cultures should flow to her, finding a home in her hospitable soil, and that many a caravan should rest here…. Eleven hundred years of common history (of Islam

and Hinduism) have enriched India with our common achievements. Our languages, our poetry, our literature, our culture, our art, our dress, our manners and customs, the innumerable happenings in our daily life, everything bears the stamp of our joint endeavour.... These thousand years of our joint life have moulded us into a common nationality.... Whether we like it or not, we have now become an Indian nation, united and indivisible. No fantasy or artificial scheming to separate and divide can break this unity.

Interestingly, Pakistan's former Foreign Minister Khurshid Mahmud Kasuri has eloquently described in late 2015 the 'fusion of Indo-Muslim culture' over the centuries across the Indian subcontinent as under:[108]

... the relationship of various communities living in this region cannot be cast in black and white; it lies in the grey area... there have been long periods in the history of the subcontinent when Muslims and Hindus have lived peacefully under humane rulers who promoted tolerance and harmony. The Mughal legacy illustrates how different communities existed side by side in the subcontinent. The Mughal Empire was founded by Zahir-ud-din Muhammad Babur, who emphasised culture, not religion.... In the Mughal era, relations between the Sikhs and Muslims also improved.

.... The beautiful arches, with elaborate motifs, delicate stone masonry, slender marble columns, rich calligraphy, well-designed gardens, elaborate fountains, and ornate palaces are also characteristic of the historic fusion of Indo-Muslim culture. The Muslim architecture came in contact with Indian architecture resulting in new Indo-Muslim architecture.... After Muslim conquests, the practitioners of 'Sufism' arrived in India for the purpose of spreading Islam.... They all preached a message of love, brotherhood, harmony and peace, and through this message they were responsible for a number of conversions. The *dargah* (shrine) of Khwaja Moinuddin Chisti in Ajmer Sharif attracts pilgrims from different religions and is an excellent example of communal harmony.... Sufi music is also marked by the synthesis that was initiated under Amir Khusrau's (1253–1325) auspices between Indo-Islamic musical traditions which have grown steadily, thus producing a lasting feeling of cultural kinship between major communities of the subcontinent irrespective of religion....

It must be understood and emphasised that cultural fusion was not restricted to the arts in the subcontinent; rather it touched almost every aspect of a person's life. An astute understanding of South Asian history includes understanding all the features of a person's life that this culture has influenced: Meat and vegetable dishes, rice, and pudding were all part of Indo-Muslim culture and so were scents, jewellery designs, and most of all, the traditions of romance, poetry, plays, and musical instruments.

Kasuri writes that while 'even a few miles apart, it is possible to find a different set of dialects, customs, cultures, religions, and traditions', these are 'organically bound'.[109] He asserts that:[110]

... the people of the subcontinent are united by the shared experience of being burned by the summer sun, the sheer joy of the monsoon rains breaking the summer heat, and the memories of foreign invasions.

Many geographical occurrences are particular to South Asia. Rain is a discomfort to many parts of the Western world; in South Asia it causes the land to acquire a life of its own, and is a season to celebrate. Poets and musicians generate a string of melodies about the magic of rainfall, the elderly order steaming cups of *chai* (tea), and those obliged to stay indoors gaze dolefully outside their windows wishing to be part of the celebrations while stunned foreigners gape at the locals, taken aback by the extent of their elation.

Kasuri goes on to refer to the great rivers originating in the Himalayas and running through the subcontinent, like the Indus and the Ganges, which determined the culture and the behaviour of the people that populated the region.[111] He discusses the common practices, common food, common passion for *qawwalis* (devotional music) and *ragas* (classical music) and musical instruments such as *harmonium*, *tabla*, and *dholak*, the similar cinematic themes, and the love for the same sports, especially hockey and cricket, across the subcontinent.[112]

It may be pointed out here that while such affinity remains self-evident amongst the people across the Indian subcontinent, the description of a 'humane' Mughal rule may not be wholly accurate, in light of the instances of terrible religious persecution of the Hindus during the Mughal rule that have been documented. Indeed, several commentators refer to the religious differences to argue that the British did not create the Hindu–Muslim divide. Hodson asserts that:[113]

It is not possible to divide and rule unless the ruled are ready to be divided. The British may have used the Hindu–Muslim rivalry for their own advantage, but they did not invent it. They did not write the annals of India's history, nor prescribe the conflicting customs of her communities, nor foment the murderous riots that periodically flared between the Hindus and Muslims in her villages and cities. They were realists, and if they did use India's divisions for their advantages, the divisions themselves were already real.

But then, as Gandhi told Mountbatten, the then Viceroy, on 1 April 1947 that while one 'did not hold the British responsible for the origin of the Hindu–Muslim animosity, their policy of "divide and rule" had kept the hostility very much alive'.[114] What Gandhi perhaps was unaware of at that time was that the British had gone a step further. The British did not only intentionally pit Hindus and Muslims against each other through communal politics, they also pitted Muslims against each other through the avowed policy of making Jinnah, having little or no political base, the sole representative of all Indian Muslims, who would then single-handedly deliver a friendly 'Pakistan' to them. As will be evident shortly, the British deliberately required Jinnah to be intransigent and unreasonable in his demands, ostensibly on behalf of the Indian Muslims, so as to ensure the failure of any effort made by Indian leaders to placate or persuade him to give up 'Pakistan', whose creation was in the interests of the British for its Great Game.

Looking back, the two-nation theory was obviously fallacious. Religion could not keep even West Pakistan and East Pakistan united, leading to the birth of Bangladesh. The Muslims who migrated to West Pakistan, or the Mohajirs as they are termed there, have been up in arms ever since 1947 at the treatment meted out to them. Taking cue from Muslim-populated Balochistan, which seeks *azadi* (freedom) from Islamic Pakistan, a section of these Muslims were moving towards such azadi, if their protests outside the UN in early October 2015 are any indication.[115]

On the other hand, the rest of the subcontinent survives as one secular entity, India. Of course, Hindus and Muslims were, and will remain, different communities with a different way of life. Divisions have existed between them for centuries, just as they exist within communities in Britain and in the US. Persons belonging to different communities and faiths in Britain or in the US do not cease to be British or American on that ground. Similarly, the existence of differences between Hindus and Muslims does not imply that they could not coexist within one state. The fact that, notwithstanding periods of religious persecution, Hindus and Muslim coexisted for centuries before the British arrived on the Indian subcontinent was conveniently ignored. So was the fact that the 30 million Muslims left out of Pakistan would have to coexist with the Hindus in modern India following partition in 1947. It is worthwhile to mention that, as of date, there are more Muslims in India than in Pakistan.

It was because the northwestern region of colonial India, so crucial for British interests, was predominantly Muslim that the British formulated the two-nation theory to portray that the partition of British India (though not of the princely Indian states) was necessary to accommodate differences between Hindus and Muslims. This approach also came handy in resisting the US pressure to give freedom to the Indian subcontinent and to keep it united. It may be recalled that the Atlantic Charter had been signed on 12 August 1941 by the then US President Franklin Delano Roosevelt and the then British Prime Minister Winston Leonard Spencer-Churchill. The Atlantic Charter laid down certain common principles that the US and the UK wanted to follow for a better future for the world and these included the declaration that 'they respect the right of all peoples to choose the form of government under which they will live'. Hodson points out that the US 'was now Britain's ally, and American opinion, not least that of President Franklin Roosevelt, had been critical of British imperialism and specially anxious for a display of liberal aims in India, a move which it now believed to be essential if the subcontinent were to be saved from Japan'.[116] Further, the US had been advising Britain for years to keep colonial India united, fearing India's balkanization would help the communists. In fact, as late as 4 April 1947, Dean Gooderham Acheson, the then Under Secretary of the US Department of State, had wired to the US Embassy in London that '[o]ur political and economic interest in that part of the world would best be served by the continued integrity of India'.[117]

The British were obliged to give India her freedom. Sarila writes that the way out for the British was therefore to build a propaganda around the theme that 'it was not a question whether Great Britain is prepared to give India her freedom but whether India is in a position to exercise it, in view of the serious differences between the Hindus represented by the Congress Party and the Muslims represented by the Muslim League'.[118] Moreover, there was little the US could do if partition for such an ostensible reason was consented to by the Indian leadership.

Let us now consider how the British gave effect to their policy of partitioning the Indian subcontinent, and its people, in order to realize the British strategic and imperial interests in the region. I have dealt with this at length because in the words of the Pakistan scholar, Ayesha Jalan:[119]

> India's partition along ostensibly religious lines in 1947 is simply the most dramatic instance of postwar decolonization based on arbitrary drawing of boundaries. The forced migration of an estimated fourteen million people, the murder of perhaps two million men, women and children, devastated subcontinental pysches.... There can be no understanding of India, Pakistan, and Bangladesh without a full grasp of the lasting impact of partition on their self-imaging, political contestations and national projections.

Notes and References

1. Hodson writes that the 'concept of "Dominion Status", meaning full nationhood within the British Commonwealth, had been developed after the adoption of the famous Balfour Report on Inter-Imperial Relations by the Imperial Conference of 1926.... By convention and by law under the Statute of Westminster, 1931, it had come to embody complete constitutional freedom... and an assured and undenied right to secede from the Commonwealth'. See Hodson, H.V. 1969. *The Great Divide: Britain–India–Pakistan*, pp. 300–301. London: Hutchinson & Co (Publishers) Ltd.
2. *White Paper on Indian States*, 1950. Ministry of States, Government of India, p. 17.
3. *Supra* Note 1, p. 24.
4. Ibid.
5. *Madhav Rao* v *Union of India*: (1973) 3 SCR 9 at p. 76.
6. Sarila, Narendra Singh. 2005. *The shadow of the Great Game: the Untold Story of India's Partition*, p. 75. New Delhi: HarperCollins.
7. Khan, Wali. 2004. *Facts are Facts: The Untold Story of India's Partition*, p. 10. Available online at http://www.awaminationalparty.org/books/factsarefacts.pdf (downloaded on 1 October 2015).
8. Extracted in ibid.
9. Ibid., p. 11.
10. *Supra* Note 6, p. 75.
11. *Supra* Note 7, p. 2.
12. Singh, Jaswant. 2009. *Jinnah: India–Pakistan Independence*, pp. 304–305. New Delhi: Rupa & Co.
13. Ibid., p. 29.
14. Ibid., p. 30.
15. *Supra* Note 6, p. 75.
16. Extracted in *Supra* Note 12, p. 47.
17. Ibid., pp. 526–530.
18. Ibid., p. 527.
19. Ibid.
20. Ibid., p. 568.
21. *Supra* Note 6, p. 76.
22. *Supra* Note 12, p. 49.
23. Ibid., p. 51.
24. Ibid., p. 532.
25. Ibid., p. 51.
26. *Supra* Note 7, p. 13.
27. Ibid.
28. Guha, Ramachandra, 2007. *India after Gandhi*, p. 27. London: Macmillan: (Picador).
29. *Supra* Note 7, p. 14.
30. Ibid.
31. Ibid., p. 15.
32. Ibid.
33. Ibid., p. 16.
34. Ibid.

35. Ibid., pp. 16, 18.
36. Extracted in Krishan, Yuvraj. 2013. *Partition and Pakistan: Jinnah the Founder, British the Architects*, p. 230. New Delhi: Mosaic Books.
37. *Supra* Note 1, p. 81.
38. *Supra* Note 36, p. 230.
39. *Supra* Note 12, p. 537.
40. *Supra* Note 7, p. 175.
41. Cited in *Supra* Note 6, p. 92.
42. *Supra* Note 1, p. 76.
43. *Supra* Note 12, p. 263.
44. *Supra* Note 1, pp. 83–84.
45. *Supra* Note 6, p. 37.
46. *Supra* Note 12, pp. 263–264.
47. *Supra* Note 6, p. 18.
48. Ibid., p. 9.
49. Ibid.
50. Cited in ibid., p. 21.
51. *Supra* Note 36, p. 140.
52. Cited in *Supra* Note 6, p. 103.
53. *Supra* Note 7, pp. 2, 32, 34, 69–71.
54. *Supra* Note 1, Introduction.
55. Ibid.
56. *Supra* Note 6, p. 10.
57. Cited in ibid., pp. 61–62.
58. *Supra* Note 7, p. 40.
59. Ibid.
60. *Supra* Note 12, pp. 640–641.
61. Ibid., p. 641.
62. *Supra* Note 6, p. 57.
63. Ibid., p. 57.
64. *Supra* Note 7, pp. 32, 41–42, 45.
65. Ibid., pp. 32, 48.
66. Ibid., p. 37.
67. Extracted in ibid., p. 62.
68. *Supra* Note 1, p. 80.
69. *Supra* Note 6, p. 78.
70. *Supra* Note 1, p. 16.
71. Ibid., p. 17.
72. *Supra* Note 6, p. 78.
73. *Supra* Note 12, p. 103.
74. Ibid., p. 607.
75. Cited in ibid., p. 123.
76. *Supra* Note 36, p. 258.
77. *Supra* Note 12, pp. 169–170.
78. Ibid., p. 203.
79. Ibid., p. 243.
80. Extracted in *Supra* Note 7, p. 27.
81. *Supra* Note 12, p. 283.

82. Ibid., p. 304.
83. Cited in *Supra* Note 6, p. 65.
84. Ibid., p. 77.
85. Ibid., pp. 77–78.
86. Ibid., p. 77.
87. *Supra* Note 12, pp. 570–574.
88. *Supra* Note 7, p. 191.
89. Kasuri, Khurshid Mahmud. 2015. *Neither a Hawk nor a Dove: An Insider's Account of Pakistan's Foreign Policy*, p. 87. Gurgaon: Penguin Books India Ltd.
90. *Supra* Note 6, p. 93.
91. *Supra* Note 12, p. 485.
92. Ibid., p. 486.
93. Extracted in *S.R. Bommai v Union of India*: AIR 1994 SC 1918 at p. 1950.
94. Extracted in Gandhi, Rajmohan. 2007. *Mohandas*, pp. 452–453. New Delhi: Penguin Books Pvt. Ltd.
95. Ibid., pp. 456–457.
96. *Supra* Note 12, p. 319.
97. Extracted in *Supra* Note 12, p. 322.
98. See *Supra* Note 36, p. 95.
99. *Supra* Note 89, p. 94.
100. Extracted in *Supra* Note 12, p. 572.
101. *Supra* Note 6, p. 66.
102. Ibid., pp. 66–67.
103. Ibid., p. 67.
104. Ibid., p. 69.
105. Ibid.
106. Ibid., pp. 67–69.
107. Extracted in *Supra* Note 28, p. 25.
108. *Supra* Note 89, pp. 124, 129–132.
109. Ibid., p. 130.
110. Ibid., pp. 130–131.
111. Ibid., at pp. 131–132.
112. Ibid., at pp. 130–131.
113. *Supra* Note 1, p. 16.
114. Ibid., p. 221.
115. *The Times of India*. 2015. 'Mohajirs, Baloch hit Pak's K-stand', New Delhi, 9 October.
116. *Supra* Note 1, p. 91.
117. Extracted in *Supra* Note 6, p. 263.
118. Ibid., pp. 153–154.
119. Jalal, Ayesha. 2013. *The Pity of Partition*, pp. 3–4. Noida: HarperCollins Publishers India.

II

Moving towards Partitioning the Indian Subcontinent

The British ruthlessly pursued their aim to divide the Indian subcontinent in order to create 'Pakistan', a friendly state in the northwest region of colonial India, which would help protect British interests in the area and check the spread of Soviet influence in the oil-rich Middle East. Having got Jinnah to mouth the two-nation theory, the British simply adopted the position that 'ignoring Jinnah's demands for a separate state would hurt the British position amongst the Muslims of the Middle East'.[1] Sarila writes that there was, however, 'no special sympathy for Jinnah or his movement in Muslim countries', many of which in fact saw 'Jinnah as a British puppet', and notes that:[2]

> In the Middle East at that time, feelings of anti-colonialism, nationalism or socialism were stronger than those of the Islamic brotherhood. The Palestinians were fighting the Jews to prevent their land from being occupied on the basis of nationalism and not on communal considerations. The secular Baath party of Lebanon, which was to spread to Syria and Iraq, and later the phenomenon of 'Nasserism' in Egypt, attempted to adopt socialism and nationalism as their planks, essentially to create an ideological platform other than one based on Islam, on which people of other faiths could join Muslims in their struggle against foreign domination. Afghanistan was so hostile to Pakistan than it was the only country in the world to vote against the latter's admission to the United Nations. There was no contact between Jinnah and Saudi Arabia.... Mohammad Mossadeq, the prime minister of Iran, who nationalized oil, was moved by a secular impulse. Iran turned pro-Pakistan after the British and the Americans helped to build up the Pakistan–Iran axis under the umbrella of the anti-Soviet Baghdad Pact and the CENTO Pact.

The Quit India Movement by the Congress in 1942 further distanced the British from the Congress, having come in the midst of the Second World

War (1939–1945) at a critical time when the British were struggling to get any military success. Indeed, this movement was perceived by Churchill, the then British Prime Minister, and the British public as a stab in the back,[3] making the creation of 'Pakistan' even more imperative. The British now had to get the Congress leadership to accept the principle of partition to make 'Pakistan' materialize. For this purpose, the British floated several 'Plans' from time to time. Before examining these 'Plans', it will be useful to first consider the constitutional framework that had been put in place by the British to govern the Indian subcontinent in line with their imperial interests.

Constitutional Framework

As noticed earlier, the Government of India Act of 1858 had contemplated the appointment of the Viceroy of India by the British Crown, who was to be instructed in the exercise of his powers by the Secretary of State. This Act was followed by successive Government of India Acts of 1912, 1915, 1919 and 1935.

The Government of India Act of 1919 sought to devolve some power to the provincial governments. However, the governor of a province had the final say, regardless of the view of the provincial government or its ministers. The Government of India remained under the Viceroy and responsible to the British Parliament through the Secretary of State. The structure of the government remained unitary.

In the early 1930s, the Round Table Conference at London, attended by the representatives of the British government, the princely Indian states and British India, was convened to consider the establishment of a federation in the Indian subcontinent between the provinces and the princely Indian states, structured in such a way that the federal government would be under British influence and would be able to accommodate essential British interests.

Churchill, who was later to become the British Prime Minister on 10 May 1940, had, however, opposed such a federation, taking the view that it could encourage the Indian political parties and religious groups to work together and initiate political unity and self-rule in the subcontinent. For Churchill, 'India was a geographical expression, a land that was no more a single country than the equator', and it did not matter how many pieces it was broken up into.[4]

Churchill preferred to trifurcate India into three mutually antagonistic entities: 'A Muslimstan, a Hindustan and a Princestan', as disclosed by

Linlithgow to Jinnah on 13 March 1940.[5] Churchill was anxious not to encourage and promote Hindu–Muslim unity as he argued that such 'unity was, in fact, almost out of the realm of practical politics, while, if it were to be brought about, the immediate result would be that the united communities would join in showing us the door'.[6] Archibald Wavell, who succeeded Linlithgow as Viceroy of India, also recorded, after his meeting with Churchill on 29 March 1945 at London, that Churchill 'seems to favour partition of India into Pakistan, Hindustan and Princestan'.[7] Such a trifurcation would help the British play the Muslims, the Hindus and the rulers of the princely Indian states against each other and thus govern the Indian subcontinent for decades to come. Churchill himself summed up his view as under:[8]

> We hope once and for all to kill the idea that the British in India are aliens moving out of the country as soon as they have been able to set up any kind of governing organisation to take their place. We shall try to inculcate the idea ... that we are there forever as honoured partners with our Indian fellow subjects whom we invite in all faithfulness to join with us ... in the higher function of governments for their lasting benefits and for our own....

Churchill had, therefore, denounced the proposed all-India federation in the British Parliament as a 'gigantic quilt of jumbled crochet work, a monstrous monument of shame built by pygmies',[9] and 'the possibility that India would gradually move towards becoming a dominion as being "criminally mischievous"'.[10]

The British Parliament, nonetheless, did enact the Government of India Act of 1935, which provided for the formation of a federation in the Indian subcontinent. Churchill sent intermediaries to the Indian subcontinent to persuade the rulers of the princely Indian states not to join the proposed federation.[11] The officers of the Indian Political Service, who dealt with these rulers, quietly supported Churchill.[12] The part of the Government of India Act of 1935 that dealt with the federation never became effective. While the Government of India continued to function as constituted under the Government of India Act of 1919, some departments in the provinces were administered with the aid of ministers, who were to be popularly elected and in a sense responsible to the electorate. However, the Governors of the provinces could still act in their discretion without consulting the ministers in respect of certain matters. The administration thus continued to function as an agent of the British Parliament.

The decision to detach parts of the Indian subcontinent to serve as a defence bastion for the British gathered momentum during the period that Churchill was the British Prime Minister.[13] It has, indeed, been a matter of speculation whether it was Churchill's friends who had earlier 'inspired' 36-year-old Rahmat Ali to propose the creation of a separate sovereign state in the northwestern region of colonial India, and to coin the term 'Pakistan' for such state in a pamphlet titled *Now or Never* that he had published in 1933 from Cambridge in England.[14] Hodson discloses that the Muslim League delegation to London, which included Jinnah, dismissed the idea of 'Pakistan'.[15] Hodson writes that:[16]

> Mr. C Rahmat Ali claims, with evident reason, to be the founder of the Pakistan movement. In 1933 he and three other young Muslim Indians in England circulated a leaflet declaring that 'on behalf of our thirty million Muslim brethren who live in PAKISTAN—by which we mean the five northern units of India—viz., *P*unjab, North-West Frontier Province (*A*fghan Province), *K*ashmir, *S*ind and Baluchis*tan*' ... they protested against the federal constitution then being adumbrated at the Round Table Conference, and repudiated the claim of the Indian Muslim delegation—which of course included Mr. Jinnah—to speak for their community. India, they wrote, was not the name of one single country, or the home of one single nation. The Muslims of PAKISTAN, a distinct nation, 'demand the recognition of a separate national status'.
>
> Delegates of the Muslim League and the All-India Muslim Conference, [when] asked about a scheme 'under the name of Pakistan' [while] giving evidence to the Joint Select Committee of Parliament, dismissed it as 'only a students' scheme' and 'chimerical and impracticable'.

However, as far as the British were concerned, the partition of the Indian subcontinent to create 'Pakistan' was a foregone conclusion for the reasons discussed earlier. Let us now examine the 'Plans' drawn by the British to get the Congress to concede 'Pakistan'.

Stafford Cripps Plan

The Stafford Cripps Plan, formulated in London in February 1942, contemplated that India could, immediately after the war, 'have full independence ... [a]nd in the interim period, the leaders of the Indian political parties would be asked to enter the Viceroy's Executive Council and enjoy considerable autonomy except for the conduct of the war that would remain in British hands'.[17] Hodson records that Stafford Cripps arrived at Delhi on 22 March 1942 and addressed the press on 29 March 1942, following which he released a draft declaration to the effect that:[18]

1. Immediately after the end of the war an elected body would be set up in India with the task of framing a new constitution....
2. His Majesty's Government undertook to accept and implement forthwith the constitution so framed subject to ... the right of any province that was not prepared to accept the new constitution to retain its existing constitutional provision, provision being made for its subsequent accession, should it so decide. His Majesty's Government will be prepared to agree with a non-acceding province a new constitution, arrived at by a similar representative process, and giving it the same status as the Indian Union itself....
3. During the war and until the new constitution could be framed the British Government must control and direct the defence of India.... His Majesty's Government invited the immediate and effective participation of the leaders of the principal sections of the Indian people in the counsels of their country, of the Commonwealth and of the United Nations.

In other words, the British promised that once the war was over, they would recognize the provinces that chose not to accept the new constitution of India as separate national governments. All that the provinces had to do was to stay out of the proposed Indian Union. Significantly, the then Secretary of State Leopold Amery by his letter of 24 March 1942 to the then Viceroy Linlithglow pointed out: 'Jinnah ... will be content to realise that he has now got his Pakistan in essence, whether something substantive, or a bargaining point'.[19]

The Stafford Cripps Plan contemplated partition of the Indian sub-continent in such a manner that the fractured units would continue to be dependent on the British. Amery, in his letter of 24 March 1942 to Linlithglow, referred to the Plan as under:[20]

As regards that plan, the more I think of it the more probable it seems to me that in some form or other the Viceroy will have to remain, not merely as a constitutional Governor General, but as representative of broader imperial aspects of the government, for a good long time to come, and to be equipped with the instruments of power required to carry out its functions. After all, supposing that Pakistan does come off, there will possibly be two Muslim areas, the whole of the States, Hindu British India (if that does not divide itself up!).... It is obviously absurd to think that each of these is going to have its own air force and navy or even its own mechanized ground forces on any scale that is going to be of use for the defence of India. There will have to be someone in the absence of a central self-governing federal scheme, to take control of these matters.... So whatever else you do or agree to, you had better keep in mind the desirability of retaining Delhi and a considerable area around it as the ultimate federal territory of an eventually united India, and not let it pass into the hands of any one of the 'Dominions' that may temporarily emerge out of the first experiment in constitution framing.... When the entire country is thus broken up and there is no strong Central Government, it would be impossible for the various units to maintain their Military, Naval and Air strength. Therefore, once again they will become dependent on the British.

The intent of offering the Congress leaders 'considerable autonomy' in the British-run Government of India during the interim period was clear—to tempt them with a whiff of power in order to soften them for partition. Should the Congress wish to assume office in the British-run Government of India, pending the formulation of the new constitution of India after the war, it would first have to accept the principle of partition of India at the time of independence. Sarila notes that the 'provincial option'—namely, that the Indians must accept the right of any of the provinces to stay out of independent India if they chose to do so—remained a constant feature in subsequent British policies, including the Cabinet Mission Plan of 1946 and in the announcement on 20 February 1947 by the then British Prime Minister Clement Richard Attlee of British withdrawal from the Indian subcontinent.[21]

The Congress was put in a fix by the introduction of such 'provincial option', having preached about self-determination in the past.[22] While the Congress Resolution of 11 April 1942 opposed the Stafford Cripps Plan because of its 'acceptance beforehand of the novel principles of non-accession for a Province … [which would be] a severe blow to the conception of Indian unity', the same resolution also stated that it 'cannot think in terms of compelling the people in any territorial unit to remain in an Indian union against their declared and established will'.[23] The Congress stuck to this position throughout, with its Working Committee resolution of September 1945 being couched in the same terms. Hodson writes that this was 'a hole in the dyke which Mr. Jinnah was determined to widen', since the device of the 'provincial option' had opened 'the door to the principle of Pakistan' which, as noted above, had been 'vaguely endorsed by the Congress in the words of the Working Committee's resolution'.[24]

Sarila asserts that Wavell, the Viceroy from 1943 to early 1947, had also understood that Britain, 'a fading power in India', would have to withdraw from the subcontinent; the 'primary usefulness' of the Indian subcontinent for Britain in future 'would be for defence and not any more a market'; that the Congress, which would 'rule India after the British withdrew, was unlikely to cooperate with Britain on military matters and foreign policy, whereas the Muslim League, which wanted a partition of India, would be willing to do so'.[25] Accordingly, Wavell too subscribed to the view that the British defence interests in the Middle East and the Indian Ocean area could be served 'if the Muslim League were to succeed in separating India's strategic northwest from the rest of the country'.[26] Wavell believed that the way forward was to promote 'the ambitious Jinnah and, with his co-operation, to withdraw the British forces into the Muslim-majority provinces, including the strategic northwest of India—and the port of Karachi—as they were the most suitable areas to counter any Soviet expansionist designs'.[27] Such separate state, 'Pakistan', was, of course, to become a dominion of the British Commonwealth.[28] Churchill, who had by then become the British Prime Minister, endorsed such view.

On 5 May 1945, the day Germany surrendered, Churchill directed the Post-Hostilities Planning Staff of the War Cabinet to assess 'the long-term policy required to safeguard the strategic interests of the British Empire in India and the Indian Ocean', the report in respect of which was submitted on 19 May 1945.[29] The report emphasized that 'Britain *must* retain its military connection with the subcontinent so as to ward off the Soviet Union's threat to the area', citing four reasons for the 'strategic importance of India to Britain'—India's 'value as a base from which forces could be suitably deployed within the Indian Ocean area, in the Middle East and the Far East'; it serving as 'a transit point for air and sea communications'; it being 'a large reserve of manpower of good fighting quality'; and the strategic importance of the northwest region to threaten the Soviet Union.[30] Following such report, 'the British Chiefs of Staff became enthusiastic proponents of a Pakistan that would cooperate with Britain in military matters' and provide 'strategic facilities such as the port of Karachi and airbases in North West India and the support of Muslim manpower'.[31] In a subsequent report, the Chiefs of Staff asserted that 'British strategic interests in the subcontinent should be focused on Pakistan' as the 'area of Pakistan [West Pakistan or the northwest of India] is strategically the most important in the continent of India and the majority of our strategic requirements could be met … by an agreement with Pakistan alone'.[32] Sarila states that:[33]

The crux [of the British policy was that the] Indus Valley, western Punjab and Baluchistan [the northwest] are vital to any strategic plans for the defence of [the] all-important Muslim belt … the oil supplies of the Middle East. If one looks upon this area as a strategic wall (against Soviet expansionism) the most important bricks in the wall are: Turkey, Iran, Afghanistan and Pakistan. Only through the open ocean port of Karachi could the opponents of the Soviet Union take immediate and effective countermeasures. The sea approaches to all other countries will entail navigation in enclosed waters directly menaced by Russian air fleets ... not only of the sea lanes of approach, but also the ports of disembarkation. If the British Commonwealth and the United States of America are to be in a position to defend their vital interests in the Middle East, then the best and most stable area from which to conduct this defence is from Pakistan territory. In light of the Cripps offer, the British still hoped that some large princely states would become independent and it may however be possible ... to use the territory of independent [princely] Indian States.

The British, having mooted the two-nation theory, having hand-picked the politically ambitious Jinnah to propound such theory in order to demand 'Pakistan', and having formulated the 'provincial option' to enable the creation of 'Pakistan', now spared no effort to paint Jinnah and his Muslim League as the sole representative of all Indian Muslims. Jinnah, with little or no political base, but claiming to represent all Indian Muslims, would then stand firm on his demand for 'Pakistan' and effectively ensure that there was no settlement that would make the British irrelevant or compromise British interests.

Interestingly, it appears that even at this point of time, the Muslim League itself was unsure of whether it would get 'Pakistan' and did not want the British to transfer the power presumably in the hands of the Congress. Wali Khan documents that the Muslim League was:[34]

> in fact, anxious to impress upon the British that the Muslims of India did not want them to leave. The Viceroy of India, Lord Wavell, wrote that the British should stay on in India for a while; at least the Muslims did not want to see them go. 'He [Liaquat Ali Khan] said that in any event we [British] should have to stop for many years yet, and that the Muslims were not at all anxious that we should go ... [Jinnah] maintained that India did not need any final transfer of power, and that those who made such demands were unaware of the existing conditions. Democracy could not prevail in a country like India'.

Let us now consider how the British played up the differences between the Congress and the Muslim League, and then, citing possible civil war, required them to settle their differences as a condition precedent to the transfer of power, while instructing Jinnah to veto any possible settlement.

Simla Conference of 1945

On his return from London, Wavell declared at Delhi on 4 June 1945 that he planned to call a political conference in Simla on 25 June 1945, and that:[35]

I propose, with the full support of His Majesty's Government, to invite Indian leaders both of central and provincial politics to counsel with me with a view to the formation of a new Executive Council, more representative of organised political opinion. The proposed new Council would represent the main communities and would include equal proportion of caste Hindus and Muslims....

Thus, the stage was set by the British for the Muslim League to claim 'equal proportion' of the representation in the government on behalf of the Muslims of India, though Muslims formed less than one-fourth of the total population.

The Indian leaders were asked to meet Wavell at the Viceregal Lodge at Simla on 25 June 1945. Though the purpose of this Simla Conference was stated to be the '*Indianization* of the Viceroy's Executive Council' within the framework of the Government of India Act of 1935,[36] the idea was to give Jinnah a platform to make a long statement to highlight Hindu–Muslim differences, argue fully the case for 'Pakistan' and claim to represent all the Muslims of India.[37] Sarila writes that:[38]

According to Durga Dass, a journalist of great integrity, Jinnah told him in the lift of the Cecil Hotel, Simla (towards the end of the conference), that he had been assured by friends in England, through a member of the Viceroy's Executive Council, that 'if he remained firm on the demand [of exclusively representing the Muslims and thus breaking the conference] he would get Pakistan.' One of the two secretaries of the Simla Conference has written: 'Hossain Imam, who attended the conference in his capacity as the leader of the Muslim League party in the Council of States, stopped me on my way to the Cecil Hotel and said that a member of the Viceroy's Executive Council was advising Jinnah to stand firm.'

Wavell held several interviews with Indian political leaders on the eve of the Simla Conference, during which Wavell deliberately sought to undermine non-Muslim League leaders by dismissively telling Gandhi that Indian Muslims trusted only the Muslim League. Hodson records that:[39]

The Viceroy had interviews with Mr. Gandhi, Mr. Jinnah and Maulana Azad on 24th June. Out of these talks three clear points emerged. Both Maulana Azad and Mr. Gandhi insisted that the Congress, without wishing to fight on the issue of parity, must have a say in the representation of communities other than Caste Hindus, and would not accept the nomination of Muslims by only one communal organisation. Mr. Gandhi also claimed that in the provinces minorities should be represented in the Government by members of their communities belonging to the Congress, to which the Viceroy tartly retorted that the vital point was that they should be represented by people they trusted. Mr. Jinnah, on the other hand, claimed that under the proposals the Muslims would have always been in minority, for the Sikhs and Scheduled Castes would vote for the Congress. He asked that no matter should be decided in the Executive Council by vote if the majority of the Muslim members opposed. And he claimed for the Muslim League the right to nominate all the Muslim members, and specifically objected to including representatives of the Punjab Unionist Party or of Congress Muslims.

Sarila points out that:[40]

the conference failed as it was planned to fail, because Wavell refused to veto Jinnah's claim to represent all Muslims, being fully aware that both the Punjab and the NWFP ministries of Muslims opposed to Jinnah were in office and commanded majorities in the legislatures. Wavell had before him the top-secret and personal telegram sent by Sir Bertrand James Glancy, the governor of the Punjab, dated 3 July 1945, stating: 'Jinnah's claim to nominate all Muslims appears to me in light of League's meager hold on Muslim-majority Provinces, to be outrageously unreasonable. If he is given three nominations out of, say, five Muslim seats he should account himself [sic] fortunate indeed.' Wavell knew all along that Jinnah would stick to his guns, a stand that would be unacceptable to the Congress Party. He also knew that London would never agree to overrule Jinnah's demand, however absurd it may be; or let the Congress Party enter his 'cabinet', without the countervailing presence of the Muslim League in it. Therefore, 'enacting' the Simla Conference had no other purpose except to build up Jinnah against his Muslim rivals in the Punjab and to head off renewed American pressure for Indian self-government. And in this, Wavell succeeded brilliantly. The results of Simla were recorded by the Punjab governor as follows: 'Since Jinnah succeeded by his intransigence in wrecking the Simla Conference his stock has been standing very high with his followers and with a large section of the Muslim population. He has openly come out that the [coming] election will show an overwhelming verdict in favour of Pakistan. The uninformed Muslim would be told that the question he is called on to answer at the polls is—Are you a true believer or an infidel or a traitor? Against this slogan the Unionists have no spectacular battle cry.

Wali Khan agrees that Wavell had convened the Conference 'to tell the world that he was prepared to make a settlement, but whom should he settle with if the Hindus and the Muslims persisted in their mutual disagreement?', and that the 'conference was not expected to find a solution to the problem' but 'was held to bring the leaders face to face so that the situation could reach an impasse and subsequently deteriorate'.[41] He describes the happenings at the Conference as under:[42]

The Simla Conference approved Wavell's first suggestion that a Central Executive Council be formed. At the start he had indicated that there would be a Muslim and a non-Muslim party. Jinnah became adamant on the point that no one else had the right to represent the Muslims, and, moreover, no one had the right to appoint any Muslim Minister on this Council. His intention was clear: that the Muslims and non-Muslims should have equal representation. At one end of the political spectrum was Jinnah and on the other all the inhabitants of India; Hindus, Sikhs, Christians and Parsis. India had a population of forty crores of which ten crores were Muslims. While the Muslim League had not formed the Government in a single province, the Congress had formed the Government in eight provinces, which included provinces with Muslim majority. Muslim League had not whiffed at the sweet smell of success even in the Muslim provinces! Of the one hundred and seventeen seats in Bengal, the Muslim League had won forty and of the eighty-four in Punjab, only one. They had no seat in Sind or in the Frontier.

Wavell asked Jinnah how many Muslim Ministers should there be on the Council? Jinnah expressed the view that, 'They must all be nominated by the League and must all be Leaguers. None, except himself, as head of the Muslim League, could nominate the Muslims on the new Council'.

The Muslim League's obstinacy enabled the British to say that since the Indians could not reach agreement, the power should remain with the British Government. H.V. Hodson wrote 'A minority party with unsupportable claim had been allowed to veto the whole project for advancing India's Self Government'.

Wali Khan highlights the British attempt to persuade the Congress to accept that the Muslim League would represent all Indian Muslims:[43]

Lord Wavell concluded the defunct Simla Conference on the note that the Congress should recognize the League as the sole representative of the Indian Muslims. Dr Khan Sahib, who was present, asked Wavell, 'I am the Chief Minister of the largest Muslim Province, but not a member of the Muslim League. What do you have to say to me?' ... The British ... were insistent that unless the Congress accepted the Muslim League as the sole representative of all Muslims, there could be no agreement.... The British were using the Muslim League for its own private game.... These games were being played to tell the world that while the British were ready to relinquish power, the Indians were not ready to assume it.... Therefore, at the Simla Conference held in 1945, the British had only one purpose; to impress upon the Muslims that if anyone wanted to be recognized and represented, his only course was to sign up with the Muslim League'.

Yuvraj Krishan terms the Conference to be 'Churchill–Amery–Wavell' conspiracy 'to proclaim the British policy on "The Problem of India" to be: acceptance of (i) the two nation theory (ii) that India was not one country but "two lands"—Hindustan and Pakistan, (iii) the Muslim League truly represented the majority of Muslims of India; and (iv) above all, the Muslims' fears of suffering oppression and injustice at the hands of the Hindu majority were genuine'.[44] Indeed, Wavell wrote to Amery on 15 July 1945 that:[45]

> ... the immediate cause of the failure of the Conference was Jinnah's intransigence about Muslim representation and Muslim safeguards. The deeper cause was the real distrust of the Muslims, other than the Nationalist Muslims, for the Congress and the Hindus. Their fear that the Congress, by parading its national character and using Muslim dummies will permeate the entire administration of any United India is real, and cannot be dismissed as an obsession of Jinnah and his immediate entourage.

Hodson concludes that:[46]

> The immediate effect was greatly to heighten the prestige of the Muslim League and its leader at a time when its fortunes in the provinces had not altogether prospered.... In the Punjab—the crucial area for Pakistan—Sir Khizar, the Premier ... [of] the Unionist Party ... was still confidently in office. In Bengal, Khwaja Sir Nazimuddin, the Muslim League Premier ... had been defeated in the Assembly in March 1945.... In the North-West Frontier Province ... in March 1945, a Congress Ministry had been formed under Dr. Khan Sahib. Mr. Jinnah's demonstration of imperious strength at the Simla conference was a shot in the arm for the League and a serious blow for its Muslim opponents, especially in the Punjab. Some observers thought that Lord Wavell's sudden abandonment of his plan [Simla Conference] was the decisive move that made the partition of India inevitable.

And thus continued the British policy to lead Jinnah and his Muslim League to the point of partition. In the process, the British proceeded to undermine the secular provincial governments. Punjab or 'the heart of Pakistan', as Yuvraj Krishan terms it, was run by the Unionist Party of 'rural, secular Muslims, Hindus and Sikhs, till 1945 when this non-communal, secular citadel was demolished by Jinnah with the assistance of Wavell'.[47]

The British were playing a very dangerous game by stoking religious frenzy. Betrand Glancy had warned that '[i]f Pakistan becomes an imminent reality we shall be heading straight for bloodshed on a wide scale'.[48] Sarila records that the British:[49]

ignored the warnings of their governors, Henry Craik and Betrand Glancy, that strengthening Jinnah's Muslim League in the Punjab at the expense of the Muslims of the Unionist Party, who were opposed to partition—Shaukat Hayat used to call it 'Jinnahstan'—would result in a blood bath in the province. Wavell did forward Glancy's warning to London, but the policy to build up Jinnah as the sole spokesman of the Muslims continued.

Indeed, even British Supreme Commander, Field Marshall Claude Auchinleck, in his secret Note of 11 May 1946, was to concede that the 'separation of Hindustan from Pakistan instead of eliminating the fundamental enmity of the Hindu for the Muslim is likely to inflame it'.[50]

Blueprint of Partition

Unfazed by the dangers of communalizing the Indian subcontinent, the British put into operation the plan to convert the strategic north-west of colonial India into the dominion of Pakistan, and to withdraw the British forces from the rest of colonial India into such dominion of Pakistan. The blueprint of the partition plan of British India was drawn up by Wavell in New Delhi towards the end of 1945 and communicated in a top-secret telegram to the Secretary of State on 6 February 1946,[51] while British ministers continued to make noises favouring a united India.[52] The blueprint of the future 'Pakistan', which was implemented almost to the letter when the Indian subcontinent attained independence 18 months later, was as under:[53]

(1) If compelled to indicate demarcation of genuinely Moslem areas I recommend that we should include:

(a) Sind, North-West Frontier Province, British Baluchistan, and Rawalpindi, Multan and Lahore Divisions of Punjab, less Amritsar and Gurdaspur districts.

(b) In Bengal, the Chittagong and Decca Divisions, the Rajshahi division (less Jalpaiguri and Darjeeling), the Nadia, Murshidabad and Jessore districts of Presidency division; and in Assam the Sylhet district.

(2) In the Punjab the only Moslem-majority district that would not go into Pakistan under this demarcation is Gurdaspur (51 per cent Moslem). Gurdaspur must go with Amritsar for geographical reasons and Amritsar being sacred city of Sikhs must stay out of Pakistan …

(5) We should make it clear in any announcement that this is only an indication of areas to which in HMG's view the Moslems can advance a reasonable claim, modifications in boundary might be negotiated and no doubt

the interests of Sikhs in particular would be carefully considered in such negotiations. Some saving clause is indicated by importance of preventing immediate violence by Sikhs.

(6) In Bengal the three Moslem-majority districts of Presidency divisions must I think be included in Pakistan, though this brings frontier across the Ganges. The demarcation includes in Pakistan all Moslem-majority districts and no Hindu-majority districts.

(7) There is no case for including Calcutta in Pakistan.

The Moslems will probably try to negotiate for it being made a free port. If negotiations fail Eastern Bengal's prospects as a separate autonomous State will be seriously affected. But Moslems, if they insist on Pakistan, must face up to this problem.

The Labour Party came to power in England in 1945. Wavell had suggested that the British government make an award to divide India in terms of his plan; however, Attlee, the new British Prime Minister, wanted this to come across as an Indian decision.[54] Attlee was known to be sensitive to the US view that Britain should not partition the Indian subcontinent. Attlee also wanted to do the seemingly impossible—partition the Indian subcontinent to create Pakistan and yet maintain good relations with the Indian leadership.[55] While Pakistan would safeguard British interests in the Middle East, a friendly India would cooperate with the British in South East Asia.[56] Also, if partition was presented as an Indian decision, Britain would be absolved of responsibility for the terrible butchery, destruction and misery that was bound to follow. Thus, the assent, or at least the acquiescence, of the Congress in the partition of the Indian subcontinent was essential.[57] Let us examine the steps taken towards this end.

Cabinet Mission Plan

Attlee had declared on 19 February 1946 that a Mission of three British Cabinet ministers would be sent to India to explore the possibility of an immediate settlement of the political stalemate. This Cabinet Mission reached India in March 1946. The tone was set by the press conference held by the then Secretary of State Pethwick-Lawrence, immediately on the arrival of the Cabinet Mission, during which he declared that 'while the Congress are representative of large numbers, it would not be right to regard the Muslim League as merely a minority political party—they are in fact majority representatives of the great Muslim community'.[58]

The Cabinet Mission Plan, circulated on 16 May 1946, contemplated the setting up of a single constituent assembly to draft a constitution, with autonomous provinces having the 'provincial option' not to accede to the 'Union of India'. The device now evolved by the British to create 'Pakistan' was the compulsorily grouping of the provinces into three Sections. Section A, the 'Hindu' majority-group—comprised Madras, Bombay, United Provinces, Bihar, Central Provinces and Orissa. Section B, the 'Muslim'-majority group—had Punjab, North-West Frontier Province (NWFP) and Sind. Section C comprised the Muslim-majority province of Bengal and the non-Muslim-majority province of Assam, making the group as a whole having Muslim majority.

The Plan provided for a preliminary meeting of the constituent assembly followed by each of the three Sections meeting separately to draw up the provincial constitutions. It would be open to the provinces within each Section to draft a constitution for the entire Section. The Sections would then frame a constitution for India together with the representatives of the princely Indian states. The Plan stated:[59]

> As soon as the new constitutional arrangements have come into operation, it shall be open to any province to elect to come out of any Group in which it has been placed. Such a decision shall be taken by the new legislature of the province after the first general elections under the new constitution.

Thus, until such constitutional framework materialized, the provinces did not have the choice to opt out of the Sections in which they had been placed by the British. Consequently, Punjab, though marginally having Muslim majority, and the NWFP, though held by the Congress, could not opt to join the 'Hindu' Section A but would be under the control of the 'Muslim' Section B.

Again, should the Muslim-majority provinces in Section B be persuaded not to accede to the 'Union of India', they would form West 'Pakistan'. And as, Yuvraj Krishan points out, Group C 'was constituted absolutely arbitrarily by including Assam therein' so as to make East 'Pakistan' 'economically viable', since a Group C 'consisting only of the Muslim majority East Bengal districts and Sylhet district of Assam would have been a "rural slum"—"a sick child"—an economic burden for [East] Pakistan'.[60]

Further, the Cabinet Mission Plan provided for vesting of the powers in the provinces and limited the authority of the 'Union of India' to three subjects: defence, external affairs and communications. The idea was to keep the 'Union of India' so weak that it would be compelled to depend on the

British. Pethick-Lawrence told the Cabinet Delegation at a meeting on 4 April 1946, which was also attended by Wavell and Jinnah, that:[61]

[India] would not be able to stand up at all at sea and as a land power only to some extent. Therefore the British Government presumes that they will be invited to assist in India's defence since the logic of events will make this necessary....

The setting up of a single constitution-making body (which suited the Congress) and the 'provincial option' coupled with grouping of the provinces along communal lines (which suited the British and the Muslim League) led to both the Congress and the Muslim League giving varying interpretations to the terms of the Cabinet Mission Plan. Hodson records that:[62]

[O]n 6th June the Council of the Muslim League passed by a big majority a resolution accepting the Cabinet Mission's plan, though with an observation of their own. Reiterating that a sovereign Pakistan remained the unalterable objective of Muslims, but having regard, said the resolution ... to the fact that the basis of Pakistan was inherent in the grouping of the Muslim areas in sections B and C, the League accepted the scheme and was willing to join the constitution-making body. It kept in view, however, the implicit opportunity of secession of provinces or groups from the Union, and reserved the right to revise its policy at any time if the course of events so required.

.... Maulana Azad communicated the Congress Working Committee resolution of 25th June and said that 'Congress accepted the statement of 16th May while adhering to its own interpretation of some of its provisions, for instance regarding the grouping of provinces'.

.... The position when the Cabinet Mission departed (on 29 June 1946) was that the Muslim League had accepted the main plan (the statement of 16th May) without qualification, though with the express intention of continuing to work within it for secession and Pakistan; the Congress had nominally accepted the plan, but with reservations or interpretations which could have nullified its central provision of grouping.

The Muslim League eventually rejected the Cabinet Mission Plan, taking the view that it would not participate in any single constitution-making body, and demanded two separate constituent assemblies for the people of Pakistan and Hindustan. When the Cabinet Mission Plan ran into difficulties, Wavell gave a memorandum to the Cabinet Mission on 30 May 1946 to the effect that:[63]

.... We should hand over the Hindu Provinces [the Congress-ruled ones] by agreement and as peacefully as possible to Hindu rule, withdrawing our troops, officials and nationals in an orderly manner [into Muslim-majority provinces] and should at the same time support the Muslim Provinces of India against Hindu domination and assist them to work out their own constitution. We should make it quite clear to the Congress [Party] that it would result in the division of India.... This might compel them [the Congress] to come to terms with the Muslim League, i.e., agree to partition.

Direct Action

Meanwhile, the British encouraged the Muslim League to make its presence felt. Jinnah announced on 27 July 1946 in Bombay that the Muslim League was not bound by the Cabinet Mission Plan and announced that the League should 'bid goodbye to constitutional methods and take "direct action"',[64] inasmuch as '[t]oday we have also forged a pistol and are in a position to use it'.[65]

Yuvraj Krishan refers to the report of the Director of the Intelligence Bureau, of October 1946, to the Viceroy which 'defined "Direct Action" as using violence to achieve the goals/agenda of the Muslim League', and which warned that:[66]

...

(ii) 'Direct Action' could lead to bloodshed, butchery, slaughter of Hindus of East West Bengal and Sind, (iii) 'Direct Action' would lead to violence which would result from (a) the movement for establishment of Pakistan fostered by Jinnah and (b) from the incitement to violence by the Muslims ...; (iv) 'Direct Action' would take the form of sabotage: collection of arms and ammunition and acts of terrorism.

Such acts would clearly qualify as criminal offences, inviting prosecution of political leaders calling for such 'direct action'. Indeed, as Wavell had himself observed, '[i]n any other country, they would have been dismissed and arrested'.[67] However, Jinnah, with the backing of the British, sought to decriminalize such violence by deliberately colouring the commission of communal violence by Muslims against non-Muslims as a jihad. Accordingly, it was portrayed as the religious duty of the Muslims to take 'direct action' against the 'infidels'.

Jinnah had declared 16 August 1946 as the 'direct action day'. Not surprisingly, the British Brigadier in charge of law and order in Calcutta, J.P.C. Makinlay, 'ordered his troops confined to barracks for the day, leaving the city naked for the mobs'.[68] Hodson documents that:[69]

In Calcutta the League Ministry under Mr. Suhrawardy, who had adopted a much more bellicose attitude than Mr. Jinnah, declared 16th August a public holiday, an extremely dangerous thing to do when communal passions were inflamed.... In the next three days some 20,000 people were killed or seriously injured in Calcutta. Whole streets were strewn with corpses—men, women and children of all communities—impossible to count, let alone identify. If the Muslims gave the provocation and started the holocaust, they were certainly its worst victims, for they were in a minority in the city, and the Sikhs in particular, a comparatively small community in Calcutta but tough and armed and largely motorised, being the mechanics and drivers of Bengal as of so many places, swept furiously through the Muslim quarters slaying mercilessly as they went.... The Governor, Sir Frederick Burrows, could have overridden his Ministers in calling in the Army earlier, but he declined to do so until his Government demanded it.... the Great Calcutta killings set in train a sequence of catastrophes which did not end until many more thousands had died of communal violence and revenge throughout India and Pakistan, indeed which might be said even now to be continuing in the Indo-Pakistani confrontation.

Wali Khan describes the happenings on 16 August 1946 as under:[70]

.... Suhrawardy ... announced Direct Action as Government policy and declared a general holiday so that official demonstrations could be arranged.

.... The result was predictable. Rioting broke out. The Muslims ignited the spark while the Hindus poured oil. Then the Sikhs created more havoc. In Calcutta the Muslims were in minority. The Sikhs controlled the transportation in the city. All the taxis were owned by Sikhs.... Calcutta was the commercial centre. Thousands of labourers and mill workers converged on the city. There was a large influx of people from the neighbouring State of Bihar which was relatively poor and under-developed. These transients were mostly non-Muslims. The Calcutta riots drove these people back to Bihar. There they related horrifying stories of killing, rape, arson and other atrocities resulting from the Muslim League's Direct Action. These stories, often exaggerated, led to full scale mass murders in the nearby states.... One fact emerged as the undisputed truth. The only ones which benefited from this rioting were the British. Their one hundred year old communal policy reached a resounding climax: the Muslims and non-Muslims sharpening their blades and preparing themselves to slit each others' throats.

Sarila writes that the violence unleashed in Calcutta on 16 August 1946 led to the killing of about 5,000 people belonging to both communities and injuring about 20,000 persons.[71] He records that 'the British archives contain a copy of the Muslim League's proclamation of "Direct Action Day", published on 13 August 1946, which was forwarded to London and to New Delhi from the Governor's office', and which left 'little doubt that the Governor had received advance notice of the League's intentions'.[72] However, 'Jinnah was never held responsible' for the Calcutta killings; rather, Wavell, in his telegram of 28 August 1946 to the Secretary of State, 'exonerated the Muslim League by noting "[b]oth sides had made preparations, which may or may not have been defensive"'.[73] Wavell then went a step further. As reported by Leonard Mosely, Wavell actually cited the Calcutta killings to pressurize Gandhi and Nehru during their meeting on 27 September 1946 to concede to the demands of the Muslim League, warning that else 'India is on the verge of civil war'.[74]

The British had also encouraged the Congress, led by Nehru, to accept office in the interim government under the British, as the implication of such acceptance of office was the inevitability of partition. Sarila writes that the British knew that 'Pakistan is likely to come from "Congresstan"', that is, from 'the acceptance of office' by the Congress.[75] Nehru was made the Vice President of the Viceroy's Executive Council on 2 September 1946 in the interim government and was referred as the 'Prime Minister'. Jinnah dismissively remarked '[y]ou cannot turn a donkey into an elephant by calling it an elephant'.[76]

As soon as Nehru was sworn in as 'Prime Minister', Wavell started to press him to invite the Muslim League to enter the interim government without requiring Jinnah to first enter the existing all-India Constituent Assembly.[77] Otherwise, Jinnah, by entering the all-India Constituent Assembly, would have had to accept the Cabinet Mission Plan that contemplated a single constitution-making body. Wavell did not require Jinnah to even call off his 'direct action' campaign.[78]

On 2 October 1946, Nehru, out of 'sheer exasperation' of being 'pestered' by Wavell, acquiesced in the Muslim League joining the interim government.[79] It was announced on 15 October 1946 that the 'Muslim League had decided to join the Interim Government'.[80] The Muslim League proceeded to sabotage the working of the government from within. Yuvraj Krishan notes that:[81]

Wavell could not have been unaware of Jinnah's purpose in agreeing to the induction of the militant Muslim Leaguers in the Interim Government which, in the words of Sardar Patel, was 'to achieve Pakistan by sabotage inside and disorder outside'.... At the Simla Conference 1945, Wavell had helped Jinnah to become the Quaid-i-Azam, the supreme leader of the Muslims of India. By manipulating the induction of the ideologues of 'Direct Action' in the Interim Government even though they had publicly declared that the Muslim League would continue its policy of 'Direct Action' instead of constitutional means to achieve Pakistan, Wavell had driven the last nail in the coffin of United India.

Wali Khan records that:[82]

India was burning in the fire of Direct Action. Frequent riots were taking place in different parts of the country. In October (1946), Hindu–Muslim riots occurred in the Noakhali district of East Bengal. Thousands of innocent people were killed. Stories of the riots in Calcutta and Noakhali spread in the country. While Hindus were killed in Noakhali, Muslims were slaughtered in Bihar. These riots, which occurred in the month of November, are associated with the most horrendous stories. The whole of India was aflame with communal hatred, enmity and prejudice. Wavell was confident that the increased hatred between these two communities would result in the British becoming indispensable for India. His plan would then materialize, i.e. the British would move their entire belongings to the Muslim majority provinces, namely, Pakistan. The Muslim League, too, wanted to prove to the world that it had become impossible for the Hindus and Muslims to co-exist. Partition was the only recourse left.

Hodson confirms such communal violence as stemming from the 'direct action' commenced by the Muslim League in Calcutta. He writes that:[83]

The chain reaction from Calcutta had given rise to a series of explosions. In October 1946 there were serious outbreaks in Noakhali and Tipperah in East Bengal, in which the Muslim majority were the aggressors and Hindus the victims. There was evidence that this was an organised operation and not a spontaneous combustion of individual communal hatred: there was virtually no outbreaks in larger towns, where the police and military could be more effective than in scattered villages. Reactions to Noakhali were widely distributed, by far the worst were in Bihar, where many Bengali Hindu refugees had fled, and where their tales of horror had excited some of the local population to a massacre of their Muslim neighbours in November....

Ramachandra Guha writes that by 'November 1946 the all-India total of deaths in rioting was in excess of 5,000 ... [a]s an army memo mournfully observed: "Calcutta was revenged in Noakhali, Noakhali in Bihar, Bihar in Garmukteshwar, Garmukteshwar in???"'.[84] In this communally charged environment, Attlee, the British Prime Minister, made a statement in the British Parliament on 20 February 1947 to the effect that:[85]

1. His Majesty's Government wish to make it clear that it is their definite intention to take the necessary steps to effect the transference of power into responsible Indian hands by a date not later than June 1948.

2. If it should appear that such a constitution (as proposed by the Cabinet Mission) will not have been worked out by a fully representative Assembly before the time mentioned.... His Majesty's Government will have to consider to whom the powers of the Central Government in British India should be handed over, on the due date, whether as a whole to some form of Central Government for British India or in some areas to the existing Provincial Governments, or in such other way as may seem reasonable and in the best interests of the Indian people.

The British, by fixing the date for transfer of power, and declaring that they would transfer power to the provincial governments if a constitution had not been worked out by a fully representative Assembly by that date, ensured that all that Jinnah had to do to get 'Pakistan' was not to join that Assembly by that date. Indeed, Hodson writes that:[86]

Those in India who did not want a single nation to succeed to British power had only to play out time, by making a fully representative Constituent Assembly impossible, in order to oblige His Majesty's Government to hand over to two or more successors.... The statement of 20th February 1947, in the context of Indian politics, was thus an open licence for Pakistan in some form or the other.

Notwithstanding the Opposition in the British Parliament denouncing the British policy and asserting that 'far from moderating Indian differences it would heighten them',[87] the 'British Government advised the League to get rid of the Unionists if they wanted Punjab and to throw out the Khudai Khidmatgars' if they wanted the NWFP included in 'Pakistan'.[88] Wali Khan writes that:[89]

.... After this the entire concentration of the Muslim League and its supporters was on these two Provinces. They were desperate to establish their control over them. Having lost the election in both provinces, they had no legal or democratic right. So they had to resort to illegal means.... If Hindu–Muslim riots could be started [in Punjab], ... the Sikh and Hindu members would be chased away, then the decision would come down in favour of the Muslim League....

The Punjab

Ramchandra Guha documents that '[a]t the end of 1946, one province that had escaped the rioting was the Punjab', where in 'office there were the Unionists, a coalition of Muslim, Hindu and Sikh landlords'.[90] Hodson notes that:[91]

> [i]n becoming the heart of a sovereign, anti-Hindu Pakistan, the Punjab became also its most suffering victim.... At the Provincial elections of 1936 the Muslim League had little success in the Punjab. The great majority of Muslim seats went to the supporters of the Unionist Party, a three community group, founded by Sir Fazl-i-Husain in the 1920s as a genuine attempt at intercommunal co-operation and representing mainly rural interests against the urban and commercial classes from which the Congress drew its principal strength in the province.... An essentially Punjabi organisation, wielding Muslims, Hindus and Sikhs under Muslim leadership on a provincial economic basis, the Unionist Party was inherently inimical to the League....

Guha writes that:[92]

> Unlike the Hindus of Bengal, the Sikhs of Punjab were slow to comprehend the meaning and reality of Partition. At first they doggedly insisted that they would stay where they were. Then, as the possibility of division became more likely, they claimed a separate state for themselves, to be called 'Khalistan'. This demand no one took seriously, not the Hindus, not the Muslims, and least of all the British.

> The historian Robin Jeffrey has pointed out that, at least until the month of August 1947, the Sikhs were 'more sinned against than sinning'. They had been abandoned by the British, tolerated by the Congress, taunted by the Muslim League, and above all, frustrated by the failures of their own political leaders.... It was the peculiar (not to say tragic) dilemma of the Sikhs that best explains why, when religious violence finally came to Punjab, it was so accelerated and concentrated....

Hodson refers to the report of Evan Jenkins, the then Governor of Punjab, on the happenings since 4 March 1947 when he assumed office. According to Jenkins, the disturbances had occurred in three main phases:[93]

> Phase One, from 4th to 20th March, was characterised by rioting in the cities, including Lahore, Amritsar, Multan and Rawalpindi, and massacres of Sikhs and Hindus in rural areas of the Rawalpindi Division and Multan District, with very heavy casualties and much burning, especially in Multan and Amritsar. The urban slaughter was without precedent (in Multan city

about 130 non-Muslims were killed in three hours) and the wholesale burnings and rural massacres were new....

In Phase Two, up to 9th May, there were minor incidents in many districts, serious rioting and burning in Amritsar with repercussions in Lahore, and the first outbreaks in Gurgaon. This period of relative quiet was used by the communities for preparations, and there was much practising with bombs.

Phase Three, from 10th May onwards, launched the 'communal war of succession'. Lahore and Amritsar suffered much incendiarism, stabbing and bombing....

The Governor proceeded to give figures of casualties reported in all three phases by areas upto 2nd August.... In rural Rawalpindi alone 2,164 killings had been reported, most of them murders of Sikhs and Hindus by Muslims....

Revenge for Rawalpindi was now to make the pendulum swing again. As 15th August [the date of partition] approached, the situation grew steadily worse.... In and around Amritsar, the Sikhs formed large armed bands which raided Muslim-majority villages at a rate of three or four a night.... Muslim bands were organised for a like purpose in Lahore District.... The police became more and more communal, and thousands deserted—Muslims from East Pakistan and non-Muslims from West. Even before 15th August, hundreds of thousands of people had lost or left their homes and were on the move; after 15th August, the stream of migration became a torrent....

Yuvraj Krishan has detailed the report of Lieutenant General Messervy, general officer commanding (GOC; Western Command), and Jenkins, the Punjab Governor, on the nature and scale of violence in West Punjab—Rawalpindi division and Multan division—as under:[94]

Messervy, headquartered at Rawalpindi had reported in March 1947 that in rural areas large mobs of Muslim peasants from different villages had 'bonded together to destroy and loot Hindu and Sikh shops and homes, hacking or beating men, women and children to death, burning their houses, forcible conversion of males and abduction of females' above all 'to rid many areas of all Sikh and Hindus entirely for ever'. Jenkins, the Punjab Governor, in his reports of 17 and 20 March 1947 to Wavell, had confirmed that 'there was a regular butchery of non-Muslims, particularly the Sikhs....

In the report of 20 March 1947, Jenkins observed 'what had happened in Rawalpindi, Attock and Chakwal and the Chakwal sub-Division was a general massacre of the most beastly kind ... the massacre has been conducted in the name of the Muslim League and senior Military Officers thought it had been carefully planned and organised.

The members of the Constituent Assembly for Punjab, in a note of 1 May 1947 to Hastings Lionel Ismay, the Viceroy's Chief of Staff, stated that:[95]

> The terrible happenings in the Punjab have revealed that an organised and well planned '*Jehad*' was preached and carried out against the unoffending non-Muslim minorities particularly in the Rawalpindi and Multan Divisions of the Province ... a regular holocaust of murder, loot, arson, abduction, rape and forcible conversion of the members of the minority communities ... such a state of affairs cannot be described as riots or communal fracas ... innocent Hindus and Sikhs were butchered or burnt alive, property worth crores of rupees was looted, or wantonly destroyed....

Major General T.W. Rees, who was appointed as the Commander of the Punjab Boundary Force that had been set up from 1 August 1947, reported that when he took over:[96]

> Communal bitterness was at its peak, and the masses were egged on ... and inflamed by shock-troops of resolute and well-armed men determined to fight.... Throughout, the killing was pre-medieval in its ferocity. Neither age or sex was spared; mothers with babies in their arms were cut down, speared or shot, and Sikhs cried 'Rawalpindi' as they struck home. Both sides were equally merciless.

E.P. Moon describes the pogrom in West Punjab in the following words:[97]

> [T]o kill a Sikh had become almost a duty; to kill Hindu was hardly a crime, to rob them was an innocent pleasure carrying no moral stigma; to refrain was a mark not of virtue but of lack of enterprise. On the other hand to try to stop these things was at best a folly, at worst a crime.

Unmoved by such communal violence, the British persisted with their policy of partition in order to create 'Pakistan', which assumed added urgency in light of the resolution of the Congress-dominated all-India Constituent Assembly with regard to India's intention to leave the Commonwealth. Let us examine this facet briefly.

The Congress and Foreign Policy

Nehru had declared in the Constituent Assembly in January 1947 that 'it is inconceivable that India can be a Dominion like other Dominions.... India must sever her connection with Great Britain'.[98] Nehru told Mountbatten at their first meeting on 24 March 1947 that 'under no conceivable circumstances is India going to remain in the British Commonwealth'.[99] Such step would have removed the British influence from the region and resulted in non-cooperation of Indian armed forces in the defence of the Commonwealth. Ismay had written to Prime Minister Attlee on 20 September 1946 that the 'Chiefs of Staff ... would like to suggest for your consideration ... the necessity to do everything possible to retain India within the Commonwealth'.[100] The British Chiefs of Staff had, in their report of 8 September 1946 on the strategic value of India to the British Commonwealth, pointed out that the 'oil from the Persian Gulf is essential to the British Commonwealth and its safe passage must be ensured', that if 'India became dominated by Russia with powerful air forces ... we should have to abandon our command of the Persian Gulf and the northern Indian Ocean routes'; that 'India is an essential link in our Imperial strategic plan', 'because with the coming of atomic warfare there is increased necessity for space and India has this space' and that for 'the Commonwealth to undertake military operations on a large scale in the Far East, India is the only suitable base [and] one of India's most important assets is an almost inexhaustible supply of manpower'.[101]

Further, the interim government's foreign policy under Nehru had fuelled mistrust between the Congress and the British. Sarila writes that the British Foreign Office, in a joint memorandum with the India Office, expressed concern to the British Cabinet stating that:[102]

> Many of the leaders of the Congress Party, and Pt. Nehru in particular, have well-defined views on this intriguing brand of administration, with a lack of experience in the field, and an impatience to carry out ideas formed in conditions of irresponsibility ... without regard for [their] wider implications.... In the UN General Assembly of 1946 clashes between the British and the Indians had already occurred on the question of apartheid in South Africa and on colonial matters in the UN Trusteeship Council. India might offer public support to the Indonesians against the Dutch and to Vietnam against the French. It should not be forgotten that the independence movements in Burma, Malay and Ceylon might demand the return of Portuguese and French possessions ... [British interests] on the Arab shore of the Persian Gulf ... make it necessary that the charge of these interests should be in reliable hands and under [British] direct control. We must not risk any Indian interference with our essential interests in the area.

With the Congress declaring its intention of having independent India leave the Commonwealth and voicing foreign policy on matters in a manner inimical to British interests, it became even more imperative for the British to create a separate state in the Indian subcontinent on which the British could rely.

The Last Bastion: The NWFP

The Congress, on its part, was banking on frustrating the creation of 'Pakistan' by denying the NWFP to the Muslim League, since without the NWFP, 'Pakistan' would be a mere enclave within India.[103] Jinnah and the Muslim League would not accept such 'Pakistan'. Also, should such 'Pakistan' be created, it would eventually return to India. The Congress reasoned that all that it had to do was to retain the NWFP.

The NWFP, which was strategically crucial for Britain's Great Game given its proximity to the then Soviet Union, had the largest majority of Muslims in British India. The support offered by Gandhi to the Khilafat movement had resulted in the NWFP, inhabited mainly by Pathans and led by Khan Abdul Ghaffar Khan (popularly known as the 'Frontier Gandhi'), being ruled by the Congress.[104] Hodson writes that:[105]

> The origins of the ... predominance of the Congress in this overwhelming Muslim province, right upto 1947, ... go back to the Khilafat movement of 1919, when Mr. Gandhi urged Hindus to make common cause with the Muslims in a united mass campaign to restore the Ottoman Caliphate, uprooted by the Treaty of Sevres, and to win self-government for India. The Congress thus became an ally of the Khilafat Committee, whose greatest strength was in the north-west....

The fact that the NWFP was 95 per cent Muslim ensured that the communal division could not be exploited.[106] In the 1936 general election held under the Government of India Act of 1935, the Congress had routed the Muslim League all over the NWFP.[107]

After the Congress party had resigned from office in 1939 in protest of India being dragged into the Second World War, there was a political vacuum in the region. Linlithgow asked Jinnah to install a Muslim League ministry in the NWFP.[108] Jinnah sought the support of the Governor of the NWFP, George Cunningham, to be able to do so, to which Linlithglow agreed.[109] Wali Khan, in his book *Facts Are Facts: The Untold Story of India's Partition*, has detailed the steps taken by Cunningham in this regard.[110]

When Jinnah declared the 'Pakistan scheme' on the basis of the two-nation theory in early 1940, the Pathans in the NWFP were asked to choose between the 'Hindu' India and an Islamic state. However, the Pathans did not want the Islamic state, as was evidenced in the general elections of 1945, in which the Congress won 30 seats as against 17 seats of the Muslim League.[111] Even in the following elections for the all-India Constituent Assembly held in July 1946, the Congress won three of the four seats allotted to the province.[112]

The British knew that a 'Pakistan', which was a mere enclave within India, would have no strategic value for their Great Game. The British now had to remove the Congress influence in the NWFP for a strategically valuable 'Pakistan' to be formed. Since the NWFP could not 'be detached from India as long as its representatives to the Constituent Assembly supported its affiliation to India',[113] the way 'to bypass them would be to have another election in the NWFP, despite one being held just a few months ago, and ask the electorate to vote directly on the province's future'.[114] But then, the necessary conditions would first have to be created in the NWFP for the wholly Muslim and fiercely independent electorate to join Islamic 'Pakistan' or at least choose independence.

Wavell had, in March 1946, posted Olaf Caroe as the Governor of the NWFP. Caroe was assigned to keep an eye on the northwest frontier of colonial India should the Russians seek to extend their influence to the oil wells of the Persian Gulf or to Afghanistan.[115] Interestingly, when Mountbatten, as Viceroy, later went to the NWFP in June 1947, and met its Chief Minister, Khan Abdul Jabbar Khan (known popularly as Khan Sahib), and his ministers at the Government House, he was told by the Khan Sahib that the Muslim League in the NWFP was run, not by Jinnah, but by the 'Governor and his officials'.[116]

Nehru, as the Minister-in-Charge of Tribal Affairs, decided to visit the NWFP in late 1946. Caroe and the Muslim League reportedly orchestrated such demonstrations against Nehru that he reportedly 'lost all dignity and his temper and commenced shouting at the Jirga [tribal assembly]',[117] and later even suffered injuries.[118] Caroe reported to Wavell on 23 October 1946 regarding Nehru's visit that what the Jirga 'particularly disliked was talk of a regime of love coupled with an arrogant loss of temper'.[119] Wali Khan documents the complicity of the Political Agent of the Khyber Agency and of government officials in fomenting violence during Nehru's visit.[120] Soon after Nehru's visit to the NWFP, Wavell himself went there to assure the Jirga that 'after the British withdrawal from the Indian subcontinent, their territories would be returned to them'.[121] The intention was 'to mobilize opinion in favour of a fresh election in the NWFP in order to bypass the elected representatives of the province', who were inclined to participate in the all-India Constituent Assembly.[122]

The Congress, however, remained convinced that 'Pakistan' would not materialize as it would retain the NWFP. Further, Jinnah had demanded, amongst other territory, the whole of Punjab and Bengal for 'Pakistan'. The Congress was of the view that should it demand division of Punjab and Bengal, Jinnah would not accept a 'moth eaten Pakistan'. Also, the British would not accept such division at the cost of civil war, and would hand over these provinces to the Congress. Sardar Patel, in his letter of 4 March 1947 to Kanji Dwarkadas, erroneously reasoned that:[123]

> Before next June, the Constitution must be ready and if the League insists on Pakistan, the only alternative is the division of the Punjab and Bengal. They cannot have Punjab as a whole or Bengal without civil war. I do not think that the British Government will agree to division. In the end they will see the wisdom of handing over the reins of government to the strongest party. Even if they do not do so, they will not help the minority in securing or maintaining division and a strong centre with the whole of India except Eastern Bengal and a part of Punjab, Sindh and Baluchistan, enjoying full autonomy under that centre, will be so powerful that the remaining portions will eventually come in.

The Congress Working Committee, therefore, resolved on 8 March 1947 that to avoid violence in Punjab this 'would necessitate a division of the Punjab into two provinces, so that the predominantly Muslim part may be separated from the predominantly non-Muslim part'.[124] Nehru, while forwarding the Congress resolution to Wavell on 9 March 1947, wrote in the covering letter that '[t]his principle [of communal division in the Punjab] would, of course, apply to Bengal also'.[125]

Later, analysing this resolution of the Congress, the US *chargé d'affaires* in India, George Merrell, wired to the US State Department on 22 April 1947:[126]

> The Congress efforts to make Pakistan as unattractive as possible—by demanding partition of the Punjab and Bengal—Congress leaders have in effect abandoned the tenets which they supported for so many years in their campaign for united India. They have also agreed by implications [to] Mr Jinnah's allegation that Hindus and Muslims cannot live together, a charge which in the past Congress has—quite rightly I believe—denied.

With Britain having decided to partition the Indian subcontinent, Mountbatten was sent to India to replace Wavell as Viceroy, with a mandate to make the partition of the subcontinent look like an Indian decision as Attlee had desired. Mountbatten was to persuade the Congress to let go of the NWFP so as to make 'Pakistan' come into being, and Jinnah to forgo his claim for the whole of the Punjab, Bengal and Assam to make partition feasible as per the resolutions of the Congress.[127] Further, while 'Pakistan' was to serve Britain's strategic interests, good relations with the Indian leadership also had value. As discussed earlier, the resolution in the all-India

Constituent Assembly declaring independent India's intention to leave the British Commonwealth had come as a jolt to Britain. Mountbatten's task was to persuade New Delhi to remain in the British Commonwealth, thereby enhancing British prestige worldwide; 'Pakistan' was expected to do so anyway.[128] Let us now examine how Mountbatten fulfilled his mandate.

Notes and References

1. *Supra* Note 6, Chapter I, p. 204.
2. Ibid.
3. Ibid., p. 136.
4. Extracted in ibid., p. 53.
5. Ibid., p. 183.
6. Extracted in *Supra* Note 12, Chapter I, p. 283.
7. Extracted in *Supra* Note 6, Chapter I, p. 183.
8. Extracted in *Supra* Note 36, Chapter I, p. 33.
9. See *Supra* Note 1, Chapter I, p. 48.
10. Extracted in *Supra* Note 6, Chapter I, p. 36.
11. Ibid.
12. Ibid.
13. Ibid., p. 23.
14. Ibid., p. 69.
15. *Supra* Note 1, Chapter I, pp. 81–82.
16. Ibid.
17. *Supra* Note 6, Chapter I, p. 101.
18. *Supra* Note 1, Chapter I, p. 96.
19. Extracted in *Supra* Note 7, Chapter I, p. 50.
20. Extracted in *Supra* Note 36, Chapter I, pp. 8–9.
21. *Supra* Note 6, Chapter I, p. 102.
22. Ibid., p. 111.
23. Ibid., p. 110.
24. *Supra* Note 1, Chapter I, p. 105.
25. *Supra* Note 6, Chapter I, pp. 24–25.
26. Ibid., p. 25.
27. Ibid., p. 177.
28. Ibid.
29. Ibid., p. 22.
30. Ibid.
31. Ibid., p. 26.
32. Ibid., p. 28.
33. Ibid., p. 29.
34. Extracted in *Supra* Note 7, Chapter I, pp. 23, 170.
35. Extracted in *Supra* Note 12, Chapter I, pp. 544–545.
36. *Supra* Note 36, Chapter I, p. 27.

37. *Supra* Note 6, Chapter I, p. 186.
38. Ibid.
39. *Supra* Note 1, Chapter I, pp. 121–122.
40. *Supra* Note 6, Chapter I, pp. 186–187.
41. Extracted in *Supra* Note 7, Chapter I, pp. 93–94.
42. Ibid., pp. 94–96.
43. Ibid., pp. 96–97.
44. *Supra* Note 36, Chapter I, p. 29.
45. Extracted in ibid.
46. *Supra* Note 1, Chapter I, pp. 126–127.
47. *Supra* Note 36, Chapter I, p. 96.
48. Cited in *Supra* Note 6, Chapter I, p. 187.
49. Ibid., p. 410.
50. *Supra* Note 12, Chapter I, pp. 557–559.
51. *Supra* Note 6, Chapter I, pp. 194–195.
52. Ibid., pp. 191, 207.
53. Ibid., pp. 195–196.
54. Ibid., p. 199.
55. Ibid., p. 200.
56. Ibid.
57. Ibid., p. 199.
58. Extracted in *Supra* Note 1, Chapter I, p. 134.
59. Ibid., p. 149.
60. *Supra* Note 36, Chapter I, pp. 46–47.
61. Extracted in ibid., pp. 145–146.
62. *Supra* Note 1, Chapter I, pp. 153, 158, 161.
63. Extracted in *Supra* Note 6, Chapter I, p. 217.
64. Ibid., p. 222.
65. *Supra* Note 1, Chapter I, p. 166.
66. *Supra* Note 36, Chapter I, p. 58.
67. Ibid., p. 62.
68. *Supra* Note 6, Chapter I, p. 223.
69. *Supra* Note 1, Chapter I, pp. 167–168.
70. *Supra* Note 7, Chapter I, pp. 113–114.
71. *Supra* Note 6, Chapter I, p. 222.
72. Ibid., p. 224.
73. Ibid., p. 225.
74. *Supra* Note 12, Chapter I, p. 553.
75. *Supra* Note 6, Chapter I, p. 228.
76. Ibid.
77. Ibid., pp. 235–236.
78. Ibid., p. 235.
79. *Supra* Note 1, Chapter I, p. 173.
80. Ibid., p. 172.
81. *Supra* Note 36, Chapter I, p. 61.
82. *Supra* Note 7, Chapter I, pp. 119–120.
83. *Supra* Note 1, Chapter I, p. 180.
84. *Supra* Note 28, Chapter I, p. 11.

85. *Supra* Note 1, Chapter I, pp. 199–200.
86. Ibid.
87. Ibid., p. 200.
88. *Supra* Note 7, Chapter I, p. 126.
89. Ibid.
90. *Supra* Note 28, Chapter I, p. 11.
91. *Supra* Note 1, Chapter I, p. 269.
92. *Supra* Note 28, Chapter I, p. 13.
93. *Supra* Note 1, Chapter I, pp. 341–345.
94. *Supra* Note 36, Chapter I, pp. 63–64.
95. Extracted in ibid., p. 64.
96. Extracted in *Supra* Note 1, Chapter I, p. 345.
97. Ibid.
98. *Supra* Note 36, Chapter I, p. 130.
99. Ibid.
100. *Supra* Note 6, Chapter I, p. 239.
101. Ibid., pp. 239–240.
102. Extracted in ibid., p. 242.
103. Ibid., pp. 38, 264.
104. Ibid., p. 245.
105. *Supra* Note 1, Chapter I, p. 277.
106. *Supra* Note 6, Chapter I, p. 245.
107. Ibid.
108. Ibid., p. 49.
109. Ibid.
110. *Supra* Note 7, Chapter I.
111. *Supra* Note 6, Chapter I, pp. 245–246.
112. Ibid., p. 247.
113. Ibid., p. 280.
114. Ibid.
115. *Supra* Note 7, Chapter I, p. 126.
116. *Supra* Note 1, Chapter I, p. 286.
117. *Supra* Note 6, Chapter I, p. 247.
118. Ibid.
119. Ibid.
120. *Supra* Note 7, Chapter I, pp. 140–141.
121. *Supra* Note 6, Chapter I, p. 249.
122. Ibid.
123. Extracted in *Supra* Note 12, Chapter I, p. 417.
124. Ibid., p. 418.
125. Extracted in *Supra* Note 6, Chapter I, p. 264.
126. Extracted in ibid., p. 264.
127. Ibid., p. 273.
128. Ibid.

III

Partition

Mountbatten, the last Viceroy of India, reached the Indian subcontinent on 22 March 1947. The communalization of the Indian polity was by now complete. Hodson records that:[1]

'the whole country', wrote Lord Mountbatten in a letter to London a week after his arrival in India, 'is in a most unsettled state. There are communal troubles in the Punjab, N.W.F.P., Bihar, Calcutta, Bombay, U.P., and even here in Delhi.' The same story continued week after week. On 17th April he reported to the Secretary of State:

In the Punjab, the Gurgaon area (near Delhi, where there had been a serious disturbance) is quieter, but there have been riots in Amritsar which have necessitated a 24-hour curfew. In the N.W.F.P., rioting, looting, and arson have been reported from Dera Ismail Khan. Half the city is in flames and there is severe communal fighting ... the tension in both the Punjab and the N.W.F.P. is still very high.... In Bengal, there were more incidents at Calcutta on Sunday 13th April. In Bombay a curfew at night has been imposed, and similarly at Benaras....

The places varied but the story did not. As in a tinder-dry forest, fires would break out here and there, lit by a spark from the embers of earlier conflagrations and fanned by the hot wind of communal fear and hatred.

Significantly, it was in such state of affairs that Mountbatten mooted, on 2 April 1947,

the possibility of handing over power to the different areas of India according to the wishes of the inhabitants, that is to say, presumably to a Hindu India, a truncated Pakistan, the several larger States and groups of small States, all under a central authority for defence, external affairs, communications, and possibly food.[2]

On reaching India, Mountbatten had called for various political leaders. Hodson records Liaquat Ali Khan (representing the Muslim League) telling Mountbatten, whom he met on 24 March 1947 and 3 April 1947, that if Mountbatten 'was prepared to let the Muslim League have only the Sind desert', they would 'still prefer to accept that and have a separate Muslim state in those conditions' than to remain in undivided India with the Congress.[3]

Jinnah, according to Hodson, was 'more emphatic than ever that he would have nothing to do with the Cabinet Mission plan' at the meeting on 10 April 1947;[4] though Mountbatten sought to reason with him that the 'Cabinet Mission plan gave him ... a really worth-while and workable Pakistan'.[5]

As regards the NWFP, Mountbatten launched 'Operation Frontier', the plan being to once again provide for an election in the NWFP on the pretext that 'freedom to become independent had not been a choice in the last election'.[6] Should the electorate in the NWFP choose independence or join an Islamic state, with 'Pakistan' materializing, the Congress would, in any event, lose its control over the NWFP.

Hodson records that Nehru 'protested vehemently' against the 'proposal to hold fresh elections in the N.W.F.P.', denouncing it as a policy that 'was giving way to violence', and declared that the Congress would not contest the elections if this issue was forced upon it.[7]

Nehru, according to the Viceroy's report, did, however, 'agree in principle that it would be desirable to obtain the views of the people before the final turnover of power was effected'.[8] Sarila records that:[9]

> Meanwhile, the Muslim League agitation and 'direct action' had started to take their toll, communalizing the situation in the NWFP as the Sikhs and Hindus came under attack. The viceroy's report mentioned certain areas such as Dera Ismail Khan, Bannu and Tank, where 'property amounting to millions of rupees was damaged and bitter hatred was laid [sic] by massacres, forcible conversions and atrocities.... The riots in the Punjab raised communal tensions in the NWFP (lying to its west) and in Sind (lying to its south) giving a boost to communal forces there and helping the Muslim League in these Muslim provinces'.

Sarila documents further that towards the end of April 1947, Mountbatten 'was able to convince Nehru to accept a referendum in the NWFP on the simple issue of 'Pakistan or the new India' instead of a fresh election',[10] thereby bypassing the elected representatives of the NWFP sitting in the all-India Constituent Assembly.

Equally important, if not more, was the timing of the referendum. The British wanted to announce the agreement between the Congress and the Muslim League to partition the Indian subcontinent prior to the referendum, so as to drive home the point that Islamic 'Pakistan' was a reality to which the predominantly Muslim NWFP could accede.

Ismay, the Viceroy's Chief of Staff, flew to London on 2 May 1947 and reported 'the shocking deterioration that is taking place in so many Provinces', that 'the Viceroy had found communal feeling in India to be far more bitter than he had expected' and that it 'had become an obsession with both Hindus and Muslims and had been much intensified by the statement of 20th February [on the transfer of power by June 1948]'.[11] Hodson further details the proposals made by Mountbatten to London on the transfer of power following the partition[12] and notes that the 'proposals were designed to place the responsibility of dividing India conspicuously on the Indians themselves'.[13] Ramchandra Guha writes that Evan Jenkins, the then Governor of Punjab, meanwhile urged Mountbatten in early May 1947 to:[14]

> reconsider the terms of any early announcement embodying a solution of the Indian political problem. In the Punjab we are going to be faced with a complete refusal of the communities to co-operate on any basis at all. It would clearly be futile to announce a partition of Punjab which no community would accept.

The 3rd June Plan

The British, however, proceeded to announce, on 3 June 1947 at Delhi, the partition of the Indian subcontinent. As regards the NWFP, the British linked the future of that province to whether any part of Punjab decided not to join the all-India Constituent Assembly, knowing full well that its partition blueprint dividing Punjab would necessarily result in a part of Punjab not joining the existing all-India Constituent Assembly. Para 11 of the 3rd June statement asserted that:[15]

> The position of the North-West Frontier Province is exceptional. Two of the three representatives of the Province are already participating in the existing [all India] Constituent Assembly. But ... in view of its geographical situation, and other considerations, if any part of the Punjab decides not to join the existing Constituent Assembly, it will be necessary to give the North-West Frontier Province an opportunity to reconsider its position. Accordingly, in

such an event, a referendum will be made to the electors ... in the North-West Frontier Province to choose which Dominion, India or Pakistan, the people of N.W.F.P. would like to join.

Yuvraj Krishan states that:[16]

> The British military strategists were more explicit; protection of British Imperial and strategic interests made it absolutely essential that the British must control North West Frontier of India (which in the present context meant the N.W.F.P.). In July 1946, Auchinleck, the then Commander-in-Chief, had said that the British must control North-Western India as a bulwark against Russian expansion towards South East Asia. The Chief of Staff Committee of the UK, in its report of 18 March 1947 on India's defence arrangements, had observed: from a military point of view 'we should wish to support the power controlling the Western Frontier and the Indus valley, probably Pakistan....' This was fully endorsed by the British Cabinet which observed, whatever form the division (of India) might take ... it would be necessary to give Pakistan military assistance....

The then British Secretary of State for Foreign Affairs, Ernest Bevin, went on record to explain at the Labour Party Annual Conference in June 1947 at Margate in England that 'the British withdrawal from India will help to consolidate Britain in [the] Middle East'.[17] It is astounding that the Indian leadership could not even now see that the real cause of partition was the political, strategic and defence interests of the British. Vengalil Krishnan Krishna Menon, soon to be India's first High Commissioner to the UK, wrote to Mountbatten on 14 June 1947 in response to Bevin's statement as under:[18]

> Is this frontier [the northwest of India abutting Afghanistan and Iran] still the hinterland of the Imperial strategy? Does Britain still think in terms of being able to use this territory and all that follows from it? There is considerable amount of talking in this way; and if Kashmir, for one reason or another, chooses to be in Pakistan, that is a further development in this direction. I do not know of British policy in this matter. I do not know whether you would know it either. But if this be the British intent, this is tragic.... As it becomes more evident, the attitude of India would be resentful and Britain's hold on Pakistan would not improve it. I think I have said enough. Perhaps a bit too much.

Surely the eminence of the Indian leaders of undivided India alone cannot rescue them from their seeming innocence of politics, nor absolve them of the tragic consequences of their irresponsible actions, their misplaced confidence as also their penchant for reckless public posturing on volatile and delicate political issues. It is inconceivable that the Indian leaders were not aware of the Great Game or the significance of the north-western region of the Indian subcontinent for the British strategists for decades, or that they had to ask Mountbatten, the symbol of British imperialism in India, if he knew of it. The Indian leaders must have been aware that their half-baked policies to pre-empt partition, such as demanding the division of Punjab and Bengal to make the notion of 'Pakistan' unattractive, would not deter the British, or for that matter, even Jinnah. Indeed, Maulana Azad acknowledged that the British government's 'surrender to the demands of the Muslim League' was 'due more to its anxiety to safeguard British interests than its desire to please the Muslim League', since a state 'dominated by the Muslim League would offer a permanent sphere of influence to the British'.[19] It mattered little to the British that the 'Pakistan' they were creating was 'moth-eaten' as long as it included the territories marked by Wavell to be essential for British interests. And Jinnah, having been left dangling for power for years now, would accept whatever came his way, even if it was merely the Sindh desert.

At least Jinnah and the Muslim League seemed to know exactly why 'Pakistan' was being created. Pakistan's former Foreign Minister Khurshid Mahmud Kasuri while explaining how the Great Game stemmed from the 'conflict between two great imperial powers: the Czarist Empire of Russia and the British Empire', the latter being concerned that its Indian possessions could be threatened by 'Czarist Expansionism',[20] asserts that 'even before Partition, there was talk of the geostrategic importance of a future Pakistan and the role of its armed forces'.[21] Mountbatten, to whom Krishna Menon wrote, in fact spelt out the US policy as under:[22]

> The American object in India was to capture all the markets to step in and take the place of the British, that their aim might even be to get bases in India for ultimate use against Russia. In fact, backed by the British and American arms and technique, Pakistan would in no while, have armed forces immensely superior to that of Hindustan.... Places like Karachi would become big naval and air bases.

Jinnah started to woo the Americans right away. Wali Khan documents that:[23]

> On 1 May 1947 two Americans, Ronald A. Hare, Head of the Division of South Asian Affairs, and Thomas E. Weil, Second Secretary of U.S. Embassy in India, visited Jinnah. A detailed account of this visit was sent by the American Charge D' Affairs to Marshall, the Secretary of State. According to

this account Jinnah ... sought to impress on his visitors that the emergence of an independent, sovereign Pakistan would be in consonance with American interests. Pakistan would be a Muslim country. Muslim countries stand together against Russian aggression. In that endeavour they would look to the United States for assistance, he added.... This is a variation on the old British game of hanging around the Soviet neck, the 'albatross' of Islam. The second problem Jinnah presented to these Americans was also a part of the British scheme. If the British left a United India in the hands of the Congress it would have disastrous consequences for the western world. The Congress ... would be unwilling to protect their interests in the Middle East and the Gulf. Jinnah coupled the danger of Russian aggression with another menace that Muslim nations might confront. That was 'Hindu imperialism'. The establishment of Pakistan was essential to prevent the expansion of Hindu imperialism to the Middle East.... Jinnah was trying to persuade the United States that it was politically expedient to build an Islamic bastion against the Russians. If India was allowed to remain unified then the bastion stretching from Turkey to China would be incomplete. This message was being communicated by Jinnah through every American Agent. The slogan was, 'Create Pakistan and save the western world!'

Khurshid Mahmud Kasuri writes that '[d]uring the Cold War, Pakistan's geostrategic significance cemented its role as a frontline ally of the West against the Communist bloc, particularly the Soviet Union'.[24] In contrast, Nehru alienated the US even before India attained independence by telling Henry Grady, the then US Ambassador to India, as reported by the latter to the US State Department on 9 July 1947, that New Delhi did not desire to be involved with any bloc and that the Indian economy would probably follow the trend of the British economy under socialist government, with nationalization of large industries.[25]

Jaswant Singh records the voices of dissent and sharp exchanges[26] at the Congress Working Committee meet of 14 and 15 June 1947 in Delhi to adopt the resolution accepting the 3rd June announcement of partition, and quotes Leonard Moseley as under:[27]

Pandit Nehru told Michael Brecher, his biographer (in 1956, the reasons for accepting the Partition of India): 'Well, I suppose it was the compulsion of events and the feeling that we wouldn't get out of that deadlock or morass by pursuing the way we had done; it became worse and worse. Further, a feeling that even if we got freedom for India with that background, it would be very weak India; that is a federal India with far too much power in the federating units. A larger India would have constant troubles, a constant disintegrating pulls. And also the fact that we saw no other way of getting our freedom—in the near future, I mean. And, so we accepted it and said, let us build up a strong India. And if others do not want to be in it, well how can we and why should we force them to be in it?...'.

Acharya Kripalani, the then President of the Congress, described the factors that made the Congress accept partition at this meet as under:[28]

> The Hindu and Moslem communities have vied with each other in the worst orgies of violence.... I have seen a well where women and their children, 107 in all, threw themselves to save their honour. In another place, a place of worship, fifty young women were killed by their menfolk for the same reason. I have seen heaps of bones in a house where 307 persons, mainly women and children, were driven, locked up and then burnt alive by the invading mob.... The fear is that if we go on like this, retaliating and heaping indignities on each other, we shall progressively reduce ourselves to a stage of cannibalism and worse. In every fresh communal fight the most brutal and degraded acts of the previous fight become the norm.

Jaswant Singh notes that Gandhi too grappled with the inevitability of 'Pakistan', as is evident from the fact that:[29]

> He wrote in the *Harijan* in 1942 that if the vast majority of Muslims want to partition India they 'must have the partition', and in 1944 he actually carried out negotiations with Jinnah on this very basis. And yet, when the crucial moment for final decision arrived, he told on 3 March 1947, before he met Mountbatten: 'if the Congress wishes to accept partition, it will be over my dead body. So long as I am alive, I will never agree to the partition of India. Nor will I, if I can help it, allow Congress to accept it'. According to Azad, a great change came over Gandhi after he had interviewed Mountbatten. Gandhi no longer spoke so vehemently against it (partition)....

With the Congress accepting the 3rd June 1947 announcement of partition, the British Parliament passed the Indian Independence Act of 1947 on 18 July 1947 and amended the prevailing Government of India Act of 1935, to provide the constitutional framework for the partition of British India and to deal with the princely Indian states. The date 15 August 1947 was reflected in the British statutes as the date for transfer of power to Indian hands, instead of June 1948 as originally proposed. This date was not chosen due to any geopolitical realities or considerations of peaceful and smooth transition, but was casually chosen by Mountbatten. Indeed, Mountbatten admits that when 'I named August 15 ... I chose the anniversary of the surrender of the Japanese in Singapore but I had to name a date, and it was a good date'.[30]

The Sikh Hiccup

But then, there were the claims of the Sikhs to be addressed, the huge majority of whom were residents of Punjab, which was also home to their religion and their historic places of worship. The partition of Punjab would divide the Sikhs and their homeland. However, should the claims of the Sikhs for a separate homeland be conceded, 'Pakistan' would not be economically viable. Yuvraj Krishan notes:[31]

> [F]rom the viewpoint of the Muslim League, the Sikh demands for the establishment of a Punjabi Subba, in the central districts of Lahore Division and Sikhistan or Khalistan, from out of the Majha (pre-partition central Punjab districts) and Malwa and Doaba areas of East Punjab, had the potentiality of becoming the most serious threat to the establishment of an economically viable Pakistan whose borders would not be vulnerable. Again a Western Pakistan without the canal colonies—the neo-homelands of the Sikhs of the central districts of Lyallpur and Montgomery—was unthinkable. The districts of West Punjab were 'for the most part either desert or waste and the soil of very poor quality and almost unproductive, in certain districts mostly rock or ravine—hilly or desert.' The Muslim League, therefore, contended that 'west Punjab cannot be robbed of its fertile districts' (the Central districts).

The British, therefore, could not afford to create a 'Sikhistan or Khalistan' at the cost of 'Pakistan'. The Secretary of State, by his letter of 9 May 1947 to Mountbatten, pointed out that:[32]

> .... There is no doubt that the Sikhs are a very dangerous element in the situation. Under your proposals they will be divided and I do not think that any subsequent adjustment of boundaries can possibly begin to satisfy the claims they put forward. I understand from Ismay that they are asking that the Lahore Division be kept out of partition you propose pending a Boundary Commission at which Sikh claims would be considered.... But if you are satisfied that a Boundary Commission, with terms of reference such as will keep the Sikhs quiet until the transfer of power, can be set up without provoking hostility of the two major communities, I shall be ready to support your view to my colleagues....

The Boundary Commission was eventually constituted to demarcate the boundaries between the dominions of India and Pakistan, and its terms of reference required it to take into consideration 'other factors'. Yuvraj Krishan asserts that Mountbatten 'tricked' the Sikh leaders to accept the partition plan 'by assuring them' that the Boundary Commission 'would safeguard their legitimate interests by considering the Sikh demand for Sikhistan' under the term 'other factors',[33] knowing fully well that such term could not empower the Boundary Commission to carve out a third nation, Sikhistan, on the Indian subcontinent. Cyril Radcliffe, a British judge, was sent to the Indian subcontinent in the first week of July 1947 to head the Boundary Commission. Since the dominions of India and Pakistan were to be born on 15 August 1947, Radcliffe had less than five weeks to draw the boundaries between the dominions, and that too, when he had no prior knowledge of India, and with 'maps at his disposal ... out of date, and the Census Returns almost certainly incorrect'.[34] Radcliffe, realizing the precarious nature of his assignment, wrote to his nephew that:[35]

> nobody in India will love me for the award about the Punjab and Bengal and there will be roughly 80 million people with a grievance who will begin looking for me. I do not want them to find me....

The NWFP Referendum

Now that 'Pakistan' was emerging as a reality, the British went ahead with the referendum in July 1947 in the NWFP. The Congress decided to abstain from participating in the referendum. Yuvraj Krishan describes the farce of the referendum as under:[36]

> Referendum was, truly speaking, a subterfuge to bypass the Provincial Legislature ... [it] was in actual practice converted into an issue of faith—Islam and *kufr* (blasphemy), between Pakistan (the sacred land) and Hindustan (the land of infidel).... Voting for India was thus made an act of infidelity.... Further the referendum was held in highly charged communal atmosphere. Since March 1947, the Muslim League had launched a violent civil disobedience movement as part of its programme of Direct Action to establish the inability of the Congress Government to maintain law and order in the Province. The Muslim League cadres had indulged in organised violence especially against the Hindu and Sikh minorities. The Muslim League aroused anti-India, rather anti-Hindu and Sikh, feelings among the mass of common people by popularizing such blatantly communal and provocative slogans: *Bihar ka badla sarahad main layange* (Bihar riots will be avenged in the Frontier (N.W.F.P.).... In the words of Mountbatten, the Muslim League had 'laid up bitter hatred by massacres, forcible conversions and horrible atrocities.' ... [In] the months of March and April 1947 about 200,000 Hindus and Sikhs had migrated from their homes

in the N.W.F.P.…. Further, even the Khudai Khidmatagars, the followers of the pro-Indian Pathan leader, Khan Abdul Gaffar Khan, popularly known as the Frontier Gandhi, and the Congress MLAs led by the Chief Minister, Dr Khan Sahib, were too scared to vote in the referendum as they ran the risk of 'commit-ting sin and being damned' for violating the *fatwa*, religious decree directing the voters to vote for Pakistan…. Khan Abdul Gaffar Khan justly bemoaned that it was an act of treachery on part of the Congress to have agreed to the referendum being held in the N.W.F.P.: it threw the Khudai Khidmatagars to the wolves. The Khudai Khidmatagars had been the real backbone of the Congress….

Wali Khan notes that 'the referendum was held only in six districts of the province, and six Agency areas adjacent to the Frontier were excluded along with the tribal areas' and so were Swat, Dir, Chitral and Amb States.[37] The result of the referendum was declared on 20 July 1947. Wali Khan docu-ments that the total number of votes was 572,799 out of a population of 7–8 million of the NWFP, and 289,244 votes were in favour of 'Pakistan', that is 50.5 per cent.[38] Thus, less than 0.3 million people out of a population of 7–8 million made 'Pakistan' materialize.

Sarila records that in Baluchistan, the votes were cast by members of the Jirga and of the Quetta Municipality; the result was predictably in favour of 'Pakistan'.[39]

The Indian subcontinent was accordingly to be partitioned by the British in terms of the Wavell plan, though now with immediate transfer of power and a verbal assurance made by Mountbatten to Nehru to persuade a majority of the princely Indian states to accede to the dominion of India in lieu of New Delhi's consent to remain part of the British Commonwealth. With the Indian leadership accepting partition, Britain would be absolved of all responsibility of dealing with the conflagration in Punjab and else-where on the subcontinent. With India assuming dominion status within the Commonwealth and remaining on good terms with Britain, despite being divided, Britain would enhance its prestige worldwide. With the creation of 'Pakistan' in the strategic north-western region of the Indian subcontinent to cooperate with Britain, Britain would satisfy its political, strategic and defence interests. Pakistan's former Foreign Minister Khurshid Mahmud Kasuri concedes that '[i]n our initial years, our foreign policy was greatly influenced by the British connection' and that '[w]e became part of military alliances where the UK with the US played a dominant role'.[40] Wali Khan records that the first Government of Pakistan:[41]

> [D]id precisely what the British had expected them to do. Almost all key positions were given to the British. When the names of the new Governors of the Provinces were announced, with the exception of Sind all the provinces

had British Governors: (1) Sir Frederick Bourne, East Bengal; (2) Sir Francis Mudie, Punjab; (3) Sir George Cunningham, NWFP; and (4) An Englishman as Agent in Baluchistan. Sir Ghulam Husain Hidayatullah was the only Pakistani, who was appointed the Governor of Sind. This appointment was made because the capital of Sind was Karachi which also happened to be the capital of Pakistan. The Government House of Sind was occupied by Jinnah, the Governor-General of Pakistan. Therefore another residence had to be arranged for the Governor of Sind!

The British were appointed the Chiefs of the Pakistan Army, Air Force and Navy: (1) General Sir Frank Messervy, Commander-in-Chief, Army; (2) Air Vice-Marshal Perry Keane, Chief of Air Force; and (3) Rear Admiral Jefford, Chief of Naval Staff. There were five British Secretaries in the Central Government of Pakistan. In addition, Defence and other Central Ministries were placed under British officers. In his autobiography, Iskander Mirza profusely praised these British officers, saying how hard they worked for the consolidation of Pakistan…. The situation in the North West Frontier Province deserves special mention, because, as viewed from the British angle, this was the most sensitive area…. In this province a large number of British officers still hung around; it was difficult to say that the British had departed and we had attained independence. The Governor of the province was British. British officers were in key positions such as Chief Secretary, Secretaries to the State Government, Police Chief, and even Secretaries of Public Works Department and Department of Electricity….

The British strategy now, with the dominion of Pakistan having come into being, was to withdraw as early as possible from the rest of the Indian subcontinent. Jaswant Singh notes that 'almost entirely the focus of the British withdrawal was on self-preservation, a quick getaway, orderly if possible, but any how, even disorderly if that is what it was to be; but 'exit quickly before total chaos' overtook the occupiers; that was all that mattered'.[42]

The Boundary Commission under Cyril Radcliffe was to pronounce its partition award before 15 August 1947. Just before the said date, the tribals of the Chittagong Hill tracts on the eastern part of the Indian subcontinent had learnt that the area was likely to be allotted to 'East Pakistan', notwithstanding the fact that the tribals, who were almost a quarter of a million, were not Muslim. This led to the tribal leaders meeting the Congress leaders, who assured them that their area would not fall in 'Pakistan'. Following a meeting with the delegation of the tribal leaders during the morning of 13 August 1947, Patel wrote to Mountbatten on the same day that '[a]ny award against the weight of local opinion … or without any referendum to ascertain the will of the people concerned, must, therefore, be construed as a collusive or partisan award and will therefore have to be repudiated by us'.[43] Hodson records that:[44]

The Viceroy had received warnings of this storm at a meeting with his staff on 12th August, when he was informed that the award would probably allot the Chittagong Hill Tracts to Pakistan. Mr. V. P. Menon said that this would have a disastrous effect on the Congress leaders, who had been committing themselves unequivocally on the matter. If the details of the award were given before 15th August, he thought they might well refuse to attend the meeting of the Constituent Assembly which the Viceroy was to address on that day, or the State Banquet in the evening ... Lord Mountbatten ... decided that somehow the details of the awards must be kept back from the leaders until after 15th August ... [d]espite the great administrative disadvantages of not knowing, at the creation of the two Dominions, what their precise areas would be, with the result that the administration of the potential border districts would be completely in the air....

The first indication the Viceroy had that the awards were almost ready was on or about 9th August ... Lord Mountbatten had a meeting with Sir Cyril Radcliffe to discuss the date on which the awards were to be announced. He asked whether Sir Cyril could hold his reports until after 15th August. Sir Cyril replied firmly that he could not delay beyond the 13th at the very latest. The Viceroy agreed that the reports should be sent to his office on the 13th. He was leaving for Karachi that afternoon and would not have time to see them until he returned on the evening of the 14th, which would automatically delay publication until the 15th or later. This was the plan that was followed.

Sarila writes that the pronouncement of the award was deliberately delayed till 17 August 1947 so that the celebrations of Independence Day in India, 'that helped so much to bury past Indian animosity to Britain' as Mountbatten put it, remained 'joyous and tumultuous', and that the 'excuse then contrived for delaying the announcement of the verdict was to put it in a safe on receipt and to say that it was received from Lord Radcliffe on 13 August, after the Viceroy had left for Karachi to take part in the Pakistan Independence Day celebrations there on 14 August'.[45]

The British were fully aware that each day of delay in pronouncing the award would lead to graver disorder. Ramchandra Guha records that:[46]

'Rees [Commander of the Punjab Boundary Force] predicted that the boundary award would please no one entirely. It may well detonate the Sikhs'. This was said on 7 August; on the 14th, the commander-in-chief of the British Indian Army, Field Marshall Sir Claude Auchinleck, observed that 'the delay in announcing the award ... is having a most disturbing and harmful effect. It is realized of course that the announcement may add fresh fuel to the fire, but lacking the announcement, the wildest rumours are current, and being spread by mischief makers of whom there is no lack.'

On 22 July, after a visit to Lahore, Lord Mountbatten [had written] to Sir Cyril Radcliff asking him to hurry up, for 'every extra day' would lessen the risk of disorder. The announcement of the boundary award before Independence would have allowed movements of troops to be made in advance of the transfer of power. The governor of Punjab was also very keen that the award be announced as soon as it was finalized. As it happened, Radcliff was ready with the award on 9 August itself. However Mountbatten changed his mind, and chose to make the award public only after the 15th, his explanation for the delay was strange, to say the least: 'Without question, the earlier it was published, the more the British would have to bear the responsibility for the disturbances which would undoubtedly result'. By the same token, 'the later we postponed publication, the less would the inevitable odium react on the British'.

The Horrors of Partition

The emotional celebrations on 15 August 1947 in the streets of Delhi of having attained freedom, with the Mountbattens joining the crowds, did add enormously to British prestige in the world. It is another matter that the cataclysmic upheaval in Punjab had begun and the war for the PIS of J&K was only a few weeks away.

Jaswant Singh writes that:[47]

Even at this stage, no one knew how this ancient land stood divided, or where the boundary actually ran, not even where it might finally get delineated. Many million laments then filled the air, hauntingly, in India and in Pakistan.... The loss was not just individual, nor in Punjab and Bengal alone. Established geographical and economic entities, ancient cultural unities, having evolved over millennia into a distinct and unique oneness, got fragmented; this historical synthesis of an ancient land, its people, its culture and its civilisation was deliberately broken into pieces.

D.F. Karaka summed up the sombre mood as under:[48]

[T]hat day which witnessed the consummation of a long struggle for freedom, too saw the tragedy of a rupture within the nation. A people who had battled together against a common enemy, moved by the same pulsations of patriotism and the same vision of freedom, were now to be divided. A country that was one through long centuries of historical development and by virtue of geographical frontiers was to be artificially bisected into two dominions.

Partition was unnatural. Geographically the country was indivisible and by historical association, the two communities were inseparable. Their cultures had nourished each other so long that they were indistinguishable. Now a frontier would have to be created, tearing through bonds of association. Not the surgeon's healing knife but the butcher's destructive axe would be in operation. The country would be disrupted, the orderly threads of 400 million human lives which were interwoven to form the fabric of India, would be torn.... Like a nightmare, one could see the tragedy of division, the chaos it would bring and the violence it was likely to entail....

Pakistani scholar Ayesha Jalan quotes Saadat Hasan Manto, the widely respected Urdu writer, as under:[49]

In this land, once called India, such rivers of blood have flowed over the past few months that even the heavens are bewildered.... Blood and steel, war and musket, are not new to human history. Adam's children have always taken interest in these games. But there is no example anywhere in the colourful stories of mankind of the game that was played out recently.

Ayesha Jalan writes that:[50]

Shocked by the catastrophic impact of India's partition in 1947, Saadat Hasan Manto (1912–1955), the greatest Urdu short story writer of the twentieth century, marvelled at the stern calmness with which the British had rent asunder the subcontinent's unity at the moment of decolonization. Even the coolest of Indian minds had no time to think. Those renowned for their statesmanship, acumen, and farsightedness were left blinking their eyes. Human beings had instituted rules against murder and mayhem in order to distinguish themselves from beasts of prey. None was observed in the murderous orgy that shook India to the core at the dawn of Independence.

'Now before our eyes lie dried tracks of blood, cut up human parts, charred faces, mangled necks, terrified people, looted houses, burned fields, mountains of rubble, and overflowing hospitals. We are free. Hindustan is free. Pakistan is free, and we are walking the desolate streets naked without any possessions in distress.'

The partition of India did more than rip apart the territorial unity of the subcontinent. Looting of property and the indiscriminate murder of innocent men, women, and children, purportedly because of their religious identity, destroyed the psychological equilibrium of people, now divided into two separate and mutually hostile nations.

Ramchandra Guha asserts that the trouble in Punjab 'was made worse by the noticeably partisan attitude of the Governor of West Punjab, Sir

Francis Mudie', who was 'inveterate of the Congress' and did not find himself limited by his ministers; Jinnah, on his part, remained in Karachi and visited Lahore 'only in purdah and was most carefully guarded'.[51] As late as 30 July 1947, Evan Jenkins had cautioned Mountbatten that 'the prospect of Independence with Partition evoked anger rather than enthusiasm' in Punjab.[52] Hodson documents that:[53]

> Independence Day in Punjab was a day of violence and terror. That afternoon, in a town of East Punjab, a mob of Sikhs were reported to have seized Muslim women, stripped and raped them, and paraded them naked on the streets, some of them being then slaughtered and burnt. Across the border, on the night of 15th August a ... large Muslim mob burnt down a Gurdwara (Sikh temple), killing and incinerating its occupants to a number of about a score—'it was impossible to count the victims properly in the confused heap of rubble and corpses'.

Along with the orgy of violence, millions of people were forced to leave their homes. Hodson records that 'gruesome attacks were made on refugee trains' and that between '20th and 23rd September, 2,700 Muslims and 600 non-Muslims were killed or wounded on trains'.[54] By that month, the problem of refugees assumed catastrophic proportions, with columns of millions of people moving in opposite directions with their loved ones and meagre belongings. Ramchandra Guha refers to a press report by a Punjab correspondent of the weekly, *Swatantra*, who wrote that:[55]

> There is another sight I am not likely to forget. A five mile-long caravan of Muslim refugees crawling at a snails pace into Pakistan over the Sutlej bridge. Bullock-carts piled high with pitiful chattels, cattle being driven alongside. Women with babies in their arms and wretched little tin trunks on their heads. Twenty thousand men, women and children trekking into the promised land—not because it is the promised land, but because bands of Hindus and Sikhs in Faridkot State and the interior of Ferozepur district had hacked hundreds of Muslims to death and made life impossible for the rest.

Glyn Paterson quotes a then 22-year-old partition survivor as recounting the 'horrendous sight' of people moving on foot from one dominion to another as under:[56]

> The poorest, the most helpless, old, sick, weak, and with hardly any belongings in the world—people were forced to move in long caravans. They were preyed upon again and again along the way. Robbed, abducted. And then, all this misery was compounded by rains. It rained and rained and the floods came and thousands of these caravans were swept away....

The fact that the monsoons on the Indian subcontinent would peak in the month of August resulting in heavy floods was evidently irrelevant to Mountbatten, when he casually chose 15 August 1947 as a 'good date' to effect partition.

Wali Khan describes the situation in Karachi as under:[57]

In the country thousands of communal fires were continuing to smolder; it was looking as though every one was intent upon cutting the other's throat. Young boys and girls and children who had led sheltered lives and had never stepped outside their carpeted drawing rooms were brutally murdered. While houses were set on fire, and streams of blood flowed in towns and cities, parades were held, bugles were sounded, salutes given. In the city of Karachi unending streams of refugees were escaping from their burning homes while murderers' bullets were riddling human bodies. Families who had never stirred out of their homes were walking barefoot on the roads and open spaces.

Wali Khan recounts Gandhi telling him at a meeting post the partition as under:[58]

The objective before me was not just to attain freedom, but also to remove all the social ills in the society which had festered during the 200 years of the British rule. They have practically divested us of our traditions of tolerance and harmony, and, instead, fomented hatred and discord through their communal policies. I had thought that we could change the entire system and people of this country and would live together like brothers, in love, harmony, and peace, so that coming generations may be blessed with all of that, which, thanks to the British, we have been deprived of.... If you look around at India today, you will see that all the empty spaces and bazaars of Srinagar are crowded with Hindu and Sikh refugees from NWFP. Similarly, in Bengal, Bihar and Delhi, Muslims are suffering the trauma of partition. The Punjab situation is, by far, the worst. Caravans of Muslim refugees are going towards Pakistan, and, similarly, unending streams of Hindu and Sikh refugees are coming to India. They are being massacred enroute. Men have turned brutes. Barbarism is rampant; every group of refugees is faced with well-organised attacks. Bloodshed has become a daily occurrence; people are being killed irrespective of their age or sex.... Today, when I see Hindus and Muslims separated, with a more or less permanent gulf, I feel politically and spiritually defeated....

It mattered little to the British that the partition of the Indian subcontinent would leave the dominions of both India and Pakistan vulnerable, whether in matters of defence, economy or even communications. While India would be stripped of its natural frontiers on both the north-west and north-east and such borders handed over to Pakistan, West Pakistan and East Pakistan (now Bangladesh) would be separated by thousands of miles, with Indian territory wedged in between. Factories lay on one side of the border, raw materials and markets on the other. Rivers and important ports fell in one dominion, affecting navigation and transportation in the other. The communalization of the Indian polity would perpetuate the cycle of conflict between the two dominions. Both dominions, though plagued with poverty, disease and illiteracy, would spend their scarce resources in trying to outdo the other in the arms race. Surely the British, who had governed the subcontinent for about 200 years, knew of the interdependence of the people in the provinces and, indeed, of the provinces and the princely Indian states. Surely the British were well aware that the communal partition of the Indian subcontinent and of the identity of its people would be a prelude to continuous internal warfare within the Indian subcontinent, complete with gory bloodshed and dismembered lives for generations to come. Surely the British were fully conscious that the partition would leave millions of men, women and children slaughtered, and millions more uprooted from places where they had been born and raised, only to be transplanted in essentially foreign soil to start life afresh in poverty and degradation.[59] Yet the British had ruthlessly pursued their policy of partition to create a friendly 'Pakistan', viewing the dead and dispossessed in the Indian subcontinent as merely incidental damage. Mountbatten dismissively commented:[60]

> Now if you just say: '200,000 people died', it sounds terrible. But what is 200,000? Out of 400 million? That is one person in 2000 isn't it? Work it out. It is 0.01 per cent, something of that order. It is a fractional percentage.

Indeed, Mountbatten spelt out the British view when he remarked that 'in a way, the massacres were a tribute to British power, and the belief in British protection' and that it 'was the removal of the British protection that caused it'.[61]

This narration of independence of the Indian subcontinent from the British colonial rule indicates how thoroughly the partition had been scripted by the British to secure their interests to the very end with the creation of 'Pakistan'. What made this remorseless act even more unconscionable was the fact that the British had indulged in the same kind of politics in the Middle East in the early part of the 20th century, causing similar sufferings there. A reference to the role of the British in the happenings in the Middle East would leave no scope for doubt that the partition of the Indian subcontinent, and everything around it, was a deliberate design of the British.

British Politics and the Middle East

The multiethnic Ottoman Empire, which ruled much of the Arab world, was founded in 1299 by Islamic Turkish tribes in Anatolia (Asia Minor) and became, over the next six centuries, a transcontinental power controlling lands around the Mediterranean basin. The Ottoman Empire was dissolved in 1923 by the Treaty of Lausanne, and was succeeded by the Republic of Turkey (which came into being on 29 October 1923) as also the new states in south-eastern Europe and the Middle East.

A few decades before the East India Company arrived in Surat (Gujarat), a few English merchants, organized in the form of an association known as the Levant Company, had engaged with the Ottoman Empire for permission for English ships to trade in Ottoman ports. The English traders employed William Harborne, a businessman, in 1578 to travel to Constantinople, the capital of the Ottoman Empire, for this purpose. Harborne secured such permission and became the English Ambassador to the Ottoman Empire in 1583. Over time, trade thrived between England and the Ottoman Empire. The turn of the 20th century saw the British supporting the Ottoman Empire which, like the north-western frontier of the Indian subcontinent, served as an Islamic buffer against Russian expansionism during the Great Game. The emergence of Germany as a commercial rival to Britain around this time led to the British employing their particular brand of politics.

It will be useful to examine the similarities between the happenings in the Middle East and the situation in the Indian subcontinent. Pat Walsh writes that:[62]

> Britain acted as an ally of the Ottoman Empire for most of the century before the Great War [First World War]. During this period Britain was determined to preserve the Ottoman State as a giant buffer zone between its Empire and the expanding Russian Empire. It was part of what was known as the Great Game in England that the Russians should not have Constantinople and the warm water port that this would have given them. It was for this reason that England fought the Crimean War. Later on in the century the British Prime Minister Benjamin Disraeli negotiated the Treaty of Berlin to help preserve the Ottoman Empire against another attempted Russian expansionism in the region.... England, with the French, helped preserve the Ottoman Empire in a weak, dependent state through devices like the Capitulations so that outlying Ottoman territories could be absorbed into the British Empire in a gradual process (for example, Egypt) when a favourable opportunity arose.

A similar state of affairs had existed in the Indian subcontinent, with the British using the Islamic north-western frontier of colonial India to check the Russian influence during the Great Game. The British did their best to delay the transfer of power, and then floated 'Plans' that were calculated to fracture the Indian subcontinent with a weak centre, which would continue to be dependent on the British. The British insisted on the 'provincial option' in the hope that parts of the Indian subcontinent would not join the Union of India and would choose to be absorbed into the British sphere of influence by treaty. And when the British were forced to transfer power, they ensured the creation of Islamic Pakistan, complete with the strategic NWFP, which would continue to serve as such buffer zone.

Pat Walsh writes further that:[63]

.... Britain had always practiced a Balance of Power policy with regard to Europe. For centuries Britain had built its empire by keeping Europe divided and by giving military assistance to the weaker powers against any power that might be emerging on the continent. Whilst Europe was preoccupied with war England was able to get on with its business of conquering the rest of the world. It had the great advantage of being an island and therefore it could meddle with Europe and then retire from the continental battlefield and let others continue the fighting when enough had been gained.

The British followed the 'balance of power' policy in the Indian subcontinent as well through its divide and rule strategy, and by propping up Jinnah and strengthening the Muslim League in order to check the growing power and influence of the Congress. Following partition, the British policy was to give military and other assistance to Pakistan, knowing fully well that it would be used against India. While the Indian leadership was preoccupied with communal warfare, both in undivided India and later in divided India, the British were able to get on with their Great Game with Russia. The British could meddle in the Indian subcontinent and then watch, from a safe distance of thousands of miles, the Congress and the Muslim League (later India and Pakistan) fighting at the cost of their people.

Pat Walsh explains the reason for the British later sacrificing the Ottoman Empire by joining hands with the Russians to check Germany as a commercial rival:[64]

.... Germany had begun to show interest in the Ottoman Empire. In 1898 the Kaiser made a celebrated visit to Istanbul to show Germany's good faith to Turkey. What worried Britain about the German involvement with the Ottoman Empire was that it was not a parasitic relationship like the other imperialist powers. The German objective seems to have been to rejuvenate and modernize the Ottoman Empire in exchange for commercial rights there. England and Russia had seen the Ottoman Empire as the sick man of

Europe and they had been waiting around for his death but now they looked on as Germany threatened to revive the health of the sick man, and dash their dreams of conquest.

.... During the 19th century Britain's traditional enemy in Europe had been France and her traditional rival in Asia was Russia. However, in the early years of the 20th century England gradually decided that Germany was the coming power to be opposed. Therefore, it was decided to overturn the foreign policy of a century and to establish alliances with its traditional enemies, France and Russia, so that Germany could be encircled and then when war came about Britain would join the conflict and destroy Germany as a commercial rival....

.... The problem for Britain was that the Russians ... had no real reason to fight Germany. Therefore, something had to be promised to the Czar for his help in destroying Germany. That something was Constantinople.

It may be recalled that until the 'Mutiny' of 1857, Britain's traditional enemy were the Muslims. With the Hindu middle class asserting itself, the British overturned their policy of over a century and established alliances with prominent Muslim leaders. However, Muslim-majority provinces of British India had no reason to insist on partition of the Indian subcontinent to create an Islamic 'Pakistan'. The British, therefore, hand-picked the politically ambitious Jinnah to demand partition on the basis of the two-nation theory. Something had to be promised to Jinnah for his help in partitioning the Indian subcontinent, and that something was the British patronage to promote Jinnah, having little or no political base, as the undisputed leader of all Indian Muslims and to consequently install him as the head of state of 'Pakistan'.

In order to draw out further similarities between the British politics in the Indian subcontinent and in the Middle East, it will be necessary to have an overview of how the British dealt with the Ottoman Empire during, and post, the First World War (1914–1918). Firas Alkhateeb writes that:[65]

.... In the summer of 1914, war broke out in Europe.... On the 'Allied' side stood the empires of Britain, France, and Russia. The 'Central' powers consisted of Germany and Austria-Hungary.

At first, the Ottoman Empire decided to remain neutral.... After trying to join the Allied side and being rejected, the Ottomans sided with the Central Powers in October of 1914.

The British immediately began to conceive of plans to dissolve the Ottoman Empire and expand their Middle Eastern empire. They had already had control of Egypt since 1888 and India since 1857. The Ottoman Middle

East lay right in the middle of these two important colonies, and the British were determined to exterminate it as part of the world war.

The British were successful in exterminating the Ottoman Empire by triple-crossing the Arabs. Alkhateeb records that the British made 'three different agreements with three different groups promising three different political futures for the Arab world'. The first agreement was with Sharif Hussein bin Ali, the emir of Mecca, who was promised his own Arab Kingdom if he organized an Arab revolt against the Ottoman Empire. Alkhateeb writes that:[66]

.... One of the British strategies was to turn the Ottoman Empire's Arab subjects against the government. They found a ready and willing helper in the Hejaz, the western region of the Arabian Peninsula. Sharif Hussein bin Ali, the amir (governor) of Makkah entered into an agreement with the British government to revolt against the Ottomans.... In return, the British promised to provide money and weapons to the rebels to help them fight the much more organized Ottoman army. Also, the British promised him that after the war, he would be given his own Arab kingdom that would cover the entire Arabian Peninsula, including Syria and Iraq. The letters in which the two sides negotiated and discussed revolt were known as the McMahon-Hussein Correspondence, as Sharif Hussein was communicating with the British High Commissioner in Egypt, Sir Henry McMahon.

In June of 1916 Sharif Hussein led his group of armed Bedouin warriors from the Hejaz in an armed campaign against the Ottomans. Within a few months, the Arab rebels managed to capture numerous cities in the Hejaz (including Jeddah and Makkah) with help from the British army and navy. The British provided support in the form of soldiers, weapons, money, advisors (including the 'legendary' Lawrence of Arabia), and a flag. The British in Egypt drew up a flag for the Arabs to use in battle, which was known as the 'Flag of the Arab Revolt'. This flag would later become the model for other Arab flags of countries such as Jordan, Palestine, Sudan, Syria, and Kuwait.

The second agreement that the British entered into was with the French to divide the Arab world between them, in direct conflict with what the British had promised Sharif Hussein bin Ali. Alkhateeb documents that:[67]

Before the Arab Revolt could even begin and before Sharif Hussein could create his Arab kingdom, the British and French had other plans. In the winter of 1915–1916, two diplomats, Sir Mark Sykes of Britain and François Georges-Picot of France, secretly met to decide the fate of the post-Ottoman Arab world.

According to what would become known as the Sykes–Picot Agreement, the British and French agreed to divide up the Arab world between themselves. The British were to take control of what is now Iraq, Kuwait, and Jordan. The French were given modern Syria, Lebanon, and southern Turkey. The status of Palestine was to be determined later, with Zionist ambitions to be taken into account. The zones of control that the British and French were given allowed for some amount of Arab self-rule in some areas, albeit with European control over such Arab kingdoms. In other areas, the British and French were promised total control.

…. The Sykes–Picot Agreement directly contradicted the promises the British made to Sherif Hussein and caused a considerable amount of tension between the British and Arabs….

The third agreement the British made was with the Zionists for establishing a Jewish state in the Holy Land of Palestine. Alkhateeb refers to the letter sent on 2 November 1917 by Arthur Balfour, the Foreign Secretary for Britain, to Baron Rothschild, a leader in the Zionist community, which 'declared the British government's official support for the Zionist movement's goals to establish a Jewish state in Palestine'.[68] He writes that:[69]

…. The Arabs insisted they still get their Arab kingdom that was promised to them through Sharif Hussein. The French (and British themselves) expected to divide up that same land among themselves. And the Zionists expected to be given Palestine as promised by Balfour.

In 1918 the war ended with the victory of the Allies and the complete destruction of the Ottoman Empire… all the former Ottoman land was now under European occupation. The war was over, but the Middle East's future was still in dispute between three different sides.

…. In the aftermath of WWI, the League of Nations (a forerunner to the United Nations) was established. One of its jobs was to divide up the conquered Ottoman lands. It drew up 'mandates' for the Arab world. Each mandate was supposed to be ruled by the British or French 'until such time as they are able to stand alone.' The League was the one to draw up the borders we see on modern political maps of the Middle East. The borders were drawn without regard for the wishes of the people living there, or along ethnic, geographic, or religious boundaries—they were truly arbitrary. It is important to note that even today, political borders in the Middle East do not indicate different groups of people. The differences between Iraqis, Syrians, Jordanians, etc. were entirely created by the European colonizers as a method of dividing the Arabs against each other.

Through the mandate system, the British and the French were able to get the control they wanted over the Middle East. For Sharif Hussein, his sons were allowed to rule over these mandates under British 'protection'. Prince Faisal was made king of Iraq and Syria and Prince Abdullah was made king of Jordan. In practice, however, the British and French had real authority over these areas.

For the Zionists, they were allowed by the British government to settle in Palestine, although with limitations. The British did not want to anger the Arabs already living in Palestine, so they tried to limit the number of Jews allowed to migrate to Palestine. This angered the Zionists, who looked for illegal ways to immigrate throughout the 1920s–1940s, as well as the Arabs, who saw the immigration as encroachment on land that had been theirs since Salah-al-Din liberated it in 1187....

It may be noted that the Ottoman Empire had initially tasted victories against the Allied forces at the Battle of Gallipoli and the Siege of Kut and had held the upper hand for almost two years. It was the British-inspired Arab Revolt that helped the British defeat the Ottoman forces in 1917 and partition the Ottoman Empire under the Treaty of Sèvres. Alkhateeb points out that the 'British did not have to look hard for an Arab man' while hand-picking Sharif Hussein to lead the Arab Revolt, as he, 'the disgruntled local emir (Governor) of Mecca', also 'had dreams of becoming an independent ruler of Hejaz (the west of the Arabian Peninsula), and perhaps even king of all the Arabs'.[70] Alkhateeb writes that:[71]

It is important to note that the Arab Revolt did not have the backing of a large majority of the Arab population. It was a minority movement of a couple thousand tribesmen led by a few leaders who sought to increase their own powers. The vast majority of the Arab people stayed away from the conflict and did not support the rebels or the Ottoman government....

Alkhateeb records that in:[72]

[A] series of letters from late 1915 to early 1916, the British enticed [Sharif Hussein] to rebel, and promised to supply him with money, weapons, ships, and men, believing that this would snowball into a large-scale Arab revolt.... Sharif Hussein declared his rebellion against the Ottoman Empire in early June of 1916. Word was sent out (with British help, of course) to Arabs throughout the empire to join Sharif Hussein as he built a new Arab kingdom, free from Ottoman domination. The response was lackluster, to say the least. Besides a few thousand desert warriors from Sharif Hussein's own tribe, absolutely no Arabs flocked to Sharif Hussein's side....

.... His small group of tribesmen had no artillery or machine guns, which had to be provided and manned by British soldiers, usually from Egypt and

India. Also instrumental was the role played by a young British army officer, who would later be famously known as Lawrence of Arabia. It is doubtful that without such British support, Sharif Hussein's effort would have even survived the first few months after the revolt was declared.

.... Sharif Hussein did not seem to be interested in Arab nationalism at all. His only motivation seems to have been to create a kingdom that he would personally be the ruler of. The resurgence of Arab identity, literature, and culture did not interest him nearly as much as personal power....

The similarities in the British strategy with respect to the Ottoman Empire and the Indian subcontinent are striking, whether they relate to the British pitting Muslims against Muslims, to the hand-picking of the politically ambitious but disgruntled Sharif Hussein and Jinnah, both of whom lacked popular support to lead the 'revolt', to the building up of both Hussein and Jinnah as the sole representatives of the Muslims, to the drawing of borders arbitrarily and to the installing of regimes in new states that would let the British exercise the real authority. Returning to Pat Walsh's narrative:[73]

In making war on the Ottoman Empire, and in pursuing the Zionist objective, the British Empire not only destroyed the prosperous and content Jewish communities across the Ottoman possessions but also sowed the seeds for generations of conflict with the local inhabitants of Palestine who would find themselves the chief victims of this great act of conquest and ethnic cleansing.

.... The British conquering of Mesopotamia and establishment of Iraq was another consequence of the Great War on Turkey. In this conquest Britain put together an unstable mix of peoples from the Ottoman vilayets of Basra, Mesopotamia and Mosul in the strategic interests of the Empire, and for the oil of Mosul.

Originally the intention was to just incorporate the Basra region into British India to create a new buffer to replace the Ottoman buffer. Arnold Wilson, who was put in charge of the conquered territories, came with pre-war Imperial understandings and an expectation that British power would be fully utilized to govern Iraq in the firm manner that had been applied to the Indian Empire.... The system established by Britain in Iraq was the worst of all possible worlds. The old Ottoman system had the virtue of governing the intermingled peoples of Mesopotamia as the other peoples of the Empire, within a large multi-ethnic unit where local rivalries were largely kept in check.... However, the system that emerged after 1918 was neither strong nor purposeful. It put three distinct groups into a pseudo-nation and created a pressure-cooker environment for them to conflict with each other for power. And it was not surprising that afterwards this system could only be made functional by ruthless strongmen.

If one reads this narration in the context of the Indian experience, it is eerie to see the similarity in how the British sowed the seeds of conflict for generations to come between Hindus and Muslims, and between India and Pakistan. It may be recalled that the persistent demand of the Indian leadership during the freedom struggle was that the British must transfer power into Indian hands, leaving the Indian subcontinent to govern itself as a sovereign republic having no relations with the British Commonwealth. That threatened the British strategy for the Great Game as also British imperial interests in the region. So, just as the British detached Kuwait and Palestine from the Ottoman Empire to protect their interests, the British strategy in the Indian subcontinent revolved around detaching the north-western region of colonial India to create the friendly state of 'Pakistan'. To this end, the British spun smokescreens so effectively that hardly any European national was targeted during the gory partition violence; rather, the Indians, both Hindus and Muslims, focused on wiping each other out in the most brutal manner. The pre-British system had the virtue of governing the intermingled peoples of the Indian subcontinent sharing the fusion of Indo-Muslim culture. The steady communalisation of the Indian polity by the British created the pressure-cooker environment for them to conflict with each other for power. Even with respect to Pakistan, the British put distinct groups into a pseudo-nation of West Pakistan and East Pakistan, which simply could not function.

Alkhateeb records that the Ottoman Empire, 'made up of Turks, Kurds, Greeks, Armenians, Bosnians, Serbians, Persians, Arabs, and others', did not 'for the most part... suffer from its diversity'.[74] While referring to the Armenians, the ethnic minority within the Ottoman Empire, Pat Walsh recalls that 'Britain always sought to undermine enemies or states it saw as rivals by destabilizing them through their national minorities', and writes that:[75]

The Armenians were used by England and Russia as a means of destabilizing the Ottoman Empire and disrupting the Turkish resistance to invasion behind their lines ... its main effect was to make the ordinary Armenians position impossible within the Ottoman Empire. It was made impossible for them to remain a loyal community and a functional part of the Empire, which they had been for centuries....

Nationalism was a most unsuitable thing to promote in the region covered by the Ottoman Empire where a great patch-work of peoples were inter-mingled and were inter-dependent. Its promotion in the region by the Western powers was as disastrous for the many Moslem communities of the Balkans and the Caucuses, who were driven from their homes of centuries, as it was for Christians caught up in the inevitable consequences of the simplifying process it encouraged. The same forces in Europe unleashed by the Versailles settlement did much to make the position of Jews untenable within societies that they had dwelt in for centuries.

The important point that should be borne in mind is that it was not in the Turkish interest that the Armenians should rebel and resort to war but it was very much in the Russian and British interest that they should do so.

Unfortunately for the Armenians, they, like other peoples in strategically important areas found themselves being used as pawns in a new Great Game. And after being encouraged to rise and form themselves into a national entity, that was never a practicality given their dispersion across Ottoman territories, they were quickly discarded and forgotten when their interests no longer coincided with those of their sponsors.

.... The Russians and British raised some people's expectations so that they were willing to exact retribution on people they had grievances against and in turn those people exacted revenge on them. No one quite knew under whose authority they would exist when the war was over and therefore all restraint was removed on behaviour. It was under these circumstances and in this context that the relocation of Armenians took place and the killing of both Christian and Moslem peoples.... Essentially the responsibility for what happened to the Armenians and the other minorities that existed relatively peacefully within the Ottoman Empire for centuries must be placed at the hands of those who attempted to destabilize and ultimately destroy this multinational Empire.

The script could have been written for the Indian Muslims dispersed throughout the Indian subcontinent. The British used the Indian Muslims to sabotage the freedom struggle spearheaded by the multi-faith Congress. It was not in the interests of the Indian Muslims to rebel or indulge in communal violence, but it was very much in the interests of the British that they should do so. The Hindus and Muslims were led to exact retribution and invite revenge. The main effect of the British strategy was to make the position of the ordinary Muslim who stayed on in India suspect. The Indian Muslim community is often forced to express its loyalty to India in order to remain a functional part of the Indian society, despite it having been so for centuries.

Pat Walsh writes about the propaganda machinery set up by the British to justify their actions in the Middle East to the world, and to the US in particular:[76]

Wellington House was a secret propaganda department set up at the start of the war under Charles Masterman. Masterman was later replaced by John Buchan, the famous author of The 39 Steps. Buchan and other notable literary figures and historians of the time were recruited to the propaganda drive through a covert meeting held just after the outbreak of the war.... The intention was to establish a propaganda drive against Germany which would use the talents of all these writers in the construction of a great output of material that would demonize the enemy from all possible angles—accusing them of terrible atrocities, having violent natures and instincts, producing aggressive and expansionist ideas etc. etc.

.... A classic example was Mark Sykes famous article in The Times called The clean fighting Turk—a spurious claim. Sykes was the man charged with secretly carving up the Middle East with the French at the same time as Britain was openly promising an Arab state on the same territory to the Arabs.

Another example, amongst dozens of others, was the book called Crescent and Iron Cross by E.F. Benson. Benson was a famous novelist and writer of ghost stories. As far as I know he had little interest in the history of the Ottoman Empire or Turkish affairs before the Great War. Suddenly he produced a book which demonized the Turks and made all sorts of allegations about the Ottomans and particularly about their treatment of the Armenians.

... the sheer volume and range of all these publications produced the same effect as poison gas in the trenches—attacking all the senses and creating something that was very difficult to avoid penetrating the mind.

Two and a half million books and pamphlets reached an audience of at least 13,000 contacts in the United States.... [in] order to justify ... the conquest of the Middle East.... The idea was to implant in the American mind the view that once Britain had liberated the Arab areas from the Ottoman Empire they would all become Gardens of Eden and that the British Empire only had the noblest of motives and the interests of native peoples in mind in fighting and conquering in the region.

When one recalls the propaganda created by the British, painting the Congress as a Hindu party, and building the theme for US consumption that the British were ready to give India her freedom but India was not in a position to exercise it due to serious differences between the Hindus, represented by the Congress, and the Muslims, represented by the Muslim League, one can easily imagine how such false perceptions would have been spread.

The similarities do not end there. The decades of instability in the Middle East, as also the European refugee crisis, have been linked to the politics of the British (and its allies) in the Middle East. Alkhateeb points out that the 'political mess that Britain created in the aftermath of

WWI remains today', with the 'competing agreements and the subsequent countries that were created to disunite Muslims from each other [leading] to political instability throughout the Middle East'.[77] It may well be argued that just as terrorism in the Indian subcontinent can be traced directly to the British politics to settle 'The Problem of India', the turbulence in the Middle East due to the policies of the British (and its allies) has led to the rise of the Islamic State. The 13/11 Paris attacks focused world attention on the Islamic State that controlled chunks of Sunni-majority lands in west Iraq and Syria—an area larger than the UK—and which split Iraq on Shia–Sunni–Kurd lines.[78] Reports narrate how the division of territory on sectarian lines goes back to the 'solutions force-fitted', when West Asia was being 'settled' following the defeat of the Ottoman Empire,[79] and how 'nations that were created as a result of colonial pacts like the Sykes–Picot agreement are simply falling apart'.[80]

The British politics in the Middle East also led to enhanced hatred and heightened nationalism between Turkey and Greece, the latter having also been a part of the Ottoman Empire, and to the exchange of population between these states on the basis of religion. Pat Walsh describes the British role in pushing Greece into war with Turkey as under:[81]

> That brings us to the issue of the Greeks. The political and military assault launched by Britain on neutral Greece and the devastating effect this ultimately had on the Greek people across the Balkans and Asia Minor is almost completely forgotten about in Western Europe. The Greek King Constantine and his government tried to remain neutral in the war…. So England made offers to the Greek Prime Minister, Venizlos, of territory in Anatolia which he found too hard to resist. The Greek King, however, under the constitution had the final say on matters of war and he attempted to defend his neutrality policy. King Constantine was then deposed by the actions of the British Army at Salonika, through a starvation blockade by the Royal Navy and a seizure of the harvest by Allied troops. This had the result of a widespread famine in the neutral nation that forced the abdication of Constantine.

> These events led to the Greek tragedy in Anatolia because the puppet government under Venizlos, installed in Athens through Allied bayonets, was enlisted as a catspaw to bring the Turks to heel after the Armistice at Mudros. They were presented with the town of Smyrna first and then the Greeks, encouraged by Lloyd George, advanced across Anatolia toward where the Turkish democracy had re-established, at Ankara, after it had been suppressed in Constantinople. Britain was using the Greeks and their desire for a new Byzantium in Anatolia to get Atatrk (the Turkish President) and the Turkish national forces to submit to the Treaty of Sevres, and the destruction of not only the Ottoman State but Turkey itself.

But the Greek Army perished just short of Ankara after being skillfully maneuvered into a position by Atatrk in which their lines were stretched. And the two thousand year old Greek population of Asia Minor fled on boats from Smyrna, with the remnants of their army after Britain had withdrawn its support, because the Greek democracy had reasserted its will to have back its King.

By the end of 1922, there was a mass exodus of Orthodox Christians from Turkey to Greece, including the Asia Minor Greeks. Greece and Turkey entered into the Convention Concerning the Exchange of Greek and Turkish Populations on 30 January 1923, which required a compulsory exchange of population of about 1.5 million Christians from Turkey to Greece and around 500,000 Muslims from Greece to Turkey. This compulsory population exchange based solely on religious identity was under the auspices of the League of Nations, complete with guarantees of protection of possessions and resettlement of the refugees. The British had this precedent of population exchange before them in 1947. The British, while creating mutually hostile dominions of India and Pakistan in a communally charged and violent environment, being fully aware of the warnings of their own British officers of a bloodbath accompanying partition, chose to prepone the partition from June 1948 to 15 August 1947, without putting in place any credible administrative or policing national or international machinery, and, instead, proceeded with the partition with the people across the subcontinent not even knowing the boundaries of the two dominions.

The British politics in the Middle East confirms that the partition of the Indian subcontinent was scripted by the British. And while scripting the partition, the British had assumed that the strategically located, and Muslim-majority, PIS of J&K would accede to Pakistan or at least be associated with it, and thus form part of their Middle-Eastern sphere of influence to protect British interests in the region and to check the spread of Soviet influence in the oil-rich Middle East. However, when the PIS of J&K chose not to accede to Pakistan, the die had been cast for the genesis of the Kashmir issue. That takes us to the princely Indian states in the Indian subcontinent, and in particular to the PIS of J&K.

Notes and References

1. *Supra* Note 1, Chapter I, p. 266.
2. Ibid.
3. Ibid., p. 224.
4. Ibid., p. 229.

5. Ibid., p. 230.
6. *Supra* Note 6, Chapter I, p. 280.
7. *Supra* Note 1, Chapter I, p. 287.
8. *Supra* Note 6, Chapter I, p. 281.
9. Ibid., pp. 282, 286.
10. Ibid., p. 282.
11. *Supra* Note 1, Chapter I, pp. 293–294.
12. Ibid., p. 296.
13. Ibid., p. 294.
14. *Supra* Note 28, Chapter I, p. 32.
15. Extracted in *Supra* Note 36, Chapter I, p. 75.
16. Ibid., p. 77.
17. *Supra* Note 6, Chapter I, p. 309.
18. Extracted in ibid., pp. 15–16.
19. *Supra* Note 36, Chapter I, p. 106.
20. *Supra* Note 89, Chapter I, p. 494.
21. Ibid., p. 142.
22. Extracted in ibid., pp. 142–143.
23. *Supra* Note 7, Chapter I, pp. 133–134.
24. *Supra* Note 89, Chapter I, p. 143.
25. *Supra* Note 6, Chapter I, p. 310.
26. *Supra* Note 12, Chapter I, pp. 451–456.
27. Extracted in ibid., pp. 457–458.
28. Extracted in ibid., pp. 459–460.
29. Ibid., p. 458.
30. Collins, Larry & Dominique Lapierre. 1984. *Mountbatten and Independent India: 16 August 1947–18 June 1948*, p. 26. New Delhi: Vikas Publishing House Pvt. Ltd.
31. *Supra* Note 36, Chapter I, p. 88.
32. Extracted in ibid., p. 91.
33. Ibid., p. 90.
34. *Supra* Note 28, Chapter I, p. 13.
35. Extracted in ibid.
36. *Supra* Note 36, Chapter I, pp. 78–91.
37. *Supra* Note 7, Chapter I, p. 153.
38. Ibid.
39. *Supra* Note 6, Chapter I, p. 303.
40. *Supra* Note 89, Chapter I, p. 766.
41. *Supra* Note 7, Chapter I, pp. 194–195.
42. *Supra* Note 12, Chapter I, pp. 422–423.
43. *Supra* Note 1, Chapter I, p. 350.
44. Ibid., pp. 350–351.
45. *Supra* Note 6, Chapter I, p. 327.
46. *Supra* Note 28, Chapter I, pp. 14, 33.
47. *Supra* Note 12, Chapter I, p. 460.
48. Extracted in Sengupta, Vivek. 1984. 'Mountbatten and Nehru', *Sunday*, p. 23 at 26. Ananda Bazar Patrika, Calcutta, 8 April–14 April.
49. Extracted in *Supra* Note 119, Chapter I, p. 1.
50. Ibid., pp. 1, 2, 145.

51. *Supra* Note 28, Chapter I, p. 16.
52. Ibid., p. 32.
53. *Supra* Note 1, Chapter I, p. 403.
54. Ibid., p. 412.
55. *Supra* Note 28, Chapter I, p. 15.
56. Glyn Paterson. 2015. 'A Time to Remember', *Eye*, The Sunday Express Magazine, New Delhi, 6 September.
57. *Supra* Note 7, Chapter I, p. 149.
58. Ibid., pp. 162–163.
59. *Supra* Note 48, p. 26.
60. *Supra* Note 30, p. 24.
61. Ibid., p. 19.
62. Walsh, Pat, 2010. 'Britain's Great War on Turkey: An Irish Perspective'. 26 October. Available online at http://www.turkishweekly.net/2010/10/26/article/britains-great-war-on-turkey-an-irish-perspective (downloaded on 5 November 2015).
63. Ibid.
64. Ibid.
65. Alkhateeb, Firas. 2012. 'How the British Divided Up the Arab World', 26 December. Available online at http://lostislamichistory.com/how-the-british-divided-up-the-arab-world/ (downloaded on 15 November 2015).
66. Ibid.
67. Ibid.
68. Ibid.
69. Ibid.
70. Alkhateeb, Firas. 2014. 'The Arab Revolt of World War One', 4 August. Available online at: http://lostislamichistory.com/the-arab-revolt-of-world-war-one/ (downloaded on 15 November 2015).
71. *Supra* Note 65.
72. *Supra* Note 70.
73. *Supra* Note 62.
74. *Supra* Note 70.
75. *Supra* Note 62.
76. Ibid.
77. *Supra* Note 65.
78. Deshpande, Rajeev. 2015. 'Kill 129, IS claims responsibility', *Sunday Times of India*, New Delhi, 15 November.
79. *Sunday Times of India*. 2015. 'IS territory provides sanctuary to jihadis', New Delhi, 15 November.
80. Deshpande, Rajeev. 2015. 'Sectarian divide allows IS to grow as power centre', *The Times of India*, New Delhi, 16 November.
81. *Supra* Note 62.

IV

Princely Indian States and Kashmir

It has been noted that there were two kinds of territory in the Indian subcontinent under the British colonial rule. One was that of the British-annexed provinces, namely, British India, and the other was that of 560-odd princely Indian states owing allegiance to the British Crown.

The British carved out 'Pakistan' from the British-annexed territory in terms of the two-nation theory, while declaring that the allegiance of the princely Indian states to the British Crown would lapse on 15 August 1947. The PIS of J&K was one of these 560-odd princely Indian states. Upon the lapse of allegiance of the PIS of J&K to the British Crown on 15 August 1947, both India and Pakistan claimed that the PIS of J&K belonged to them.

New Delhi's stand was that with the grant of independence on 15 August 1947, it became the successor government of the Indian subcontinent and, therefore, New Delhi alone was sovereign in India.[1] Consequently, those princely Indian states on the subcontinent that did not accede to the newly created dominion of Pakistan continued to remain under New Delhi's sovereignty. Further, since the monarch of the PIS of J&K did, as will be discussed shortly, execute an Instrument of Accession in favour of India on 26 October 1947, the state became an integral part of India.

Pakistan viewed the Muslim-majority PIS of J&K, which is contiguous to Pakistan, as rightfully belonging to it. Pakistan argued that the basis of the partition of the Indian subcontinent following independence from British rule in 1947 was 'that Pakistan would be constituted by the contiguous Muslim-majority areas in the northwest and the northeast of the subcontinent, and India would comprise contiguous non-Muslim-majority areas'.[2] Pakistan contended that it 'was thus universally assumed that, following the basis adopted for Partition', princely Indian states with 'a Muslim majority in population contiguous to Pakistan would accede to

Pakistan'.[3] Pakistan refused to recognize the accession by the PIS of J&K in favour of India.

I have argued elsewhere[4] that the Kashmir issue has generally been viewed as a political one, having legal and constitutional ramifications. However, a political stance must invariably be consistent with the political decisions accepted and crystallized into law. Accordingly, the respective claims of India and Pakistan should be examined in light of the legal status of the PIS of J&K at the time when both countries attained independence from the British on 15 August 1947, pursuant to the decisions accepted by their political leadership and crystallized into the Indian Independence Act of 1947, and the Government of India Act of 1935, as amended. Simply put, should New Delhi have succeeded to the British Crown in the Indian subcontinent, so as to claim sovereignty over those princely Indian states that had not acceded to Pakistan, India could stake a claim to the PIS of J&K, regardless of the subsequent accession by the PIS of J&K to India. Should the future of the PIS of J&K be dictated by it being a Muslim-majority state and being contiguous to Pakistan, Pakistan may have a point in staking a claim to it. However, should the PIS of J&K have been a sovereign state in international law as on 15 August 1947, it would have had the competence to decide its own future. More importantly, in that event, neither the dominion of India nor Pakistan could have staked a claim to a sovereign PIS of J&K as of 15 August 1947.[5] But then, the PIS of J&K did accede to the dominion of India, an accession disputed by Pakistan. In order to appreciate the legal status of the PIS of J&K, and other legal issues that stem from the subsequent accession of the PIS of J&K to India, one would necessarily have to consider the relations of the princely Indian states in general, and of the PIS of J&K in particular, with the British Crown.

Accordingly, this chapter first discusses the status of the monarchical rulers of the princely Indian states in relation to the British Crown. It then examines the happenings in the PIS of J&K and its constitutional status up to the date of its accession to the dominion of India.

Princely Indian States and the British Crown

The fact that the rulers of the princely Indian states owed allegiance to the British Crown did not mean that the rulers of the states possessed no sovereignty at all. It is settled law that independent states may 'have their sovereignty limited and qualified in various degrees, either by the character of their internal constitution, by stipulations of unequal treaties of alliance, or by treaties of protection or of guarantee made by a third Power'.[6] There are judicial precedents in common law for the proposition that 'a state may, without ceasing to be a sovereign state, be bound to another more powerful state by an unequal alliance'.[7]

Thus, merely because the monarchial rulers of the princely Indian states ceded certain powers to the British Crown, they did not cease to be sovereign. In fact, this position has been recognized by the Indian Supreme Court with respect to the PIS of J&K itself. The Supreme Court held in *Premnath Kaul*[8] that insofar as 'the internal administration and governance of the State' were concerned, the ruler was 'an absolute monarch' even under British sovereignty and that 'all powers legislative, executive and judicial in relation to his State and its governance inherently vested in him'.[9]

The British Cabinet Mission Plan of 16 May 1946, referred to earlier, therefore stated that with the attainment of independence by colonial India, the paramountcy of the British Crown over the princely Indian states 'can neither be retained by the British Crown nor transferred to the new Government (of India or Pakistan)'.[10] The memorandum dated 12 May 1946 of the British Cabinet delegation had explained that the British Crown 'will cease to exercise the power of paramountcy, and therefore, all the rights surrendered by the States to the Paramount Power will return to the States'.[11] In other words, the rulers of the 560-odd princely Indian states were to regain absolute sovereign powers upon the lapse of British sovereignty in 1947. This consequence of the lapse of the British sovereignty was reflected in the British statutes transferring power to Indian hands.

British Statutes and the Princely Indian States

Prior to 1947, the constitutional law in force in colonial India was the Government of India Act of 1935 enacted by the British Parliament. On 18 July 1947, the British Parliament enacted the Indian Independence Act of 1947 to make provision for the setting up of two independent dominions in the Indian subcontinent (India and Pakistan) and to amend the prevailing Government of India Act of 1935.

Section 2 of the Indian Independence Act of 1947 specified the territories of the new dominions. The territory of Pakistan was to be the territories of a partitioned Punjab and Bengal as described in the schedules to the 1947

Act, the province of Sind and the Chief Commissioner's province of British Baluchistan. The Act provided for referendum in the Muslim-majority NWFP and Sylhet district of the Assam province, and for such territories to form part of the territory of Pakistan should Pakistan win the referendum.

With regard to the princely Indian states, however, Section 7 of the 1947 Act declared that as of 15 August 1947 'the suzerainty of His Majesty over the Indian States lapses'. The amended Government of India Act of 1935 provided in Section 6 that a princely Indian state shall be deemed to have acceded to either of the dominions on the acceptance of the Instrument of Accession executed by the Ruler thereof.

Thus, the inescapable conclusion is that the princely Indian states ceased to owe any allegiance to the British Crown upon the lapse of the British paramountcy or sovereignty, and became legally sovereign in the full sense of the term. Pakistan has, right from 1947 until the present, taken this correct view of the lapse of the British paramountcy. Pakistan has consistently stated, in national and international fora, that 'with the lapse of paramountcy on the transfer of power by the British, all Indian States ... automatically' regained 'full sovereign and independent status', and were 'therefore free to join either of the two Dominions or to remain independent'.[12]

Pakistan took this stand to rebut New Delhi's contention that it had succeeded to the British Crown on 15 August 1947 as the paramount power on the Indian subcontinent and that those princely Indian states that did not accede to the newly created dominion of Pakistan remained under the supposed paramountcy of the dominion of India. New Delhi had reasoned that:[13]

> a declaration issued by the Crown terminating its relationship with the princely Indian states could determine only the Crown's own future relationship with the states: it could not have the effect of divesting the successor government of its status vis-à-vis the states and its rights and obligations in relation to them inhering in it as the supreme power in India.

New Delhi had argued that all the 'factors which established the paramountcy of the British Government over the states operated to assign a similar position to the Government of India', and hence it was 'the duty of the Government of India to ensure that the vacuum caused by the withdrawal of the British did not disturb the peace and tranquility of the country'.[14] New Delhi, therefore, took the view that 'none of the Indian States had sovereign rights in the full sense of the term; nor did they have individually the necessary resources to claim or enjoy the attributes of a sovereign independent power'.[15]

With regard to the PIS of J&K, Nehru wrote that 'even if Kashmir did not decide whether to go to Pakistan or India … that did not make Kashmir independent and our responsibility even then continued as the continuing entity if anything happened to Kashmir whether Kashmir acceded to India or not'.[16] According to Nehru, India was entitled to intervene regardless of accession inasmuch as 'there is a certain inherent paramountcy in the Government of India which cannot lapse—an inherent paramountcy in the dominant State in India…. Paramountcy must exist'.[17]

The fact that New Delhi's stand on it possessing paramountcy was legally misconceived has been concluded by the judicial authority of the Indian Supreme Court. In *Madhav Rao*,[18] the Supreme Court found it 'strange' that New Delhi should have claimed that the Government of India inherited any aspects of the paramountcy exercised by the British Crown. The Court observed that paramountcy as claimed by the British rulers was one of the manifestations of imperialism, a power exercised by a superior sovereign over the subordinate sovereign.[19] The Court held that the 'paramountcy of the British Crown was not inherited either by India or Pakistan, [but] was allowed to lapse',[20] and that on 15 August 1947, the rulers of the princely Indian states 'became absolute sovereigns. In law they were free to accede to either of the dominions of India or Pakistan or to remain independent'.[21]

As far as the PIS of J&K was concerned, both the Indian Supreme Court in *Premnath Kaul*[22] and the Jammu and Kashmir High Court in *Magher Singh*[23] held that with the lapse of the British paramountcy, the PIS of J&K became an independent and sovereign state in the fullest sense in international law.

The British were well aware of this legal position at the time of transfer of power to Indian hands. Britain, in fact, had toyed with the idea of using some of the independent princely Indian states as military bases, as noted earlier. Hyderabad, in particular, could provide air-transit facilities to British aircrafts going eastwards. However, few of the 560-odd princely Indian states could, given their size, hope to survive as sovereign countries. Moreover, the princely Indian states lay interspersed with the provinces of British India and had become interdependent in matters of communications, currency, security and so on so forth. Should the Indian subcontinent drift into anarchy due to the emergence of several entities, it would seriously damage British prestige worldwide. Further, a fractured subcontinent with 560-odd fully sovereign princely Indian states could lead to the balkanization of India, much to the consternation of the US. It, therefore, suited the British to have the princely Indian states accede to either the dominion of India or of Pakistan prior to 15 August 1947, instead of becoming independent states. Such strategy meant that the two dominions of India and Pakistan would take over the entire subcontinent from the British on 15 August 1947, thereby relieving the British from all responsibility of the subcontinent drifting into anarchy.

The British, therefore, decided to use the princely Indian states to leverage the deal with the Indian leadership, as discussed in the previous chapter. In exchange for Congress's acceptance of the partition of the Indian subcontinent and its consent to remain part of the British Commonwealth, Britain used the good offices of Mountbatten to push the majority of the princely Indian states to accede to the dominion of India. The Indian leadership eventually succumbed to the British demands, and to adopting a legal framework by which the princely Indian states could accede to the dominions prior to the date of Indian independence.

Negotiations for the accession of almost all of the 560-odd princely Indian states were concluded through instruments of accession executed by their respective rulers. Mountbatten played his part by making it clear to the rulers that they would need to keep in mind the compulsions of geographical continuity, viability, security and other practical considerations, and so they should choose to accede rather than retain independence.[24] As far as the dominion of India was concerned, the accession of the princely Indian states was initially confined only to three subjects of defence, external affairs and communications with an express assurance given to the rulers that they would retain their sovereignty except for the accession in respect of these subjects. New Delhi took pains to point out that there was no intention of the dominion of India to encroach upon the internal autonomy or the sovereignty of the princely Indian states or to fetter their discretion in respect of their acceptance of the new constitution for India.[25]

Constitutional Process

By virtue of the Indian Independence Act of 1947, the all-India Constituent Assembly was vested with the power to enact a constitution and to make laws which were not to be void or inoperative on the ground that they were repugnant to the laws of England or the provisions of the said Act. The all-India Constituent Assembly, which had first met on 9 December 1946, re-assembled after the midnight of 14 August 1947 as the sovereign Constituent Assembly for modern-day India, and began its task of drafting the constitution for India. After due deliberations, the draft was declared as passed on 26 November 1949 and became the Constitution of India.

As provided by Article 394 of the Constitution, only specified Articles came into force as of 26 November 1949, with the remaining provisions to come into force as of 26 January 1950, the latter date being referred to in the Constitution as the date of its commencement.

Meanwhile, further negotiations between the dominion of India and the princely Indian states that had acceded to it in terms of the instruments of accession led to the states executing instruments of merger integrating the territories of the acceded princely Indian states into the Union of India. A few days before 26 November 1949, a large majority of the princely Indian states proclaimed that the Constitution of India would be the constitution for their respective territories and would supersede and abrogate all other existing constitutional provisions inconsistent therewith. The Indian Supreme Court, in *Madhav Rao*,[26] held that such proclamations and the execution of the merger agreements resulted in the complete extinction of the princely Indian states as separate units. The rulers of these states ceased to retain any vestige of sovereign rights or authority qua their states. Instead, the rulers acquired the status of citizens of India. In *Keshavananda Bharti*,[27] the Indian Supreme Court reiterated that with the coming into force of the Constitution of India there was 'repeal' of the prevailing constitutions in the princely Indian states.

It will at once be noticed that it was only with the merger of the acceding princely Indian states into the Union of India that such states lost their identity as sovereign states, and that the Constitution of India eventually replaced the constitutional law prevailing in such states. It, therefore, becomes imperative to mention here that, unlike all other acceding princely Indian states, the PIS of J&K did not execute any instrument or agreement to merge into the Union of India. Instead, it sought to retain its sovereignty by limiting its accession to the dominion of India to only the three subjects ceded in the terms of its Instrument of Accession. That brings us now to the PIS of J&K.

The PIS of J&K: A Historical Perspective

The White Paper on Jammu and Kashmir describes the PIS of J&K as under:[28]

> The State of Jammu and Kashmir is situated in the extreme north of the Indian sub-continent covering an area of 84,471 square miles, and is the largest of the Indian states. It consists of three Provinces—the Frontier

Districts, Kashmir Province, and Jammu Province which includes the Jagirs of Poonch and Chenani. To the northeast it is bordered by Tibet, to the north by Chinese Turkestan (Sinkiang) and to the north-west by the Soviet Republic of Turkestan and Afghanistan....

The country is almost entirely mountaneous, and it may be geographically divided into three areas: Tibetan and semi-Tibetan tracts in the north, containing the districts of Ladakh and Gilgit; the middle region of the 'Happy Valley' of Kashmir; and the large level areas of Jammu in the South. These three regions are divided from each other by the snow-bound outer Himalyan ranges.

The modern history of the PIS of J&K started with the reign of Raja Gulab Singh, the Hindu Dogra ruler of Jammu. By 1846, Raja Gulab Singh held Ladakh and Baluchistan and entered into the Treaty of Amritsar of 16 March 1846 with the British to 'buy' Kashmir for a sum of Rs 7.5 million. Kashmir and Gilgit had been ruled by the Sikhs of Lahore, but had been defeated by the British that year.[29] The Imperial Gazetteer records that:[30]

The general and practical result, therefore, of the Treaty of Amritsar was to confirm Gulab Singh in what he already possessed, and to transfer to him the Province of Kashmir with its newly acquired authority over Gilgit.

Raja Gulab Singh thus brought the distinct regions of the PIS of J&K under one rule—the Hindu Dogra rule. The PIS of J&K, like other princely Indian states, owed allegiance to the British Crown. The British were quite happy to let Raja Gulab Singh extend the territories of the PIS of J&K up to Tibet at state expense, since such extension took the outposts of the British Empire into Central Asia.

The reign of Raja Gulab Singh, followed by that of Raja Ranbir Singh, Raja Pratap Singh and Raja Hari Singh, saw the establishment of an elaborate system of administration. However, the Kashmiri Muslims were excluded from important posts in the civil services as well as the armed forces, and the consequent resentment snowballed into a movement with the slogan 'State for the State's People'.[31] Indeed, it was the freedom struggle in other parts of colonial India against British rule which influenced the movement of the Kashmiri Muslims led by Sheikh Abdullah's National Conference against communal discrimination. The popular unrest compelled Raja Hari Singh, who had succeeded Raja Pratap Singh in 1925, to promulgate successive enactments, the latest being the Jammu and Kashmir Constitution Act of 1939. Such enactments ostensibly sought the involvement of the people in the matter of legislation and administration of the state, but were premised on the ruler's supremacy and on the principle that he was the repository of all powers with regard to the state and its subjects. The Indian Supreme Court, in *Premnath Kaul*, examined the provisions of these enactments, including the Jammu and Kashmir Constitution Act of 1939, to find that they emphatically brought out the fact that the ruler, like his predecessors, was an absolute monarch enjoying all legislative, executive and judicial powers, along with prerogative rights.[32]

This position continued even after the lapse of paramountcy of the British Crown on 15 August 1947, the only difference being that the PIS of J&K, like other princely Indian states, was now legally sovereign without any allegiance to the British Crown. Hence, Raja Hari Singh remained the sole repository of power in the state and was held to be so by no less than the Indian Supreme Court in *Premnath Kaul*'s case.

It may be recalled that the mechanism of accession of princely Indian states to the dominions of India or Pakistan, as contained in Section 6 of the Government of India Act of 1935, as amended, provided that a princely Indian state shall be deemed to have acceded to either of the dominions on the acceptance of the Instrument of Accession executed by the Ruler thereof. The British statutes that created both modern India and Pakistan, and which were accepted by both India and Pakistan, thus mandated that, regardless of the religious complexion of its population, it was only the sovereign ruler, and not the people of a princely Indian state, who could decide the future of that state—that is, whether to remain independent or to accede to either of the dominions of India or Pakistan.

The PIS of J&K and Its Accession to India

The PIS of J&K had borders with both India and Pakistan and was capable of acceding to either dominion. It was against this background that the question arose as to whether the sovereign ruler of the PIS of J&K would accede to either of the dominions of India or Pakistan, or, in the alternative, choose to remain independent. Let us consider the circumstances that helped the ruler, Raja Hari Singh, make up his mind.

The White Paper on Jammu and Kashmir records that according to the 1941 census, the total population of the state was 4,021,616. This comprised 77.11 per cent Muslims, 20.12 per cent Hindus and 2.77 per cent Sikhs, Buddhists and others.[33] Muslims were in majority in the Gilgit region, the Kashmir Valley and in the Doda, Rajouri and Poonch districts of Jammu. The majority of the population in Jammu was Hindu. In Ladakh, the biggest region of the state area-wise but having the least population, the Buddhists were the majority followed by Muslims.[34]

The PIS of J&K, having a predominantly Muslim population, and being adjacent to Pakistan, had a Hindu Dogra ruler, who was unlikely to be in favour of Islamic Pakistan. On the other hand, Raja Hari Singh had directed the arrest of Nehru, the future first Prime Minister of independent India, on 10 June 1946, for defying a ban on his entry in Kohala.[35] Raja Hari Singh was also well aware of the close association that Nehru had with the Kashmiri popular leader, Sheikh Abdullah, who had remained a constant source of irritation to Raja Hari Singh since 1931. Sheikh Abdullah had been arrested several times between 1931 and 1946 and was sentenced to three years' imprisonment for launching the 'Quit Kashmir' movement against Raja Hari Singh in 1946.[36] Raja Hari Singh was in no mood to release him, even on the advice of Gandhi, who had met the Raja in Srinagar in July 1947.[37] Nehru, on his part, had declared that 'Highnesses and Excellencies do not count in the new conditions of India and the mood of the people' and had sought the release of Sheikh Abdullah.[38] The reluctance of Raja Hari Singh to negotiate with Sheikh Abdullah, who had raised the slogan of 'Quit Kashmir' against him, was coupled with the apprehension that with Nehru as Prime Minister of the dominion of India, he would be reduced to the status of a mere figurehead and would be required to hand over power to Sheikh Abdullah.[39] Raja Hari Singh, therefore, nurtured the hope of retaining his sovereignty over the PIS of J&K.

New Delhi's Policy on Disputed Accessions

Around the same time, there had been the somewhat controversial instances of the accession of the princely Indian states of Hyderabad and Junagadh. While the PIS of J&K had a predominantly Muslim population and a Hindu ruler, the Hindu majority of the princely Indian states of Hyderabad and Junagadh had Muslim rulers. The Nizam of Hyderabad, like the ruler of the PIS of J&K, had expressed his inclination to retain his independence. But it was in the matter of the accession of Junagadh that Jinnah outwitted the Congress into laying down the policy that the people of a princely Indian state should decide the future of the state. The Muslim League could not have propounded such policy, since Jinnah had consistently been, as documented by Wali Khan,[40] 'against according any democratic right to the people who lived in the Princely States' and the Muslim League 'did not consider it necessary to consult the people of the states'.

If the rule contained in the Indian Independence Act of 1947, and the Government of India Act of 1935, as amended, was adhered to—that is, the sovereign ruler of the princely Indian state alone would decide the question of accession—Pakistan could, at best, secure the accession of Junagadh, whose territory was only about 4,000 square miles. Moreover, Junagadh was not contiguous to Pakistan but was surrounded by states that had ceded to India. Thus, should the Nawab of Junagadh have acceded to Pakistan, it would have been a liability for Pakistan. However, if the 'wishes of the people' were to be the deciding factor on the question of accession of a princely Indian state, instead of the will of the sovereign ruler of that state, Pakistan could at least stake a claim to the Muslim-majority PIS of J&K, with a territory of 84,471 square miles.[41] Jinnah's trap was to get New Delhi to formulate and act upon such policy, so that Pakistan could then take advantage of this policy for the 'parallel case' of the PIS of J&K.

Hodson detailed Pakistan's strategy as under:[42]

.... Junagadh ... enmeshed with Princely India, having a Muslim Ruler but a predominantly Hindu population, [was] sacred to Hindu sentiment for two reasons—death-place of Lord Krishna and as the site of the famous temple of Somnath.... Junagadh was inherently important as a State of 700,000 people, fronting on the ocean ... in the midst of the great Indian region of Kathiawar.... The complexities themselves implied that its handling would be full of traps, and there was good reason to suspect that some of these traps had been deliberately laid by Pakistan. At the start of the story, all the signs were that Junagadh would eventually join India and that the Nawab favoured an association of the Kathiawar states in which he would participate. Then in May 1947, during his absence in Europe, a 'palace revolution' placed in power as his Dewan a Muslim League politician from Sind, Sir Shah Nawaz Bhutto, who was soon in correspondence with Mr. Jinnah and obeyed the latter's advice to 'keep out under all circumstances until 15th August'....

Why, we may ask, should Mr. Jinnah and his Government have been so keen to get, and have gone to such extent to hold, a poor communally divided State whose geography would make her adherence as great an embarrassment for Pakistan as her defection made for India, even without the extravagant promises of defence and economic help that were given in Karachi to the Nawab and his emissaries? ... the accession of Junagadh to Pakistan placed India into an acute dilemma from which any escape could be turned to the advantage of Pakistan. If the Indian Government acquiesced, admitting the undoubted legal right of the Ruler to decide which way to go, the precedent of a Muslim Prince taking a Hindu-majority State into Pakistan, notwithstanding geographical and communal arguments to the contrary, could be applied to a bigger prize of Hyderabad. If the Indian Government intervened with force, besides the harm it would do to itself with outside opinion, it would set up a contrary precedent, to be applied by Pakistan to Kashmir, were the latter's Maharajah to accede to India. If India demanded, as an alternate to force, a plebiscite in Junagadh, this could be adopted as a general principle which when applied to Kashmir and Jammu would, in Karachi's estimation, take the State to Pakistan.

The British were well aware that Pakistan was laying a trap for New Delhi, which will become relevant when one examines the British stand subsequently before the United Nations Security Council (UNSC) on the Kashmir issue. Hodson quotes from Mountbatten's report to Albert Frederick Arthur George, or simply George VI, the King of the United Kingdom, as under:[43]

> I had spoken to Mr. Liaquat Ali Khan, who was in Delhi for a meeting of the Joint Defence Council, about the situation in Junagadh. He used one phrase, which in view of my belief that the issue had been planned by Pakistan as a trap, I considered of considerable significance. This was: 'All right. Go ahead and commit an act of war and see what happens.'

> Lord Ismay also spoke to Mr. Liaquat Ali Khan. He had referred to the principle ... that a referendum should be held in Junagadh, and that the issue of the State's permanent accession should be decided according to the will of the people. Mr. Liaquat Ali Khan had asked Lord Ismay why, if it was suggested that a referendum should be held in Junagdh, one should not also be held in Kashmir.

> These reports of conversations with Mr. Liaquat Ali Khan were considered at the meeting on 22nd September. Lord Ismay gave his view that one of the objects of the Pakistan Government was to use Junagadh as a bargaining counter for Kashmir.

Hodson writes that:[44]

> At the first meeting of the Defence Committee of the Indian Cabinet on 30th September, Pandit Nehru ... concluded ... that wherever there is a

dispute in regard to any territory, the matter should be decided by a referendum or plebiscite of the people concerned. We shall accept the result of this referendum whatever it may be as it is our desire that a decision should be made in accordance with the wishes of the people concerned....

Thus Pandit Nehru ... committed himself to the general policy ... before the Kashmir dispute blew up but in the knowledge that Junagadh may well be a trap designed to exploit the case of Kashmir. He repeated his commitment in a talk with Mr. Liaquat Ali Khan which Lord Mountbatten engineered.... Lord Mountbatten's account of this conversation ... in his report to the King, continues:

.... Pandit Nehru then declared that he considered that, in difficult cases like this, the will of the people should be ascertained. He said India would always be willing to abide by a decision obtained by a general election, a plebiscite or a referendum, provided that it was conducted in a fair and impartial manner.

I emphasised the importance of Pandit Nehru's statement to Mr. Liaquat Ali Khan, and assured him that the Government of India would abide by it, and that Pandit Nehru would agree that this policy would apply to any other State, since India would never be party to trying to force a State to join their Dominion against the wishes of the majority of the people. Pandit Nehru nodded his head sadly. Mr. Liquat Ali Khan's eyes sparkled. There is no doubt that both of them were thinking of Kashmir.

It may be noted here that the instances of the accession of Hyderabad and Junagadh were raised at the UNSC. In the case of Hyderabad, Pakistan alleged that its ruler, the Nizam, had sought to retain independence for his state but New Delhi refused to accept that position and demanded that the state should accede to India unconditionally.[45] The Yearbook of the United Nations, 1948–49, records that the representative of India 'pointed out that, as early as August 1947, the Indian Government had suggested a plebiscite on the issue of Hyderabad's accession, but the Hyderabad Government had rejected that proposal'.[46] Pakistan claimed that when the Nizam did not agree, New Delhi marched its troops into Hyderabad and announced that the Nizam had acceded to India.[47] New Delhi denied the allegation and contended that the Hyderabad government had been forcibly taken over as the result of a coup d'état carried out by extremist elements in the state. New Delhi claimed that the Nizam had ceased to be a free agent and had, after being released from the control of a group of extremists, voluntarily acceded to the dominion of India.[48]

As regards Junagadh, New Delhi went a step further before the UNSC—it refused to even locate the question of accession of a princely Indian state in law, but termed it to be essentially a 'political decision'. Gopalaswami Ayyangar (India) declared before the UNSC:[49]

> With regard to the question of Junagadh's accession…. Both the application for and acceptance of accession are acts of a political nature. The letter of the law cannot exclusively govern a political situation of that nature…. The fact remains that in deciding a particular case, the Security Council will not concentrate on the merely legalistic aspect of the matter. As I have contended, it was essentially a political decision, and that while certain things can be done from a strictly legal point of view, in the transactions of States and Governments, we have to take into account factors which should, perhaps, persuade one party or the other to take a decision which, though it might not be in accordance with the letter of the law, would still be in the best interests of all the parties concerned.

New Delhi declared before the UNSC that it would be prepared to accept any democratic test in respect of the accession of Junagadh to either of the two dominions.[50] Junagadh acceded to Pakistan on 15 September 1947. New Delhi termed such accession 'as an encroachment on Indian sovereignty and territory' and sought a plebiscite in the state.[51] Pakistan alleged that a 'Provisional Government of Junagadh was set up in Indian territory' and then, on 9 November 1947, India 'marched its troops into Junagadh and forcibly annexed the State which had acceded to Pakistan'.[52] Subsequently, 'a farcical plebiscite was held—India was in military occupation of the state—and the state was formally incorporated into the Indian Dominion'.[53] New Delhi refuted this version of the happenings in Junagadh. New Delhi informed the UNSC that the Dewan (Prime Minister) of Junagadh, who was in Karachi with the Nawab of Junagadh and 'in very close touch with members of the Pakistan Government', wrote to the Government of India, asking the latter to take over the responsibility of the princely Indian state of Junagadh, which had acceded to Pakistan, because the popular view in Junagadh had been that the administration of the state be handed over to the Union of India.[54] Indeed, such unfolding of events is documented by Hodson, who writes that:[55]

> On 8th November, the Dewan of Junagadh, Sir Shah Nawaz Bhutto, sent Major Harvey Jones, the Senior Member of the Junagadh State Council with a letter to Mr. Buch, the Indian Regional Commissioner at Rajkot. This letter requested Government of India to take over the administration of Junagadh 'in

order to save the State from complete administrative breakdown and pending an honourable settlement of the several issues involved in Junagadh's accession'. The Dewan of Junagadh ... had telegraphed to Mr. Liaquat Ali Khan telling him that he was making this request which, he said, was supported by the public of Junagadh.... He had received telegraphic instructions from the Nawab, who had a short time previously flown to Karachi....

New Delhi evidently did not find it strange that the Dewan of Junagadh, sitting in Karachi with the Nawab of Junagadh and being 'in very close touch with members of the Pakistan Government', should write to the Government of India at all. Ironically, New Delhi had declared before the UNSC that 'some of the action of the Pakistan Government in this particular matter, with the assistance of the Nawab of Junagadh was calculated as a device to tease the Government of India into taking precipitative and aggressive action', but the Government of India was 'particularly careful to avoid doing anything as the result of which it might fall into a trap of this nature'.[56]

But the trap was obvious—it was not to 'tease' New Delhi into taking 'precipitative and aggressive action', but to induce New Delhi to reiterate and act upon its policy that the 'wishes of the people' would settle the question of accession of the princely Indian state as discussed above. And New Delhi did just that—it even held a plebiscite in Junagadh to declare before the world that the people had voted in favour of accession of the state to the dominion of India. New Delhi happily told the UNSC that New Delhi was quite prepared to hold another plebiscite under international auspices.[57]

Pakistan simply adopted the stand before the UNSC that the only question regarding Junagadh, which 'lawfully acceded to Pakistan but have since been forcibly occupied by India, is the settling of conditions under which a plebiscite could and may be held'.[58] Mohammed Zafrullah Khan (Pakistan) stated that:[59]

> Our submission is that the Security Council is concerned with the question of principle. If, irrespective of the history of the matter, the principle is today accepted by the two Dominions that in order to put an end to the disputes between them over these two States the question of the accession of each shall be decided by means of a plebiscite, then, in the name of all that is fair and just, let the plebiscite in each case be free and unfettered.... That is the crux of the matter, both with regard to Junagadh and with regard to Kashmir.

Thus, the significance of the accession of Hyderabad and Junagadh to the dominion of India lay in the formulation of the policy, and that too by New Delhi, that in the case of a dispute regarding the accession of a princely Indian state to either of the dominions, the 'wishes of the people' would prevail. New Delhi apparently did not pause to even consider that such policy was, in fact, politically unnecessary in view of the geographical location of Junagadh and Hyderabad. As Mountbatten put it:[60]

> I always said in all the speeches I made about accession that there were certain geographical compulsions. I mean the idea that Junagadh could join Pakistan, across all the other Kathiawar states was just stupid. The idea that Hyderabad could join Pakistan was equally stupid.

British Policy on Kashmir

The PIS of J&K had, right from the beginning, engaged British strategists during the Great Game because of its geographical location. As noted earlier, the state abutted Central Asia and had international boundaries with Tibet to the north-east, with Chinese Turkestan to the north, and with the Soviet Republic of Turkestan and Afghanistan to the north-west. Gilgit, the northern portion of the PIS of J&K, lay to the north and east of the equally crucial NWFP, and stretched to the Chinese Turkestan with only a narrow strip of Afghan territory separating it from the erstwhile Soviet Union. The more the Soviets moved southwards during the Great Game, the more the British started exercising control in the territory through political agents.

The areas of Gilgit, Baltistan and Frontier Illaqas comprising Hunza, Nagir, Punial, Yasin, Kuh-Ghizar, Ishkoman and Chilas together formed the Northern Areas of the PIS of J&K.[61] The British, with a view to secure this area, had pressurized Raja Pratap Singh, the then ruler of the PIS of J&K, to part with a portion of Gilgit to form the Gilgit Agency. V.P. Menon records that the British first appointed a political agent in Gilgit in 1877 but he was withdrawn in 1881.[62] The Agency was re-established in 1889,[63] and the de facto administration of the Gilgit frontier passed into British hands. By 1935, Soviet Russia had taken virtual control of Sinkiang, making it necessary for the British to take over the administration and defence of the entire Gilgit region from the PIS of J&K on a 60-year lease. Sarila documents that 'the region was administered by the British from Delhi in the same way as agencies in the NWFP, such as Malakand or Khyber, with political officers stationed there reporting to the Viceroy through Peshawar',[64] and that 'a carefully chosen force capable of rapid movement in mountainous territory, and controlled by British officers (called the Gilgit Scouts), provided muscle to the administration'.[65]

Sarila has summarized the strategic importance of the Northern Areas of the PIS of J&K for the British as under:[66]

> After the czars had incorporated the Muslim sultanates of Khokand, Bokhara and Khiva, including the cities of Tashkand and Samarkand, into their empire in the 1860s and 1870s, they brought Russia's frontier to within a few hundred miles of India (in Kashmir). The northwest frontier of India had become, for the British, the most sensitive of all the frontiers of their vast Empire. And it was here that the pick of the British Indian Army was quartered (and where, incidentally, Winston Churchill had served with the Malakand Field Force in 1898). The British had fought three wars in Afghanistan, incorporated in the 1880s parts of eastern Afghanistan into the North West Frontier Province and Baluchistan (now in Pakistan), built a railway network to the Khyber and Bolan Passes leading to Afghanistan, helped the Dogra Rajput ruler of Jammu under their paramountry to extend his rule into Kashmir right up to the Sinkiang border, constructed a road from Gilgit in Hunza in northern Kashmir through the 13,000-feet-high Mintaka Pass in the Karakoram mountains to Kashgar in Sinkiang, posted agents there to monitor Russian activities across the border in Uzbekistan and the Pamirs, and bribed and threatened the Shahs of Persia—all in order to keep the areas of India's western approaches from slipping under Russian influence.

Given such strategic importance of the Northern Areas of the PIS of J&K, the British could not conceive losing control over the region. Indeed, Wavell, in his memorandum of 30 May 1946 to the Cabinet Mission, had stated that 'Kashmir ... would remain within the British sphere of influence in the northwest' and that 'this arrangement should be a permanency ... that would amount to a Northern Ireland in India'.[67] Olaf Caroe, the Governor of the NWFP, had even discussed on 27 May 1947 with Ely E. Palmer, the US diplomat in Afghanistan, the possibility of Soviet penetration of the Northern Areas, as also 'the desirability of the establishment of Pakistan'.[68] The British expected that the PIS of J&K, being predominantly Muslim, would accede to Islamic Pakistan contiguous to it or at least remain independent and be associated with the British defence policy.

It is well documented that the British sought to persuade the then ruler of the PIS of J&K, Raja Hari Singh, to accede to Pakistan. Noorani records that Mountbatten visited the PIS of J&K in June 1947, where he told Ram Chandra Kak, the then Prime Minister of the state, that while it was entirely for the state to decide to which dominion it should accede, '[y]ou must consider your geographical position, your political situation and composition of your population and then decide', to which Kak responded, '[t]hat means that you advise us to accede to Pakistan'.[69] Sarila records that Mountbatten, in his personal report to the Secretary of State in July 1947, suggested 'the possibility of Kashmir joining Pakistan'.[70] Mountbatten himself describes his state visit to the PIS of J&K in July 1947, during which he told Raja Hari Singh that:[71]

.... I've come up with full authority of the present government of the future Dominion of India.... I've come to tell you that if you decide to accede to Pakistan, they'll think it a natural thing to do, because the majority of your population are Muslims. It'll only not cause no ill-feeling, but they'll give you all support and help they can.

'I don't want to accede to Pakistan on any account', he said.

'Well', I said, 'it's up to you. I think you might be wise to accede, because majority of your people are Muslims'.

'Yes', he said, 'but don't forget that with Sheikh Abdullah, who's madly pro-Nehru, most of my people would really wish to join India....'

In August 1947, Ismay, then the Viceroy's Chief of Staff, visited Kashmir 'on a holiday' and raised the same issue with the Maharaja, who, however, argued that the Kashmiri Muslims were different from the Punjabi Muslims.[72] Mountbatten, in his interview given to Larry Collins and Dominique Lapierre, goes on to say:[73]

I must tell you honestly. I wanted Kashmir to join Pakistan. For one simple reason, it made Pakistan more viable.... I was convinced that East Pakistan would never work. The whole concept of two different peoples being held together over all those miles by the same religion was absolute nonsense. But West Pakistan was something else, I wanted it to work. I wanted it to be viable. After all, I was responsible for it. I wanted Kashmir with them. I didn't want to muck up my own creation, for God's sake.

The Boundary Commission under Cyril Radcliffe had (like Wavell in his blueprint of partition) awarded Gurdaspur to India. This facilitated the land link to the PIS of J&K from India. Referring to such award, Mountbatten lamented in his interview that:[74]

.... Radcliffe let us in for an awful lot of trouble by making it possible for them to accede to India. If he hadn't made that award, the Maharaja would really have had no option but to join Pakistan.... The pressures on the

Maharaja would have built to where he had to accede to Pakistan.... I am sure Radcliffe had no notion of the consequences.

The accession of the PIS of J&K to India could have been fatal to Britain's Great Game. The British were not going to take any chances. Regardless of whether or not the PIS of J&K acceded to India, the British identified two areas of the state that had to be kept free of Indian presence. One was the Northern Areas so crucial for the Great Game, and the other was the western strip of territory along the border of Pakistani Punjab so as to secure Pakistan in a possible war with India over the PIS of J&K.

Consequently, as soon as the sovereign PIS of J&K acceded to the sovereign dominion of India, the British carved out the Northern Areas from the sovereign state through the pre-planned coup of Gilgit, hoisted the Pakistani flag there and invited Pakistan to take control of the region. Let us examine how clinically this coup was given effect to by the British in violation of every conceivable principle of international law.

Coup of Gilgit

With the impending lapse of British paramountcy over the princely Indian states, Gilgit had reverted back to Raja Hari Singh on 1 August 1947, and this area was handed over to the state by Lieutenant Colonel Roger Bacon, the British Political Agent.[75] The Raja appointed Brigadier Ghansar Singh Jamwal as the Governor of Gilgit, who accordingly assumed office two weeks prior to the transfer of power by the British on 15 August 1947.[76] The British sent Bacon to the Khyber post based in Peshawar (that fell in Pakistan), from whom Major William Alexander Brown, the then Commander of the Gilgit Scouts, and his immediate junior, Captain A.S. Mathieson, took instructions.[77] The two British officers had, according to the *Bulletin of Military Historical Society of Great Britain,* discussed '[t]he broad post-partition plans' in June 1947, and after Mathieson arrived in Gilgit, as second in command, 'the two British Officers refined contingency measures, should the Maharaja take his State over to India'.[78] The posting of Bacon at Peshawar ensured perfect coordination between the Gilgit Scouts and Peshawar.[79] Menon records that when the Governor, accompanied by Major General H.L. Scott, Chief of Staff of the Jammu and Kashmir Army, reached Gilgit on 30 July, they found that 'all the officers of the British Government had opted for service in Pakistan', and that 'the Gilgit Scouts also wanted to go over to Pakistan'.[80]

Following the accession of the PIS of J&K to India on 26 October 1947, Major Brown sought to deliver Gilgit and other parts of the northern region of the PIS of J&K to Pakistan on the night of 31 October 1947. Snedden documents that the local Gilgit Scouts, under the command of Brown, surrounded the Residency, took the Raja's Governor, Ghansar Singh Jamwal, and some other non-Muslims into 'protective custody'.[81] Peshawar (in Pakistan) was then informed by Brown about the accession of Gilgit to Pakistan.[82] After asking the Pakistan government to send troops to Gilgit, Brown, along with Mathieson, established a military government on 1 November 1947 and even hoisted the Pakistani flag at his headquarters on 2 November 1947, while informing the force that they now served the government in Karachi, the then capital of Pakistan.[83] Brown and Mathieson were instructed by George Cunningham, the new Governor of the NWFP, which was by then in Pakistan, 'to restore order' in Gilgit.[84] Snedden writes that, on 16 November 1947, Pakistan sent a 'Political Agent' to the Gilgit area.[85]

Pakistan's former Foreign Minister Khurshid Mahmud Kasuri admits to the 'exploits of Major W. Brown who was the Commander of the Gilgit Scouts and under whose leadership the people of the area revolted successfully against Dogra rule and publicly declared their intention to join Pakistan', as also to the role of 'Colonel Pasha (real name of Major Muhammad Aslam Khan who later rose to the rank of Brigadier) in the liberation of the Northern Areas from Dogra rule'.[86] Alistaire Lamb notes that Colonel Beacon, British Political Agent (Khyber), and Colonel Iskander Mirza, Pakistan's Defence Secretary, were not 'particularly unhappy' about this coup.[87]

Britain thus succeeded in keeping the Northern Areas of the PIS of J&K under the de facto control of Pakistan and, consequently, under its own influence, for the Great Game. Nothing can be more telling of the British footprint on the coup than the entry in the 1948 *London Gazette*, which read: 'The King has been graciously pleased on the occasion of the celebration of His Majesty's Birthday to give orders for the following appointments to the Most Exalted Order of the British Empire: "Brown, Major (Acting) William Alexander, Special List (ex-Indian Army)"'.[88] Not surprisingly, Pakistan, too, awarded Brown its 'Sitara-e-Pakistan'.

'Azad Kashmir'

The other territory of the PIS of J&K that the British had to ensure would remain free of India's presence, regardless of the accession of the state to India, was the western strip of land covering 13,528 square kilometres from

Naushera to Muzaffarabad lying along the border with Pakistani Punjab.[89] Sarila explains the British view for putting this area under Pakistan's control as under:[90]

> Occupation of Bhimber and Mirpur [two important places in that areas] will give India the strategic advantage of ... sitting on our doorsteps, threatening the Jhelum bridge which is so vital for us. It will also give them control of the Mangla Headworks placing the irrigation in Jhelum and other districts at their mercy.... Furthermore, loss of Muzaffarabad-Kohala [a strategically located place] would have the most far-reaching effect on the security of Pakistan. It would enable the Indian Army to secure the rear gateway to Pakistan through which it can march in at any time it wishes ... it is imperative that the Indian Army is not allowed to advance beyond the general line Uri-Poonch-Naoshera.

Let us consider how the British did ensure that this territory was ostensibly liberated from the Raja's rule by the 'Azad Army' and christened as 'Azad Kashmir'. The 'Azad Army' was united under the leadership of General 'Tarik', who was 'subsequently identified as Colonel Akbar Khan, a Pakistan Army regular determined to deliver the PIS of J&K to Pakistan'.[91]

Much has been written, and documented, about the tribal-led Pakistani invasion of the PIS of J&K on 22 October 1947.[92] However, it appears that as soon as the partition plan was announced on 3 June 1947, Pakistan started putting in place plans and schemes to infiltrate into the state with a view to incite communal violence there.

Ramchandra Guha records that:[93]

> There was, indeed, discontent in one part of Kashmir. This was the district of Poonch, which lay west of Srinagar.... On 14 August several shops and offices in Poonch had flown Pakistani flags, indicating their allegiance lay to that country, and not to the still unaffiliated state of Kashmir. In the following weeks clashes between the Dogra troops and local protestors were reported. By the beginning of September dozens of Poonch men had equipped themselves with rifles obtained from 'informal' sources in Pakistan. They had also established a base in the Pakistani town of Murree; here were collected arms and ammunition to be smuggled across the border to Kashmir. Pakistani accounts acknowledge that both prime minister, Liaquat Ali Khan, and a senior Punjab Muslim League leader, Mian Iftikharuddin, knew and sanctioned assistance to the Poonch rebels. Overseeing the operation was Akbar Khan, a colonel in the Pakistan Army. Khan had collected 4,000 rifles from army supplies and diverted them for use in Kashmir. More fancifully, he had adopted the nom de guerre 'General Tariq', after a medieval Moorish warrior who had fought the Christians in Spain.

What is less known is the complicity of the British in these plans and schemes. Sarila refers to 'some circumstantial evidence that certain people in the Commonwealth Relations Office (CRO) were aware of Pakistan's designs, the Principal Staff Officer to the Secretary of State, General Geoffrey Scoones (an ardent supporter of Pakistan) ... amongst them'.[94] Menon writes that:[95]

> It is a fact that several top-ranking British officers serving in Pakistan did have an inkling of these preparations and plans.... We came to know later that, as soon as the June 3rd plan was announced, Kashmir became the subject of attention and study in certain military circles. Why was there a demand on the Survey of India for so large a number of maps of Kashmir? What was the mysterious 'Operation Gulmarg', copies of orders in respect of which fell into hands of those who were not meant to receive them?

If one goes back into the chronology of events, there exists sufficient material to establish that much before the tribal invasion of 22 October 1947, Pakistan had been cutting off essential supplies to the state in violation of the standstill agreement between Pakistan and the state that provided for the continuance of economic and administrative relations, and applying military pressure along the PIS of J&K and Pakistan border, the complaints in respect of which had been made by the PIS of J&K to the British Prime Minister, Mountbatten (who had been appointed by New Delhi as the first Governor General or independent India) and to Pakistan itself.[96] The cable of 15 October 1947 sent by Mehr Chand Mahajan, the then Prime Minister of the PIS of J&K, to the British Prime Minister detailed such facts, recorded the threats of invasion by Pakistan and pointed out that:[97]

> It is actually conniving at the influx of its armed people into Poonch Jagir area of the State.... As a result of obvious connivance of the Pakistan Government the whole of the border from Gurdaspur side up to Gilgit is threatened with invasion which has actually begun in Poonch. It is requested that the Dominion of Pakistan may be advised to deal fairly with the Jammu and Kashmir State and adopt a course of conduct which may be consistent with the good name and prestige of the Commonwealth of which it claims to be a member....

However, the British simply did not respond to these complaints.[98] Pakistan's actions were calculated to instigate communal violence so as to justify an invasion by Pakistan into the PIS of J&K to 'save the Muslims'. Pakistan, however, could not stir up communal violence in the state. Sarila records that:[99]

Even in the west, along the Punjab border, there was no massive spontaneous revolt against the maharaja to justify an incursion by Pakistan to save the Muslims. According to H.V. Hodson, the trouble that broke out in Poonch was 'sporadic for most part' and there was 'some evidence of Pakistan taking part'. He says: 'The above was nothing surprising or pretentious in view of Punjab happenings.... To justify action (by Pakistan) in Kashmir on the above basis would be incorrect.' The reports of Webb, the British resident in J&K, and of the British commander-in-chief of the Kashmir State Forces, General Victor Scott, confirm Hodson's assessment. According to Webb, 'relations between Hindus and Muslims began to grow uneasy and in some areas strained as communal violence flared up in the plains around the State. Kashmir remained free from communal disturbances. The unease was more confined to Jammu and along the frontier areas adjoining Pathan Tribal Agencies'. General Scott reported in September 1947 that: 'The State troops had escorted one lakh Muslims through Jammu territory on their way to Pakistan and an equal number of Sikhs and Hindus going the other way', signifying that the communal situation in J&K was totally different from that in the Punjab. Lars Blinkenberg, the Danish diplomat, has pointed out: 'The Maharaja with Mehr Chand Mahajan [his prime minister] toured the western part of Jammu from 18 to 23 October 1947. The local revolt in the areas of Poonch and Jammu made out by Pakistan was therefore not sufficiently powerful to obstruct the Maharaja's circulation'.

With Pakistan mounting pressure, Raja Hari Singh had no option but to tilt towards the dominion of India. However, New Delhi was now in a quandary. Having taken the stand internationally that it was the 'wishes of the people' that would prevail in cases of disputed accession, it could not now treat the decision of the Hindu ruler as the basis of accession of the largely Muslim state to India.

New Delhi sought to reconcile this position by seeking the affirmation of the popular leader in the state (read Sheikh Abdullah) of the accession of the PIS of J&K to India so that the ruler's decision to accede to India was seen to be in conformity with the wishes of the people. Nehru, in his letter dated 21 October 1947 to Mehr Chand Mahajan, the then Prime Minister of the PIS of J&K, pointed out that having 'accepted a policy in regard to States which necessarily leads to a referendum where there is a dispute', New Delhi cannot object to it, and that the 'best way' at present would be to have a popular interim government functioning.[100]

New Delhi's plans, however, were overtaken by the Pakistan-sponsored tribal invasion of the PIS of J&K on 22 October 1947. The brutality of the invaders has been well documented not only in the White Paper on Jammu and Kashmir, but also in the record of the subsequent reference of the Kashmir issue to the UNSC by New Delhi. Several persons who witnessed such horrors firsthand also describe how the invaders stripped town after town of its wealth and young girls, butchered the inhabitants including children, and committed large-scale arson and loot. Menon, who was the person chosen by the Defence Committee of the Indian Cabinet to shuttle between New Delhi and Srinagar to assess the situation in the state, and later to formalize the accession with Raja Hari Singh, has given in his book, *Integration of the Indian States*, published in 1956, graphic details, day-by-day, of the ghastly devastation, plunder, rapine and orgy by the raiders in the PIS of J&K, with wholesale murder of non-Muslims and abduction and auctioning of Kashmiri girls.[101]

The fact that the tribal invasion was sponsored by Pakistan has been expressly admitted by Pakistan's former Foreign Minister Khurshid Mahmud Kasuri who refers to the tribal invasion as 'the 1947 war on Kashmir' and writes that 'had it not been for the Pakistan Army and the volunteers, Pakistan would have had nothing of Kashmir'.[102] The evidence in this regard can be found in abundance in both Indian and Pakistani statements before the UNSC. The overt involvement of Pakistan in the invasion has been recorded in writing by Raja Hari Singh himself in his letter dated 26 October 1947[103] to Mountbatten, as also by Shiekh Abdullah, the popular leader of the sovereign PIS of J&K.[104] Mounbatten, in fact, reasons that had Radcliffe not awarded Gurdaspur to India, the PIS of J&K would have had to accede to Pakistan, and that '[t]his would have meant that they wouldn't have had to put the tribes in'.[105] Indeed, at the meeting at Lahore on 1 November 1947 between Mountbatten, Ismay and Jinnah, when Jinnah proposed that both sides withdraw at once and simultaneously from the PIS of J&K, and Mountbatten asked Jinnah as to how the tribesmen could be induced to remove themselves, Jinnah replied 'If you do this I will call the whole thing off'.[106] Sarila gives an account of Pakistan's involvement as under:[107]

> Time was obviously running out for Jinnah. To avoid an open conflict with India, pro-Muslim League tribesmen from the frontier areas (Masoods, Afridis and Hazzars) would be used as proxies, enticed with the promise of loot and more. They would be recruited by Pakistani officers of the old Indian Political Service who had a vast knowledge of the tribes and armed and transported by Pakistan and led by Pakistani officers.... Colonel (later major general) Akbar Khan of the Pakistan Army has described in his book how the 'tribal operation' was planned under the direct supervision of Prime Minister Liaqat Ali Khan. Akbar Khan was the military member of the Liberation Committee. He has written in his book:

Upon my seeking a clarification of our military objective, the Prime Minister said that all he wanted was to keep the fight going for three months which would be enough time to achieve our political objective by negotiations and other means.

The Pakistani attempt to seize Srinagar failed. The Dogra commander of the J&K Forces, Rajinder Singh, held back the tribal hordes (the first attack was by about 5,000 tribesmen) for three days at the entrance of the valley, till he was killed. Then two days were lost by the invaders in pillage and rapine in Baramulla, at the entrance of the valley. Moreover, according to one source, 'the rapidity with which Indians flew into Srinagar was outside Jinnah's calculations' … Uri (where we found Akbar Khan stranded), Naoshera to Uri's south on the southern side of the Pir Panjal range and Tithwal to Uri's north were approximately at the eastern extremities of the belt of territory which General Douglas Gracey had argued was necessary for Pakistan's security.

Ramchandra Guha has documented that:[108]

[The tribal] incursion into Kashmir was openly encouraged by the prime minister of North-West Frontier Provinces, Abdul Qayyum. The British governor, Sir George Cunningham, turned a blind eye. So did the British officers who then served with the Pakistan army. As Jinnah's American biographer observes, 'trucks, petrol and drivers were hardly standard tribal equipment, and British officers as well as Pakistani officials all along the northern Pakistan route they traversed knew and supported, even if they did not actually organise and instigate, the October operation by which Pakistan seems to have hoped to trigger the integration of Kashmir into the nation'.

Pakistan would have succeeded in capturing Srinagar had the raiders not stayed on in Baramulla for plunder and rape. Guha writes that:[109]

At Baramula the greed of the tribesmen conclusively triumphed over religious identity. For here they 'invaded the houses of peace-loving Kashmiri Moslems as well. They looted and plundered the latter's houses and raped their young girls. Shrieks of terror and agony of those girls resounded across the town of Baramula'.

Faced with such a situation, Raja Hari Singh had no option but to turn to the dominion of India. Let us examine now how New Delhi dealt with the matter.

PIS of J&K and New Delhi

Menon records that it was in the evening of 24 October 1947 that New Delhi received a desperate appeal for help from Raja Hari Singh, which was considered in the morning of 25 October 1947 by the Defence Committee presided over by Mountbatten.[110] Mountbatten, however, 'emphasised that no precipitative action should be taken until the Government of India had fuller information', and thus it was agreed that Menon would fly to Srinagar to study the situation and report to New Delhi.[111] Menon gives a firsthand account of his visit to Srinagar and his meeting with Raja Hari Singh, and states that, on flying back to New Delhi in the morning of 26 October 1947, he went directly to the meeting of the Defence Committee, where he pointed out the extreme necessity of saving the state from the raiders.[112] Menon documents Mountbatten as saying that:[113]

[I]t would be improper to move Indian troops into what was at the moment an independent country.... If it were true that the Maharajah was now anxious to accede to India ..., in view of the composition of the population, accession should be made conditional on the will of the people being ascertained by a plebiscite after the raiders had been driven out of the State and law and order had been restored....

Menon states that after the meeting of the Defence Committee, he flew to Jammu on 26 October 1947, where Raja Hari Singh had reached from Srinagar by driving overnight. Menon again gives a firsthand account of how he woke up Raja Hari Singh, who was asleep due to his overnight travel, informed him about the Defence Committee meeting and how the Raja 'was ready to accede at once' and 'also signed the instrument of accession'.[114] Menon details the letter composed that day by Raja Hari Singh to the Governor General about his desire to retain independence, the violation of the standstill agreement by Pakistan, the tribal invasion into the PIS of J&K sponsored by Pakistan and his having to seek military aid from the dominion of India to defend the territory of the state and to protect the lives and property of the citizens.[115] Menon writes that:[116]

Just as I was leaving, he told me that before he went to sleep, he had left instructions with his ADC that, if I came back from Delhi, he was not to be disturbed as it would mean that the Government of India had decided to come to his rescue and he should therefore be allowed to sleep in peace, but that if I failed to return, it meant that everything was lost and, in that case, his ADC was to shoot him in his sleep!

Menon records that he flew back to Delhi with the Instrument of Accession and the letter of 26 October 1947 of Raja Hari Singh and went straight to the Defence Committee meeting, where it was decided that the accession be accepted subject to the above quoted suggestion of Mountbatten.[117] Menon documents that even after this decision had been reached, Mountbatten and the three British Chiefs of Staff of the Indian Army, Navy and Air Force pointed out the risks in the operation.[118] The Defence Committee eventually decided that Indian troops be sent to the PIS of J&K the next morning (27 October 1947), and that the Government of India 'will accept this accession provisionally subject to their declared policy that such matters should be finalised in accordance with the will of the people'.[119]

The Instrument of Accession of 26 October 1947 was thus executed in favour of the dominion of India by Raja Hari Singh, who, as held by the Indian Supreme Court in *Premnath Kaul*,[120] was the absolute monarch of the PIS of J&K. The said Instrument was accepted by Mountbatten, the Governor General of India, on 27 October 1947, in terms of the Indian Independence Act of 1947, read with the Government of India Act of 1935, as amended. The Instrument of Accession contains the following recital:

Whereas the Indian Independence Act, 1947, provides that as from the fifteenth day of August 1947, there shall be set up an independent Dominion, known as India and that the Government of India Act, 1935, shall, with such omissions, additions, adaptations and modifications as the Governor General may by order specify, be applicable to the Dominion of India;

And whereas the Government of India Act, 1935, as so adapted by the Governor General, provides that an Indian State may accede to the Dominion of India by an Instrument of Accession executed by the Ruler thereof:

It was in the context of such recital that the Instrument of Accession set out the following terms of accession, which were accepted by the dominion of India, through its Governor General, Mountbatten:

I, Shriman Inder Mahendra Rajrajeshwar Maharajadhiraj Shri Hari Singhji, Jammu Kashmir Naresh Tatha Tibbet adi Deshadhipathi Ruler of Jammu and Kashmir in the exercise of my sovereignty in and over my said State Do hereby execute this my Instrument of Accession and

1. I hereby declare that I accede to the Dominion of India with the intent that the Governor-General of India, the Dominion Legislature, the Federal Court and any other Dominion authority established for the purpose of the

Dominion shall, by virtue of this my Instrument of Accession, but subject always to the terms thereof, and for the purposes only of the Dominion, exercise in relation to the State of Jammu and Kashmir such functions as may be vested in them by or under the Government of India Act, 1935 as in force in the Dominion of India on the 15th day of August, 1947 (which Act as so in force is hereinafter referred to as 'the Act').

2. ...

3. I accept the matters specified in the Schedule hereto as the matters specified in the Schedule with respect to which the Dominion Legislature may make laws for this State.

4. ...

5. ...

6. ...

7. Nothing in this Instrument shall be deemed to commit me in any way to acceptance of any future Constitution of India or to fetter my discretion to enter into arrangements with the Government of India under any such future Constitution.

8. Nothing in this Instrument affects the continuance of my sovereignty in and over this State, or save as provided by or under this Instrument the exercise of any powers, authority and rights now enjoyed by me as Ruler of this State or the validity of any law at present in force in this State.

9. I hereby declare that I execute this Instrument on behalf of the State and that any reference in this Instrument to me or to the Ruler of the State is to be construed as including a reference to my heirs and successors.

Given under my hand this 26th day of October Nineteen Forty-Seven.

sd/-

Hari Singh

Maharaja Dhiraj of Jammu & Kashmir

I do accept this Instrument of Accession.

Dated this Twenty-Seventh day of October, Nineteen Hundred and Forty-Seven

sd-

Mountbatten of Burma

Governor General of India

The Schedule to the Instrument of Accession specified defence, external relations, communications and certain ancillary matters, including elections to the dominion legislature (Indian Parliament), to be the matters with respect to which the dominion legislature may make laws for the state.

A perusal of the Instrument of Accession will confirm that Raja Hari Singh, the sovereign ruler of the PIS of J&K, unconditionally acceded to the dominion of India in terms of the Indian Independence Act of 1947 and the Government of India Act of 1935, as amended, and did not require 'a reference to the people to settle the accession'. Neither did the acceptance by New Delhi endorsed on the instrument itself.

However, Mountbatten, while accepting the accession on behalf of New Delhi, replied to the letter dated 26 October 1947 of Raja Hari Singh by his letter dated 27 October 1947, as under:[121]

> Your Highness letter dated 26th October has been delivered to me by Mr V.P. Menon. In the special circumstances mentioned by your Highness my Government have decided to accept the accession of Kashmir State to the Dominion of India. In consistence with their policy that in the case of any State where the issue of accession should be decided in accordance with the wishes of the people of the State, it is my Government's wish that as soon as law and order have been restored and her soil cleared of the invader the question of the State's accession should be settled by a reference to the people.
>
> Meanwhile, in response to your Highness appeal for military aid action has been taken today to send troops of the Indian army to Kashmir to help your own forces to defend your territory and to protect the lives, property and honour of your people. My Government and I note with satisfaction that Your Highness has decided to invite Sheikh Abdullah to form an interim Government to work with your Prime Minister....

It is here that the proposal for a 'reference to the people' to settle the question of the accession of the PIS of J&K to India was mooted, and, that too, as a 'wish' of the Government of India.

The White Paper on Jammu and Kashmir records that '[t]he accession was legally made by the Maharaja of Kashmir, and this step was taken on the advice of Sheikh Abdullah, leader of the All-Jammu and Kashmir National Conference, the political party commanding the widest popular support in the State'.[122] It is further recorded that 'in accepting the accession, the Government of India made it clear that they would regard it as purely provisional until such time as the will of the people of the State could be ascertained'.[123] Similarly, the White Paper on Indian States reiterated that the Government of India stood 'committed to the position that the accession of this State is subject to confirmation by the people of the State'.[124]

Thus, it will be seen that it was New Delhi that voluntarily and unilaterally expressed a wish to 'settle' the question of accession of the PIS of J&K to the dominion of India by a 'reference to the people' and declared that it would regard the accession as 'purely provisional'. New Delhi did not stop there. After raising doubts on the finality of the accession of the PIS of J&K to the dominion of India, New Delhi decided to involve the UNSC in the Kashmir issue and to commit to holding a plebiscite or referendum in the PIS of J&K under international auspices.

In order to appreciate how terribly misconceived New Delhi's stand on the Kashmir problem has been throughout, it will be useful to pause here to consider whether New Delhi was even competent to introduce the 'wishes of the people' as a factor to determine the accession of a princely Indian state to either of the dominions, let alone commit before the UNSC to a plebiscite or referendum in the PIS of J&K under international auspices.

Notes and References

1. *Supra* Note 2, Chapter I, pp. 142–144.
2. S/PV/761, p. 3, Firoz Khan Noon (Pakistan), 16 January 1957.
3. Ibid.
4. *Supra* Note 1, Introduction.
5. Ibid.
6. *Duff Development Company Limited v Government of Kelantan and Anr.* 1924 AC 797, p. 830.
7. Ibid., pp. 807–808; *Gurdwara Sahib v Piyara Singh*: AIR 1953 Pepsu.
8. *Premnath Kaul v State of Jammu and Kashmir*: AIR 1959 SC 749.
9. Ibid., p. 756.
10. *Supra* Note 2, Chapter I, p. 154.
11. Ibid.
12. See statement issued on 30 July 1947 by M.A. Jinnah, Governor-General-Designate of the Dominion of Pakistan, extracted in A.G. Noorani, 2013. *The Kashmir Dispute 1947 -2012*, Vol II, p. 2, New Delhi: Tulika Books.
13. *Supra* Note 2, Chapter I, pp. 142–144.
14. Ibid.
15. Ibid.
16. Extracted in Noorani, A.G. 1964. *The Kashmir Question*, p. 19. Bombay: Manaktalas.
17. Ibid., p. 18.
18. *Supra* Note 5, Chapter I, p. 166.
19. Ibid.

20. Ibid., p. 157.
21. Ibid., p. 154.
22. *Supra* Note 8.
23. *Magher Singh v Principal Secretary, Jammu and Kashmir*. AIR 1953 J&K 25.
24. See address of Mountbatten on 5 July 1947 at the Special Full Meeting of the Chamber of Princes extracted in Appendix VI, *White Paper on Indian States*. 1950, p. 158.
25. Ibid.
26. *Supra* Note 5, Chapter I, p. 81.
27. *Keshavananda Bharati v State of Kerala*: AIR 1973 SC 1461.
28. *White Paper on Jammu and Kashmir*. 1948, Government of India, p. 1.
29. Ibid.
30. Extracted in *Supra* Note 28, p. 1.
31. See Singh, Tavleen. 1996. *Kashmir: A Tragedy of Errors*. New Delhi: Penguin Books.
32. *Supra* Note 8, p. 756.
33. *Supra* Note 28, p. 1.
34. See Wani, Gull Mohd. 1996. *Kashmir: From Autonomy to Azadi*. Srinagar: Valley Book House.
35. Hari Jaisingh. 1996. *Kashmir: A Tale of Shame*, p. 61. New Delhi: UBS Publishers' Distributors Ltd.
36. Sharma, B.P. 1996. 'Special Status of Jammu & Kashmir: Its Genesis and Development', in *Supra* Note 34, p. 88.
37. Ibid.
38. Ibid., p. 87.
39. See Nayar, Kuldip. 1996. 'Kashmir: Re-reading its past in order to proffer a practicable solution', in Gull Mohd. Wani (Ed.), *Kashmir: From Autonomy to Azadi*, pp. 23–24. Srinagar: Valley Book House.
40. *Supra* Note 7, Chapter I, pp. 22, 169.
41. *Supra* Note 2, Chapter I, p. 17.
42. *Supra* Note 1, Chapter I, pp. 428–430.
43. Ibid., p. 432.
44. Ibid., pp. 432–434.
45. S/PV 463, p. 27, Mohammed Zafrullah Khan (Pakistan), 7 February 1950.
46. *Yearbook of the United Nations, 1948–49*, Hyderabad Question, p. 300.
47. *Supra* Note 45, p. 29.
48. *Supra* Note 46, p. 29.
49. S/PV 264, pp. 55–56, Gopalswami Ayyangar (India), 8 March 1948.
50. For discussion on New Delhi's policy on Junagadh, see *Supra* Note 2, Chapter I, pp. 112–113.
51. *Supra* Note 45, pp. 31–32.
52. Ibid., p. 33.
53. Ibid.
54. S/PV 257, pp. 328–329, M.K. Vellodi (India), 26 February 1948.
55. *Supra* Note 1, Chapter I, p. 438.
56. *Supra* Note 49, p. 55.
57. S/PV 287, p. 5, M.K. Vellodi (India), 23 April 1948.
58. S/PV 289, p. 12, Mohammed Zafrullah Khan (Pakistan), 7 May 1948.
59. S/PV 264, p. 64, Mohammed Zafrullah Khan (Pakistan), 8 March 1948.
60. *Supra* Note 30, Chapter III, p. 43.

61. *Supra* Note 12, p. 650.
62. Menon, V.P. 2014. *Integration of Indian States*, p. 353. New Delhi: Orient Blackswan Private Limited.
63. Ibid.
64. *Supra* Note 6, Chapter I, p. 332.
65. Ibid.
66. Ibid., pp. 16–17.
67. Ibid., p. 218.
68. Ibid., p. 331.
69. *Supra* Note 12, p. 828.
70. *Supra* Note 6, Chapter I, p. 346.
71. *Supra* Note 30, Chapter III, pp. 36–37.
72. *Supra* Note 6, Chapter I, p. 345.
73. *Supra* Note 30, Chapter III, pp. 39–40.
74. Ibid., pp. 43–44.
75. *Supra* Note 6, Chapter I, p. 332.
76. Ibid.
77. Ibid.
78. Ibid., p. 333.
79. Ibid., pp. 332–333.
80. *Supra* Note 62, pp. 363–364.
81. Snedden, Christopher. 2013. *Kashmir: The Unwritten History*, p. 85, Noida, UP: HarperCollins Publishers.
82. *Supra* Note 6, Chapter I, p. 333.
83. Ibid.
84. Ibid., p. 334
85. *Supra* Note 81, p. 85.
86. *Supra* Note 89, Chapter I, p. 338.
87. *Supra* Note 6, Chapter I, p. 334.
88. Ibid.
89. Ibid., p. 340.
90. Ibid., pp. 340–341.
91. *Supra* Note 81, p. 45.
92. See *Supra* Note 28, pp. 1–44.
93. *Supra* Note 28, Chapter I, pp. 65–66.
94. *Supra* Note 6, Chapter I, p. 347.
95. *Supra* Note 62, p. 372.
96. Ibid.
97. *Supra* Note 28, pp. 8–9.
98. Ibid., pp. 355–356.
99. *Supra* Note 6, Chapter I, pp. 347–348.
100. For full text, see *Selected Works of Jawaharlal Nehru*. 1996. Second Series, Vol 4, p. 274. Jawaharlal Nehru Memorial Fund, New Delhi.
101. *Supra* Note 62.
102. *Supra* Note 89, Chapter I, pp. 408–409.
103. *Supra* Note 28, pp. 46–47.
104. Abdullah, Sheikh Mohammad. 1993. *Flames of Chinar: An Autobiography*, abridged and translated by Khushwant Singh, pp. 92–94. New Delhi: Viking.

105. *Supra* Note 30, Chapter III, p. 43.
106. *Supra* Note 62, p. 364.
107. *Supra* Note 6, Chapter I, pp. 340, 351, 353.
108. *Supra* Note 28, Chapter I, p. 67.
109. Ibid.
110. *Supra* Note 62, p. 357.
111. Ibid.
112. Ibid., p. 359.
113. Ibid.
114. Ibid., p. 360.
115. Ibid. For full text of letter, see *Supra* Note 28, pp. 46–47.
116. *Supra* Note 62, p. 359.
117. Ibid., p. 360.
118. Ibid.
119. *Supra* Note 100, p. 276.
120. *Supra* Note 8.
121. *Supra* Note 28, pp. 47–48.
122. Ibid., p. 3.
123. Ibid.
124. *Supra* Note 2, Chapter I, p. 111.

V

Reference to the People

The question of whether it was open to New Delhi to introduce the 'wishes of the people' as a factor to determine accession of a princely Indian state to either of the dominions of India or Pakistan can be considered at different levels. Did New Delhi have the competence to do so under the constitutional law governing both India and Pakistan, and accepted by both countries, namely the Indian Independence Act of 1947 and the Government of India Act of 1935, as amended? Further, did the accession of the PIS of J&K to the dominion of India itself empower New Delhi to reopen the question of the accession of the state? Again, did the subsequent constitutional developments with respect to the PIS of J&K, including the adoption of Article 370 of the Constitution of India, enable New Delhi to question the accession? Finally, did the Kashmiri people, or for that matter, the people of any of the 560-odd princely Indian states that acceded to either India or Pakistan in 1947, even otherwise, have a 'right to self-determination'? Once the aforesaid aspects have been considered, the chapter examines the fallout of the stand of New Delhi on the accession of the PIS of J&K to the dominion of India.

Competence of New Delhi to Introduce 'Wishes of the People' to Determine Accession

The unilateral and voluntary desire expressed by New Delhi that the question of accession of the PIS of J&K be settled by a reference to the people was stated to be consistent with the policy of the Government of India that in case of any princely Indian state where the accession was in issue, the accession should be decided 'in accordance with the wishes of the people of the State'.

Let us consider the issue from the standpoint of the PIS of J&K. It has been noted that in view of the express provisions of the Indian Independence Act of 1947, read with the Government of India Act of 1935, as amended; the memorandum dated 12 May 1946 of the Cabinet Mission declaring that all the rights surrendered by the rulers of the princely Indian states to the British Crown will return to them; and the legal position enunciated by the Indian Supreme Court and shared by Pakistan and the UK, the princely Indian states became sovereign states under law in every sense upon the lapse of the paramountcy of the British Crown on 15 August 1947. The ruler of the PIS of J&K enjoyed sovereign powers and had, in terms of the said statutes, the sole authority to offer the accession, regardless of the religious complexion of the state.

It was, no doubt, the prerogative of the sovereign ruler of the state to negotiate the terms of accession with either of the dominions of India or Pakistan. However, Raja Hari Singh executed the Instrument of Accession on 26 October 1947, which was neither provisional nor subject to the 'wishes of the people' of the state. The Constitution Bench of the Indian Supreme Court held in *Madhav Rao*[1] that the instrument of accession was an Act of State on the part of the sovereign ruler of a princely Indian state and bound all concerned. Hence, as far as the PIS of J&K was concerned, the question of the accession already made by its sovereign ruler being further 'settled' through a 'reference to the people' or otherwise did not arise, and least of all, at the instance of New Delhi.

It has been suggested that the ruler of the PIS of J&K followed a policy of repression of Muslims in the state, resulting in a rebellion against the Raja, particularly in the Poonch area. Noorani refers to a report by an Indian Civil Service official, which was published on 10 August 1948 in the *London Times* stating that:[2]

237,000 Muslims were systematically exterminated—unless they escaped to Pakistan across the border—by all the forces of the Dogra State, headed by the Maharaja in person and aided by Hindus and Sikhs. This happened in October 1947, five days before the first Pathan invasion and nine days before the Maharaja's accession to India.

There are, however, also studies to the contrary, a few of which have been mentioned in the previous chapter, which negate the commission of such condemnable atrocities by the Raja and the state. It is crucial to state here that even if it is assumed that the ruler of the PIS of J&K did follow a policy of repression, it does not detract from the legal position that under the constitutional law creating and governing both the dominions of India and Pakistan, namely, the Indian Independence Act of 1947, read with the Government of India Act of 1935, as amended, it was the ruler of a princely Indian state that had the sole authority to offer accession, regardless of the religious complexion of its population. If this legal principle was to be discarded on account of the immensely attractive plea that since part of the population of a given princely Indian state was being oppressed by the ruler, it ought to be the people who should decide the question of accession, it would result in challenging the accessions of several princely Indian states and undoing both Pakistan and India as they exist today.

Coming to the stand of New Delhi, it is important to recall that both India and Pakistan existed as dominions from 1947 onwards until the promulgation of their individual constitutions. Since the dominions of India and Pakistan were created by the British statutes, namely, the Indian Independence Act of 1947 and the Government of India Act of 1935, as amended, the dominions were bound by the terms of these statutes. What the British statutes did not authorize, the dominions could not do.

Now, it was open to both the dominions of India and Pakistan to either accept or reject an offer of accession made by the sovereign ruler of a princely Indian state. But the acceptance or rejection by either of the dominions of the offer of accession was to be in accordance with the Indian Independence Act of 1947, and the Government of India Act of 1935, as amended, governing both dominions. The provisions of these British statutes governing the dominions of India and Pakistan did not contemplate a provisional accession. Indeed, Menon has pointed out that:[3]

> Some rulers signed the Instrument of Accession and forwarded it with covering letters which laid down conditions subject to which the accession had been signed. They were told that the execution of the Instrument of Accession must be unconditional and [they] subsequently complied.

The question that then arises is whether the said statutes empowered the dominion of India to formulate a policy, which prescribed that the accession made by the sovereign ruler of a princely Indian state to the dominion of India would be subject to the 'wishes of the people' of that state or to regard an accession of a princely Indian state as being 'purely provisional'? There is no provision in either the Indian Independence Act of 1947, or the Government of India Act of 1935, as amended, which enabled the dominion of India, or for that matter, the dominion of Pakistan, to do so. On the contrary, such a proposition negates the very premise underlying both statutes—namely, that it is the sovereign ruler of a princely Indian state who was to decide the future of that state.

It may be recalled that as far as the provinces comprising British India were concerned, the Indian Independence Act of 1947 made specific provisions for a referendum to be held in certain territories. These provisions confirm that the British Parliament, while enacting the Indian Independence Act of 1947, was aware of the option of holding a referendum as a method for accession of a territory. Yet the said Act, read with the Government of India Act of 1935, as amended, did not prescribe such method for the princely Indian states to accede to either of the dominions of India or Pakistan.

The Indian Supreme Court, in *In re Delhi Laws Act, 1912*,[4] cited Crawford on *Statutory Construction* to the effect that 'if a statute directs certain acts to be done in a specified manner by certain persons, their performance in any other manner than that specified, or by any other person than is there named, is impliedly prohibited'.[5] It is, indeed, well settled law that '[i]f text is explicit the text is conclusive, alike in what it directs and what it forbids'.[6]

In *Keshavananda Bharati*,[7] the Indian Supreme Court held that the very fact that the Constituent Assembly did not include referendum as one of the methods of amendment of the Constitution of India would render the method of referendum, if selected for the purpose of amendment, 'extra constitutional or revolutionary'.[8] Similar precedents are available all over the world, notably of the US Supreme Court in *George S. Hawke*,[9] which found it illegal to hold a referendum for the purposes of ascertaining the true wishes of the people on the question of ratification of the 18th (Prohibition) Amendment to the US Constitution, since such procedure did not find place in Article V of the US Constitution.

Hence, when the provisions of the Indian Independence Act of 1947, read with the Government of India Act of 1935, as amended, contemplated a referendum for some of the provinces comprising British India, like the NWFP, but did not provide for a referendum as the means of settling the accession of a princely Indian state to either of the dominions, the desire expressed by New Delhi for a reference to the people to settle the question of the accession of the PIS of J&K made by its sovereign ruler to the dominion of India was extra-constitutional.

Indeed, it is difficult to appreciate how the dominion of India could act beyond the said Acts—which it had, along with the dominion of Pakistan, accepted—and promise to hold a 'reference to the people' to 'settle' the question of the accession of the PIS of J&K to the dominion of India.

But then, did the accession of the PIS of J&K to the dominion of India empower New Delhi to reopen such accession?

Legal Incidence of Accession of the PIS of J&K to the Dominion of India

The PIS of J&K was a sovereign state prior to its accession to the dominion of India. The dominions of India and Pakistan had no paramountcy rights over any princely Indian state.

However, as examined earlier, it is quite consistent with the notion of sovereignty that the sovereign may, in certain respects, be dependent on another power. Should Raja Hari Singh, notwithstanding the accession of the PIS of J&K to the dominion of India, be found to have retained sovereignty over his state, the question of New Delhi exercising powers in respect of the PIS of J&K, other than those conferred by the Instrument of Accession, simply does not arise. Rather, as laid down by the Constitution Bench of the Indian Supreme Court in *Madhav Rao*, the 'relations between the States and the Dominion of India were strictly governed by the instruments executed from time to time'.[10] The Indian Supreme Court, in *Keshavananda Bharati*,[11] reaffirmed its earlier decision in *Deep Chand*,[12] where the test laid down in *Queen v Burah*[13] had been followed; namely, the terms of the instrument by which powers are affirmatively created and by which they are negatively restricted are to be looked into.

It may also be recalled that, unlike all other acceding princely Indian states, the ruler of the PIS of J&K did not subsequently execute any instrument or agreement of merger to integrate the territory of the state into the Union of India. The refusal of the PIS of J&K to execute the instrument of merger did not, however, affect the validity or legality of the accession itself. The PIS of J&K, on accession, formed part of the dominion of India even in the absence of the instrument of merger. The legal implication merely was that the accession of the PIS of J&K to the dominion of India was limited to the terms of the Instrument of Accession.

It would, therefore, be necessary to examine the terms of the Instrument of Accession of 26 October 1947, in order to determine the powers of the dominion of India over the PIS of J&K. A perusal of the relevant terms of the Instrument of Accession, the text of which has been reproduced in the previous chapter, would show that it authorized the Indian legislature to make laws for the state only with respect to defence, external affairs, communications and certain ancillary matters. None of these empowered New Delhi to reopen the accession itself of the PIS of J&K to the dominion of India, it being an Act of State. Moreover, there is case law for the proposition that even with respect to these three areas, the ruler, notwithstanding the accession, retained a residuary sovereign power to legislate.[14] Indeed, the ruler explicitly stated in Para 8 of the Instrument of Accession that '[n]othing in this Instrument affects the continuance of my sovereignty in and over this State, or save as provided by or under this Instrument the exercise of any powers, authority and rights now enjoyed by me as Ruler of this State or the validity of any law at present in force in this State'.

Noorani argues that the accession of the PIS of J&K was provisional and conditional, since, according to him,[15]

> In law, it matters not one bit whether a condition, stipulation or a proviso is added to the principal document, or in a related, collateral document executed simultaneously. A letter granting the lessee the right of way over the lessor's ground to the leased land has the same force in law as the indenture of lease itself.

It has, perhaps, escaped consideration that the question is not whether New Delhi added a condition, stipulation or proviso to the unconditional accession offered by the sovereign ruler of the PIS of J&K, but whether New Delhi had the power under the very statutes that gave birth to India to add a condition, stipulation or proviso to such accession. Neither the Indian Independence Act, 1947, and the Government of India Act, 1935, as amended, nor the Instrument of Accession of 26 October 1947 executed by the sovereign ruler of the PIS of J&K in terms of these British statutes, conferred any such power upon New Delhi.

The matter stands concluded against New Delhi with the judicial authority of the Indian Supreme Court in *Premnath Kaul*,[16] wherein the Constitution Bench accepted the proposition that notwithstanding the accession of the PIS of J&K to the dominion of India, Raja Hari Singh retained sovereignty over the state. New Delhi, therefore, lacked competence to reopen the accession by a sovereign ruler.

A similar case is that of the princely Indian state of Bahawalpur which had acceded to Pakistan. The King's Bench Division in the UK held in *Sayce*[17] that the ruler of the princely Indian state of Bahawalpur had, notwithstanding the accession of that state on 3 October 1947, in specified areas, to the dominion of Pakistan in terms of the Indian Independence Act, 1947, and the Government of India Act, 1935, as amended, retained his sovereignty so as to entitle him to immunity as the ruler of a sovereign state from being sued in the UK.

Thus, given that the ruler of the PIS of J&K retained sovereign powers over his state, notwithstanding its accession to the dominion of India in specified areas, New Delhi had no say in the future disposition of the PIS of J&K.

This brings us to the question of whether the adoption of the Constitution of India, and in particular the application of Article 370 thereof to the PIS of J&K, affected the sovereignty of the ruler of the PIS of J&K?

Sovereignty of the PIS of J&K and Subsequent Constitutional Developments

Subsequent to the accession of the PIS of J&K to the dominion of India, Raja Hari Singh issued the Proclamation of 5 March 1948,[18] supposedly to install a 'popular interim government' headed by Sheikh Abdullah as Prime Minister of the state, which was to function under the Jammu and Kashmir Constitution Act of 1939. The 1939 Act, too, was premised on the supremacy of the Raja.[19] The Raja deputed Sheikh Abdullah, Mirza Afzal Beig, Moulana Masoodi and Pandit Moti Ram Baigra to represent the PIS of J&K in the Constituent Assembly of India, which was in the process of framing the Constitution of India.[20] The said representatives, who joined the Constituent Assembly on 16 June 1949, sought to limit the accession of the PIS of J&K to the dominion of India only to the matters listed in the schedule to the Instrument of Accession.[21] This relationship between the PIS of J&K and the Union of India was crystallized in Article 370 of the Constitution of India. Article 370 permitted the PIS of J&K to have its own constitution formulated by its own Constituent Assembly and limited the relationship between the Union of India and the PIS of J&K to the subjects specified in the Instrument of Accession until the Constituent Assembly of the PIS of J&K consented to accede further subjects to New Delhi.

The adoption of Article 370 in the Constitution of India, therefore, did not affect the sovereignty of Raja Hari Singh over the PIS of J&K, which had been retained by him in terms of the Instrument of Accession. Article 370 of the Constitution of India did not confer new powers on New Delhi qua the PIS of J&K so as to enable it to question the accession of the state to the dominion of India.

Meanwhile, Raja Hari Singh became understandably very sore at New Delhi's stand on the issue of the accession of the PIS of J&K. In his letter dated 31 January 1948, to Sardar Patel, the Raja said '.... You know I definitely acceded to the Indian Union with the idea that Union will not let us down and the State would remain acceded to the Union and its position and that of my dynasty would remain secure...'.[22]

Raja Hari Singh was 'persuaded' by New Delhi to entrust all his powers and functions with regard to the governance of the state to his son Yuvraj Karan Singh by the Proclamation of 20 June 1949.[23] The Yuvraj issued the Proclamation of 25 November 1949, which declared that 'the Constitution of India shortly to be adopted by the Constituent Assembly of India shall in so far as it is applicable to the State of Jammu and Kashmir ... govern the constitutional relationship between this State and the contemplated Union'.[24]

The Jammu and Kashmir High Court, in *Magher Singh*,[25] considered the legal effect of the adoption of Article 370 of the Constitution of India and the Proclamation of 25 November 1949 of Yuvraj Karan Singh on the sovereignty of the ruler of the PIS of J&K. The High Court found that since Raja Hari Singh continued to remain sovereign even after executing the Instrument of Accession, Yuvraj was granted his powers by an authority as sovereign as the British Parliament. The High Court observed that Article 370 of the Constitution of India indicated that the Instrument of Accession executed on 26 October 1947 was still the real basis of the relationship between the Union and the state. This matter stands yet again concluded by the Constitution Bench of the Indian Supreme Court in *Prem Nath Kaul*,[26] which considered the above constitutional developments and held that 'it was not, and could not have been, within the contemplation, or competence of the Constitution makers to impinge even indirectly' on the plenary powers of the ruler of the PIS of J&K.[27]

Thus, the position that emerges is that the Constitution of India applies to the PIS of J&K by virtue of the Instrument of Accession of 26 October 1947 and subject to its terms and conditions. With the accession of the PIS of J&K to the dominion of India, the Indian Parliament was given the jurisdiction to legislate for the PIS of J&K on matters pertaining only to external affairs, defence and communications and certain ancillary matters. The sovereignty of the ruler over the PIS of J&K was expressly retained by him under the Instrument of Accession, and recognized by Article 370 of the Constitution of India. Neither the Instrument of Accession, nor Article 370 of the Constitution of India, nor the Proclamation of 25 November 1949, detracted from the sovereignty enjoyed by the ruler over the PIS of J&K upon the lapse of the British paramountcy on 15 August 1947. Rather, the ruler continued to be legally sovereign, with the Indian Supreme Court expressly ruling that it was not within the competence of the Indian Constitution-makers to even impinge upon the powers of the ruler. It follows that New Delhi did not get a say in the disposition of the territory of the PIS of J&K.

The constitutional position that the accession of the PIS of J&K to the dominion of India in 1947 was final, irrevocable and complete, and that it was legally impermissible to require it to be 'settled' by a 'reference to the people', would lead to the inevitable conclusion that the 'wishes of the people' of the PIS of J&K were quite irrelevant to determine the question of accession. But then, would such a proposition not be in derogation of a right of the Kashmiri people to self-determination?

Right of the Kashmiri People to Self-determination

Before this issue is examined, it may be worthwhile to refer to certain other developments in the PIS of J&K that render this issue academic.

After the accession of the PIS of J&K to the dominion of India in limited areas, Yuvraj Karan Singh, the then sovereign ruler of the PIS of J&K, had issued the Proclamation of 1 May 1951,[28] directing that a state constituent assembly, consisting of representatives of the people elected on the basis of adult franchise, shall be constituted forthwith for the purpose of framing the constitution for the state. The preamble to this Proclamation stated that the Yuvraj was satisfied that it was the general desire of the people that a constituent assembly be brought into being for the purpose of framing a constitution for the PIS of J&K and that it was commonly felt that the convening of the said assembly could no longer be delayed without detriment to the future well being of the state.

The elections to the Constituent Assembly of the PIS of J&K were held in September 1951. Seventy-five members were elected from various constituencies, while 25 seats were kept vacant for the state subjects living in areas occupied by Pakistan.[29] The state Constituent Assembly began its task of framing a constitution for the PIS of J&K. On 12 November 1952, the state Constituent Assembly formally terminated the monarchical rule in the state. In *Ghulam Rasul*,[30] the Full Bench of the Jammu and Kashmir High Court reviewed the constitutional history of the PIS of J&K to hold that with the Constituent Assembly of the PIS of J&K coming into existence, all the rights, authority and jurisdiction of the ruler were surrendered to the people of the state, who were represented at the Constituent Assembly through their elected representatives.

The state Constituent Assembly endorsed on 15 February 1954, after much debate, discussion and consideration, the accession of the PIS of J&K

to India. The Constitution of Jammu and Kashmir of 1957, framed by the state Constituent Assembly, declares the PIS of J&K to be an integral part of the Union of India and puts a limitation on the legislative power to amend the Constitution of Jammu and Kashmir of 1957 to alter this position. In *S. Mubarik Shah Naqishbandi*, the Jammu and Kashmir High Court considered this aspect of the Kashmir issue to hold that 'the wishes of the people were fully ascertained as promised by [Mountbatten] in the shape of election of the representatives of the people who framed the present Constitution of the State'.[31]

Hence, should the people of the PIS of J&K have had a right to self-determination, the people, through their elected representatives in the Constituent Assembly of the PIS of J&K, reaffirmed the decision of the sovereign ruler to accede to India. Therefore, the question of a plebiscite or further self-determination does not, even otherwise, arise, whether legally or morally.

Be that as it may, let us consider whether, independent of these developments, the Kashmiri people could claim, or be promised, the right to self-determination.

It may sound incongruous, in light of current international opinion, to deny the existence of a 'right to self-determination' to any section of people around the world. However, it must be emphasized that when the monarchical PIS of J&K became fully sovereign in 1947, the sovereignty vested in the ruler and not in the people of the state. This was a period when most of the American, British and German scholars had attacked the notion of 'right to self-determination' as 'being wrong in principle and worthless in practice'.[32] The British statutes, namely, the Indian Independence Act of 1947, and the Government of India Act of 1935, as amended, which created both India and Pakistan and which were accepted by both, did not recognize at all a 'right to self-determination' in respect of the people of the 560-odd princely Indian states that acceded to the dominions of India or Pakistan. It was in terms of the said British statutes that the princely Indian states became part of India or of Pakistan. The PIS of J&K, upon its accession to the dominion of India in 1947, thus became a member state within the Union of India.

It is in this context that the question arises as to whether the Kashmiri people could claim, or be conferred, the right to self-determination in the matter of accession of the PIS of J&K to the dominion of India. To put it differently, can a section of the people within the Indian Union claim a 'right to self-determination'?

The import of the right to self-determination is often misunderstood and has been the subject of intense discussion within the UN itself. In the Debates of the Special UN Committee on Friendly Relations between States in 1970, it was clarified that, first, the right to self-determination was applicable only to peoples struggling to free themselves from colonial and foreign domination. Second, this right was not to be utilized for 'authorising or encouraging any action which would dismember or impair totally or in part the territorial integrity or political unity of sovereign and independent states'. The UN, at its 50th anniversary session, passed a resolution which, while affirming the 'right of self-determination of all peoples', clarified that it should not be construed as 'authorising or encouraging any action that would dismember or impair ... the territorial integrity or political sovereignty of sovereign and independent nations'.

The legal position was correctly summarized in 1970 by U. Thant, the then UN Secretary General, who asserted that 'self-determination of peoples does not imply self-determination of a section of population of a particular member State', and that when 'a state applies to be a member of the UN and when the UN accepts that member then the implication is that the rest of the membership of the UN recognises the territorial integrity, independence and sovereignty of this particular member state'.[33]

It has been overlooked by those propounding a right to self-determination for the Kashmiri people that the UN has accepted both India and Pakistan as sovereign countries, as created in terms of the Indian Independence Act of 1947, and the Government of India Act of 1935, as amended. It follows that the membership of the UN, including Pakistan, has recognized the territorial integrity and political sovereignty of India in terms of these very Acts, which would include the entire territory of the PIS of J&K described in Schedule I to the Constitution of India to be part of the Union of India. Significantly, the PIS of J&K does not form part of Pakistan under Pakistan's own Constitution. The question of the people of a portion of India, whether it is in Kashmir or in any other state, having a right to self-determination does not, therefore, arise. If the provisions of the Charter of the United Nations of 1945 (the UN Charter) are to be ignored to confer upon the people of the PIS of J&K a right to self-determination, such right would also have to be conferred upon the people of every other princely Indian state that acceded to the dominion of India or Pakistan, as well as upon the Irish in the UK and the Texans in the US.[34]

New Delhi would be within its rights to remind the international community about what the latter had to say when India spoke the language of the right to self-determination for the people in East Pakistan, now Bangladesh, before the UNSC. Kulaga (Poland) had admonished New Delhi by asserting that '[i]f some people in East Pakistan were disgruntled— and we should not set ourselves up here as judges concerning whether they were right or wrong—they should compose their differences with their

Government, without interference from outside' and that '[i]f we encourage such secessionist movements, we may have to gerrymander many countries and prepare a new map of the world'.[35]

Significantly, even Pakistan endorses such a view of the right to self-determination, as is evident from its stand before the UN on East Pakistan that became an independent nation, Bangladesh, in 1971. Referring to the right of self-determination of the people of East Pakistan, it asked the UN as to '[h]ow is self-determination involved in Bengal, in East Pakistan' when 'East Pakistan is a part of Pakistan, an inextricable part of Pakistan, united with Pakistan for 24 years'.[36] The script could have been written for PIS of J&K—which acceded to India and became an inextricable part of India—not because I say so, but because the Acts which gave birth to both India and Pakistan, namely, the Indian Independence Act of 1947, and the Government of India Act of 1935, as amended, and which remain on the British statute book, say so.

It may be worthwhile to examine India's stand before the UN on the right to self-determination. Article I of the Covenant on Civil and Political Rights, as also the Covenant on Economic, Social and Cultural Rights, provides that 'all peoples have the right of self-determination. By virtue of the right they freely determine their political status and freely pursue their economic, social and cultural life'.

India, while ratifying the Covenants in 1979, set out the qualification that the 'Government of the Republic of India declares that the words the right of self-determination appearing in Article I apply only to the peoples under domination and these words do not apply to sovereign independent states or to a section of people or nation—which is the essence of national integrity'.[37] Maurice Mendelson opines that the aforesaid reservation made by India at the time of ratification of the Covenants, even otherwise, denied applicability of this right to the Kashmiri people or for that matter, any 'peoples' or state in India.[38]

To summarize, the 'wishes of the people' were alien to the question of accession of a princely Indian state to either of the dominions of India or Pakistan under the Indian Independence Act of 1947, and the Government of India Act of 1935, as amended. The Instrument of Accession dated 26 October 1947 was executed by Raja Hari Singh in respect of the PIS of J&K under such constitutional law governing both the dominions. New Delhi was not legally competent to require that this accession be further 'settled' by a 'reference to the people' of the PIS of J&K. Nor could it regard the accession as being 'provisional'. The accession of the PIS of J&K to the dominion of India in 1947, made by its sovereign ruler, was unconditional, final, irrevocable and complete in view of the provisions of the said British statutes.

New Delhi, however, appeared to be blissfully unaware of this legal position. This is evident from the pronouncements made ad nauseam by New Delhi on every conceivable occasion to reiterate, as noted below, that it had accepted the accession of the PIS of J&K to the dominion of India provisionally and subject to the final decision to be taken in accordance with the wishes of the Kashmiri people.

Fallout of New Delhi's Stand

It may be recalled that Indian troops flew into the PIS of J&K on 27 October 1947. Nehru, in his cable dated 25 October 1947 to Attlee, the then British Prime Minister, had detailed the tribal invasion and emphasized that the 'question of aiding Kashmir in this emergency is not designed in any way to influence the State to accede to India' and that India's view 'which we have repeatedly made public is that the question of accession in any disputed territory of State must be decided in accordance with wishes of the people'.[39] Nehru, in his cable dated 28 October 1947 to Attlee, detailed Pakistan's complicity in the tribal invasion and declared that India's 'military intervention is purely defensive in aim and scope, in no way affecting any future decision about accession that might be taken by the people of Kashmir ultimately', since '[w]e have laid down the principle that accession of every State, whether Junagadh or Kashmir or Hyderabad, should depend on the ascertained wishes of the people concerned'.[40]

Nehru, in his cable dated 28 October 1947, to Liaquat Ali Khan, the then Prime Minister of Pakistan, in fact reassured Pakistan that the accession 'is subject to reference to people of State and their decision',[41] and went on in his cable of 31 October 1947 to say that:[42]

> Kashmir's accession to India was accepted ... on the condition that as soon as the invader has been driven from Kashmir soil, and law and order restored, the people of Kashmir will decide the question. It is open to them to accede to either Dominion then.... Our assurance that we shall ... leave the decision about the future of the State to the people of the State is not merely a pledge to your Government, but also to the people of Kashmir and to the world.

New Delhi kept reiterating this stand whether it was before the Constituent Assembly of India, in its White Paper on Jammu and Kashmir, or in press statements and radio broadcasts. New Delhi even sent cables to world leaders that it would withdraw its troops from the PIS of J&K as soon as order was restored and leave it to the people of the state to decide their future.[43]

New Delhi's commitment that such plebiscite be held under UN auspices was just as unequivocal. While Nehru, in his letters dated 31 October 1947 to Mehr Chand Mahajan,[44] the then Prime Minister of the PIS of J&K, and to Sheikh Abdullah,[45] suggested UN involvement, he explicitly advised Shiekh Abdullah in his letter dated 1 November 1947 that the question of accession be decided by the people 'under the auspices of the United Nations'.[46] Nehru went on to announce on All India Radio from New Delhi on 2 November 1947:[47]

[I]t has been our policy all along that where there is a dispute about the accession of a State to either Dominion, the decision must be made by the people of that State. It was in accordance with this policy that we added a proviso to the Instrument of Accession.... We have declared that the fate of Kashmir is ultimately to be decided by the people. That pledge we have given ... not only to the people of Kashmir but to the world. We will not, and cannot back out of it. We are prepared when peace and law and order have been established to have a referendum held under international auspicies like the United Nations....

Nehru, by his cable of 3 November 1947 to Liaquat Ali Khan, referred to his broadcast as under:[48]

I wish to draw your attention to the broadcast on Kashmir which I made last evening. I have stated our Government's policy and made it clear that we have no desire to impose our will on Kashmir and to leave final decision to the people of Kashmir. I further stated that we have agreed to an impartial international agency like the United Nations supervising any referendum. This principle we are prepared to apply to any State where there is a dispute about accession. If these principles are accepted by your Government there should be no difficulty in giving effect to them.

New Delhi, in fact, proposed through a cable dated 8 November 1947 to Liaquat Ali Khan that on restoration of law and order in Kashmir, 'the Governments of India and Pakistan should make a joint request to the United Nations to undertake a plebiscite in Kashmir at the earliest possible date'.[49] New Delhi called upon Pakistan to accept

[T]he principle that, where ruler of a State does not belong to community to which the majority of his subjects belong, and where the State has not acceded to that Dominion whose major community is same as the State's, the question whether the State has finally acceded to one or other Dominion should be ascertained by reference to the will of the people.[50]

Nehru followed up by another cable dated 21 November 1947 to Liaquat Ali Khan to the same effect.[51]

It appears that the National Conference in the PIS of J&K had opposed New Delhi's enthusiasm to make a reference to the UNSC. Nehru, in his letter dated 21 November 1947 to Sheikh Abdullah, reasoned that 'it is not easy for us to back out of the stand we have taken before the world', as it 'would create a very bad impression abroad and more specially in the U.N. circles'.[52]

Nehru declared on 25 November 1947 in the Constituent Assembly of India that:[53]

> We made it clear that as soon as law and order has been restored in Kashmir and her soil cleared of the invaders, the question of the State's accession should be settled by reference to the people ... we have suggested that when the people are given the chance to decide their future this should be done under the supervision of an impartial tribunal such as the United Nations Organisation....

Nehru deemed it fit to eventually write to the sovereign ruler of the PIS of J&K, Raja Hari Singh, on 1 December 1947, about the proposed reference regarding his state, acknowledging that the Raja did 'not like the idea of a plebiscite; but we cannot do away with it without harming our cause all over the world'.[54]

These pronouncements have been referred to in some detail to establish that as far as the international community was concerned, it was New Delhi that was itching for a referendum or plebiscite in the PIS of J&K under the auspices of the UN, and also to explain why New Delhi's subsequent denial before the UN and the world that it had ever regarded the accession as being 'provisional' failed to impress the international community. No one took India seriously when it later pleaded that it had not given any commitment to have a plebiscite under international auspices to settle the accession of the PIS of J&K to India. I have detailed elsewhere how the more New Delhi sought to avoid holding the plebiscite, the more justified the propaganda of Pakistan appeared to Western public opinion, being heavily influenced by the Western media.[55] Francois Gautier, a French reporter covering the 1999 invasion by Pakistan into India, wrote that irrespective of whether India ultimately wins the battle, there is:[56]

> [O]ne war, which India has been constantly losing since 1947. It is the public relations battle. Look at this particular case. Not only is Pakistan the aggressor—It trained, armed, and financed the Kashmiri separatists, put them under the command of Pakistani soldiers in civil and Afghan Mujahideens and pushed them into Indian held territory—but now it is able

to portray itself as a peacemaker (and blackmail the world with the threat of a nuclear war).

What an irony … whatever the Indian government says, Western public opinion is still not on its side, as Kashmir proves. For 15 years, various Indian governments have been saying that Pakistan was sponsoring, arming and training Kashmiri militants. In the beginning, we foreign journalists were a bit skeptical, but after some years, it became obvious to a few of us that it was the truth, because it made sense, it was logical—we were even shown aerial photographs of training camps inside Pakistan. Yet today, if we dare to mention in our dispatches on Kashmir 'the Pakistan-trained Kashmiri militants', some of our editors in Paris, London or New York will immediately correct the text to: 'India says that the Kashmiri militants are backed by Pakistan'.

The BBC as well as several other Western media channels till date continue to refer to the PIS of J&K as India-administered Kashmir and Pakistan-administered Kashmir, thereby perpetuating the 'disputed' status of the state. Incomprehensible as it may sound, the BBC World News, on 2 August 1998 at 18.58 GMT, informed the world that:[57]

[U]nder an agreement signed in 1949, the Western third of Kashmir went to Pakistan, while the rest remained under Indian occupation, and the two sides agreed to hold a UN-supervised plebiscite to determine the future of the Muslim-majority state…. But, the vote was never held and the territory became a battlefront in the war between India and Pakistan'.

The crucial fallout of New Delhi's misconceived stand on the accession of the PIS of J&K to the dominion of India has been on world opinion, which still feels that it is India that has refused to honour its word—a perception that has altered the entire international political discourse on the Kashmir issue. When Pakistan makes itself hoarse, protesting against the denial of 'the right to self-determination' of the Kashmiri people, one does not even expect a rebuttal from New Delhi, having itself introduced the 'wishes of the people' to determine accession. Despite being the aggressor, Pakistan has been able to paint India, the victim, black. Indeed, the current international opinion, as discussed later in the book, is that while it may not be feasible to hold a plebiscite in the PIS of J&K today, the state remains a 'disputed territory' between India and Pakistan and that the Kashmir issue must be resolved keeping in mind the wishes of the Kashmiri people.

But then, it does become pointless for New Delhi to rebuke the international community for its opinion when some Indian political leaders continue to endorse the legally untenable proposition that the accession of the PIS of J&K to the dominion of India was provisional and subject to the final decision to be taken in accordance with the wishes of the Kashmiri people. For instance, Rajmohan Gandhi writes that 'the Kashmiris have had, and continue to nurse, real and deep grievance', namely 'that their inclusion in India in 1947 was the Maharaja's decision, not their choice', and that 'New Delhi went back on early commitments it gave (not just to the UN but also to the people of Kashmir) that the state's future would be for its people to decide'.[58] Politicians are not alone; the legally flawed stand of New Delhi has polarized the academia across the country with recurrent misconceived debates in universities on whether the Indian security forces in the state are, in fact, 'occupation forces' brutally suppressing the Kashmiri 'right to self-determination'.

Indian commentators perpetuate this misconception. Zafar Meraj argues that '[s]weeping promises were made to the Kashmiris by the tallest of Indian leaders that their distinct identity would be maintained and preserved and their aspirations and wishes respected' and that 'the bottom line has to be acknowledged that the people of Jammu and Kashmir state, that includes Azad Kashmir, the northern areas of Gilgit and Baltistan are the ultimate arbiters of their fate'.[59] Minoo Masani contends that 'to this day the people of Kashmir Valley have been denied the right to self-determination'.[60] S.K. Mehera reasons that the accession of Kashmir to India is a 'historical aberration' as 'had Kashmir been a province of British India, it would have gone to Pakistan in 1947, virtually automatically or after some form of partition like Punjab and Bengal'.[61] Noorani asserts that while the UN Resolutions are 'wrecked', one of the 'propositions of enduring worth [that does] survive the wreckage ... is the reiteration ... of the principle that the people of Kashmir would decide their future, not the Constituent Assembly'.[62] In his view, 'a plebiscite in Kashmir was a moral imperative, besides being a democratic necessity',[63] particularly in light of the unabated, smouldering Kashmiri resentment against the Treaty of Amritsar of 16 March 1846 and the ill-treatment during the reign of Raja Gulab Singh.[64]

One does not even look at New Delhi to correct Kashmiri politicians who seem to share this perception. It said nothing when Abdul Ghani Lone of the People's Conference declared before a well-attended convention in the Kashmir Valley that while 'it was India who made Pakistan a party to the issue by taking the matter to the UN', the people of the state were the third party to the Kashmir issue.[65] It kept silent when the People's Conference adopted a resolution calling upon the Governments of Pakistan and India to involve the 'people of POK (Pakistan Occupied Kashmir) and J&K (Jammu and Kashmir)' in any dialogue to resolve the Kashmir issue.[66]

Similarly, there was a stony silence from New Delhi when Hurriyat leaders like Yassin Malik claimed that the Kashmir issue was 'directly concerned with the people of Jammu and Kashmir', who were not 'animals' to have their future decided by India or Pakistan,[67] or when he expounded the view that 'self-determination is our birthright' and that '[w]e were promised it in the instrument of accession'.[68] Again, when Mirwaizi Umar Farooq declared that the Kashmir problem could be resolved only 'in accordance with the wishes of the Kashmiri people' who were entitled to 'self-determination',[69] there was no response from New Delhi. New Delhi was clueless as to how to react when Syed Ali Shah Geelani took pains to clarify that the 'struggle' in the PIS of J&K was not based on any enmity against India, nor on account of it being a Hindu-majority country, but merely because India had reneged on its promise that 'we would be allowed to decide our own future' and that he wanted 'India and its people to prosper and to do justice to the oppressed people of J&K'.[70] New Delhi had no answer when Geelani gave a press statement on 31 August 2010, explaining that:[71]

> We, the people of Jammu Kashmir have been engaged in a struggle for our inalienable right of self-determination, for which we have been made to suffer immensely. Our right to self-determination has been acknowledged by India herself in the United Nations Security Council and also in their repeated public pronouncements from 1947 to 1953.... Our resistance has always been met with violence from the Indian State, resulting in killing of 120,137 persons, disappearance of almost 10,000 people, rapes and molestations of thousands of women, incarcerations, torture, extra judicial murder, humiliation of our people and destruction of our property worth billions of dollars....

The other fallout of New Delhi's misconceived stand has thus been to create and allow to fester for decades a feeling of injustice amongst the Kashmiri populace. It is this feeling of injustice that makes the common Kashmiri want to tear things down. The turmoil in the PIS of J&K could not have sustained over the decades but for the perception of the common person in the state that he or she has been wronged by New Delhi.

This sad state of affairs could have been averted if New Delhi had simply realized that it was not even competent to introduce the 'wishes of the people' as a factor to determine the accession of the PIS of J&K to the dominion of India, let alone promise a right of self-determination to the people of the state.

The matter did not end here. New Delhi went a step further to involve the UNSC in the Kashmir issue, and to commit before the UNSC to hold a plebiscite in the state under international auspices.

It is necessary to point out here that New Delhi was pressed by the British to do so. Just as the British got Jinnah to mouth the two-nation theory, they got Nehru to first commit to hold the plebiscite in the PIS of J&K to 'settle' the accession, and later to make the reference to the UNSC. The British would then ensure, through the UNSC, that such territory of the PIS of J&K that would serve British interests for the Great Game remained with Pakistan, free of Indian presence. Let us consider these happenings in some detail.

Notes and References

1. *Supra* Note 5, Chapter I, p. 37. The Supreme Court explained on page 53 that '[a]n act of State is a sovereign act which is neither grounded on law nor does it pretend to do so' and that it is 'a catastrophic change constituting a new departure'.
2. *Supra* Note 12, Chapter IV, p. 480.
3. Extracted in Noorani, A.G. 2013. *The Kashmir Dispute 1947–2012,* Vol I, p. 24, New Delhi: Tulika Books.
4. *In re Delhi Laws Act, 1912:* 1951 SCR 747.
5. Ibid., p. 946.
6. *The Judicial Committee in Attorney General for Ontario v Attorney General for Canada*: 1912 A.C. 571.
7. *Supra* Note 27, Chapter IV.
8. Ibid., p. 1639.
9. *George S. Hawke v Harvey C. Smith*: 253 US 221 (1919).
10. *Supra* Note 5, Chapter I, p. 93.
11. *Supra* Note 27, Chapter IV, p. 1682.
12. *Deep Chand v State of Uttar Pradesh*: (1959) Supp. 2 SCR 8.
13. *Queen v Burah*: (1878) 5 Ind App 178 at pp. 193–194.
14. *Rehman Shagoo v State of Jammu and Kashmir*: AIR 1958 J&K 29.
15. *Supra* Note 3, p. 24.
16. *Supra* Note 8, Chapter IV.
17. *Sayce v Ameer Ruler Sadiq Mohammad Abbasi Bahawalpur State*: 1952 All. E.R. 326.
18. *Proclamation of 5 March 1948,* Jammu and Kashmir Government Gazette Extraordinary, Vol 60, Part 1-B, 5 March 1948.
19. See *Supra* Note 8, Chapter IV; *Supra* Note 23, Chapter IV.
20. See *Supra* Note 36, Chapter IV, p. 104.
21. Noorani, A.G. 2000. 'Article 370: Law and Politics', *Frontline*, p. 90, 29 September.
22. *Supra* Note 36, Chapter IV, pp. 92–93.
23. Extracted in ibid., p. 97.
24. Cited in *Supra* Note 23, Chapter IV.
25. Ibid., p. 30.
26. *Supra* Note 8, Chapter IV.
27. Ibid., p. 758.
28. *Jammu and Kashmir Government Gazette* No. 22, dated 1 May 1951.
29. *Supra* Note 36, Chapter IV, p. 99.
30. *Ghulam Rasul v State of Jammu and Kashmir*: AIR 1956 J&K 17.
31. *S. Mubarik Shah Naqishbandi v The Income Tax Office*: AIR 1971 J&K 120 at p. 123.
32. See Hingorani, N.H. 1995. 'Kashmir Insurgency: Misconception in Geneva', *The Indian Express*, New Delhi, 24 October.

33. Cited in Jha, C.S. 1995. 'Self-determination II: State has the last word', *The Indian Express*, New Delhi, 16 May.
34. *Supra* Note 32.
35. S/PV 1608 at p. 24, Kulaga (Poland), 6 December 1971.
36. S/PV 1611 at pp. 18–19, Z.A. Bhutto (Pakistan), 12 December 1971. Also see S/PV 1613 at p. 28, Z.A. Bhutto (Pakistan), 13 December 1971.
37. Cited in *The Times of India*. 1995. 'Kashmiris have no right to self-determination: UK expert', New Delhi, 25 May.
38. Ibid.
39. *Supra* Note 100, Chapter IV, p. 274.
40. Ibid., pp. 288–288a.
41. Ibid., p. 288a
42. Ibid., p. 296.
43. For a list of pledges made by New Delhi in this regard, see *Supra* Note 3, pp. 124–131.
44. *Supra* Note 100, Chapter IV, p. 292.
45. Ibid., p. 294.
46. Ibid., pp. 299–300.
47. *Supra* Note 28, Chapter IV, pp. 53, 55.
48. Ibid., p. 55.
49. Ibid., pp. 61–62.
50. Ibid.
51. For text, see ibid., pp. 65–67.
52. *Supra* Note 100, Chapter IV, pp. 336–337.
53. *Supra* Note 28, Chapter IV, pp. 69, 71.
54. *Supra* Note 100, Chapter IV, pp. 349–350.
55. *Supra* Note 1, Introduction.
56. Gautier, Francois. 1999. 'Losing the PR battle', *Hindustan Times*, New Delhi, 15 June.
57. *Hindustan Times*. 1998. '1949 Pact gave one-third Kashmir to Pak-BBC', New Delhi, 8 August.
58. Gandhi, Rajmohan. 2000. 'Drama, Beyond Statistics', *Hindustan Times*, New Delhi, 25 September.
59. Meraj, Zafar. 2001. 'Deciding Kashmir's future', *The Times of India*, New Delhi, 5 July.
60. Masani, Minoo. 1996. 'Case for Self-Determination', in *Supra* Note 34, Chapter IV, p. 99.
61. Mehera, S.K. 1998. 'Kashmir Issue–I', *The Statesman*, New Delhi, 7 July.
62. Noorani, A.G. 1997. 'UN & Kashmir–III', *The Statesman*, New Delhi, 30 July.
63. *Supra* Note 3, p. 6.
64. See *Supra* Note 12, Chapter IV, pp. 88–91.
65. *The Times of India*. 2000. 'Involve people of POK, J&K in talks: Lone', New Delhi, 9 October.
66. Ibid.
67. *The Times of India*. 2001. 'Pak has ditched Kashmiris: Yasin', New Delhi, 30 June.
68. See *Supra* Note 31, Chapter IV, p. 231.
69. *Sunday Times of India*. 2001. 'Should Kashmir be handled the Punjab way?', New Delhi, 29 July.
70. See *The Times of India*. 2001. 'Hurriyat to suspend stir ahead of summit', New Delhi, 11 June.
71. Extracted in *Supra* Note 3, pp. 79–80.

VI

Britain, Kashmir and Reference to the United Nations

It has been noted earlier that the PIS of J&K had, right from the beginning, engaged British strategists during the Great Game because of its geographical location. One of the factors that weighed with the British while demarcating areas that would comprise a reliable state, 'Pakistan', in the north-western region of colonial India was that the PIS of J&K would permanently remain within the British sphere of influence. It was assumed that the predominantly Muslim state would accede to Islamic Pakistan contiguous to it or at least remain independent and satisfy essential British interests.

The British and the Accession of the PIS of J&K to India

The accession of the PIS of J&K to the dominion of India on 26 October 1947 was simply inconvenient for the British. On 31 October 1947, the British Secretary of State for Commonwealth Relations, in an internal top-secret policy directive to the British High Commissioners in Delhi and Karachi, formulated the British view as under:[1]

> It would have been natural for Kashmir to eventually accede to Pakistan on agreed terms.... On the one hand Pakistan had connived at the tribal invasion into Kashmir, 'supplied artillery and transport' for the same and on the other India had made 'provocative mistakes' in accepting Kashmir's accession since that was not really required for sending military help (to prevent tribal depredations) ... had not consulted Pakistan and [had] used Sikh troops.

While the British had secured the Northern Areas of the state as detailed earlier, there remained the danger of India going to war with Pakistan to vacate the tribal invasion. That was to be avoided at all cost. For Britain to use the Northern Areas of the state, along with the NWFP and other frontier outposts, for the Great Game, Pakistan had to survive. These areas also had to be free of Indian control. War between India and Pakistan over the PIS of J&K at that time could have liquidated Pakistan and defeated the very rationale of partition of the Indian subcontinent. The British had to outwit the Indian leadership yet again to ensure that New Delhi was not able to vacate the Pakistani invasion in the PIS of J&K, and that the two areas of the state marked by the British to be kept free from Indian control remained free of such control, notwithstanding that these areas had legally become part of the dominion of India.

The British first had to scuttle the legal effect of the accession. Sarila documents that the British Prime Minister Attlee wired to Liaquat Ali Khan on 31 October 1947 that:[2]

> If in the talks with the Indians [scheduled for the next day] there was agreement that accession 'is not to prejudice in any way the ultimate decision of the future of Kashmir...[then Liaquat] and Jinnah would make such appeal in the way you will know best to ensure those not immediately under your control may fully weigh your counsel to them'.

Sarila notes that this was 'an extraordinarily convoluted way of referring to the tribesmen in order to absolve Pakistan of blame for the invasion' and that the message was clear—'If there was no agreement and if India used the Instrument of Accession to justify its position in Kashmir, you stay put (do not pull back the tribals)'.[3]

The next step was to check the advance of the Indian Army to vacate the tribal-led invasion. Inter-dominion war between India and Pakistan had also to be ruled out. It is important to emphasize here that both India and Pakistan existed as dominions from 1947 onwards until the promulgation of their individual constitutions in 1950 and 1956, respectively. Thus, both dominions, even after independence, retained the British monarch as a ceremonial head of state, who was generally represented in the dominion by a Governor General. Accordingly, George VI, King of the United Kingdom, who had been 'Emperor of India', now acted as the 'King of India' as also as the 'King of Pakistan' during the dominion phase. While George VI ceased to be the King of India in 1950, he remained King of Pakistan until his death in 1952. His then 26-year-old daughter, Elizabeth Alexandra Mary, or Elizabeth II, succeeded him as the Queen of Pakistan till 1956.

Further, neither dominion had yet established full control of their respective armies so as to be able to act speedily with decisive results. It was British officers which were heading the armies in both the dominions, with General Roy Bucher being the Acting Commander-in-Chief of the Indian Army and General Doughlas Gracey being the Acting Commander-in-Chief of the Pakistan Army, and who were both reporting to the British government. In fact, when Jinnah learnt of the accession of the PIS of J&K to India on 26 October 1947, he directed Gracey to rush regular troops to the state. The British Supreme Commander, Field Marshall Claude Auchinleck, fearing inter-dominion war, flew into Lahore on 28 October 1947 and threatened to pull out British troops from the Pakistan Army, if Pakistan did not cancel its orders to Gracey to send in regular troops into the PIS of J&K.[4] Mountbatten describes the situation as under:[5]

> [Jinnah] exploded with rage. He called General [F.W.] Messervy and told him, 'This is going too far, we shall have to declare war. We'll have to invade Kashmir and throw the Indians out'.
>
> Messervy said, 'You realise this will mean real war?'
>
> 'Yes'.
>
> 'I must warn you that this will entail severe repercussions and I must report this to the Supreme Commander,' Messervy said. He then called Auchinleck who said 'You will not take Jinnah's order to advance into Kashmir until he appreciates that the moment he invades, every British officer now serving in the Pakistan army must be stood down before the order is given'. Auchinleck reported this to me. It stopped the war in its tracks'.

The two British Generals, heading the Indian and Pakistani armies, felt free to make their own private arrangements, of course with consent from London at every stage. Hodson records that:[6]

> One extraordinary aspect of the situation was that the armies of both nations were commanded by British officers (Generals Bucher and Gracey) who were in direct personal touch and had [even] come close to arranging a qualified *de facto truce* at the end of March....

The fact that it was the British General Bucher heading the Indian Army came in handy for the British to ensure that Bucher stopped the advance of his own army. Bucher had no compunctions in indicating to Gracey that he would try to get the Indian troops withdrawn from Poonch,[7] and that:[8]

> '[H]e had no wish to pursue an offense into what is effectively Azad Kashmir-controlled territory, i.e., to Mirpur and Poonch sector' and that.... The

object of these arrangements is to reach a situation in which each side will remain in undisputed military occupation of what are roughly their present positions.... An essential part of the process ... is that three battalions of the Pakistan army should be employed in Kashmir opposite the India forces at Jhangar in or around Poooch and at Uri.... The Pakistan Prime Minister is aware of the exchanges I have reported above, but I understand he feels unable at present to endorse this officially'.

That Mountbatten had a considerable hold over Nehru is well documented. Indeed, if Mountbatten is to be believed, Nehru and Patel handed independent India back to Mountbatten in the wake of the Punjab conflagration and violent scenes in Delhi. In his interview to Larry Collins and Dominique Lapierre, Mountbatten recounts how he was asked to urgently return to Delhi from Simla and discloses the conversation he says he had with Nehru and Patel, the 'chastened schoolboys', as under:[9]

The thing was deteriorating and they said, 'We don't know how to hold it'. I said, 'Why not? You have taken over power'. And Nehru said, 'While you were exercising the highest command in the war, we were in prison. You're a professional, a high level administrator. We're not amateurs, we just know nothing. You can't turn over this country to us, having stayed with us all our lives with all your knowledge and experience, then leave us, without any experience or knowledge how to do it. Will you run the country?.... You must understand.... You've got to take it. We'll do whatever you say. We'll be more obedient than when you were Viceroy. Please, take over the country'.

I said, 'Well, look, it's terrible, for if it were known that you'd turned over the country to me, you'd be finished. You'd be a laughing stock. The Indians keep back the British Viceroy and then turn the country back to him? This is out of the question!'

They said, 'Well, we may find ways of disguising this, but if you don't do it, we can't manage it'.

'All right', I said, very reluctantly. 'I'll do it, and of course, I can pull the country together because I do know how to do it, but I think you must all agree that nobody must know about this. Nobody must know that you have made this extravagant offer to me, or these requests; we shall find a solution which will be done in such a way that it will appear to be constitutionally normal, correct and proper'.

Mountbatten goes on to disclose that this 'constitutionally normal, correct and proper' solution was to set up an 'Emergency Committee' in the Indian Cabinet, which Mountbatten would chair, with Nehru sitting on his right and Patel on his left. Mountbatten was to go through the motions of consulting Nehru and Patel, who were to simply accept the decisions taken by Mountbatten. Mountbatten, in his interview to Larry Collins and Dominique Lapierre, details his exchange with Nehru and Patel as under:[10]

'So you two will ask me to set up an Emergency Committee in the Cabinet, and I will agree. Will you do that?'

'Yes'.

'All right. You've asked me. I will take the chair because you invite me to?'

'Yes, we invite you'.

'The Emergency Committee will consist of the people I will nominate'.

'Oh, we must have the whole Cabinet!'

'The whole Cabinet?' I said, 'It would be disastrous. I don't want your odds and sods, I just want the key people. And I want the Director of Civil Aviation, the Director of Railways'.

'You can have the Minister'.

I said, 'I don't want the Minister at all, I want the civil servants who are doing it. I want the Chief of Police, I want the head of the Indian medical services, I want my wife, who will immediately set up a council for all the voluntary organisations, and she will represent them. The Secretary will be General Erskine-Crum, my Conference Secretary. The minutes will be kept by British stenographers. They will be typed in the course of the meeting and handed to people as they go away and be acted on at once. In every case, you invite me to do this'.

'Yes, we invite you'.

'Nobody will know that you asked me to tell you what to do. All you're doing is you've left me in the chair. The Prime Minister sits on my right, the Deputy on my left, and every time I'll always go through the motions of consulting you, and whatever I say, you're not going to argue with me, we haven't got time. I'll say, 'I'm sure you wish me to do this,' and you'll say, 'Yes, please'. That's all I want. I don't want you to say anything else'.

Patel said, 'Well, can't we have …'

I said, 'Not if you're going to delay things. You can go through the motions of arguing with me so long as you finally do what I say. Do you want me to run the country or are you going to try and make a mess of it yourself?'

'Ah, all right', he said. 'You run the country'.

Incredulous as it may seem, Mountbatten used to routinely send reports to the King in the UK, post India's independence, detailing the happenings in New Delhi, as also the decisions and policies of the Indian Cabinet. Hodson records that:[11]

> According to [Mountbatten's] own report to H.M. the King, after a Cabinet meeting on 6th September Nehru told him that it had unanimously been decided that an Emergency Committee of the Cabinet should be set up and invited him to take the chair ... the Indian leaders, conscious that the situation had got beyond their inexperienced capabilities, asked the Governor-General in effect to cease from being purely constitutional and to assist in governing: 'hoping that he will grip the situation ... enlist his active and overriding authority'. While he had been attaining experience of emergency administration at the highest level, said Pandit Nehru, his Ministers had been in prison.... Lord Mountbatten ... offered the device of an Emergency Committee over which he would preside.... The plan was immediately accepted....

> The Committee met daily in Government House, with Pandit Nehru on the Governor-General's right and Sardar Patel on his left. Lord Mountbatten's secretariat under Colonel Erskine Crum kept the minutes and issued instant instructions in writing on the Committee's authority.... The Committee's instructions were never questioned.

Hodson documents that Mountbatten, 'as Chairman of the Emergency Committee of the Indian Cabinet ... was deeply involved in the formation and execution of a policy'.[12] Such policy was duly communicated to the British; Hodson details Mountbatten's report to the King five days later on 11 September 1947, describing what had transpired at the meeting, the decisions taken and the orders issued to the minutest detail.[13]

The matter did not end there. Hodson records that:[14]

> .... Lord Mountbatten proposed, and it was at once accepted, that there be set up a Defence Committee of the Cabinet.... The Cabinet invited Lord Mountbatten ... to become Chairman of the Defence Committee, and to this he agreed without hesitation or reluctance.... In the vital field of defence he now presided over the formation of policy and became committed to its consequences.

> [Further] the Joint Defence Council was set up to complete the division [between India and Pakistan] of the Armed Forces and their plant, equipment and stores; to control the general administration, discipline, pay, food, clothing and medical services of the Armed Forces for an interim period; and to control any forces overseas and any force operating under joint command in disturbed areas near the new frontiers.... By invitation of both India and Pakistan, [Mountbatten] was also chairman of their Joint Defence Council....

… and as Chairman of the Joint Defence Council he could and did bring to bear upon Indian policy, through his Chairmanship of the Indian Defence Committee, a moderating or impartial influence in the interests of peace and co-operation between the two Dominions.

Indeed, as Mountbatten himself asserted to the King, he, by his 'own physical presence as the Governor-General of India was the best insurance against the actual outbreak of war with Pakistan'.[15]

It is crucial to note here that it was the Defence Committee of the Indian Cabinet that decided the Kashmir war policy, and not the Indian Cabinet as a whole.[16] Accordingly, 'all the key decisions of the Government of India about Kashmir at the end of October 1947 were taken under the leadership of the Governor-General, for they were decisions in terms of defence against the tribal invasion'.[17] And since Mountbatten chaired the Defence Committee of the Indian Cabinet, he could support Bucher, the acting British Commander-in-Chief of the Indian Army, in opposing the plan of General Kulwant Singh, GOC, Kashmir Operations in November 1947 to clear the territory of the PIS of J&K of the Pakistani invasion.[18]

While Mountbatten sought to 'neutralize' Indian military initiatives,[19] Attlee urged Nehru, the first Prime Minister of independent India, to desist from armed intervention in the PIS of J&K, opining that it would only aggravate the problem and lead to an open military conflict between India and Pakistan.[20] Attlee even raised doubts on the legality of armed intervention by India to resist Pakistan's invasion. Nehru had written to Mountbatten that under 'international law we can in self-defence take any military measures to resist it [the invasion], including sending our armies across Pakistan to attack their bases near the Kashmir border'.[21] Attlee wrote to Nehru that he 'was gravely disturbed by [Nehru's] assumption that India would be within her rights in international law if she were to send forces to Pakistan in self-defence'.[22]

It is necessary to recall here that the PIS of J&K had acceded to India in terms of the British statutes that were binding on the British government. As per the British statutes, the PIS of J&K had become part of India. Each country has the right under international law to protect its own territory. Attlee's incredulous and legally untenable view was evidently intended to ensure that New Delhi did not disturb Pakistan's control over the two areas of the state earmarked by the British to be vital for British interests.

Following the accession, the British had also mooted to New Delhi, as early as November 1947, the idea of partition of the PIS of J&K, which would have left the part of the state crucial for British interests with Pakistan. Nehru, in his letter to Krishna Menon, the then Indian High Commissioner in the UK, on 20 February 1948, recorded that:[23]

The British attitude, to begin with, that is six months ago was definitely in favour of Kashmir going to Pakistan. Subsequently, they have talked of partition, meaning thereby that Jammu should come to India and Kashmir Valley and the rest should go to Pakistan. That is totally unacceptable to us. The real bone of contention is the Kashmir Valley. Even Mountbatten has at various times hinted at partition. Recent suggestions referred to the Poonch-Mirpur area being added on to Pakistan while Kashmir Valley, Jammu etc., might remain with India....

In fact, in May 1948, Mountbatten tried to get Pakistan's Prime Minister to visit New Delhi to discuss partition. Maps were marked and discussed with Nehru and the Chief of Army Staff, but Liaquat Ali did not come.[24] Hodson quotes from Mountbatten's report to the King as under:[25]

The solution of the Kashmir problem which I could have backed, if Liaquat Ali Khan had come, would have been based on the partition of the State. At my request Mr. Gopalaswami Ayyangar and Mr. V.P. Menon had worked out a compromise which they said that the Indian cabinet would accept if Mr. Liaquat Ali Khan put it up. It was my intention to have suggested to Mr. Liaquat Ali Khan that he should put this forward as a proposal....

Indeed, Mountbatten often used his influence to weigh on New Delhi to concede on issues that would otherwise adversely affect Pakistan, the British creation. Hodson writes about Mountbatten's intervention with regard to the division of the cash assets of pre-partition Government of India as under:[26]

.... Rs 20 crores had been allocated to Pakistan as a preliminary cash balance.... Pakistan's share of the cash assets was fixed at Rs 75 crores, of which, therefore, Rs 55 crores remained to be paid.... In the middle of December, however, the Government of India decided not to implement the various financial agreements until there was a settlement on Kashmir. This policy, of which warning had been given, was particularly sponsored by Sardar Patel but was endorsed by Pandit Nehru and the whole Cabinet.... On 12th January ... [t]he Governor-General told [Gandhi] that he viewed it as unstatesmanlike and unwise, and as the only conscious act taken, to his knowledge, by the Government of India which he regarded as dishonourable....

.... The next day Lord Mountbatten saw Sardar Patel and to him also he used the word 'dishonourable'. Patel protested. Clear notice had been given to Pakistan, within two hours of the meeting at which the cash agreement had been reached, that India intended to link implementation with a settlement in Kashmir. If the Government of Pakistan had not accepted this caveat it would not have signed, several days later, a letter withdrawing the various financial matters from the Arbitral Tribunal. Lord Mountbatten withdrew the word 'dishonourable', while doubling his emphasis on 'unstatesmanship and unwise', and passed a message to this effect to Mahatma Gandhi. The latter's approach to Pandit Nehru and Sardar Patel proved irresistible during a fast in which his life was in danger, and which he declined to break until they adopted the 'honourable' course towards the cash balances. On 16th December the Government of India decided to pass orders releasing the Rs 55 crores to Pakistan.... It was widely believed that Mr. Gandhi's fast had been the leverage of pressure on the Government; so this righting of a palpable wrong may well have been a proximate cause of his assassination by a rabid Hindu extremist.

Hodson gives another instance of how Mountbatten intervened to protect Pakistan's interests:[27]

> The ... incident concerned canal waters ... when [the interim agreement] expired [on 31st March 1948] East Punjab Government shut off the water, arguing that the Ministers from West Punjab had failed to come to frame a new agreement, that the water should be paid for, and that in any case they needed most of it for themselves. At a meeting of Ministerial representatives from India and Pakistan on 3rd May, Dr. Ambedkar, for India, insisted that no water could be supplied until Pakistan accepted India's legal claim that all the water belonged to East Punjab, who had the right to do with it as they wished. The chief Pakistan representative, Mr. Ghulam Mohammed, came to see Lord Mountbatten after the meeting had broken down on this point. The Governor General immediately phoned Pandit Nehru and expressed his disgust that miserable peasants and refugees were being made to suffer when the matter was still under negotiation. Pandit Nehru agreed and undertook ... to break the deadlock.

British Strategy Post the Accession of the PIS of J&K

I believe that following the accession of the sovereign PIS of J&K to the dominion of India, the British were keen for Pakistan to get some standing in the PIS of J&K, and for that it was imperative that Pakistani presence be recognized in the PIS of J&K. Further, international weight was needed to be brought upon New Delhi to let go of the PIS of J&K or to at least partition the state so as to let Pakistan keep the strategic northern part of it so necessary for British interests. The simplest way to do so was to involve the

UNSC in the matter. In order to appreciate the reason for this, one needs to refer to the practice that had evolved in the League of Nations since the 1920s that in the event of a conflict, the League would immediately issue a 'ceasefire' order in order to maintain international peace. If the parties to the conflict accepted such order, peace would be restored. If one party refused, that party would have itself branded as the aggressor and would invite immediate measures against it. This practice, which put the aggressor on a par with the victim, had the advantage that it did not involve identifying any state as an aggressor at the outset. However, if the ceasefire order was not followed, it provided a clear criterion for determining against whom action would follow. As Wright[28] points out, a state which refused to comply with such order was likely to be regarded not only as an aggressor, but as dangerous, by third states, who would take an immediate interest in acting to suppress it. He notes that this method proved effective in the history of the League, especially in the Greco-Bulgarian dispute of 1925, the Mosul issue of 1925, the Shanghai affair of 1932 and the Leticia issue of 1932.[29]

The UN, the successor organization to the League of Nations, was set up on 24 October 1945, and was virtually run by the US, Britain and China at that time. Sheikh Abdullah asserts that 'three out of its five permanent members were in full control of the United Nations—the United States, Great Britain and China', and while 'Britain usually followed in the footsteps of the United States', the 'US paid attention to the advice of Great Britain since she had ruled over India for about 200 years and was well-acquainted with her innards'.[30] Pakistan's former Foreign Minister Khurshid Mahmud Kasuri agrees with the assessment that the US had 'a special relationship with the UK and consulted it regularly on issues concerning South Asia'. [31]

I believe that the British were well aware that once the UNSC got involved in the PIS of J&K, they could ensure—and did ensure, as will be evident later—that the UNSC would issue a ceasefire order *without first requiring the Pakistani aggression to be vacated* and would place India on the same footing as Pakistan—which it did—and that if India thereafter sought to wrestle back the strategic territory of the PIS of J&K illegally occupied by Pakistan through aggression, India would have paradoxically been termed as the aggressor. Simply put, by involving the UNSC, the British would make sure that Pakistan got to retain de facto control over the strategic territory of the PIS of J&K that it had occupied and that India got reduced to a mere spectator, making occasional impotent protests at the overt annexation of such territory by Pakistan and the subsequent impudent cession by Pakistan of 2000 square miles of the occupied territory of the PIS of J&K to China under the Sino-Pakistan Boundary Agreement of 2 March 1963.[32] This gift of Indian territory to China by Pakistan was in addition to the territory of the PIS of J&K that China had occupied in military intrusions in 1953 and another 6000 square miles of territory, known as Aksai Chin, which China quietly occupied in 1959.[33] As of date, China—which does not have even a semblance of claim to the PIS of J&K—holds about 20 per cent of the territory of the PIS of J&K.[34]

It may be recalled that the division of the conquered Ottoman lands between the British and French was routed through the League of Nations, the forerunner to the UN. This was evidently done to confer legitimacy upon the modern political map of the Middle East. The British now apparently sought to route the division of the PIS of J&K through the UNSC, whose ceasefire line would effectively partition the state, leaving the crucial areas occupied by Pakistan undisturbed for British interests.

The only hitch in this British strategy was to somehow get New Delhi to agree to involve the UNSC. Just as responsibility for the partition of the Indian subcontinent was to be put squarely on Indian shoulders, the proposal to involve the UNSC in the PIS of J&K must emanate from New Delhi. Let us, at this stage, refer to the relevant provisions of the UN Charter.

Chapter V of the UN Charter pertains to the UNSC, and confers, in Article 24(1), upon the UNSC the 'primary responsibility for the maintenance of international peace and security'. Article 24(2) provides that '[i]n discharging these duties the Security Council shall act in accordance with the Purposes and Principles of the United Nations' and that the 'specific powers granted to the Security Council for the discharge of these duties are laid down in Chapters VI, VII, VIII, and XII'. The International Court of Justice (the ICJ) has, in *Namibia*,[35] construed the powers of the UNSC under Article 24 as under:

110.... The reference in paragraph 2 of (Article 24) to specific powers of the Security Council under certain chapters of the Charter does not exclude the existence of general powers to discharge the responsibilities conferred in paragraph 1. Reference may be made in this respect to the Secretary-General's Statement, presented to the Security Council on 10 January 1947, to the effect that 'the powers of the Council under Article 24 are not restricted to the specific grants of authority contained in Chapters VI, VII, VIII and XII ... the Members of the United Nations have conferred upon the Security Council powers commensurate with its responsibility for the maintenance of peace and security. The only limitations are the fundamental principles and purposes found in Chapter 1 of the Charter'.

Further, Article 25 states that '[t]he Members of the United Nations agree to accept and carry out the decisions of the Security Council in accordance with the present Charter'.

Chapter VI of the UN Charter provides for the 'Pacific Settlement of Disputes'. Article 34(1) enables the UNSC to 'investigate any dispute, or any situation which might lead to international friction or give rise to a dispute, in order to determine whether the continuance of the dispute or situation is likely to endanger the maintenance of international peace and security'. Article 35(1) states that '[a]ny Member of the United Nations may bring any dispute, or any situation of the nature referred to in Article 34, to the attention of the Security Council or of the General Assembly'.

Article 33 requires that the 'parties to any dispute, the continuance of which is likely to endanger the maintenance of international peace and security, shall, first of all, seek a solution by negotiation, enquiry, mediation, conciliation, arbitration, judicial settlement, resort to regional agencies or arrangements, or other peaceful means of their own choice'.

Article 36(1) empowers the UNSC to recommend 'at any stage of a dispute of the nature referred to in Article 33 or of a situation of like nature … appropriate procedures or methods of adjustment'. Article 36(2) states that the UNSC 'should take into consideration any procedures for the settlement of the dispute which have already been adopted by the parties'.

An obvious legal infirmity in invoking these provisions would be that it was irregular tribal raiders who had invaded the PIS of J&K, and such irregular raiders, even though sponsored by Pakistan, could not be treated in law to be a 'state', which could then be dragged to the UN or be made party to a dispute or be subject to a ceasefire order. The British strategized that should New Delhi purport to act under Article 35(1) of the UN Charter to bring to the notice of the UNSC the tribal invasion into the PIS of J&K, the UNSC would wink at such infirmity, and assume the jurisdiction to investigate the matter. The UNSC could then exercise its general power under Article 24(1) to pass the ceasefire order, without requiring Pakistan to first vacate the aggression, and to require New Delhi to accept and carry it out in terms of Article 25. Pakistan would thereafter move regular troops into the state—which it did—to consolidate the occupation of the areas crucial for British interests.

Further, should New Delhi assert, and Pakistan accept, that the accession of the PIS of J&K to India or Pakistan was required to be decided by the people of the state through a plebiscite or referendum, the UNSC could simply ask New Delhi to proceed to hold such plebiscite under international auspices on the terms formulated by the UNSC so as to ensure the 'impartiality' of the plebiscite. This would, after all, be a procedure 'for the settlement of the dispute' in terms of Article 36(2) of the UN Charter. Pakistan would thus get the standing in what would become the Kashmir issue, while the PIS of J&K would be conferred with a 'disputed territory' status.[36] In fact, Pakistan's former Foreign Minister Khurshid Mahmud Kasuri admits that 'the legal basis of our position on Kashmir' was provided by the fact that it was put on 'the UN agenda'.[37]

The question before the British now was to get New Delhi to act in terms of Article 35(1) of the UN Charter and to commit to hold a plebiscite in the PIS of J&K under international auspices. It is here that the policy of the Congress on disputed accessions of princely Indian states—namely, 'the people of the states must have a dominating voice in any decisions regarding them' became helpful. Should New Delhi agree to a plebiscite to ascertain the wishes of the Kashmiri people, the British (and Pakistan) could insist that such plebiscite be held under international auspices (read, the UNSC) to ensure its neutrality. Indeed, Mountbatten's draft letter of 10 February 1948 to Nehru, which, while referring to the reply from Attlee to the telegram he had sent on 8 February 1948, stated as under:[38]

> Mr Attlee is firm in his belief that it will not be possible to convince the majority of the members of the Security Council that plebiscite in Kashmir is going to be a fair one if it is held under the existing administration and while the State is still occupied only by Indian troops. Furthermore, he points out that the promise of a plebiscite under these conditions is not likely to enable the Pakistan Government to convince either their own people, or the tribesmen (whom they have to convince before they can induce them to withdraw), that it would be fair.... It is only by reaching an agreement on how fair a plebiscite—and above all a plebiscite that will look fair in the eyes of the world—can be held, that the whole problem will be solved....

Mountbatten's Role

Mountbatten, the representative of the British Crown, played a pivotal role in giving effect to the afore-mentioned British strategy. Just as Mountbatten had, as the Viceroy of India, outwitted the Indian leadership to gift away the Congress-ruled NWFP to Pakistan, he, as India's Governor General after independence and Chair of the Defence Committee of the Indian Cabinet, was to restrain New Delhi from recovering the crucial northern part of the PIS of J&K from Pakistan so that such territory remained under British influence.

It will be recalled that the British had wanted the PIS of J&K to accede to Pakistan, and that Mountbatten had tried his best to dissuade the sovereign ruler of the state from acceding to the dominion of India, emphasizing that the majority of the population in the state was Muslim. Sarila documents that Mountbatten met the Prime Minister of the PIS of J&K as late as 10 October 1947 to inform him that if the state acceded to India against the wishes of the majority of the population 'such a step would not only mean immense trouble for Kashmir but might also lead to trouble for the dominion of India' and that '[w]hatever the future of Kashmir, a plebiscite must be the first step'.[39]

Earlier, in September 1947, Gandhi had approached Mountbatten with a suggestion that the British Prime Minister Attlee be requested to mediate between India and Pakistan to avert a clash between the two countries as a result of the Punjab happenings. Gandhi wanted Attlee to ascertain 'in the best manner he knows who is overwhelmingly in the wrong and then withdraw every British officer in the service of the wrong party'.[40] Mountbatten wrote that '[a]n alternative means is to ask the UNO to undertake this enquiry and you will have no difficulty in getting Pakistan to agree to this'.[41]

As discussed earlier, the Junagadh issue had arisen prior to the question of the accession of the PIS of J&K, and Mountbatten in his own report to the King had detailed how he had 'emphasized' New Delhi's policy on disputed accessions to Liaquat Ali Khan, and assured him that New Delhi would never be party to trying to force a state (read the PIS of J&K) to join India against the wishes of the majority of the people.[42]

Mountbatten discloses in an interview to Larry Collins and Dominique Lapierre that he got the first news of tribesmen sweeping down into Kashmir at a reception on 23 October 1947. Though Mountbatten himself had explained to the King that '[i]t would still be correct to send troops at request to a friendly neighbouring country even if it did not accede ...',[43] Mountbatten recounts in the interview that:[44]

> I went straight to Nehru and said, 'This is a very serious situation. Let's look at it, let's face it. Kashmir is an independent place. We have no right to go to its defence.... You cannot intervene at the request of the Maharaja unless in fact he accedes....'

The obvious reason for Mountbatten to raise the question of accession at that point of time was to delay intervention by New Delhi in the PIS of J&K, so as to enable the raiders to overrun the state.

As noted earlier, the Defence Committee of the Indian Cabinet took decisions on the Kashmir war policy, and Nehru had, notwithstanding India having attained independence, let Mountbatten, the representative of the British Crown, chair this Defence Committee. It was Mountbatten who again insisted at the Emergency Meeting of the Defence Committee that New Delhi should accept the request of the PIS of J&K for assistance only after Raja Hari Singh accedes to the dominion of India. In his words:[45]

> When it was decided to send troops, I said, 'You cannot do it until Kashmir is part of India. You can only do it, therefore, if he accedes. If he doesn't I shall have to advise you, you are not entitled to send troops in…'.

Hodson records that at the Emergency Meeting of the Defence Committee on 25 October 1947:[46]

> …. The Governor-General suggested as a possible solution that Kashmir might temporarily accede to India, which would come to its aid, subject to the proviso that the will of the people should be ascertained as soon as law and order was generally restored…. Sardar Vallabhbhai Patel said he saw nothing to prevent India from sending armed assistance whether or not Kashmir acceded, and Pandit Nehru agreed…. The Defence Committee … directed the Secretary of the Ministry of States, Mr. V.P. Menon, to fly to Srinagar….

Mountbatten further reveals in his interview that by the time Menon returned to Delhi from the PIS of J&K with the Instrument of Accession duly executed by its ruler, Mountbatten had made up his 'mind how to handle it'.[47] He states that:[48]

> I said to Nehru, Here's the instrument of accession. As a Constitutional Governor-General, I'll only sign it at your request. *But I also added, 'I'll only countersign it on condition you offer a plebiscite'.* Then we discussed the plebiscite. Nehru made one stipulation to which I agreed. That this could only be done in peaceful conditions, with the tribesmen withdrawn…. [emphasis added]

Thus, by Mountbatten's own disclosure, it was he who required Nehru to 'offer a plebiscite' before he (Mountbatten) accepted the accession on New Delhi's behalf. In his interview to Larry Collins and Dominique Lapierre, Mountbatten reiterates time and again that 'I urged (Nehru) to have a plebiscite to decide which way Kashmir wanted to go. He immediately agreed, with the proviso we mentioned earlier'.[49] Hodson records that 'Mountbatten suggested that this plebiscite should be on three choices: to join India, to join Pakistan, or to remain independent'.[50]

It was accordingly at Mountbatten's instance that the Defence Committee, on the accession of the PIS of J&K on 26 October 1947, decided that New Delhi would accept the accession 'provisionally' subject to its 'declared policy that such matters should be finalised in accordance with the will of the people'.[51] It was Mountbatten, who followed the acceptance of the Instrument of Accession of Raja Hari Singh with the covering letter of 27 October 1947, expressing the 'wish' of the Government of India that as soon as 'law and order have been restored and the soil cleared of the invader the question of the State's accession should be settled by a reference to the people'. And it was Mountbatten, who would often 'negotiate' the possible resolution of the Kashmir situation on behalf of New Delhi with Pakistan.

Sarila records that Mountbatten, who had no authority from the Government of India to propose the induction of Pakistan's forces into the PIS of J&K, met Jinnah at Lahore on 1 November 1947, along with his Chief of Staff, Ismay, to commit on behalf of New Delhi that:[52]

> [I]t is the sincere desire of the Government of India that a plebiscite should be held in Kashmir at the earliest possible date and in the fairest possible way.... They suggest that UNO might be asked to provide supervisors for this plebiscite, and they are prepared to agree that a joint India-Pakistan force should hold the ring while the plebiscite is being held.

The cable dated 8 November 1947 sent by Nehru to Liaquat Ali Khan documents that Mountbatten had, on his return from Lahore, given Nehru a full account of the talks he had had with Jinnah and that:[53]

> Lord Mountbatten reported that Mr. Jinnah had expressed the view that there was no hope of a fair plebiscite under the present Kashmir authorities. To meet this point Lord Mountbatten had suggested that it could be conducted under the auspices of UNO.

Mountbatten held a meeting with Nehru and Liaquat Ali Khan in Delhi on 26 November 1947, in which he summarized the proposal for plebiscite to be held under the auspices of an independent body like the UN.[54]

Whenever the Indian leadership contemplated a full scale war against Pakistan to vacate Pakistani aggression in the PIS of J&K, Mountbatten intervened to suggest that alongside the preparation for such war, help should be sought from the UN since, in his opinion, India had a strong case. Mountbatten even mischievously asserted 'that the UN would promptly direct Pakistan to withdraw the raiders, which would make war unnecessary'.[55] When Nehru, at the meeting of the Defence Committee of the Indian Cabinet on 20 December 1947, spoke of striking at the invaders' camps and line of communication inside Pakistan, Mountbatten immediately intervened to suggest a reference to the UN, assuring Nehru that India had a 'cast-iron case'.[56] Earlier, at a meeting at the Government House, Lahore, on 8 December 1947, with Nehru, Sardar Baldev Singh, Gopalaswami Ayyangar, Liaquat Ali Khan and Ghulam Mohammad, Mountbatten undermined New Delhi's position by declaring that General Messervy (of Pakistan) 'had categorically assured him that Pakistan Army had not issued arms to the raiders',[57] that is, India's Governor General, in the presence of the Indian Prime Minister, virtually gave a clean chit to the Pakistan Army, which New Delhi had accused of engineering the tribal invasion into the PIS of J&K. Mountbatten admits he was privy to the communications between the British Commanders-in-Chief of India and Pakistan on the Kashmir war. In fact, in his record of his meeting with Nehru on 30 March 1948, Mountbatten notes that:[58]

> I told the Prime Minister I was aware of the exchange of telegrams between the two Dominion Commanders-in-Chief on the subject of the fighting in Kashmir.... I asked him if he minded my requesting General Bucher to send his complete file on this matter to me, and he replied, 'Certainly, of course'.

Right from the Pakistan-sponsored tribal invasion on 22 October 1947 till the time when a ceasefire was declared on 1 January 1949 that left occupied territories of the PIS of J&K under the de facto control of Pakistan (and thus of the British), Mountbatten managed to dis-engage the Indians in order to remove the military threat to Pakistan to vacate its aggression.[59]

It appears that Nehru himself was not entirely convinced about the role of the UN in the Kashmir affair. Liaquat Ali Khan, vide his Statement issued on 16 November 1947, had declared that Pakistan was:[60]

> [R]eady to request U.N.O to appoint its representative in Jammu and Kashmir State in order to put a stop to fighting and to the repression of Muslims in the State, to arrange the programme of withdrawal of outside forces, to set up an impartial administration of the State till a plebiscite is held and to undertake the plebiscite under its direction and control for the purpose of ascertaining the free and unfettered will of the people of the State on the question of accession.

Nehru, in his cable to Liaquat Ali Khan of 21 November 1947, responded as under:[61]

> .... The specific suggestions regarding the reference to the United Nations in your press statement are:

(i) 'That U.N.O. should immediately appoint representatives in Jammu and Kashmir State in order to put a stop to fighting, and to the repression of Muslims in the State'. Since United Nations have no (repeat no) forces at their disposal, we do not see how they can put a stop to the fighting or to the alleged repression of the Muslims. This can be done only by an organised military force, and is being done by our troops. The fighting would also stop as soon as the raiders withdraw and I have repeatedly asked your co-operation in stopping transit and supplies to the raiders through Pakistan territory.

(ii) 'To set up an impartial administration in the State'. It is not clear to me what U.N.O. can do in the present circumstances in Kashmir till peace and order have been established. We are convinced that Sheikh Abdullah's administration is based on the will of the people and is impartial. Anyone who goes to Kashmir and sees things for himself can appreciate this ...

(iii) 'To undertake the plebiscite under its direction and control for the purpose of ascertaining the free and unfettered will of the people of the State on the question of accession'. I have repeatedly stated that as soon as raiders have been driven out of Kashmir or have withdrawn and peace and order have been established, the people of Kashmir should decide the question of accession by plebiscite or referendum under international auspices such as those of the United Nations....

Again, the minutes of the meeting convened at Government House, Lahore, on 8 December 1947 by Mountbatten and attended by Nehru, Sardar Baldev Singh, Gopalaswami Ayyangar, Liaquat Ali Khan and Ghulam Mohammad, record that Mountbatten drew attention to the great benefits an approach to the UN would have and that time was devoted to efforts to induce Nehru to accept a reference to the UN. The record of what exactly transpired at that meeting is as under:[62]

.... His Excellency suggested that UNO should be asked to send out observers or advisers in some capacity to help the two Dominions solve the impasse which had reached. The UNO representatives could hold meetings with the two Prime Ministers. They could discuss the draft agreement, and ways and means of implementing it. They could set up a committee consisting of the principal contending parties in Kashmir. Would the two Governments agree in making a joint approach to the UNO or that one or other should make the approach?

.... Pandit Nehru said that he would entirely reject the idea. Only when hostilities had ceased was he prepared to ask UNO to send representatives for the plebiscite. The plebiscite only came into the picture when peace was restored.... Nearly all the rest of the time was devoted to efforts to induce Pandit Nehru to accept a reference to the UNO.

Pandit Nehru was extremely adamant. He went to the extremity of saying that he intended to clear Kashmir with the sword, whatever happened. He asked under what section of the Charter any reference to the UNO could be made. He asked how Pakistan came into the picture at all. He reiterated his insistence that the first step was to drive out the raiders.

His Excellency drew attention to the great benefits an approach to UNO would have. It was the only way to solve the present impasse, and stop the fighting…. Mr Liaquat Ali Khan reiterated that he would not mind in what manner the approach to the UNO was made. He would even agree that it should be in form of an accusation by India that Pakistan was assisting the raiders. He agreed with His Excellency that the first thing that the UNO Commission would probably do would be to ask Pakistan to use their influence to withdraw the raiders and stop further influxes. In these circumstances, his own position would be so immensely strengthened that he would be able to issue the appeal with impunity.

The position, as finally left, was that Pandit Nehru should examine the UN Charter and see if there was any way in which he could agree to a reference being made.

Nehru, in his cable of 12 December 1947 to Liaquat Ali Khan, stated as under:[63]

> We have given further thought … to the question of inviting the United Nations to advise us in this matter. While we are prepared to invite U.N.O. observers to come here and advise us as to the proposed plebiscite, it is not clear in what other capacity the United Nations' help can be sought. According to your own declaration to us you are not parties to the present struggle in Kashmir. We cannot treat with irregular invaders as a State….

Liaquat Ali Khan, in his cable of 16 December 1947 to Nehru, received on 17 December 1947, emphasized that:[64]

> The problem can be solved only by an act of statesmanship in light of the basic realities of the situation and not by legal disputations as to how Pakistan is party to dispute or how U.N.O. can be brought in….

A brief reference to the correspondence and notes of Nehru would confirm the manner in which Mountbatten had egged him on into making the reference to the UNSC, and to agree to hold the plebiscite under UN auspices in the PIS of J&K.

The Note of 19 December 1947 reflected the growing dismay of Nehru at the turn of events.[65] Nehru detailed in this Note how Pakistan was encouraging the raiders and how Pakistan Army officers and men were being 'given leave, known as Kashmir leave' to assist and fight with the raiders.[66] He recorded that 'there has been a progressive deterioration and the initiative appears to have been with the enemy most of the time' and that apart 'from the larger question of our whole approach to this Kashmir affair, it seems to me that our outlook has been defensive and apologetic, as if we were ashamed of what we were doing and we are not quite sure of how far we should go'.[67]

Yet, the minutes of the talks held two days later—on 21 December 1947—with Mountbatten and Liaquat Ali Khan recorded that it was Liaquat Ali Khan who was in a very chastened mood and eager for a settlement; a desire not normally associated with the winning side. Nehru disclosed that 'Lord Mountbatten referred to the great increase in the prestige of India all over the world if we could bring about a settlement' and that 'the settlement of course should essentially be on the lines we have repeatedly laid down i.e. reference to the U.N.O. to stop the fighting'.[68] Nehru wrote further that 'Lord Mountbatten said he agreed with that reference but could not we add to it that after law and order has been restored U.N.O. would supervise and carry out a plebiscite as we had previously declared?' and that 'Lord Mountbatten was anxious that I should somehow talk on the plebiscite in some form or other'.[69]

Mountbatten seemed to be in a tearing hurry that Nehru should refer the matter to the UN without much ado; in his Note dated 22 December 1947, Nehru recorded that during his meeting with Mountbatten on that day at New Delhi, the latter suggested to Nehru that he 'draft a formal application' to the UN, without even waiting for the reply of Liaquat Ali Khan to Nehru's letter of 22 December 1947, wherein India had officially called upon Pakistan to stop assisting the tribal invaders.[70]

This is how Mountbatten himself records his series of meetings with Nehru and Liaquat Ali Khan on 21 and 22 December 1947:[71]

Pandit Nehru and Mr Liaquat Ali Khan, December 21

.... I then proceeded to enlarge on how necessary it was to bring in UNO at the earliest possible moment to stop the fighting. I told Mr Liaquat Ali Khan that I had conveyed to Pandit Nehru his insistence that, once the UNO was brought in, it should deal with the whole problem of Kashmir, including the supervision of the plebiscite; and that Pandit Nehru had replied that the immediate appeal to bring about the cessation of the fighting could only be made to the Security Council, and that the Security Council was not competent to deal with the plebiscite. I pointed out that Pandit Nehru had accepted the fact that the discussions on the plebiscite, and the calling in of the UNO team for the plebiscite, would be the logical consequences of the stopping of the fight....

Pandit Nehru, Mr Liaquat Ali Khan, Mr Gopalaswami Ayyangar and Mr Mohammad Ali, December 22

.... Pandit Nehru reiterated that the reference which he intended to make to UNO would be on the question of whether or not Pakistan supported the aggression against Kashmir.... Pandit Nehru then handed to Mr Liaquat Ali Khan the letter, which represented the first step in making a reference to the UNO.... I suggested that Pandit Nehru should draft the formal application to UNO without waiting for Mr Liaquat Ali Khan's reply....

Mountbatten, by his letter dated 25 December 1947 to Nehru, opined that it would be 'a fatal illusion to believe that war between India and Pakistan could be confined to the subcontinent or be finished off quickly in favour of India without further complications; and that embroilment in war with Pakistan would undermine the whole of Nehru's independent policy and progressive social aspirations.[72] Mountbatten reiterated that 'surely the main object should rather be to bring U.N.O. here ... to get a team nominated to come out and deal with the business and help to stop the fighting...'.[73] Nehru finally gave in to Mountbatten's pressure to refer the matter to the UN, as recorded in his letter dated 26 December 1947 to Mountbatten.[74] In this letter, Nehru wrote as under:[75]

The present situation is that the Frontier Province and a considerable part of west Punjab have been turned into military training grounds where vast numbers of tribesmen, ex-service men and others are being armed and trained and then sent on to invade Kashmir. The resources of Pakistan are being employed to this end ... the only inference to draw from this is that the invasion of Kashmiris is not an accidental affair resulting from the fanaticism or exuberance of the tribesmen, but a well-organised business with the backing of the State....

From the strictly legal and constitutional point of view it is our right and our duty to resist this invasion with all our forces. From the point of view of international law we can in self-defence take any military measures to resist it, including the sending of our armies across Pakistan territory to attack their bases near the Kashmir border.

My conclusion is that we should immediately proceed along two parallel lines of action:

1. Reference to the U.N.O....
2. Complete military preparations to meet any possible contingency that might arise. If grave danger threatens us in Kashmir or elsewhere on the West Punjab frontier then we must not hesitate to march through Pakistan territory towards the bases.

Interestingly, Nehru wrote to Patel on 29 December 1947, stating that '[a]mong the consequences [of war] to consider are the possible effect on the British Officers in the Army and also the reaction of the Governor-General'.[76]

Mountbatten's role in the Kashmir affair did not end with New Delhi making the reference, which was communicated to the UNSC on 1 January 1948. Rather, he continued, post the reference, to influence New Delhi's Kashmir policy. Before examining such role, it will be useful to note the steps taken by the British to make the US fall in line with its strategy, given that the Americans, along with the British and Chinese, ran the UN at that point of time.

Handling the Americans

On the eve of the reference to the UNSC, Archibald Carter, the Permanent Under Secretary of the Commonwealth Relations Office, summoned the US *chargé d'affaires* to say that 'Prime Minister [Attlee] is disturbed by GOI assumption [that] GOI will be within its rights in international law … to move forces into Pakistan in self-defence', that the 'Prime Minister doubts whether it is in fact juridically correct and is afraid that it would be fatal from every other point of view' and 'whether U.S. Government would be willing to instruct the U.S. Embassy in Delhi to approach Nehru immediately, and without reference to the Nehru–Attlee correspondence, advise him "not to take any rash action such as invading Pakistan territory which would also prejudice irretrievably world opinion against India's case"'.[77]

The British transferred Ismay from Delhi in January 1948 to act as the Principal Adviser to the Commonwealth Secretary, Noel-Baker, so as to give effect to the British policy at the UN.[78] The other British officer involved was General Geoffrey Scoones, the Principal Staff Officer of Noel-Baker, who had been reportedly privy to Pakistan's designs in respect of the tribal invasion of Kashmir.[79] Sarila records that:[80]

> Noel-Baker, accompanied by the two generals, reached New York hard on the heels of the Indian complaint lodged at the UN [on 1 January 1948]. Their first call was on Senator Austin on 8 January 1948. They told Austin that a UN decision should be firmly and promptly made and that military policing would be required for a plebiscite, for which the Pakistani troops would be the most suitable because peace in Kashmir had to guarantee the security of the Muslims there. 'The whole affair, according to my visitors,

started with the massacre of Muslims instigated by the Prince [Hari Singh]', wired Austin to the US secretary of state on 8 January 1948. On 10 January 1948 the delegation shifted to Washington where Noel-Baker and Ismay met undersecretary of state, Robert Lovett. They suggested to him a joint Anglo-US approach at the UN based on the following points:

(1) movement of Pakistan forces to the Northern Areas;
(2) the withdrawal of Indian troops to the southern (Hindu) part;
(3) a joint occupation of the [Kashmir] Valley by the Indian and Pakistani forces; and
(4) the establishment of a UN Commission in Srinagar, the military commander of which might exercise Interim Government administration in Kashmir [i.e. Abdullah to be out].

Another telling document in this regard is the Memorandum of 6 February 1950 written to the US Secretary of State, Dean Acheson, by the Assistant Secretary of State for Near Eastern, South Asian and African Affairs, George Mcghee, and the Assistant Secretary of State for United Nations Affairs, John Hickerson, which records that:[81]

.... It is the view of the United Kingdom Attorney General and Foreign Office legal advisers that the Maharajah's execution of the Instrument of Accession to India was inconsistent with Kashmir's obligations to Pakistan, and for that reason, perhaps invalid.... This question is an important element in the dispute; and in the proceedings before the Security Council neither party is entitled to assert that rights were finally determined by the Maharajah's execution of an Instrument of Accession ... efforts to deal with the Kashmir question on the basis of legal considerations alone—or to assess original responsibilities for the difficulties that have arisen in Kashmir— would not be fruitful.... The Security Council should not permit this question to divert it from its basic task of bringing about a political solution to the Kashmir problem.

The US Secretary of State eventually wrote to the US Embassy in Britain on 11 February 1950 to the effect that:[82]

Debate on legality of accession or blame for origin is irrelevant to common purpose of peaceful solution. In US view Maharajah's act did not definitively settle rights of parties and offers India no basis for superior moral position ...

It may be recalled that the British were bound by their own Indian Independence Act of 1947 and the Government of India Act of 1935, as amended, and were, therefore, bound to accept as valid the accession of the PIS of J&K to the dominion of India by its sovereign ruler in terms of these British statutes. The British were consequently bound to view the PIS of J&K as part of India, and the Pakistan-sponsored tribal invasion into the state as pure and simple aggression. While Mountbatten pressurized New Delhi to make the reference to the UN, asserting that it had an 'cast-iron case' and 'that the UN would promptly direct Pakistan to withdraw the raiders', the British advised the US post the reference that the accession was invalid as being inconsistent with 'Kashmir's obligations to Pakistan' when they knew there were none, that the complaint against Pakistan's aggression need not be assessed at all, and that, instead, the UNSC should direct a plebiscite in the state, with military policing by Pakistani troops and removal of the Sheikh Abdullah government. It was at the instance of the British that the US took the stand that a '[d]ebate on legality of accession or blame for origin is irrelevant to common purpose of peaceful solution'. It was, in any case, politically expedient for the US to side with Pakistan. As the Belgian Ambassador to India, Prince de Ligne, told Nehru on 27 January 1948 that:[83]

> [T]he U.S. approach to [the] Kashmir issue would be influenced less by intrinsic merits than by effect of solution on broad considerations of American world strategy in [the] present state of tension between [the] USA and [the] USSR.... If Pakistan should be willing to cooperate similarly with the USA it is to be expected that the USA would try to befriend Pakistan in solution of her dispute with India over Kashmir.

After all, in the words of Yakub Malik, the then Soviet representative, 'in international politics decisions are not based on justice and fair play but on vested interests: 'You support us, we will support you. You safeguard our interests and we will safeguard yours'.[84] While New Delhi was in sore need of lessons in international politics, that by itself did not, however, relieve the British from adhering to their own political decisions on the manner and mode of accession of the princely Indian states; decisions that were subsequently crystallized into binding statutes passed by the British Parliament.

Mountbatten Post the Reference

Ramchandra Guha writes that a 'striking feature of the UN discussion on Kashmir was the partisanship of the British', and their 'representative, Philip Noel-Baker, vigorously supported the Pakistani position'.[85] Mountbatten himself records that Gopalaswami Ayyangar, who was representing New Delhi at the reference before the UNSC, had told him at the meeting on 17 February 1948, which was also attended by Nehru and Patel, that:[86]

> [I]f the British delegation had taken a definite stand at Lake Success in favour of the issue which India had raised being considered first, things would have been different. He said that one question which he had not been able to get anybody to answer satisfactorily was why the Security Council had passed a Resolution calling upon Albania, Yugoslavia and Bulgaria to stop giving help to Greek guerrillas; and had indeed appointed a Commission to ensure that this direction was complied with.

Hodson refers to Mountbatten's report to the King in which he recalls how Nehru had told him that he now bitterly regretted going to the UN and that:[87]

> Pandit Nehru said he was shocked to find that power politics and not ethics were ruling the United Nations Organisation and was convinced that the United Nations Organisation was being completely run by the Americans, and that Senator Warren Austin, the American representative, had made no bones of his sympathy for the Pakistan case. He considered that the United Nations Organisation did not intend to deal with the issue on its merits but merely to help Pakistan against India. He said that he thought that Mr. Noel Baker (the Secretary of State for Commonwealth Relations and the leader of the United Kingdom Delegation) had been nearly as hostile to India as Senator Warren Austin ... the belief spread during the first part of February, being founded on the assumption that the United Kingdom wished to appease the cause of the Muslim solidarity in the Middle East, and that the United States wished to rehabilitate their position vis-à-vis the Arabs after their advocacy of partition in Palestine.

It is astounding that despite having noticed such mischievous stand of the British before the UNSC, New Delhi continued to let Mountbatten shape its Kashmir policy. Interestingly, Mountbatten did everything possible to deflect from the true reason behind the UNSC siding with Pakistan. And so, when on 10 February 1948, Nehru, in the words of Mountbatten, 'said he could not understand what was going on at UNO' and 'remained unconvinced that motives of power politics were not influencing the outlook of the majority of the members of the Security Council,'[88] Mountbatten recorded that:[89]

> .... I informed him of my view that one of the main reasons why India's case had gone so badly at the Security Council was because the Indian delegation was

completely outclassed by the Pakistan delegation. Not only was Mr Gopalaswami Ayyangar completely the wrong type to send, not being a good social mixer and having a harsh, inaudible voice; but also there was nobody to compare with Mr Mohammad Ali for doing background work behind the scenes....

I told Pandit Nehru that I remained unashamed and unrepentant at having persuaded him to make a reference to the UNO in connection with Kashmir ... I told him that I like to take as much as possible the responsibility for having made the reference off his shoulders....

The very next day, on 11 February 1948, Mountbatten went on to persuade Patel that 'Mr Gopalaswamy Ayyangar was quite the wrong type to be selected on account of his husky inarticulate way of speaking and his teetotal, and early bed-going habits'.[90] Mountbatten even introduced the idea to Nehru, on 14 February 1948, of the British General Bucher representing India at the UNSC, which Nehru fortunately rejected while expressing his 'great appreciation at this loyal offer'.[91]

Again, Mountbatten, at the meeting on 25 February 1948 with Nehru, Sardar Patel, Gopalaswami Ayyangar and Patrick Gordon-Walker, the visiting British Secretary of State for Commonwealth Affairs, acknowledged his role in persuading New Delhi to make the reference to the UNSC in response to New Delhi expressing its loss of faith in the UNSC. The record of this meeting of 25 February 1948 documents:[92]

Pandit Nehru said that it had been an act of faith by the Government of India, at a time when the situation was rapidly deteriorating, to make their reference to the Security Council in the first place ... Sardar Patel said that Pandit Nehru had in particular great faith in the institution of UNO. But the Security Council had been meddling in power politics to such an extent that very little of this faith was left. He pointed out that it had been the Governor-General who had induced the Government to make the reference to the UNO in the first place. With this the Governor-General agreed....

Yet Mountbatten unabashedly persisted in trying to influence New Delhi to take further steps with regard to the PIS of J&K that could protect British interests. To take an instance, Mountbatten, at the meeting on the very next day, i.e. 26 February 1948, sought to widen the scope of the proposed plebiscite by suggesting that it should be held constituency wise coupled with the inclusion of a vote for independence of the PIS of J&K. The record of the meeting on 26 February 1948 discloses:[93]

The Governor-General said that he assumed that the plebiscite would be run constituency-wise. That Pandit Nehru confirmed. The Governor General went on to ask what the reactions of the Government would be if, for example, Poonch voted overwhelmingly for Pakistan, whilst the rest of Kashmir voted for India; or if most of the state voted for Pakistan, but Jammu voted overwhelmingly for India. Would the Government insist on the continued integrity of Kashmir as a whole?

The Governor General then suggested the possibility of including a vote for independence in the plebiscite might be put at UNO....

Kuldip Nayar points out that Dwarka Prasad Misra, who was Madhya Pradesh's Home Minister in 1947, had quoted Sardar Patel as having said that New Delhi's undertaking to hold a plebiscite was not even discussed in the Indian Cabinet.[94] Sarila notes that when the Indian Cabinet went along with the complaint about Pakistan's aggression to the UN, it did so under the impression that it was a prelude to India going to war with Pakistan, if the invasion was not withdrawn within a short time.[95] However, the fact remains that though New Delhi lodged its complaint with the UN on 1 January 1948, no military preparations had been made by the British Commander-in-Chief of the Indian Army for any such operation.[96]

Hence, with the PIS of J&K, having a predominantly Muslim population, opting to accede to the dominion of India, the British ensured that the territory of the state under Pakistan's control did not get disturbed. The British did this by convincing Nehru of his 'world-statesmanship' in making the reference of the Kashmir issue to the UN and adopting the moral high ground that India would not take advantage of the circumstances in which the state found itself, but would hold a plebiscite or a referendum under UN auspices to determine 'the will of the people'. The British ensured that the US, and the UNSC, fell in line with the British strategy. As detailed in the next chapter, the UNSC did its best to obtain a ceasefire without first requiring Pakistan to vacate its aggression, thereby preventing New Delhi from recovering the territory of the PIS of J&K occupied by Pakistan, and enabling Pakistan to consolidate its control over such territory so as to let Britain retain the crucial Northern Areas of the state for its Great Game. The UNSC, while explicitly bypassing the charge of aggression against Pakistan, shifted the focus on to the holding of a plebiscite in the PIS of J&K under UN auspices, which permitted the international community to recognize Pakistan's presence in the state, gave Pakistan locus standi in the state and conferred a 'disputed territory' status on the state. The reference of the Kashmir issue to the UNSC was a trap laid by the British for its strategic interests during the Great Game. New Delhi fell for it. And, as Hodson notes, Mountbatten 'did dissuade his Prime Minister from withdrawing the Indian delegation from Lake Success'.[97]

It may be argued that the UNSC is not like a court of law, and that the scheme of the UN Charter requires the UNSC to try to bring about a resolution of disputes between nations by mediation and other measures, the dominant consideration being a settlement by political means rather than the merits of the case. It is true that the reference to the UNSC was made by India under Chapter VI of the UN Charter on 'Pacific Settlement of Disputes' and not under Chapter VII on 'Action with Respect to Threats to Peace, Breaches of the Peace, and Acts of Aggression'.[98] Hence, it may be contended that the UNSC was well within its rights to bring about a settlement, rather than examining the legality of the action of a state. This reasoning overlooks that any such settlement cannot, however, be contrary to law or the UN Charter. The approach of the UNSC, as will be evident shortly, was not to facilitate a settlement within the parameters of established principles of law that it was bound to be conversant with and to follow, but to act in violation of such law and the UN Charter itself.

Looking back, the British policy to retain its influence over the strategic northern part of the PIS of J&K and, indeed, over Pakistan, has been a resounding success. India has not been able to recover till date the territory of the PIS of J&K forcibly occupied by Pakistan in 1947. On the other hand, Pakistan became a defence partner of the West in the Great Game, which later assumed global dimensions to translate into the Cold War. Pakistan joined Britain in the Baghdad Pact in February 1955, along with Iran, Iraq and Turkey, to block possible Soviet intrusions in the Middle East. With the US taking over command from Britain in the Cold War, the Baghdad Pact led to the Central Treaty Organization (CENTO). Pakistan and the US had entered into a bilateral pact in 1954. Pakistan provided the US with an airbase at Peshawar in 1958 for surveillance over Soviet activity. During the 1970s, the US used the offices of Pakistan to build relations with China so as to put pressure on the then Soviet Union from the east. During the 1980s, the US collaborated with Pakistan to create the Taliban and based its operations from Pakistan to evict the Soviets from Afghanistan, precipitating the collapse of the erstwhile Soviet Union.[99]

The happenings at the UNSC were crucial for the success of the British strategy. Let us now examine how thoroughly these were scripted as well.

Notes and References

1. Extracted in *Supra* Note 6, Chapter I, p. 355.
2. Ibid., p. 356.
3. Ibid.
4. *Supra* Note 62, Chapter IV, p. 362.
5. *Supra* Note 30, Chapter III, p. 42.
6. See *Supra* Note 1, Chapter I, p. 473.
7. *Supra* Note 6, Chapter I, p. 361.
8. Extracted in ibid., pp. 360–361.
9. *Supra* Note 30, Chapter III, pp. 32–33.
10. Ibid., p. 33.
11. *Supra* Note 1, Chapter I, pp. 413–414.
12. Ibid., p. 417.
13. Ibid., p. 414.
14. Ibid., pp. 433–434, 503.
15. Ibid., p. 430.
16. Ibid., p. 448.
17. Ibid.
18. *Supra* Note 6, Chapter I, p. 358.
19. See Ibid., p. 361.
20. See *Supra* Note 100, Chapter IV, p. 286.
21. *Supra* Note 6, Chapter I, p. 371.
22. Extracted in ibid.
23. *Supra* Note 12, Chapter IV, p. 79.
24. Ibid., p. 49.
25. *Supra* Note 1, Chapter I, pp. 471–472.
26. Ibid., pp. 504–506. See *Supra* Note 30, Chapter III, pp. 137, 139–140, for Mountbatten's record of New Delhi's efforts to link the financial agreements with Pakistan with the settlement of the Kashmir issue.
27. Ibid., pp. 506–507.
28. Wright, Quincy. 1960. *International Law and the United Nations*, p. 87. Bombay: Asia Publishing House.
29. Ibid., p. 88.
30. *Supra* Note 104, Chapter IV, pp. 105–106.
31. *Supra* Note 89, Chapter I, p. 766.
32. For full text, see Singh, Jasjit. 1995. *Pakistan Occupied Kashmir: Under the Jackboots*, p. 55–59. New Delhi: Siddi Books.
33. Ibid., p. 44.
34. See *Yearbook of the United Nations*, 1963. Communications concerning the India–Pakistan Question, pp. 45–46; *Yearbook of the United Nations*, 1965. India–Pakistan Question, pp. 159–161; S/PV 1088, p. 25, M.C. Chagla (India), 5 February 1964; S/PV 1113, pp. 1–5, M.C. Chagla (India), 7 May 1964.
35. *Legal Consequences for States of the Continued Presence of South Africa in Namibia (South West Africa) notwithstanding Security Council Resolution 726 (1970)*, Advisory Opinion: I.C.J. Reports 1971, p. 52.

36. This is, perhaps, the reason for New Delhi being led to refer the Kashmir issue to the UN under Chapter VI of the UN Charter dealing with 'Pacific Settlement of Disputes', rather than Chapter VII pertaining to 'Action with Respect to Threats to the Peace, Breaches of the Peace and Acts of Aggression', which entails the UNSC to determine the question of aggression and visit the aggressor with strict consequences.

37. *Supra* Note 89, Chapter I, p. 293.

38. Reproduced in *Supra* Note 30, Chapter III, p. 167.

39. *Supra* Note 6, Chapter I, p. 346.

40. Ibid., p. 366.

41. Ibid., p. 367.

42. *Supra* Note 1, Chapter I, pp. 432–434.

43. *Supra* Note 6, Chapter I, p. 353.

44. *Supra* Note 30, Chapter III, p. 39.

45. Ibid., p. 43.

46. *Supra* Note 1, Chapter I, pp. 448–450.

47. *Supra* Note 30, Chapter III, p. 39.

48. Ibid.

49. Ibid., p. 42.

50. *Supra* Note 1, Chapter I, p. 454.

51. See for full text *Supra* Note 100, Chapter IV, p. 276.

52. *Supra* Note 6, Chapter I, p. 356.

53. *Supra* Note 100, Chapter IV, pp. 320e–320g. Also see *Supra* Note 28, Chapter IV, pp. 61–62.

54. *Supra* Note 12, Chapter IV, pp. 72–73.

55. *Supra* Note 1, Chapter I, p. 335.

56. Ibid., p. 371.

57. *Supra* Note 30, Chapter III, p. 150.

58. Ibid., p. 179.

59. *Supra* Note 6, Chapter I, pp. 371–372.

60. *Supra* Note 28, Chapter IV, p. 65.

61. Ibid., pp. 66–67.

62. Reproduced in *Supra* Note 30, Chapter III, pp. 149, 153–154.

63. *Supra* Note 28, Chapter IV, p. 73.

64. Ibid., p. 74.

65. *Supra* Note 100, Chapter IV, p. 375.

66. Ibid., pp. 376–377.

67. See Ibid., pp. 375–377.

68. Ibid., pp. 381–386.

69. Ibid.

70. For full text of Nehru's letter, see *Supra* Note 28, Chapter IV, p. 74.

71. *Supra* Note 30, Chapter III, pp. 156 and 159.

72. *Supra* Note 6, Chapter I, p. 371.

73. *Supra* Note 100, Chapter IV, pp. 399 and 402.

74. Ibid.

75. Extracted in *Supra* Note 1, Chapter I, pp. 467–468.

76. *Supra* Note 6, Chapter I, p. 372.

77. Ibid., pp. 373–374.

78. Ibid., p. 373.

79. Ibid., p. 374.
80. Ibid., pp. 375–377.
81. Extracted in *Supra* Note 12, Chapter IV, p. 678.
82. Ibid.
83. Extracted in *Supra* Note 6, Chapter I, p. 382.
84. Cited in *Supra* Note 104, Chapter IV, pp. 105–106.
85. *Supra* Note 28, Chapter I, p. 73.
86. *Supra* Note 30, Chapter III, p. 172.
87. *Supra* Note 1, Chapter I, pp. 469–470.
88. Ibid., p. 166.
89. *Supra* Note 30, Chapter III, p. 166.
90. Ibid., p. 168.
91. Ibid., p. 170.
92. Ibid., p. 173.
93. Ibid., p. 175.
94. See *Supra* Note 39, Chapter IV, p. 28.
95. *Supra* Note 6, Chapter I, p. 372.
96. Ibid.
97. *Supra* Note 1, Chapter I, pp. 470–471.
98. *Supra* Note 12, Chapter IV, p. 677.
99. *Supra* Note 6, Chapter I, pp. 397–402.

VII

United Nations and the Reference

While several political leaders in India opposed the decision to refer the Kashmir issue to the UNSC, New Delhi eventually sent the telegram dated 31 December 1947 to India's delegation at the UN, which was transmitted to the UNSC on 1 January 1948.[1]

The formal reference detailed the facts of the invasion into the PIS of J&K to establish that the invaders were allowed transit across Pakistan; that they were allowed to use the territory of Pakistan as a base for operations; that they included Pakistan nationals; that the invaders drew much of their military equipment, transportation and supplies (including petrol) from Pakistan and that Pakistan's officers were training, guiding and otherwise actively helping them. New Delhi called upon the UNSC to ask the Government of Pakistan to desist from such activities. However, New Delhi stated in its reference that 'in order to avoid any possible suggestion that India had utilized the State's immediate peril for her own political advantage, the Government of India made it clear that once the soil of the State had been cleared of the invader and normal conditions restored, its people would be free to decide their future by the recognized democratic method of plebiscite or referendum which, in order to ensure complete impartiality, might be held under international auspices'.[2]

Pakistan, however, denied its complicity in the invasion or that it was aiding the raiders. It made a counter-complaint against India, alleging annexation of Junagadh, genocide of Muslims and an attempt to liquidate the State of Pakistan.[3] According to Pakistan, Raja Hari Singh and his government had adopted a policy of repression of Muslims in the PIS of J&K. As a result, there had been a rebellion against the Raja, particularly in the Poonch area. Pakistan claimed that this state of affairs aroused strong feelings of sympathy in Pakistan, especially among the Muslims living in the contiguous areas, who had numerous ties of relationships with the Muslims of the state, and that it was some of these people who went across to the PIS of J&K to assist their kinsmen in their 'freedom struggle' against the Hindu ruler. Pakistan alleged that the stage was thus set for the pre-planned intervention by India to quell such spontaneous uprising. It disputed the legality of the accession of the state to the dominion of India on the ground that it was fraudulent, since, according to Pakistan, the accession was achieved by the deliberate creation of certain conditions with the objective of finding an excuse to stage the accession. Pakistan asserted that the accession was based on violence, as, in its view, it was part of a plan of the state government to liquidate the Muslim population of the PIS of J&K. Accordingly, Pakistan sought that the reference to the UN be widened to cover larger ground and 'embrace all the fundamentals of the differences between the two Dominions'.[4]

Let us consider the *Jammu and Kashmir Question*, the title of which was changed, at the 231st meeting of the UNSC held on 22 January 1948, to the *India–Pakistan Question*. This change was meant to reflect the wider differences between the two dominions.

A perusal of the entire UNSC Verbatim Reports on the *Question*, which run into several thousands of pages, makes a sad reading of the legally flawed stand of both India and Pakistan, as also of the unhesitating bias of the UNSC towards Pakistan in patent contravention of the principles of international law that it was bound to be familiar with and to follow. The approach of the UNSC to the Kashmir issue is a poor reflection on the UN itself as an institution. The UNSC apparently ignored Article 24 of the UN Charter, which explains that it is only in order to 'ensure prompt and effective action by the United Nations' that 'its Members confer on the Security Council primary responsibility for the maintenance of international peace and security' and that '[i]n discharging these duties the Security Council shall act in accordance with the Purposes and Principles of the United Nations'. The primary purpose of the UN, as set out in Article 1 of the UN Charter, is to maintain international peace and security, and to that end, to take effective collective measures for the suppression of acts of aggression or other breaches of the peace. The failure of the UNSC to resolve the Kashmir problem was a foregone conclusion, the moment New Delhi realized that the UN was being subverted to suit political expediency.

It is beyond the scope of this book to detail all the ingenuous arguments made by both India and Pakistan to support their respective stands on the Kashmir issue at the UN. While the UNSC Verbatim Reports make fascinating reading, this book is confined to the stands of India, Pakistan and the UNSC relevant for the resolution of the Kashmir issue in the manner eventually suggested by this book.

Stand of India and Pakistan before the UNSC

At the UNSC, Gopalaswami Ayyangar (India) referred to Pakistan's aggression[5] and then went on to 'invite the attention of the members of the UNSC to the high-principled statesmanship characteristic of the Government of India under its present leadership', who 'have subsequently made it quite clear that they are agreeable to the plebiscite being conducted if necessary under international auspices'.[6] Ayyangar added that the 'question of the future status of Kashmir vis-à-vis her neighbours and the world at large, and a further question, namely, whether she should withdraw from her accession to India and either accede to Pakistan or remain independent, with a right to claim admission as member of the United Nations—all this we have recognized to be a matter for unfettered decisions by the people of Kashmir after normal life is restored to them'.[7] New Delhi reiterated before the UNSC that 'on the question of accession, the Government of India has always enunciated the policy that in all cases of dispute the people of the State concerned should make the decision'.[8]

Pakistan agreed with New Delhi's policy on disputed accessions, irrespective of Junagadh, Hyderabad or the PIS of J&K, and to the plebiscite under UN auspices.[9] In other words, Pakistan's claim to the PIS of J&K was premised on New Delhi's policy that the question of accession of the PIS of J&K made by its sovereign ruler would be finally 'settled' by a reference to the people. This policy was itself legally misconceived and beyond the competence of either of the dominions in view of the provisions of the Indian Independence Act of 1947, and the Government of India Act of 1935, as amended. Karachi was as oblivious as New Delhi of the fact that two wrongs did not make a right. The application of a flawed policy by one party did not entitle the other to demand its continuation to 'parallel' cases. Simply put, Pakistan's claim before the UNSC with respect to the PIS of J&K was premised on New Delhi's erroneous stand on Junagadh and Hyderabad. If New Delhi's stand goes, so does Pakistan's case.

Further, Pakistan disputed before the UNSC the legality and validity of the accession of the PIS of J&K to India as being procured by fraud and violence.[10] India rebutted the allegation. On 15 January 1948, Gopalaswami Ayyangar (India) pointed out that the 'Government of India had in fact no plans to send any military assistance to Kashmir before 25 October 1947' and that had 'India any plans ready to send troops to Kashmir before this date it would hardly have waited until the invaders had overrun half the Valley'.[11] On 23 January 1948, M.C. Setalvad (India) referred to the document signed by the British Chiefs of Staff—the Commander-in-Chief of the Indian Army, General R.M.M. Lockhart, the Air Marshal commanding the Royal Indian Air Force, T.W. Elmhirst, and the Rear Admiral of the Royal Indian Navy, J.T.S. Hall. This document detailed the true timetable of events and completely negated any theory of pre-planning or conspiracy such as had been suggested by Pakistan.[12]

Be that as it may, the real question that arises is whether Pakistan even had the standing to challenge the accession of the PIS of J&K to the dominion of India.

It is a well-known principle of international law that third states do not have a right to veto the act of accession or cession.[13] Pakistan's own stand from the very beginning has been that on the lapse of British paramountcy on 15 August 1947, the PIS of J&K became a sovereign state in the full sense of the term. Pakistan was not party to the accession of the sovereign PIS of J&K to the dominion of India, and, hence, had no locus standi in the matter. The sovereign ruler of the PIS of J&K owed no allegiance to the dominion of Pakistan. The PIS of J&K was never part of Pakistan's territory nor was the PIS of J&K ever under Pakistan's sovereignty.

According to A.S. Anand, former Chief Justice of India, the accession of the PIS of J&K to the dominion of India is analogous to that of Texas to the US.[14] The judge recalls that when Mexico separated from the Spanish Empire, Texas was a part of the new independent state of Mexico. Subsequently, Texas revolted against Mexican authorities and established itself as an independent entity. The independent status of Texas was recognized by the US and the European powers. In 1844, the Government of Texas, threatened by predatory incursions by Mexico, asked the US to annex the state. Texas's appeal was accepted by the US Congress in March 1845. The US sent its army to defend the western frontiers of Texas. Mexico protested and alleged the violation of its rights. The US reply was that '[t]he Government of United States did not consider this ... as a violation of any of the rights of Mexico, or that it offered any just cause or offence to its government; that the Republic of Texas is an independent power, owing no allegiance to Mexico, and constituting no part of her territory or rightful sovereignty and jurisdiction'.[15]

The case of the PIS of J&K is on a much stronger footing, as the PIS of J&K was admittedly never—constitutionally, legally or factually—a part of the dominion of Pakistan, whereas Texas had, at one point of time, been a part of the independent state of Mexico.[16]

Pakistan was well aware of this position. After all, the Kings Bench Division of the UK, in *Kahan*,[17] relied on the letter of 3 April 1951 of the Secretary of State for Commonwealth Relations to hold that Pakistan was an independent and sovereign state in view of the Indian Independence Act of 1947 and that no enquiry can be made into its conduct on its attaining such sovereignty. By parity of reasoning, the very statement that Raja Hari Singh was the sovereign ruler of the PIS of J&K precluded Pakistan, or for that matter, any country or authority or the UN, from challenging the accession of the PIS of J&K to the dominion of India, or from considering the question of the status of the PIS of J&K within the Union of India. Should Pakistan seek to act beyond the terms of the Indian Independence Act of 1947, read with the Government of India Act of 1935, as amended, to challenge the decision of the sovereign ruler of the PIS of J&K to accede to the dominion of India, it runs the risk of its own status as a sovereign country and of the accession of princely Indian states to the dominion of Pakistan being questioned.

The occupation by Pakistan of the territories of the sovereign PIS of J&K was, therefore, a pure and simple act of aggression. The subsequent accession of the PIS of J&K to the dominion of India conferred upon India the standing to have the aggression vacated. The UNSC ought to have found that in any view of the matter, Pakistan, a creature of the Indian Independence Act of 1947, and the Government of India Act, 1935, as amended, simply had no locus standi under these very Acts with respect to the PIS of J&K. Had the UNSC been less concerned about the identity of the parties before it, it could have even pointed out to New Delhi that the latter lacked competence to question the accession in view of the said Acts. That too, when the ruler of the PIS of J&K, who retained sovereignty over his state, was not before the UN. Significantly, the resolutions passed by the UNSC, which are discussed shortly, confirm that at least the UNSC was fully aware of the fact that the ruler of the PIS of J&K had retained sovereignty over the state and that it needed his authorization for matters relating to the PIS of J&K.

Let us now consider how the UNSC, rather than addressing the issue of aggression, simply ignored it, and instead of requiring Pakistan to vacate the aggression, highlighted New Delhi's offer to hold a UN-supervised plebiscite to merrily resolve that the question of the accession of the PIS of J&K to India or Pakistan would be decided by such a plebiscite.

Views of the UNSC

Austin (the US) referred to the wish of the Government of India contained in Mountbatten's letter dated 26 October 1947 and to the 'pledge' made to the 'whole world' by Nehru in his public broadcast to conclude that 'a plebiscite is one of the conditions attending the accession'.[18] Austin (the US) declared that he wanted on record 'a recognition of a very important fact that when India accepted the accession of Kashmir', it made its act 'conditional on fair plebiscite being held to determine the will of the people of Kashmir with respect to accession' and that 'an example was made in history at that point'.[19]

F. van Langenhove (Belgium), the then President of the UNSC, noted that 'the principle of a plebiscite has been accepted by both parties, and that it is not disputed that the plebiscite must be completely impartial and should be therefore placed under the authority of the United Nations'.[20]

Noel Baker (the UK) and Tsiang (China) agreed that the key to the problem lay in the plebiscite.[21] De La Tournelle (France) stated that it 'considers that the Indian Government has on this occasion given a striking example of its political wisdom and fairness of mind and a proof of political maturity'.[22]

Arce (Argentina) sought to clear any 'misunderstanding' by affirming that 'Kashmir is not a territory of India—no Power will either propose or accept a plebiscite to surrender a part of its territory, as India's Government did'.[23]

India stands alone in history as a country that moved the UN to complain about aggression against a part of its territory, and then readily committed at the UN to hold a plebiscite in that very territory to determine whether such territory is even part of the country.

The states comprising the UNSC were understandably forthcoming in their remarks on the 'political maturity' of the Government of India and of the fact that 'an example was made in history at that point'. The UNSC was less forthcoming in adhering to the principles of international law, discussed subsequently, which would have condemned Pakistan as the aggressor. The record of the UNSC meeting on 29 January 1948 indicates New Delhi's anguish at the UNSC for 'trying to fiddle here while India is burning',[24] with Gopalaswami Ayyangar (India) detailing the incidents as also the admissions of Pakistan itself that it was assisting the raiders who were helping the 'Azad Kashmir' government in its 'struggle for liberty' as 'volunteers'.[25]

The UNSC succeeded in not only obtaining a ceasefire without first requiring the aggression by Pakistan to be vacated, but also managed to demarcate the ceasefire line in the PIS of J&K that, unsurprisingly, left the Northern Areas and 'Azad Kashmir' under Pakistan's control and held back India from recovering such territory of the PIS of J&K occupied by Pakistan.

UN Resolutions and the Ceasefire Line

The UNSC passed numerous resolutions on the Kashmir problem, though reference is being made only to the material ones relevant for the purposes of this book.

By its resolution of 20 January 1948, the UNSC established a three-member United Nations Commission for India and Pakistan (UNCIP) 'to investigate the facts pursuant to Article 34 of the Charter of the United Nations' and to exercise 'any mediatory influence likely to smooth away difficulties'.[26] However, due to disagreement between India and Pakistan regarding its implementation, the proposed commission could not be constituted.

On 21 April 1948, the UNSC enlarged the membership of UNCIP to five and detailed how the plebiscite was to be conducted. The UN Secretary General was to nominate a Plebiscite Administrator who 'acting as an officer of the State of Jammu and Kashmir, should have the authority to ... draft regulations governing the plebiscite and such draft regulations should be formally promulgated by the State of Jammu and Kashmir'.[27]

The UNSC instructed the UNCIP to proceed to the Indian subcontinent. The UNCIP had three objectives: a ceasefire, a truce period during which the withdrawal of forces was to take place, and finally, consultations to establish the conditions by means of which the free will of the people of the PIS of J&K would be expressed.[28]

The UNCIP, so constituted, arrived in the Indian subcontinent on 7 July 1948,[29] only to find that regular Pakistan troops had moved into the territories of Kashmir under Pakistan's occupation—that is, into the state which had a sovereign ruler and which had already acceded to the dominion of India in specific areas. Pakistan admitted before the UNCIP that it had sent its regular troops to the PIS of J&K on 8 May 1948. Hodson records that:[30]

> Evidence had been accumulating, and was accepted by the (British) Chiefs of Staff in India, that troops of three regular [Pakistan] Frontier Force battalions had been operating against the Indian Army in Kashmir. Pandit Nehru sent a telegram to Mr. Liaquat Ai Khan to this effect on 10th June. The Pakistan Prime Minister's reply, a week later, did not deny the charge....

It may be recalled that it was British General Roy Bucher, heading the Indian Army, who had suggested to British General Doughlas Gracey, heading the Pakistan Army, that to ensure 'each side will remain in undisputed military occupation of what are roughly their present positions ... three battalions of the Pakistan army should be employed in Kashmir opposite the India forces'.[31] Thus, while the UNSC was 'fiddling' in New York, Pakistan, with the active connivance of the British, was overtly committing aggression by officially moving its troops into the PIS of J&K.

The UNCIP report records that Pakistan's Foreign Minister informed it 'that the Pakistan Army had at the time three brigades of regular troops in Kashmir, and that troops had been sent into the State during the first half of May [1948]' and that at 'the 19th meeting, on 20 July, a confidential cable was drafted and dispatched informing the Security Council of the presence of Pakistani troops in Kashmir'.[32] The UNSC did nothing, and did that well.

At the instance of the UNCIP, both India and Pakistan accepted two UNCIP Resolutions, one dated 13 August 1948 and the other dated 5 January 1949—both of which contemplated a ceasefire without Pakistan first vacating the aggression.

The UNCIP Resolution of 13 August 1948 (S/995) was in three parts. Part I proposed that the ceasefire order to be issued by India and Pakistan would apply to all forces under their control in the PIS of J&K and for the appointment of military observers by the UNCIP to supervise the observance of the ceasefire order. Part II of the Resolution proposed the Truce Agreement. It contemplated withdrawal of Pakistan troops as also the tribesmen and Pakistani's nationals from the PIS of J&K, following which India would withdraw the bulk of its forces from the PIS of J&K in stages to be agreed upon with the UNCIP, retaining some 'to assist local authorities in the observance of law and order'. The Resolution provided that pending 'a final solution, the territory evacuated by the Pakistani troops will be administered by the local authorities under the surveillance of the Commission'. Part III of the Resolution reaffirmed the wish of the Governments of India and Pakistan 'that the future status of the State of Jammu and Kashmir shall be determined in accordance with the will of the people'.

Interestingly, when the UNCIP had proposed in August 1948 that Pakistan's troops withdraw from the PIS of J&K, which included their withdrawal from Gilgit as well, both Britain and Pakistan panicked. Particularly since the US agreed with the UNCIP proposal, taking the view that till India lost the plebiscite, the accession of the state to India could not be questioned.[33] The British now had no option but to come clean with the US as to why it wanted Gilgit to remain with Pakistan. Ernest Bevin, the then British Secretary of State for Foreign Affairs, reasoned with George C. Marshall, the then US Secretary of State, on 27 October 1948 at Paris that the 'main issue was who would control the main artery leading into Central Asia', and that could not be left in Indian hands.[34] The US was not impressed. In its telegram of 11 November 1948 to its delegation at Paris, the State Department in Washington wrote that:[35]

Simple cease-fire order ... without provisions for truce and plebiscite would imply sanctioning of Pakistani troops and would not only be inconsistent with provisions of SC and UNCIP approach but would be highly unacceptable to GOI (Government of India).

The Government of India, however, seemed to have no problem with Pakistani troops remaining in Gilgit. Nehru, in his letter of 20 February 1948 to Krishna Menon referred to in the previous chapter, had, while dismissing the suggestion of partitioning the state so as to let the Kashmir Valley and the rest of the state, except Jammu, go to Pakistan, stated that '[a]lthough if the worst comes to the worst I am prepared to accept Poonch and Gilgit being partitioned off'.[36]

Sarila records[37] that V.P. Menon told the US *chargé d'affaires* in Delhi on 23 July 1948 that the 'Government of India will accept settlement based on accession of Mirapur, Poonch, Muzaffarabad and Gilgit to Pakistan'. Josef Korbel, who was presiding over the UNCIP, which visited Delhi in July 1948, disclosed that Nehru had told him that New Delhi would not 'insist upon the right of' its 'Army to advance and occupy the territory which would be vacated by Pakistan' and that New Delhi would be 'satisfied with the recognition of the authority of the State over all its territories and with the occupation of advanced positions important to' New Delhi 'strategically and economically', and that further, New Delhi would not be opposed to the idea of dividing the state between India and Pakistan.[38]

Such incredulous policy of New Delhi undercut the US position that, since the PIS of J&K had acceded to India, New Delhi would find it unacceptable for Pakistan's troops to remain in Gilgit. The US had no option but to drop its insistence on Pakistan withdrawing its troops from Gilgit when New Delhi eventually accepted the ceasefire, which left Gilgit, as also the rest of the territories so crucial for British interests, under Pakistan's occupation.

It may be noted that the UNCIP Resolution of 13 August 1948 did not result in the ceasefire. Subsequent negotiations led to the acceptance of the UNCIP's proposals in the communications of 23 December 1948 and 25 December 1948. A resolution embodying these proposals was adopted by the UNCIP on 5 January 1949.[39] This UNCIP Resolution of 5 January 1949 started with the acceptance of the 'principles' by India and Pakistan to the effect that '[t]he question of the accession of the State of Jammu and Kashmir to India or Pakistan will be decided through the democratic method of a free and impartial plebiscite', and that 'a plebiscite will be held when it shall be found by the Commission that the cease-fire and truce arrangements set forth in Parts I and II of the Commission's resolution of 13 August have been carried out and arrangements for the plebiscite have been completed'.

The Resolution of 5 January 1949 provided the mechanism for the holding of a 'free and impartial plebiscite' in the PIS of J&K. Though the Resolution was passed in the absence of the sovereign ruler of the PIS of J&K, the UNSC seemed to be fully aware that it was in him that powers with respect to the PIS of J&K were located. The Resolution explicitly provided for the appointment of a 'Plebiscite Administrator' by the UN Secretary General, in agreement with the UNCIP, who was to be *'formally appointed to office by the Government of Jammu and Kashmir'*. The Resolution expressly stated that the 'Plebiscite Administrator shall derive *from the State of Jammu and Kashmir* the powers he considers necessary for organizing and conducting the plebiscite and for ensuring the freedom and impartiality of the plebiscite'. Needless to add, it was the sovereign ruler of the state that comprised the government of the state at that point of time.

It was pursuant to the Resolution of 5 January 1949 that the ceasefire was declared. The UNCIP Military Adviser presented to India and Pakistan a plan for the organization and deployment of military observers in the area. This plan was put into effect on the Pakistan side on 3 February 1949 and on the Indian side on 10 February 1949. A first group of seven UN observers had arrived on 24 January 1949. Their number was increased to 20 in early February 1949. These observers, under the command of the Military Adviser, formed the nucleus of the United Nations Military Observers Group in India and Pakistan (UNMOGIP).

On 27 July 1949, the military representatives of India and Pakistan signed an agreement at Karachi, under the auspices of the UNCIP, establishing a ceasefire line. The UNCIP, not surprisingly, failed to secure the withdrawal of the forces or the creation of the conditions for a plebiscite and returned to New York in September 1949.[40] The Yearbook of the United Nations, 1950, records that the UNCIP, in its third interim report submitted on 5 December 1949, stated that 'although it had secured the agreement of India and Pakistan on a part of the permanent truce line in the State of Jammu and Kashmir, and full agreement on a cease-fire line, its proposals for implementation of the truce agreement had not been accepted' and that the 'main difficulty had arisen concerning the withdrawal of troops preparatory to the holding of the plebiscite to determine whether Jammu and Kashmir should accede to India or to Pakistan'.[41]

The Yearbook of the United Nations, 1950, records further the unsuccessful mediation efforts of the President of the UNSC as also various proposals to resolve the Kashmir issue. Significantly, all these proposals placed Pakistan and 'Azad Kashmir forces' on the same plane as Indian forces and eliminated the sovereignty of the PIS of J&K.[42]

On 14 March 1950, the UNSC terminated the services of the UNCIP and decided to appoint a UN representative to exercise all of the powers and responsibilities previously assumed by the UNCIP.

Owen Dixon of Australia, who had been appointed as the UN representative for India and Pakistan on 12 April 1950, made proposals for demilitarization, administration and plebiscite. Each proposal of Dixon, which was recorded in his report submitted on 15 September 1950, was rejected by New Delhi, which had by that time realized that it had been taken for a ride by the UNSC. The Yearbook of the United Nations, 1950, records that the UNCIP and Dixon 'had failed in their efforts to secure an agreement on practical measures for a plebiscite' and that both India and Pakistan 'concurred in the view that the possibilities of agreement had been exhausted'.[43]

New Delhi's Policy on the PIS of J&K

It appears that New Delhi had by now become reconciled to the fact that the UNSC did not intend to do anything about Pakistan's aggression. So, it took the easy way out. It simply disowned the occupied territories of the PIS of J&K as also the people living in such territories—people who are citizens of India under the Constitution of India. Since 1948 itself, the unofficial solution to the Kashmir issue touted by New Delhi has been the maintenance of status quo along the ceasefire line.

Indeed, Nehru, in his Note dated 25 August 1952 to Sheikh Abdullah, disclosed that after 'some experience of the UN, [he] came to the conclusion that nothing substantial could be expected from it', and that towards the end of 1948 he had 'ruled out plebiscite for all practical purposes', since 'we would never have the conditions which were necessary for a plebiscite', and that war with Pakistan was not 'a prospect to be welcomed'.[44] Nehru opined that the 'only possible way of putting an end to this conflict was by accepting more or less, the status quo then existing' since '[w]e were not prepared to give up any territory we possessed to Pakistan ... [b]ut we might, for the sake of peace and settlement, agree to their holding what they then had'.[45] He concluded that:[46]

> The result of all these considerations is that the only desirable future of the State is with a close association with India, retaining her autonomy in most ways; that Kashmir and Jammu should hold together; that we should consolidate our position in these areas and not care very much for what happens in 'Azad Kashmir' areas. Most important of all is that we should not have any doubts in our minds about these matters.... What is required is a firm and clear outlook, and no debate about the basic issues.

If we have that outlook, it just does not matter what the UN thinks or what Pakistan does.

.... I have held these views concisely and precisely for the last four years, and nothing has happened during this period which has made me change them in the slightest ... it has surprised me that there should be so much discussion about obvious matters.

According to Noorani, Nehru had decided against plebiscite in 1947 itself. Noorani cites the letter written by Nehru to Sheikh Abdullah on 21 November 1947 in which he 'shares the feeling' of the leadership of the National Conference against a referendum, while stating that:[47]

it is not easy for us to back out of the stand we have taken before the world. That would create a very bad impression abroad and more specially in the UN circles ... the question of referendum is rather an academic one at present.... If we said to the UNO that we no longer stand by for a referendum in Kashmir, Pakistan would score a strong point and that would be harmful to our cause....

Ramchandra Guha refers to the letter of 1 December 1947 sent by Nehru to the ruler, Raja Hari Singh, in which:[48]

[H]e outlined various forms a settlement could take. There could be a plebiscite for the whole state, to decide which dominion it would join. Or the state could survive as an independent country, with its defence guaranteed by both India and Pakistan. A third option was that of partition, with Jammu going to India and the rest of the state to Pakistan. A fourth option had Jammu and the Valley staying with India, with Poonch and beyond being ceded to Pakistan.

Such policy of New Delhi is evident from the 'tentative conclusions' it arrived at with Owen Dixon, as recorded in the Yearbook of the United Nations, 1950. These conclusions document that New Delhi had agreed that while plebiscite be held in the Kashmir Valley, the territory of 'Jammu so far as it lies east of the cease-fire line' and Ladakh (with the exception of the area above the Suru river) should go to India and that 'Gilgit, Gilgit Agency, Gilgit Wazarat, political districts, tribal territory and Baltistan and so much of the Jammu Province as lies west of the cease-fire' could go to Pakistan.[49]

Given the unofficial policy of New Delhi towards the PIS of J&K, New Delhi did not even bother to complain to the UNSC about the subsequent overt annexation of the occupied territory of the PIS of J&K by Pakistan. In fact, New Delhi told the UNSC that it did not request for a meeting as it considered it had 'a duty not to re-agitate matters' and, therefore, it had decided to 'let sleeping dogs lie so far as the actual state of affairs is concerned'.[50] New Delhi follows this policy till date. Farooq Abdullah, the former Chief Minister of the PIS of J&K with India, disclosed on 26 November 2015 that Atal Bihari Vajpayee, the then Indian Prime Minister, had, during his 1999 Lahore visit, offered the division of the state, and quotes him as saying 'I told them to keep that part of Kashmir and we will keep this part for resolution of the matter'.[51] Praveen Swami recorded in December 2015 that Narendra Modi, the Indian Prime Minister, 'has made a simple choice: to stay the course with the status quo, and see what it might deliver'.[52]

Thus, while officially New Delhi demands that Pakistan must vacate all the areas of the PIS of J&K occupied through aggression—as evidenced by the Indian Parliament's Resolution of 22 February 1994—it has viewed the conversion of the ceasefire line in the PIS of J&K (modified to the present Line of Control, LOC) into the international border between India and Pakistan as the solution to the Kashmir issue. Pakistan as also the militant outfits active in the territory comprising the PIS of J&K have consistently rejected such 'solution' to the Kashmir issue. In fact, Pakistan, reportedly acting on the 'submission' of Syed Salahuddin, the chief of the Hizbul Mujahideen, sent a letter on 9 September 2015 to the UNSC, complaining that India was planning to construct a 10-metre-high and 135-feet-wide embankment wall along the 197-km LOC, in order to convert the LOC into 'a quasi international border'.[53] Pakistan and the militant outfits view the LOC as the problem and not part of the solution to the Kashmir issue. Mercifully so, because one must pause here to consider whether New Delhi has the competence under the Constitution of India to give effect to such proposed solution. And, if not, has New Delhi been barking up the wrong tree since 1948.

Notes and References

1. For full text, see *Supra* Note 28, Chapter IV, pp. 75–79.
2. Ibid., p. 77.
3. See *Supra* Note 39, Chapter IV, p. 31.
4. S/PV 231, p. 157, Mohammed Zafrullah Khan (Pakistan), 22 January 1948.
5. S/PV 227, p. 13, Gopalaswami Ayyangar (India), 15 January 1948.
6. Ibid., p. 20.
7. Ibid., p. 29.
8. Ibid., p. 20.
9. S/PV 610, p. 15, Mohammad Zafrullah Khan (Pakistan), 23 December 1952.
10. S/PV 236, p. 274, Gopalaswami Ayyangar (India), 28 January 1948.
11. *Supra* Note 5, p. 20.
12. S/PV 234, pp. 222–223, M.C. Setalvad (India), 23 January 1948.
13. Oppenheim, L. 1961. *International Law*, edited by H. Lauterpacht, 8th Ed, Vol I, p. 550. London: Longmans.

14. Anand, A. S. 1997. 'Kashmir's accession is analogous to that of Texas', *Times of India*, New Delhi, 9 January.
15. Ibid.
16. *Supra* Note 1, Introduction.
17. *Kahan v Pakistan Federation*: 1951 (2) K.B. 1003.
18. S/PV 249, pp. 370–377, Austin (US), 4 February 1948.
19. S/PV 235, p. 261, Austin (US), 24 January 1948.
20. S/PV 236, p. 271, F. van Langenhove (Belgium), 28 January 1948.
21. S/PV 237, p. 288, Tsiang (China), 29 January 1948.
22. S/PV 237, p. 289, De La Tournelle (France), 29 January 1948.
23. S/PV 245, pp. 117–118, Arce (Argentina), 11 February 1948.
24. See S/PV 237, pp. 293–303, Gopalaswami Ayyangar (India), 29 January 1948.
25. Ibid.
26. United Nations. 1996. *The Blue Helmets: A Review of the United Nations Peace-Keeping*, p. 133, 3rd Ed. New York: Department of Public Information.
27. *Supra* Note 12, Chapter IV, p. 660.
28. *Supra* Note 26, p. 133.
29. Ibid., p. 134.
30. *Supra* Note 1, Chapter I, p. 472.
31. *Supra* Note 6, Chapter I, pp. 360–361.
32. See S/PV 763, p. 3, Krishna Menon (India), 23 January 1957.
33. *Supra* Note 6, Chapter I, p. 336.
34. Ibid. Sarila notes that this artery was the British-built track from Gilgit to Kashgar in Sinkiang, via the 4,709-metre-high Mintaka Pass, across the mighty Karakoram range, which enabled the British to maintain a presence north of the Karakoram (Ibid.).
35. Ibid., p. 337.
36. Ibid., p. 338.
37. Ibid.
38. Ibid., pp. 338–339.
39. See *Yearbook of the United Nations*, 1948–1949. The India-Pakistan Question, p. 279.
40. *Supra* Note 26, pp. 135–136.
41. *Yearbook of the United Nations*, 1950. The India-Pakistan Question, p. 304.
42. Ibid., pp. 304, 306.
43. Ibid., p. 312.
44. *Selected Works of Jawaharlal Nehru*. 1996. Second Series, Vol 19, pp. 322–323. Jawaharlal Nehru Memorial Fund, New Delhi.
45. Ibid.
46. Ibid.
47. *Supra* Note 3, Chapter V, p. 40.
48. *Supra* Note 28, Chapter I, p. 71.
49. *Supra* Note 41, pp. 311–312.
50. S/PV 769, p. 38, Krishna Menon (India), 15 February 1957.
51. Sharma, Arun. 2015. 'Pok will remain with Pak, J&K will remain part of India: Farooq', *The Indian Express*, New Delhi, 27 November.
52. Swami, Praveen. 2015. 'History of Pak engagement, calculus of Modi peace bid', *The Indian Express*, 8 December.
53. *The Indian Express*. 2015. 'Pak claims India mulling wall along IB', New Delhi, 26 September.

VIII

Territorial Status Quo

It is implicit in New Delhi's 'solution' of converting the LOC in the PIS of J&K into the international border between India and Pakistan that India would, or could, cede part of the territory of the PIS of J&K to Pakistan. But then, does New Delhi have the power to do so? Equally, did the PIS of J&K, having acceded to India, have the power to cede part of the state's territory to Pakistan, assuming that it had wanted to do so? This chapter examines the fallout of New Delhi's policy of territorial status quo. The chapter also documents the views of commentators on the Kashmir issue on such policy of New Delhi.

Competence of New Delhi to Cede Territory of the PIS of J&K

The general law may first be stated. It is, indeed, a well-settled principle of international law that the right to cede territory flows from the sovereign character of a state.[1] The reason for this is that the jurisdiction of a state over its own territories is necessarily exclusive and absolute. It would appear that New Delhi's power to cede territory of its constituent states in favour of another country would be an essential attribute of the sovereignty of India.

Having said that, there is nothing to prevent a sovereign state from imposing upon itself a limitation on the power of ceding territory. There are judicial precedents, notably of the dictum of John Marshall, the then US Chief Justice, in *The Exchange v N. Faddon*,[2] for the proposition that if such limitation can be traced to the consent of the sovereign state, it does not detract from the sovereignty of that state. The real question, therefore, is whether the Constitution of India, which represents the collective will of the people of India, puts any limitation on the power of New Delhi to cede territory of its constituent states. I believe it does, which would imply that New Delhi's policy since 1948 of territorial status quo in its constituent state of PIS of J&K is legally misconceived as well.

As a point of departure, let us consider the hypothetical situation that India and Pakistan agree to maintain status quo with regard to the territory of the PIS of J&K presently with them, and that both countries wish to draw the international border where the LOC presently exists. Such agreement would necessarily require a treaty between India and Pakistan. Indeed, the power of sovereign states to acquire and to cede territory is often located in the treaty-making power. While international law authorizes a sovereign state to negotiate treaties and assume obligations, the provisions of a treaty do not however bind the subjects of the contracting parties unless made binding by legislative action.[3] This rule prevails throughout the British Commonwealth. In other words, formal ratification of the treaty has now become an accepted part of the procedure of treaty making. The rule is reflected in the Convention of Treaties, adopted at the Sixth International Conference of American States at Havana on 20 February 1928, which provides in Article 5 that '[t]reaties are obligatory only after ratification by the contracting States, even though this condition is not stipulated in the full powers of the negotiators or does not appear in the treaty itself'.[4]

The constitutional provisions of different countries vary widely with respect to the procedure of ratification. Ratification itself is an executive act, performed by the head of the state, announcing formal acceptance of the treaty. But before the head of state can take such an action, many constitutions require the consent of one or both branches of the legislature. Seervai[5] gives the instance of the US, where it is for the President to negotiate a treaty, but his power is to be exercised on the advice and with the consent of the Senate. If the Senate refuses its consent, then the treaty does not become a law of the US as provided by Article 6(2) of the US Constitution, and would have no operation in the US, although it may involve a breach of the agreement with the foreign nation. An example was the failure of the US Senate to ratify the Comprehensive Test Ban Treaty negotiated by the US President.

In England, it has become customary for the Cabinet ratifying the treaty in the name of the Crown in Council to submit the treaty to Parliament for approval. Thus, the rule prevalent in the British Commonwealth is that an international treaty or agreement must be given domestic legislative mandate for it to take force.

As far as India is concerned, the decision of the Indian Supreme Court in *Jolly George Verghese⁶* is an authority for the proposition that an international treaty or agreement must go through the process of transformation into domestic law, before it can become an internal law or an enforceable part of the *corpus juris* of India. Article 253 of the Constitution of India empowers Indian Parliament to make any law for the whole or any part of the territory of India for implementing any treaty, agreement or convention with any other country or for implementing any decision made at any international conference, association or other body.

While on the subject of treaty-making power, the distinction between an uncontrolled constitution (like the unwritten British Constitution) and a controlled constitution (like the Constitution of India) must also be kept in mind. In an uncontrolled constitution, the difference between constituent power and legislative power disappears, because the legislature can amend, by the law-making procedure, any part of the Constitution as though it were a statute. However, with respect to a controlled Constitution, the procedure for making laws is distinct from the procedure for amending the Constitution. Seervai asserts that a 'treaty, for instance, cannot make provisions which would, in effect, amend the Constitution, or give up the form of Government set up by the Constitution, for it could not have been intended that a power conferred by the Constitution should, without an amendment of the Constitution, alter the Constitution'⁷

The Indian Supreme Court has discussed the features of a controlled constitution in *In re Delhi Laws Act, 1912.*⁸ The Court pointed out that although by the Indian Independence Act of 1947, 'the control of British Parliament over the Government of India and the Central Legislature was removed, the powers of the Central Legislature were still as those found in the Government of India Act, 1935'.⁹ Indeed, it 'is commonplace of constitutional law that a legislature created by a written constitution must act within the ambit of its powers as defined by the constitution and subject to the limitations prescribed thereby and every legislative act done contrary to the provisions of the constitution is void'.¹⁰ The reason is simple. As the Privy Council put it, 'the Dominion cannot, merely by making promises to foreign countries, clothe itself with legislative authority inconsistent with the Constitution which gave it birth'.¹¹ This rule has been applied consistently throughout the Commonwealth.¹²

With the commencement of the Constitution of India, the power of New Delhi to conclude an international treaty became subject to the express and implied restrictions imposed by the provisions of the Constitution of India. The Indian Supreme Court, in *In re Delhi Laws Act, 1912,* held that the 'Indian Parliament of the present day ... a creature of the Indian Constitution ... has to exercise its legislative powers within the limits laid down by the Constitution itself'[13] and that it is 'not a sovereign body, uncontrolled with unlimited powers'.[14]

Thus, the legal position is that not only would an international agreement entered into by New Delhi be required to be ratified by the Indian Parliament and incorporated into domestic law, such an agreement cannot also be inconsistent with any express or implied prohibition contained in the Constitution of India.

With this background, let us consider the competence of New Delhi to cede national territory. *Berubari Union*[15] dealt with this issue. In that case, an Indo-Pakistan agreement was entered into on 10 September 1958 between the Prime Ministers of India and Pakistan with a view to settle certain border area disputes. On consideration of the agreement and its background, the Indian Supreme Court held that the agreement amounted to cession or alienation of a part of the Indian territory in favour of Pakistan. The Supreme Court found that the implementation of such agreement would necessitate the amendment of Article 1, which describes India to be a 'Union of States', and of the First Schedule to the Constitution of India, which specifies the territories of India. The Court found that mere executive directives could not give effect to the agreement. The question arose as to whether Parliament could amend the Constitution of India to implement the agreement. The Court took the view that it could do so as 'under international law two of the essential attributes of sovereignty are the power to acquire foreign territory as well as the power to cede national territory in favour of a foreign State'.[16]

The argument raised in *Berubari Union* was that the Preamble to the Constitution of India, which starts by saying '[w]e, the people of India, having solemnly resolved to constitute India into a sovereign democratic Republic', postulates that India geographically and territorially must always continue to be democratic and republican and, therefore, Parliament has no power to cede any part of the territory of India in favour of a foreign State even by constitutional amendment. The Supreme Court held that the Preamble was not a part of the Constitution of India and could not impose a constitutional limitation on the power of New Delhi to cede national territory, being one of the very important attributes of sovereignty.

This approach of the Indian Supreme Court in *Berubari Union* has, however, been overruled by its 13-judge decision in *Keshavananda Bharati*.[17] In *Keshavananda Bharati*, the Supreme Court observed that the Preamble was very much a part of the Constitution of India and was, in fact, enacted and adopted by the same Constituent Assembly that drafted the Constitution. The Court held that the Preamble was drafted in light of the Objective Resolution of 13 December 1946 adopted by the Constituent Assembly, which expressly stated that:[18]

> 1. This Constituent Assembly declares its firm and solemn resolve to proclaim India as an Independent Sovereign Republic and to draw up for her future governance a Constitution.

> 2. Wherein the territories that now comprise British India, the territories that now form the Indian States, and such other parts of India as are outside British India and the States as well as such other territories as are willing to be constituted into the Independent Sovereign India, shall be a Union of them all; and....

> 7. Wherein shall be *maintained the integrity of the territory of the Republic* and its sovereign rights on land, sea and air according to justice and law of civilized nations.... [emphasis added]

The Court, in *Keshavananda Bharati,* enunciated the basic structure doctrine. It reasoned that the power of Parliament to amend the Constitution did not include the power to amend it out of existence or destroy its identity. There were, thus, some basic features of the Constitution that could not be amended by Parliament. The Court, therefore, held that it was 'convinced that the Parliament has no power to abrogate or emasculate the basic elements or fundamental features of the Constitution such as the sovereignty of India, the democratic nature of our policy, the unity of the country, the essential features of the individual freedoms secured to the citizens'.[19]

The Indian Supreme Court, in its 9-judge decision in *S.R. Bommai,* reiterated that the 'preamble of the Constitution is an integral part of the Constitution', and that '[d]emocratic form of Government, federal structure, unity and integrity of the nation, secularism, socialism, social justice and judicial review are basic features of the Constitution'.[20]

Should there have been any doubts concerning this legal position, the Constitution (Forty-Second) Amendment Act, 1976, amended the Preamble to the Constitution of India to provide the 'unity and integrity of the Nation' as one of the basic elements that 'the people of India' have solemnly resolved to secure. In view of such constitutional developments, the question of the Indian Parliament having the power to cede Indian territory can be confidently ruled out.

Interestingly, even in *Berubari Union,* the Supreme Court observed that the power of the Indian Parliament to cede territory 'is of course subject to the limitations which the Constitution' may either 'expressly or by necessary implication' impose in that behalf, and that '[s]tated broadly, the treaty making power would have to be exercised in the manner contemplated by the Constitution and subject to the limitations imposed by it'.[21] While the Court could not read any such constitutional limitation in *Berubari Union*, it did read one in *Keshavananda Bharati*. The fact of the matter, thus, is that the Indian Supreme Court has read in the Constitution of India a limitation on the power of Indian Parliament to abrogate or tinker with the 'unity of the country'. It is, no doubt, theoretically true that a larger bench of the Supreme Court could overrule *Keshavananda Bharati* as also the basic structure doctrine that has held the field since 1973. However, practically speaking, such a possibility may be ruled out, not least because the Supreme Court has through this ruling assumed for itself constituent power and wields the 'basic structure' stick for any constitutional amendment that it does not endorse. It is not likely that 15 judges of the Supreme Court would, at any point of time, concur in gifting this political power back to Parliament.

Seervai, however, locates the competence of Parliament to cede territory in its residuary legislative powers.[22] It may be noted here that the Constitution of India contains three lists in its Seventh Schedule, distributing the legislative areas between the Indian Parliament and the state legislatures. These lists contain legislative entries allotting some matters exclusively to the Indian Parliament (Union List), some exclusively to the state legislatures (State List) and some to both Parliament and state legislatures (Concurrent List). Article 248 of the Constitution provides that Parliament would have exclusive power to make any law with respect to any matter not enumerated in the Concurrent List or State List. Thus, the Constitution vests such residuary powers in Parliament, which, according to Seervai, could be exercised by Parliament to cede national territory.

It will, however, suffice to again cite the decision of the Indian Supreme Court in *Keshavananda Bharati* to rebut such view. In *Keshavananda Bharati*, the Supreme Court considered the question as to whether the power of Parliament to amend the Constitution could be located in its residuary powers. The Court held that it could not, since the Constitution-makers were 'keenly conscious' of the importance of the provision relating to the amendment of the Constitution and would not have this important power 'hidden' in the residuary powers of Parliament 'leaving it to the off chance of the courts locating that power'.[23]

It has already been pointed out that the Preamble to the Constitution of India and Article 1 thereof emphasize the unity of the nation. The

Constitution of India contains no express provision permitting Parliament, by law, to cede national territory. However, the possibility of acquiring territory was foreseen by the Constitution-makers, as is evident from the fact that Article 1(3)(c) of the Constitution of India includes in the 'territory of India' 'such territories as may be acquired'. Article 2 empowers Parliament, by law, to admit into the Union, or to establish, new states. Hence, the unity of the Union of India and the extent of the territory of India were indisputably present in the minds of the Constitution-makers. It is, therefore, difficult to believe that the Constitution-makers, who were keenly conscious of the importance of the provisions relating to the unity of the Indian Union and to the extent of the territory of India, would have left the power of Parliament to cede Indian territory hidden in the residuary powers of Parliament. If they considered that Parliament had such power, they would have surely included this power in express words in a specific constitutional provision. The obvious inference is that the Indian Parliament lacks the power to cede national territory.

It follows from the above discussion that the Constitution of India does not permit the Government of India or the Indian Parliament to cede national territory. Nor can the Indian Parliament amend the Constitution to get such competence. It is true that there is no such thing like an unamendable Constitution. However, the question here is not whether the Constitution of India is or is not susceptible to amendment—for, it is, as long it does not violate the basic structure doctrine. The point is that the Constitution of India is what the Indian Supreme Court says it is. The Supreme Court says that the Constitution of India does not permit Parliament to amend the Constitution so as to destroy its basic structure. The 'unity of the country' has been identified as part of such basic structure. It is from this finding that the constitutional limitation on the power of Parliament to cede territory can be inferred. Such a limitation also does not detract from the sovereignty of India in light of the dictum of Marshall in *The Exchange v N. Faddon.*[24] Since the restriction on the power of Parliament to cede territory has been imposed by the Constitution of India, which has been duly framed and adopted by its people, it can be traced to the consent of the people—the legitimate source of sovereignty.

It may be recalled that the Constitution of India was made applicable to the PIS of J&K through the Proclamation of 25 November 1949 of Yuvraj Karan Singh. The First Schedule of the Constitution of India specifies the territory of the PIS of J&K to be 'the territory which immediately before the commencement of this Constitution are comprised in the Indian State of Jammu and Kashmir'. This territory includes the territory of the PIS of J&K

occupied by Pakistan, and which New Delhi is not competent to cede. If we contrast this legal position with New Delhi's views on its powers, it will be evident how terribly misconceived New Delhi's approach has been. Nehru declared in Lok Sabha on 26 June 1952 as under:[25]

> And I say with all respect to our Constitution that it just does not matter what your Constitution says, if the people of Kashmir do not want it, it will not got there.... Let us suppose there is a proper plebiscite there—and the people of Kashmir said, 'We do not want to be with India', well we are committed to it, we would accept it. It might pain us but we would not send our army against them; we might accept that, however much hurt we might feel about it, and we would change our Constitution about it.

Nehru reiterated in Parliament on 7 August 1952 that:[26]

> The way out may not be completely logical, it may not be completely reasonable from the point of view of this law or that Constitution, but if it is effective, then it is a good way out, whether it offends against some legalistic arguments or logical arguments or not....

It may be argued that at the time of the reference to the UNSC and right up to 1973, the basic structure doctrine had not been propounded by the Supreme Court. However, the result would have been the same had New Delhi kept in mind the elementary proposition that the executive in India is responsible to the Indian Parliament, which, unlike the British Parliament, is not supreme but is a creature of the controlled Constitution of India, and subject to the constitutional limitations discussed earlier in this chapter. The constitutional limitation on Parliament to cede national territory was known to the executive in 1947, as is evident from the mere fact that it was Nehru himself who moved the aforesaid Objective Resolution of 13 December 1946 in the Constituent Assembly. Indeed, the first thing that the Constituent Assembly, which was set up to frame the Constitution of India, did was to adopt this Resolution, that expressly provided for the 'Union' of territories that comprise British India, the territories that form the Indian states, and such other parts of India as are outside British India and the states as well as such other territories as are willing to be constituted into the Independent Sovereign India; and mandated that 'the integrity of the territory of the Republic' would be maintained.

In light of this Resolution, New Delhi was fully aware in 1947 that it lacked competence to undo 'the integrity of the territory of the Republic'. Ironically, this was the same Resolution which was referred to and relied upon by the

Supreme Court in *Keshavananda Bharati* to formulate the basic structure doctrine.[27] Be that as it may, the question of New Delhi ceding national territory post the formulation of the basic structure doctrine does not arise.

Competence of the PIS of J&K to Cede Territory of the State

If the Indian Parliament cannot cede territory of any of its constituent states, can a constituent state cede part of its territory? This issue may be examined in light of the broader proposition, namely, whether a constituent state can secede from the Union of India? After all, if the constituent state lacks the power to secede from the Union of India, it lacks the power to cede part of its own territory.

Reference in this regard may be made to the view of the US Supreme Court. In *George W. White*,[28] the US Supreme Court considered the question of whether the State of Texas could, by the Ordinance of Secession, ratified by a majority of its citizens and given effect to by Acts of its legislature, secede from the US. Salmon P. Chase, the then US Chief Justice, held that it could not as the Constitution 'looks to an indestructible Union, composed of indestructible States' and that when 'Texas became one of the United States, she entered into an indissoluble relation'.[29]

Another case in point is that of the Commonwealth of Australia. The Commonwealth Constitution of Australia derives its legal authority from an Act of the Imperial (British) Parliament, 63 and 64 Vic. c. 12, and is the outcome of an agreement between the States named in the Preamble—New South Wales, Victoria, South Australia, Queensland and Tasmania—together with Western Australia. Section 3 of the Act provides that the states 'shall be united in a Federal Commonwealth under the name of the Commonwealth of Australia'. Nicholas notes that in 1935, the petition from the State of Western Australia to secede from the Commonwealth came before a Joint Committee of the House of Commons and the House of Lords, which was, however, unable to hold that the State had a right to secede and recommended that the petition not be allowed.[30]

As far as India is concerned, Article 1 of the Constitution of India looks to an indestructible 'Union of States'. The Indian Supreme Court, in its 9-judge decision in *S.R. Bommai*, took the view that a constituent state, 'being the creature of the Constitution ... has no right to secede or claim sovereignty'.[31]

The Constituent Assembly Debates also confirm the intention of the Constitution-makers that a constituent state, having acceded to the Union of States, had no right to secede from the Union.[32] The sovereign ruler of the PIS of J&K did accede to the dominion of India. Moreover, as already discussed, the people of a portion of India, whether it be in the territory of the PIS of J&K or any other state, did not have a right to self-determination.

Even otherwise, the Constitution of Jammu and Kashmir of 1957, framed by the Constituent Assembly of the PIS of J&K pursuant to the proclamation of the sovereign ruler of the said state, Yuvraj Karan Singh, rules out the secession of the PIS of J&K from the Union of India. The 'territory of State' is defined in Section 4 of the Constitution of Jammu and Kashmir of 1957 to be 'all territories which on the fifteenth day of August, 1947, were under the sovereignty or suzerainty of the Ruler of the State'. As noted earlier, the Constitution of Jammu and Kashmir of 1957 declares the PIS of J&K to be an integral part of the Union of India and puts a limitation, in Section 147, upon the legislative power to amend the Constitution of Jammu and Kashmir of 1957 to alter this position.

In an interesting case of *S. Mohsin Shah*,[33] the Full Bench of the Jammu and Kashmir High Court had to consider whether a resident of the PIS of J&K occupied by Pakistan could be deported from India. In that case, the petitioner was a resident of Skardu where he engaged in business. He was born and brought up in Srinagar. Since Skardu was in the PIS of J&K occupied by Pakistan, and as the border was sealed after the invasion in 1947, the petitioner was compelled to apply for a Pakistan passport to come to Srinagar. The Government of India sought to deport him to Pakistan on the ground that he was a Pakistani citizen. The High Court held that the petitioner, a resident of the PIS of J&K occupied by Pakistan, was a citizen of India under the Constitution of Jammu and Kashmir of 1957 as also the Constitution of India, since the territory comprising the PIS of J&K occupied by Pakistan was included in the Schedule of territories to which the Constitution of India applied. The petitioner was seeking to travel from one part of India to another through a foreign country. He, therefore, had to obtain a passport per force as there was no other way of visiting his home state which was also an integral part of India. The High Court observed the anomaly that even if the petitioner was deported from India, he would be deported to Skardu, which was constitutionally and legally an integral part of India, since the entire PIS of J&K had become a part of India upon the signing of the Instrument of Accession.

Thus, in light of the express provisions of the Constitution of India and the Constitution of Jammu and Kashmir of 1957, and the 13-judge bench decision of the Indian Supreme Court in *Keshavananda Bharati*,[34] the Indian Parliament and the legislative assembly of the PIS of J&K are not competent to cede the territory of the PIS of J&K nor are they in a position to even amend their respective Constitutions to enable cession of such territory. In other words, New Delhi does not possess the power, under its own Constitution, to enter into an agreement with Pakistan or any other country or authority that the LOC in the territory of the PIS of J&K be converted into the international border. There can be no Parliamentary action to give effect to any such international agreement or treaty.

It may be noted that New Delhi, under a misconception of its competence to cede national territory, issued an executive order under Article 370(1) of the Constitution of India, being the Constitution (Application to Jammu and Kashmir) Order, 1954, which added the following proviso to Article 253 of the Constitution of India:

> Provided that after the commencement of the Constitution (Application to Jammu and Kashmir) Order, 1954, no decision affecting the disposition of the State of Jammu and Kashmir shall be made by the Government of India without the consent of the Government of that State.

It would, however, be fallacious to contend that this provision, by contemplating a disposition of the PIS of J&K, implies that New Delhi has the power to cede such territory. The proviso to Article 253 of the Constitution is an executive act limiting the executive power of New Delhi to take any decision with respect to the state without its consent, and not a source of power empowering New Delhi to cede territory of the state. In any case, the state government is bound by the Constitution of Jammu and Kashmir of 1957 declaring the state to be an integral part of India. That rules out the state government giving its consent to New Delhi to make a disposition of the state.

Notwithstanding this constitutional and legal position, New Delhi continues to take the view that it would rather forget about the occupied territory of the PIS of J&K (which is Indian territory) and also its people (who are citizens of India entitled to the guaranteed rights under the Constitution of India). New Delhi has consistently worked towards the conversion of the LOC into the international border from 1948 onwards.

New Delhi, Srinagar and Status Quo

Such has been the conviction for maintaining status quo that during negotiations in Tashkent in 1966, New Delhi returned to Pakistan the crucial Haji Pir located at a height of 12,000 feet, which had been recovered heroically by the Indian forces in the 1965 Indo-Pakistan war.[35] Incredible as it may seem, India actually returned to Pakistan the territory which was, and is, legally and constitutionally a part of India and which had been forcibly and illegally captured by Pakistan during the 1947 aggression. New Delhi did not only hand over its own territory to Pakistan that was recovered at terrible cost during the 1965 war, it did so at its own peril. For, it is this area—the Haji Pir Pass and certain features in Kargil—through which terrorists infiltrate into the territory of the PIS of J&K with India. Along the mountain ranges of the snow clad Pir Panjal ranges, there are slits hiding guns overlooking the border at the LOC in the Uri Sector. Since Uri juts into the territory of the PIS of J&K under Pakistan's occupation, Pakistan dominates the borders here from three sides and uses the terrain to its advantage for infiltration and for attacking Indian posts.[36] If that was not bad enough, New Delhi committed with Pakistan in the Tashkent Declaration, signed on 10 January 1966, that 'both sides shall observe the cease-fire terms on the cease-fire line'. It is generally believed that the then Soviet Union leaned on New Delhi to do so by declining to use its veto power in favour of India should the matter be taken up by the UNSC. Interestingly, Shankar Bajpai, the then Secretary to the Indian delegation at the Tashkent Conference, disclosed in January 2016 that Moscow had signalled to the Indian delegation at the Conference that should it not come to an agreement with Pakistan, 'Moscow would not give us its usual veto in the Security Council'; Moscow's tilt towards Pakistan had apparently stemmed from its strategy to wean Pakistan away 'from its then pet hate, China'.[37]

Similarly, during the 1971 Indo-Pakistan war, New Delhi captured 93,000 Pakistani prisoners of war (PoWs) and helped create Bangladesh. New Delhi returned the PoWs to Pakistan without demanding the vacation of the territory of the PIS of J&K under the occupation of Pakistan since 1947.[38] Since New Delhi aimed for a status quo, it was content with an oral assurance from Zulfikar Ali Bhutto, the then Pakistani Prime Minister, that Pakistan would not raise the Kashmir issue again.[39] New Delhi, thus, indicated that Pakistan could keep the territory of the PIS of J&K already occupied by it.

Later, instead of demanding that Pakistan vacate the aggression, New Delhi entered into the Simla Agreement on 2 July 1972, whereby it *expressly restricted* itself from unilaterally altering the status quo and reiterated the *inviolability* of the LOC. This is the stand that New Delhi takes till date. This Agreement on Bilateral Relations between India and Pakistan states that '[p]ending the final settlement of any of the problems between the two countries, neither side shall unilaterally alter the situation'. It mandates that in 'Jammu and Kashmir the line of control resulting from the ceasefire of [17] December 1971 shall be respected by both sides without prejudice to the recognised position of either side', that '[n]either side shall seek to alter it unilaterally irrespective of mutual differences and legal interpretations' and that '[b]oth sides further undertake to refrain from the threat or the use of force in violation of this line'. New Delhi stuck to this stand in the Lahore Declaration of 21 February 1999, which reiterated 'the determination' of India and Pakistan to implement the Simla Agreement.

It is widely accepted, at least in India, that in 1972, during the negotiations leading to the Simla Agreement, Indira Gandhi, the then Indian Prime Minister, sought to pressurize Zulfikar Ali Bhutto to agree to convert the LOC into the international border with minor modifications. Ramchandra Guha writes:[40]

.... Bhutto had apparently assured Mrs. Gandhi that, once his position was more secure, he would persuade his people to accept conversion of the line of control into the international border. The ink had hardly dried on the Simla Agreement when Bhutto reneged on this (admittedly informal) promise. On 14 July he spoke for three hours in the National Assembly of Pakistan.... As a victor in war, said Bhutto, 'India had all the cards in her hands'—yet he had still forged an equal agreement from an unequal beginning. The Simla accord was a success, he argued, because Pakistan would get back its POWs and land held by Indian forces, and because it did 'not compromise on the right of self-determination of the people of Jammu and Kashmir...'.

I.K. Gujral, former Indian Prime Minister, who was at that time a member of the Indian Cabinet and was present at Simla, asserts that Bhutto had unofficially accepted the LOC as the international border but later changed his mind.[41] So, Gujral had felt it appropriate to write a letter to Kofi Annan, the then UN Secretary General, to place on record what Bhutto had accepted. New Delhi itself committed a 'cartographic surrender', when it sponsored a 16 page Supplement to be carried in the August 1982 (Vol 247, No. 3) issue of the widely read international journal, *Scientific American*, that contained a map of India, provided by New Delhi, showing the occupied territory of PIS of J&K outside the national boundaries of India.[42]

Gautam Adhikari opines that the 'Kashmir issue was in fact "resolved"' with the two nations agreeing 'that the line of actual control in India's Jammu and Kashmir state would be a de facto border'.[43] Prem Shankar Jha agrees that 'a willingness to settle on the LOC is implicit in the Simla Agreement'.[44] Shekhar Gupta points out that the 'main achievement' of the Simla Accord was to give the LOC the status of a de facto international border.[45] P.N. Dhar, a bureaucrat who was actively involved in the Simla Conference in 1972, disclosed that it was agreed that the LOC would be gradually endowed with 'characteristics of an international border' and that 'Pakistan-occupied Kashmir would be incorporated into Pakistan' for which 'India would make *proforma* protests in a low key'.[46]

Given the 'unofficial' agreement at Simla in 1972 with respect to converting the LOC into the international border, New Delhi's protests over the manner in which Pakistan has dealt with the occupied territories of the PIS of J&K have, indeed, been low key. The underlying assumption was that the gradual use of the LOC as the de facto border would reconcile people to its permanence. It certainly seems to have reconciled India's eminent politicians to its permanence, with New Delhi till date actually pleading before every international forum that it respects the 'inviolability' of the LOC, and that Pakistan must do so, too, by refraining from making incursions across the LOC. Indeed, as Noorani notes, 'no government has talked of formally demanding return of POK' after the Simla Agreement.[47] And so, when on 21 June 2015, a middle-aged woman, Shabana, resident of the territory of the PIS of J&K occupied by Pakistan inadvertently crossed the LOC in Nawshera Sector in Rajouri district, the Indian Army reportedly returned her to the Pakistan authorities from Chakan Da Bag Crossing Point in Poonch, that is, the Indian Army took the initiative of handing over a person, who was constitutionally and legally an Indian citizen, to a foreign authority.[48]

Even the Jammu and Kashmir High Court seems to have been impressed by the status quo. In *World Human Rights Protection*,[49] the High Court virtually equated the territory of the PIS of J&K occupied by Pakistan with Pakistan. In that case, a married lady, who was a resident of the PIS of J&K occupied by Pakistan, had jumped into the river Jhelum due to marital differences. She was swept to the Indian side of the river and picked up by the authorities, who handed her over to the 'police, having entered Indian territory without valid papers'.[50] The lady, whilst in jail in the PIS of J&K with India, was allegedly raped by the jail warden. The lady conceived, and gave birth to a female child while in custody. As regards the lady, the High Court took the view that 'coming over to this part of the country without permission was an offence on part of the lady' and that she was kept in detention since the 'authorities have not been able to deport her to Pakistan'.[51] Dealing with the question of the domicile of the minor child, the High Court held that because she was conceived and born in the PIS of

J&K with India, she would have to be treated as a domicile of the state, but as 'no one is sure of the fatherhood of the minor child', it was for the minor child 'to express a choice in this regard'. The High Court opined that 'the choice can be expressed by her mother also but the question as to whether she can be deported to Pakistan would depend upon the decision which the authorities in Pakistan may take in this regard'.[52] The High Court overlooked the fact that it was immaterial in which part of the PIS of J&K the child was born—whether the territory with India or in Pakistan's occupation. In either situation, the child would have been a domicile of the state. The question of deporting the child, or the lady (both being Indian citizens under the Constitution of India) to Pakistan does not arise.

In an earlier case, the High Court had, in fact, recommended to the state government not to give effect to the Jammu and Kashmir Evacuee (Administration of Property) Act, (*Samvat 2006*), as it felt that the Act dealing with evacuee property had outlived its utility after more than 40 years of its enactment. It was the Indian Supreme Court in *Mahmood Ahmed*,[53] which set aside such an observation of the High Court, holding that since a portion of the PIS of J&K was still in the hands of an alien government, there remained the possibility of a property becoming evacuee property and, hence, the provisions of the said Act could not be said to have outlived their utility.

While New Delhi preferred to disclaim the occupied territories of the PIS of J&K, Srinagar went further to expressly ask Pakistan to retain the territories under its occupation. Farooq Abdullah, who had declared in 1983, that '[a]s an Indian and a Kashmiri, there is no question of surrendering our claim to the territory forcibly occupied by Pakistan',[54] reportedly pleaded with Pakistan in January 1997, soon after assuming office in 1996 as Chief Minister of the territory of the PIS of J&K with India, that it should keep the occupied territories of state but stop the insurgency.[55] Post Kargil, Farooq Abdullah yet again reportedly declared that Pakistan should accept the LOC as the international border and settle the dispute, as it was not possible for either Pakistan or India to forcibly take away the parts of the PIS of J&K from each other.[56] Abdullah continues to maintain this position, and reportedly asserted on 26 November 2015 that while the territory of the PIS of J&K with India 'is part of India and will continue to remain so', the territory of the state occupied by Pakistan 'is part of Pakistan and it will continue to remain so'.[57] Abdullah dismissed the voices in Pakistan occupied Kashmir wanting to join India by saying that 'this will never happen'.[58] He reasoned on 28 November 2015 that nuclear-armed neighbours cannot make each other cede territory held by them.[59]

Incomprehensible as it may seem, the proposal that the LOC be converted into the international border was supported by a cross-section of former Indian Chiefs of Army, Air Force, Navy and intelligence agencies and former Indian government officials. An article[60] published in March 1999 quotes General K. Sundarji, former Chief of Army Staff, as opining that such proposal was 'realistic, practical and worth considering'. General S.F. Rodrigues, former Chief of Army Staff, viewed such a proposal in the context of an increasingly interactive world. Admiral L. Ramdas, former Chief of Naval Staff, felt that 'it could be the bottom line for a settlement on Indo-Pakistan relations'. Air Chief Marshal Arjan Singh, former Chief of Air Staff, stated that there was 'substance in the statement [of Farooq Abdullah]. And it would be the height of wisdom if both sides do agree to slight adjustment here and there'. A.K. Verma, former Chief of the Research and Analysis Wing (RAW), contended that the proposal could not be rejected without examining the possibilities it opens up. Admiral S.M. Nanda, former Chief of Naval Staff, opined that India has accepted the fact that Pakistan could retain the area beyond the LOC, and so New Delhi should accept the realities of time and get on with nation building. General V.N. Sharma, former Chief of Army Staff, felt that it was 'not a bad starting point to open discussion with Pakistan'. T.V. Rajeshwar, former Director of the Intelligence Bureau, stated that the proposal could not be 'described as outrageous' and that it 'could become one of the possible solutions'. Air Chief Marshall S.K. Kaul, former Chief of Air Staff, also asserted that this was 'one of the possible solutions'. Admiral R.H. Tahiliani, former Chief of Naval Staff, agreed, opining that 'any solution which reduces tension and allows people to live in peace should be examined expeditiously by national leaders on both sides'. Air Chief Marshal S.K. Mehra, former Chief of Air Staff, felt that it was 'the most practical thing to do'. G.C. Saxena, former Chief of the RAW and the Governor of the PIS of J&K with India, agreed that '[w]e cannot afford to be rigid. It's good that Farooq has given rise to a national debate. Now a solution has to be hammered out through quiet diplomacy'.

That the 'national debate' on such a solution, or 'quiet diplomacy' to hammer it out, would be a futile exercise lacking legal basis, did not deter scholars, intellectuals, analysts or experts on the Kashmir issue. The typical approach of such commentators is exemplified by an article written by Ishwar Sharma,[61] who claims that there are no commonalties of economic and political interest binding the people of the 'two Kashmirs' together to create a stake in its continuance as a single unit. Partition of the Indian subcontinent and the tribal invasion of the PIS of J&K destroyed whatever links had been developed during the Dogra rule. He opines that the invasion, and the resulting accession of the state to India, set into motion the process of division of the state. The subsequent ceasefire agreement under the UN extended 'legitimacy and international recognition to the fact of division'. Later, the Simla Agreement 'converted' the ceasefire line into the LOC and became the 'final seal of de jure acceptance by both India and Pakistan'. He insists that 'the reality of division of the State will inevitably be the basis of any viable political response to the current situation'.[62]

Tapan K. Bose writes that since '[n]o government in Pakistan can afford to reopen the accession of Gilgit and Baltistan which every Pakistani considers as an integral part of their country' and that 'Pakistan has already acceded territory to China from these areas', the 'dialogue between India and Pakistan gets narrowed down to the working out mechanisms for the finalisation of the present line of control in Jammu and Kashmir into the international border with minor changes'.[63]

J.N. Dixit, who was part of the Track Two diplomacy team that visited Pakistan in January 2001,[64] was critical of any attempt to reclaim the PIS of J&K occupied by Pakistan as being 'impractical',[65] and opined that 'India should convey a clear message to important powers and to the international community, that a durable solution has to be set on the basis of the LOC...'.[66]

Bharat Bhushan contends that one 'positive' fallout of the Kargil conflict was the widespread international recognition of the LOC as the de facto border.[67] He even asserts that if India 'believes in the sanctity of the LOC as described in the Simla Agreement', then all political statements about Pakistan vacating its occupation of the territories of the PIS of J&K ought to be avoided by India. He criticizes the then Indian Prime Minister Vajpayee for exhibiting his 'new found belligerence at a public meeting in Jalandhar on February 6 [2000] by saying that what needs to be discussed with Pakistan is the return of Pakistan occupied Kashmir'.[68]

B.G. Verghese argues that it would be 'mistaken' to make talks with Pakistan conditional upon its vacation of 'Azad Kashmir' and the Northern Areas, and that after 'Kargil, the world too has at last begun to accept that a settlement has to be built around the LOC and the construction of a new intra-Jammu-and-Kashmir and Indo-Pakistan relationship across that international border-in-the-making'.[69]

Kanti Bajpai agrees that the most feasible choice is the partition of the PIS of J&K and conversion of the LOC as the international border.[70] He argues that to 'make Pakistan accept L.O.C solution', there could be agreement on Siachen, Sir Creek and Wular, and free trade. He opines that Kargil, diplomatic isolation, India's success in wearing out militancy, and Pakistan's economic and internal difficulties can help change its mind.

Commentators such as Rajmohan Gandhi,[71] Swapan Dasgupta,[72] V.R. Grover,[73] Rakshat Puri,[74] A.N. Dar,[75] Jasjit Singh,[76] Rajinder Sachar,[77] Kuldip Nayar[78] and Hari Jaisingh[79] have expressed similar views. The perception of the Indian commentators is shared by some foreign commentators as well. For instance, Teresita Schaffer, former US Deputy Secretary of State for Near Eastern Affairs and the Director of South Asia Programme at the Center for Strategic International Studies in Washington, opines that it is not possible to 'change the map in Kashmir' and that 'the settlement will have to basically keep the same L.O.C., if there is a settlement'.[80] David Gore Booth, former UK High Commissioner to India, declared in April 1999 that the most viable solution to the Kashmir issue would be to recognize the LOC as the international border, since both India and Pakistan had almost reached this agreement in Simla in 1972.[81] Snedden goes further. He asserts that India only nominally claims the territories of the PIS of J&K occupied by Pakistan. According to him, 'New Delhi has shown scant interest in "its" territory since the 1949 ceasefire, or in the people's welfare therein', since 'Azad Kashmir' is 'economically backward', and possibly 'India also realised early on that to placate, then integrate, the martial, militant, anti-Indian Azad Kashmir Muslims would be a difficult—and undesirable—task'.[82] Snedden argues that it was 'easier to blame Pakistan for "occupying" this area, while concurrently leaving these rabidly pro-Pakistan elements "free" from Indian control'.[83]

While many more instances can be given, it will suffice to note that such approach towards the occupied territories of the PIS of J&K is inconsistent with the provisions of not only the Constitution of India, but also the Constitution of Jammu and Kashmir of 1957. Moreover, the Unlawful Activities (Prevention) Act of 1967, enacted by the Indian Parliament, makes it a punishable offence to engage in an 'unlawful activity', which is defined in Section 2(f) to mean

any action taken by such individual or association....

(i) which is intended, or supports any claim, to bring about, on any ground whatsoever, the cession of a part of the territory of India or the secession of a part of the territory of India from the Union, or which incites any individual or group of individuals to bring about such cession or secession;

(ii) which disclaims, questions, disrupts or is intended to disrupt the sovereignty and territorial integrity of India.

Section 2(b) of the 1967 Act defines 'cession of a part of the territory of India' to include admission of the claim of any foreign country to any such part, while Section 2(d) defines 'secession of a part of the territory of India from the Union' to include the assertion of any claim to determine whether such part will remain a part of the territory of India. And so, all those calling for the conversion of the LOC into an international border between India and Pakistan are engaging in 'unlawful activity' in terms of the 1967 Act.

New Delhi, Srinagar and almost all commentators on the Kashmir issue, in their enthusiasm to evolve a consensus that the Kashmir solution lies in disclaiming the occupied territories of the PIS of J&K and the people living in such territories, apparently remain unaware of this constitutional and legal position.

The PIS of J&K Occupied by Pakistan and Status Quo

Pakistan has no basis whatsoever to remain in any part of the territory of the PIS of J&K, the latter having been a sovereign state as on 15 August 1947, and not having acceded to the dominion of Pakistan at any point of time. As discussed in the previous chapter, the UNCIP Resolutions required withdrawal of Pakistan troops as also the tribesmen and Pakistani nationals from the PIS of J&K, following which India was to withdraw the bulk of its forces from the state. Pakistan simply did not do so and, expectedly, drew no censure from the UNSC for such blatant violation of the UNCIP Resolutions.

In the meantime, Pakistan has maintained its complete control, directly or indirectly, over 86,023 square kilometres of the territory of the PIS of J&K occupied through aggression.[84] The territory of the PIS of J&K occupied by Pakistan is not described by the Constitution of Pakistan as Pakistan's territory. Rather, Part XII of the Constitution, dealing with miscellaneous matters, provides in Article 257 that '[w]hen the people of the State of Jammu and Kashmir decide to accede to Pakistan, the relationship between Pakistan and the State shall be determined in accordance with the wishes of the people of that State'.

Let us consider Pakistan's approach to the territory of the PIS of J&K occupied by it. Given the Great Game objectives, it was inevitable that such territory would become the military outpost of Pakistan, and through Pakistan, of the Western powers. Krishna Menon (India) pointed out before the UNSC in 1957 that:[85]

> Western Kashmir is practically a province of Pakistan, administered by its central Government. It has no local government and, therefore, has become integrated in that way. The same applies to other areas, directed by the

Pakistan Army or the Pakistan Government ... in the area under Pakistan occupation, which Pakistan has illegally ... incorporated in its Dominion, airfields capable of taking military planes have been prepared.... In regard to air bases in Northern Kashmir, Gilgit and Chitral are the two important airfields; they are on the Soviet–Chinese–Indian border and, according to the reports that we have, are being expanded and developed. Of course, equipment cannot be manufactured in Pakistan. Heavy machinery and radar are reported to have arrived there. The 'Azad' Kashmir forces have no air arm of their own ... the Government of Pakistan has rendered important assistance to the 'Azad' movement; it has officered the 'Azad' forces with officers of the Pakistan Army. Units of the Pakistan Army itself are present in 'Azad' Kashmir and have operated in the closest co-operation with the local forces ... the fact does remain that the area occupied by Pakistan is not administered by local authorities such as the United Nations Commission envisaged ... it has become a military outpost of Pakistan....

The Northern Areas of the PIS of J&K have an area of 72,495 square kilometres.[86] It may be recalled that following the coup of Gilgit by the British, Pakistan had sent its Political Agent on 16 November 1947 to administer this area. Eventually, Pakistan's Ministry for Kashmir Affairs and Northern Areas exercised power through a Resident Commissioner, who wielded legislative, executive and judicial power. It was in the 1970s that the post of Judicial Commissioner was created. The Northern Areas, which comprise the road link to China and Siachen Glacier, is directly ruled by Pakistan, with Pakistan's laws being made applicable.[87] Indeed, with the enactment of The Establishment of the West Pakistan Act of 1955 by Pakistan, New Delhi pointed out before the UNSC that Pakistan had virtually annexed the Northern Areas. Krishna Menon (India) stated:[88]

The annexation of other areas is covered by section I, clause 2, sub-clause (c) of the Constitution of Pakistan, which refers to territories under the administration of the Federation but not included in either Province; that is to say, either the Pakistan Government takes any territory under its administration, and then even if it is not one of its Provinces it becomes part of Pakistan. That means annexation.

The remaining territory, 'Azad Kashmir', covers 13,528 square kilometres.[89] Snedden records that this region's relationship with Pakistan since 1947 has largely been one in which it has been progressively subsumed by Pakistan.[90] He documents various formal and legal arrangements since April 1949 that have tied 'Azad Kashmir' to Pakistan, ensured 'the nation's superior position and decreased Azad Kashmir's autonomy' and 'denied Azad Kashmiris of significant powers and responsibilities'.[91] Indeed, as Snedden asserts, 'Pakistan has totally manipulated a pliant Azad Kashmir population and denied them meaningful power'.[92] This, he confirms, was done primarily through Pakistan's Ministry of Kashmir Affairs and by providing 'lent officers' from its administrative staff to the 'Azad Kashmir' administration, who filled most senior positions.[93] Pakistan secured total control over 'Azad Kashmir', its foreign affairs, including all the UN matters, the defence, as also of the 'Azad Army'.[94] The role of the government of 'Azad Kashmir' has been that of a local authority and limited to the rump territory of the region. Given the Great Game objectives, the UN, too, dealt only with the Pakistan government on matters relating to 'Azad Kashmir', notwithstanding Pakistan's own plea that 'Azad Kashmir' was supposedly an independent state.

Pakistan gave 'Azad Kashmir' its Azad Jammu and Kashmir Government Act of 1970, which contemplated a presidential system of government. However, as Snedden records, the Pakistan Cabinet in June 1970 issued instructions to the effect that despite 'Azad Kashmir' not being part of Pakistan according to the Pakistan Constitution, 'it should for all practical [reasons] be treated like any other province.... Azad Kashmir should be brought in the mainstream of general administration'.[95]

Public denial notwithstanding, Pakistan seems to have subscribed to status quo, suggesting that there was indeed a tacit accord in 1972 at Simla to convert the LOC into the international border. Noorani points out that a 'tacit accord' came to be suspected when:[96]

on 25 September 1974 [Bhutto] formally annexed Hunza to Pakistan... President Zia–ul-Haq went further. On 3 April 1982, he nominated three observers from the Northern Areas to the Majlis-e-Shoora and claimed they were part of Pakistan. In 1987 ... Prime Minister Mohammed Khan Junejo announced that he would grant the Northern Areas representation in both Houses of Pakistan's Parliament ... from 1974 every government of Pakistan—be it of Bhutto, Zia, Junejo or Nawaz Sharif—has treated the Northern Areas as part of Pakistan and felt itself free to determine their disposition; whether to make them provinces of Pakistan or simply grant them representation in Pakistan's Parliament'.

Post the Simla Agreement of 1972, Bhutto declared at Muzaffarabad on 7 November 1973 that 'Azad Kashmir' had three choices—the status quo, 'provincial status' or a full-fledged province of Pakistan, while ruling out 'an independent status'.[97] Then came the Azad Jammu and Kashmir Interim Constitution of 1974. The preamble of this Constitution recited that the Government of Pakistan 'approved' the repeal of the 1970 Act and authorized the President of 'Azad Kashmir' to introduce the Constitution Bill 'for consideration and passage'.[98] The President, the Prime Minister, the ministers, the Speaker and all legislators of 'Azad Kashmir' had to take an oath that they 'will remain loyal to the country and the cause of accession of the State of Jammu and Kashmir to Pakistan'.[99] Section 3 of the Constitution declared Islam to be the 'State religion'.[100] The President and Prime Minister of 'Azad Kashmir' could not be non-Muslims.[101] The Constitution contemplated the 'Azad Kashmir Council', based in Islamabad, comprising Pakistani and 'Azad Kashmir' members, with the Pakistan Prime Minister as the Chairman, having overriding executive and legislative powers. Section 7(2) of the Constitution mandated that '[n]o person or political party in Azad Jammu & Kashmir shall be permitted to propagate against, or take part in activities prejudicial or detrimental to the ideology of the state's accession to Pakistan'.[102] Section 56 of the Constitution provided that nothing in the Constitution 'shall derogate from the responsibilities of the Government of Pakistan in relation to the State of Jammu and Kashmir under the UNCIP Resolutions or prevent the Government of Pakistan from taking such action as it may consider necessary or expedient for the effective discharge of those responsibilities'. Thus, 'Azad Kashmir' was officially aligned to accede to Pakistan.

Pakistan has, by taking such steps, moved towards implementing the status quo proposal of New Delhi. By ruling the Northern Areas directly and propounding the 'cause of the accession' of 'Azad Kashmir' to Pakistan, Islamabad itself has disregarded the UNCIP resolutions for plebiscite in the PIS of J&K. Further, as M.A. Niazi put it, such action:[103]

[M]ean(s) unravelling the entire fabric of Pakistan's stand on the Kashmir issue. From Pakistan's point of view, the Northern areas and Azad Jammu and Kashmir are those parts of the Dogra State in Pakistani control awaiting a UN plebiscite to be held when India, holding the remaining parts, agrees.... By absorbing the Northern Areas, Pakistan would be acknowledging by implication India's right to Ladakh, or Jammu, from Kashmir proper.

Though Pakistan rules the occupied territories of the PIS of J&K, which are admittedly not a part of Pakistan, the people of these territories have no recourse with regard to the violation of basic human rights and freedoms. Krishna Menon (India) cited before the UNSC in 1957 the memorandum to the Pakistan Constituent Assembly from the All-Jammu and Kashmir Muslim Conference, a large national organization of 'Azad Kashmir', which stated that:[104]

For the last few years the people of 'Azad' Kashmir ... have been subjected to great torture and terrorization.... The 'Azad' Kashmir Government, acting on the advice of the Ministry of Kashmir Affairs [of Pakistan], is primarily and mainly responsible for the conditions that prevail in Poonch today.... Martial law was imposed in Poonch last time without any justification.... Ruthless and random firing by mortar guns took place, resulting in many deaths.

Arrests of men, women and in some cases of children were effected. About 400 persons are still under detention in the concentration camp at Pullandri ... the people have been arrested without any warrants of arrest, on mere suspicion or personal vendetta.... They are rotting in the concentration camps at Bagh, Bari, Pullandri and Sarsawah. They are forced to live under sub-human conditions. In Pullandri jail 340 persons are detained in two rooms which have been built to accommodate only thirty-six persons. Eighteen hundred gallons of water are required daily in this prison, but only 800 gallons are supplied.... There is a concentration camp at Muzaffarabad also.... Women were arrested and subject to unbecoming and insulting treatment.

Arrests and detentions without trial are a common feature of public life now.... For the last six years, people of 'Azad' Kashmir have not been allowed to elect a government of their own. The refugees of Jammu and Kashmir, half a million of whom are on this side of the cease-fire line, are living in sub-human conditions. Their rehabilitation has been entrusted to unpopular, callous and unsympathetic so-called leaders who serve the personal purposes of the officers of the Kashmir Affairs Ministry.... The Kashmir Affairs Ministry [Pakistan] are the actual rulers of 'Azad' Kashmir.... People of 'Azad' Kashmir are stunned to see what Pakistan means to them and those in Indian-held Kashmir have become hesitant in their blind love for the Crescent....

While New Delhi maintains a grim silence in relation to the fate of these Indian citizens under foreign rule, the Government of Pakistan, led by Nawaz Sharif, told the Full Bench of the Punjab High Court (Pakistan) in 1997 that people in the Northern Areas could not be granted constitutional rights, as they were not part of Pakistan. The Government argued that the Northern Areas did not figure among the territories of Pakistan mentioned in its Constitution, and that the 'grant of constitutional rights to these will amount to unilateral annexation of these areas with Pakistan', thereby weakening its claim to the entire PIS of J&K.[105] Pakistan continues to treat the Northern Areas of the PIS of J&K as a colony without any civil or constitutional rights, as a result of which a movement is said to be underway for independence from Pakistan's rule. Harrison, while referring to the brutal suppression of the simmering widespread rebellion against Pakistan, records that Pakistan has handed over de facto control of the Gilgit-Baltistan region to China.[106] Such step, which furthers the strategic and military objectives of Pakistan and China, as discussed at a later stage in this book, compounds the already complex situation.

Pakistan had taken a similar stand before the 'Azad Kashmir' High Court, where its case was that while 'the Northern Areas do not form part of the territories of Pakistan as defined in its Constitution', these areas are not part of the territory of 'Azad Jammu and Kashmir' either.[107] The High Court in its judgement of 8 March 1993 found that 'no legitimate cause has been shown by the Respondents No. 1 (Pakistan) and 3 (POK regime), to keep the Northern Areas and their residents (State subjects) detached from Azad Jammu and Kashmir, under separate and arbitrary administrative system and deprive them of fundamental rights'.[108] Referring to the UNSC Resolutions, the High Court held that '[a]llowing integration of Northern Areas to any Province of Pakistan would tantamount to negation of Pakistan's stance at home and in the Security Council'.[109] The High Court directed the 'Azad Kashmir' government in Muzzafarabad 'to immediately assume the administrative control of the Northern Areas and to annex it with the administration of Azad Jammu and Kashmir', while requiring the Government of Pakistan 'to provide an adequate assistance and facility to the Azad Government in attainment of the said objective'.[110] This judgement of the 'Azad Kashmir' High Court was, however, set aside by the Pakistan Supreme Court on 14 March 1994, taking the view that the Azad Jammu and Kashmir Interim Constitution of 1974, itself a creation of Pakistan, did not extend to the Northern Areas, and that the High Court, being a creature of this Constitution, had no jurisdiction in the matter.[111] The Pakistan Supreme Court held that:[112]

> [T]he findings of the High Court on the point that the Northern Areas were historically and constitutionally part of the Jammu and Kashmir State before 14 August 1947 suffer from no legal infirmity; even otherwise this fact has not been challenged by the Federation of Pakistan before this Court. Thus, the said findings stand confirmed.... To summarize, in light of what has been stated, the conclusion which we reach is that the Northern Areas are a part of Jammu and Kashmir State but are not part of Azad Jammu and Kashmir, as defined in the Interim Constitution Act, 1974.

Claire Galex, a Brussels-based human rights activist, after visiting both sides of the LOC, confirmed that Pakistan maintains a vice-like grip on 'Azad Kashmir'.[113] She writes that Pakistan uses the region for training youth to fight in the Kashmir Valley, that 'Azad Kashmir' is the main entry point for militants to enter the Kashmir Valley, fuelled by the authorities to avenge the 'unbearably cruel Hindus who martyr their Kashmiri brothers' on the other side of the border, and that the 'Azad Kashmir' government has become an accomplice of the Pakistani army and the Inter-Services

Intelligence (ISI) in committing human rights violations not only in its region but beyond its own borders. She reported that Pakistan fully controls 'Azad Kashmir' on a day-to-day basis, and that the existence of the Ministry of Kashmir Affairs within the Pakistan government makes the Pakistani interference in the affairs of 'Azad Kashmir' even more obvious. Jagjit Singh, on the other hand, has detailed the fraudulent elections held in 'Azad Kashmir' from time to time.[114]

The fallout of New Delhi's misconceived policy of territorial status quo is that while Pakistan freely admits that the territories of the PIS of J&K occupied by it are not a part of Pakistan, New Delhi simply does not bother to question in any forum, national or international, the illegal presence of Pakistan and China in such territories. The UN and the international community have, in complete derogation of the principles of international law noted later in the book, chosen to do nothing about the illegality of such presence. Instead, it is India that is routinely accused by the international community and Pakistan of human rights violations in the territory of the PIS of J&K with India. New Delhi, having subscribed to territorial status quo, also does not bother to raise the issue of denial of human rights and even basic needs to its own citizens in territories of the PIS of J&K occupied by Pakistan, and by China. Nor does it rebut the incessant demand by Pakistan for granting the 'right to self-determination' to Kashmiri people in the part of the PIS of J&K with India, by pointing out that no such right has, even otherwise, been granted by Pakistan or China to the people in the territories of PIS of J&K under their occupation. Rather, such people have been subjected to foreign rule and forced to swear to the accession of the PIS of J&K to Pakistan. Indeed, the brutal suppression by Pakistan of the civilian population there was vividly captured by a video beamed by media channels on 30 September 2015, which showed Pakistan authorities mercilessly cracking down on residents in Muzzafarabad, Gilgit, Kotli and other parts of the state under Pakistan's occupation, because they were demanding azadi (freedom) and raising anti-Pakistan slogans.[115]

Thus, while Pakistan and China continue to occupy the territories of the PIS of J&K which are legally and constitutionally part of India, and continue to deprive Indian citizens of their human rights, Pakistan stakes claim to the part of the state which is with India, citing the right to self-determination. It may be recalled that Pakistan controls about 35 per cent of territory of the PIS of J&K, while China has control over about 20 per cent. Yet, the Kashmir issue has been portrayed internationally as being confined to the Muslim-dominated Kashmir Valley, which is just about 9 per cent of the PIS of J&K, where a jihad or 'struggle of independence' is said to be under way.

Sadly, even Indian commentators share this perception. For instance, Tavleen Singh opines that the 'Kashmir Valley covers an area of 8,639 square miles and forms the smallest segment of the former princely state of Jammu and Kashmir which consisted of 84,571 square miles' and that it 'is this tiny territory which constitutes the Kashmir problem'.[116] Foreign commentators tend to agree. Snedden contends that both India and Pakistan do not want to lose any part of the areas in the state 'into which they have put substantial effort and resources since 1947', and that equally neither country 'appears to want, and neither seeks to obtain, the (potentially hostile) areas' of the state "occupied" by the other'.[117] Thus, according to Snedden,[118]

> India does not want to obtain (Muslim) Azad Kashmir and (Shia Muslim) Gilgit-Baltistan; Pakistan does not want to acquire (Hindu-dominant) Jammu and remote (Buddhist/Shia) Ladakh. The only area both appear to want to possess is the (Muslim) Kashmir Valley—where, ironically, most people appear uninterested in joining either nation. The famed Kashmir Valley is the only region of contestation in J&K.

New Delhi's bungling did not end with its policy of territorial status quo. Having pledged plebiscite in the PIS of J&K under UN auspices at every conceivable occasion, New Delhi was subsequently compelled to disown before the UNSC the Constituent Assembly formed in the PIS of J&K to formulate the Constitution of Jammu and Kashmir of 1957—a Constituent Assembly and a Constitution contemplated by the Constitution of India itself in Article 370. Unbelievable as it may sound, New Delhi was forced to ask the state political leadership not to pass a resolution confirming the accession of the state to India. New Delhi had no option but to also distance itself from the Constitution of Jammu and Kashmir of 1957—a Constitution which expressly provided that the PIS of J&K was an integral part of the Indian Union. Instead, as detailed in the next chapter, New Delhi actually chose to assure Pakistan that it would still abide by its international commitment to hold a plebiscite. These developments contributed in no small measure to New Delhi losing its moral and political authority to retain the PIS of J&K and, as discussed later in the book, added to the frustration and disillusionment of the people of the state with India.

Notes and References

1. *Supra* Note 13, Chapter VII, p. 548.
2. *The Exchange v N. Faddon*: 7 Cranch, 116, 136, 144, 3 L. ed., 287, 293, 296.
3. *Walker v Baird*: 1892 A.C. 491.
4. See Fenwick, Charles. 1962. *International Law*, p. 435. Bombay: Allied Pacific Private Limited.
5. Seervai, H. M. 1991. *Constitutional Law of India*. 4th Ed., Vol 1, p. 306. Bombay: N M Tripathi Private Ltd.
6. *Jolly George Verghese v Bank of Cochin*: AIR 1980 SC 470 at p. 473.
7. *Supra* Note 5.
8. *Supra* Note 4, Chapter V.
9. Ibid., pp. 803–804.
10. Ibid., p. 857.
11. *Attorney General for Canada v Attorney General for Ontario*: 1937 AC 326 at p. 352.
12. *In re Initiative and Referendum Act*: 1919 AC 935.
13. *Supra* Note 4, Chapter V, p. 969.
14. Ibid., p. 760.
15. *Reference by the President of India under Article 143(1) of the Constitution of India on the implementation of the Indo-Pakistan Agreement relating to Berubari Union and Exchange of Enclaves*: AIR 1960 SC 845.
16. Ibid., p. 856.
17. *Supra* Note 27, Chapter IV.
18. Extracted in Shukla, V.N. 2001. *Constitution of India*, 10th Edition by M.P. Singh, p. A21–22. Lucknow: Eastern Book Company.
19. *Supra* Note 27, Chapter IV, p. 1628.
20. *S.R. Bommai v Union of India*: AIR 1994 SC 1918 at p. 2045.
21. *Supra* Note 15, pp. 856–857.
22. *Supra* Note 5, p. 305.
23. *Supra* Note 27, Chapter IV, p. 1614.
24. *Supra* Note 2.
25. Extracted in *Supra* Note 12, Chapter IV, p. 24.
26. Ibid., p. 25.
27. See *Supra* Note 27, Chapter IV, pp. 1500–1501.
28. *State of Texas v George W. White*: 7 Wall. 700 (1869) at 727.
29. Ibid., pp. 237–238.
30. Nicholas, H. S. 1948. *The Australian Constitution*. Sydney: The Law Book Co. of Australasia Pty. Ltd.
31. *Supra* Note 20, p. 2045.
32. *Constituent Assembly Debates*, VII CAD 43, Lok Sabha Secretariat, New Delhi.
33. *S. Mohsin Shah v Union Govt. of India & Ors*: AIR 1974 J&K 48.
34. *Supra* Note 27, Chapter IV.
35. See *The Indian Express*. 1995. 'Haji Pir sell out', New Delhi, 4 September; *The Indian Express*. 1999. 'Jaw-jaw, not war-war', New Delhi, 8 June.
36. *The Indian Express*. 1999. 'At post Kathi summer brings infiltrators across LoC', New Delhi, 16 April.
37. Bajpai, K. Shankar. 2016. 'Tashkent Syndrome', *The Indian Express*, New Delhi, 9 January.

38. See *The Indian Express*. 1995. 'Haji Pir sell out', New Delhi, 4 September; Chellany, Brahma. 1999. 'Blundering on Kashmir', *Hindustan Times*, New Delhi, 2 June.
39. Malkhani, K.R. 2001. 'Should the PM invite Musharraf for talks?', *Sunday Times of India*, New Delhi, 11 February.
40. Guha, Ramachandra. 2007. *India after Gandhi*, p. 465. London: Macmillan: (Picador).
41. *Sunday Times of India*. 1999. 'LOC conversion into border fell through in 1972', New Delhi, 4 July.
42. *Surya India*. 1983. 'India's gift to Zia', Jan 1–15, Vol 7, No. 6, p. 30. New Delhi: Youngmen Printers & Publishers Pvt. Ltd.
43. Adhikari, Gautam. 2008. 'Kashmir is not the issue', *The Times of India*, New Delhi, 17 January.
44. Jha, Prem Shankar. 2001. 'Architecture for peace', *Hindustan Times*, New Delhi, 15 June.
45. Gupta, Shekhar. 1999. 'Winning without a war', *The Indian Express*, New Delhi, 2 June.
46. Cited in Ramchandran, Rajesh. 2000. 'Hobson's choice', *Hindustan Times*, New Delhi, 26 March.
47. *Supra* Note 12, Chapter IV, p. 601.
48. 'POK woman crosses LoC, returned by Army'. Available online at http://www.ibnlive.com/news/india/pok-woman-crosses-loc-returned-by-army-1012467.html (downloaded on 5 August 2015).
49. *World Human Rights Protection v Union of India*: AIR 2004 J&K 6.
50. Ibid., p. 7.
51. Ibid., p. 12.
52. Ibid.
53. *State of Jammu and Kashmir v Mahmood Ahmed*: AIR 1989 SC 1450.
54. *Delhi Recorder*. 1983. 'The RSS is Anti-National', New Delhi, Vol IV, No. 1, p. 32.
55. *The Indian Express*. 1997. 'Farooq rules out talks with militants', New Delhi, 20 January.
56. *Sunday Times of India*. 2000. 'Sikhs are safer here', New Delhi, 26 March; *Hindustan Times*. 2000. 'Farooq reiterates his stand on LOC', New Delhi, 23 April; *Hindustan Times*. 2000. 'Farooq: Greater autonomy to cure all problems of J&K', New Delhi, 24 May; Joshi, Arun. (2000). 'Final solution will revolve around LOC', *Hindustan Times*, New Delhi, 7 December; *Hindustan Times*. 2000. 'Pak has no option but to push for peace', New Delhi, 12 December; *The Times of India*. 2000. 'Farooq sees movement in peace initiative', New Delhi, 19 December; *The Times of India*. 2001. 'Pak should accept LC as final border: Farooq', New Delhi, 2 February; *The Times of India*. 2001. 'Art 370 cannot be abrogated: Farooq', New Delhi, 14 April.
57. Sharma, Arun. 2015. 'Pok will remain with Pak, J&K will remain part of India: Farooq', *The Indian Express*, New Delhi, 27 November; *The Times of India*. 2015. 'Farooq: POK will remain with Pak, J&K with India', New Delhi, 28 November.
58. Sharma, 'Pok will remain with Pak'.
59. *Sunday Times of India*. 2015. 'Entire Army can't defend us against terrorists: Farooq', New Delhi, 29 November.
60. *The Indian Express*. 1999. 'Look, who else is backing Farooq Abdullah's controversial line', New Delhi, 12 March.
61. Sharma, Ishwar. 1996. 'Jammu & Kashmir Crises - I Exploring Viable Political Initiatives', in *Supra* Note 34, Chapter IV, p. 381.
62. Ibid., p. 383.
63. Bose, Tapan K. 1996. 'What's the bottom-line on Kashmir in the Indo-Pak talks?' in *Supra* Note 34, Chapter IV, pp. 296, 298.
64. *Hindustan Times*. 2001. 'Track II team headed for Pak', New Delhi, 12 January.

65. Dixit, J.N. 1998. 'Clarity on Kashmir', *Hindustan Times*, New Delhi, 22 July.
66. Dixit, J.N. 2001. 'Stamina and grit', *Hindustan Times*, New Delhi, 12 January.
67. Bhushan, Bharat. 2000. 'Pakistan-bashing as policy', *Hindustan Times*, New Delhi, 17 March.
68. Ibid.
69. Verghese, B.G. 2000. 'Clinton can't avoid Kashmir', *The Indian Express*, New Delhi, 15 March.
70. Bajpai, Kanti. 1999. 'Here's one solution to Kashmir', *Hindustan Times*, New Delhi, 25 July.
71. Gandhi, Rajmohan. 2000. 'Drama, beyond statistics', *Hindustan Times*, New Delhi, 25 September.
72. Dasgupta, Swapan. 1999. 'Diplomacy after Kargil', *India Today*, 5 July, p. 39. Delhi: Living Media Ltd.
73. Grover, V.R. 2000. 'Behind the Kashmir curtain', *Hindustan Times*, New Delhi, 20 July.
74. Puri, Rakshat. 1998. 'Time to unfreeze in Kashmir', *Hindustan Times*, New Delhi, 14 January.
75. Dar, A.N. 1998. 'Solving the Kashmir problem', *Hindustan Times*, New Delhi, 27 March.
76. *Supra* Note 32, Chapter VI, p. 18.
77. Sachar, Rajinder. 1999. 'Uneasy times in Kashmir', *Hindustan Times*, New Delhi, 23 December.
78. *Supra* Note 39, Chapter IV, p. 39.
79. *Supra* Note 35, Chapter IV, p. 209.
80. *The Times of India*. 1999. 'No redrawing maps', New Delhi, 27 September.
81. *The Times of India*. 1999. 'Kashmir solution lies in LoC: Booth', New Delhi, 15 April.
82. *Supra* Note 81, Chapter IV, p. 219.
83. Ibid.
84. *Supra* Note 32, Chapter VI, p. 3.
85. S/PV 764, pp. 8, 26–34, 40 Krishna Menon (India), 24 January 1957.
86. *Supra* Note 12, Chapter IV, p. 650.
87. Ibid.
88. S/PV 801, pp. 13–14, Krishna Menon (India), 13 November 1957.
89. *Supra* Note 32, Chapter VI, p. 4.
90. *Supra* Note 81, Chapter IV, p. 87.
91. Ibid.
92. Ibid., p. 84.
93. Ibid., p. 93.
94. See ibid., pp. 87–110.
95. Ibid., p. 100.
96. *Supra* Note 12, Chapter IV, pp. 654–655.
97. Ibid., p. 649.
98. Ibid.
99. Ibid., p. 667.
100. Ibid., p. 649.
101. Ibid., p. 668.
102. Ibid., p. 510.
103. Extracted in ibid., p. 655.
104. *Supra* Note 85, pp. 33–34.

105. *The Indian Express*. 1997. 'Northern POK residents not Pak citizens: Sharief Govt', New Delhi, 19 April.
106. Harrison, Selig S. 2010. 'The other Kashmir problem', *The Indian Express*, New Delhi, 28 August.
107. *Supra* Note 12, Chapter IV, p. 651.
108. Ibid., p. 652.
109. Ibid., p. 651.
110. Ibid., p. 648.
111. Ibid., pp. 657–658.
112. Extracted in ibid., p. 658.
113. Referred to in *The Times of India*. 1995. 'Pok residents do not favour accession to Pak', New Delhi, 7 March.
114. *Supra* Note 32, Chapter VI, p. 69.
115. *The Times of India*. 2015. 'Video showing brutal quelling of anti-Pak protests in POK', New Delhi, 1 October.
116. See *Supra* Note 31, Chapter IV, p. xiii.
117. *Supra* Note 81, Chapter IV, p. 220.
118. Ibid.

IX

Kashmir and the United Nations

It appears that the ruler of the PIS of J&K as also its political leaders were well aware of the legal position that the sovereignty of the ruler over the state was expressly retained by him under the Instrument of Accession and recognized by Article 370 of the Constitution of India. The ruler of the PIS of J&K as also its political leaders, therefore, simply ignored the stand taken by New Delhi before the UNSC to hold a plebiscite in the state to 'settle' the question of the accession. Let us consider the happenings in the PIS of J&K post the reference to the UNSC.

The Constituent Assembly of the PIS of J&K

Raja Hari Singh, as noted earlier, had entrusted all his powers and functions with regard to the governance of the state to his son, Yuvraj Karan Singh, by the Proclamation of 20 June 1949. Before doing so, Raja Hari Singh had appointed Sheikh Abdullah of the National Conference as the Prime Minister of the state on 17 March 1948. The National Conference, at the meeting of its General Council on 27 October 1950, recommended 'immediate steps for convening a Constituent Assembly based upon adult suffrage and embracing all the constituents of the State for the purpose of determining the future shape of affiliations of the State of Jammu and Kashmir'.[1]

The adoption of this resolution led to Pakistan addressing the letter dated 14 December 1950 to the President of the UNSC in protest. Pakistan's letter stated that 'the Government of India and the Maharaja's Government in Kashmir were taking steps to prejudice the holding of a plebiscite',[2] and 'nullify the international agreements between India and Pakistan' embodied in the UNCIP Resolutions of 13 August 1948 and 5 January 1949.[3]

Pakistan called upon the UNSC to require India to refrain from proceeding with the proposal of a constituent assembly.[4]

New Delhi was obviously walking on a tightrope. On the one hand, the Constitution of India itself, in Article 370, provided for the setting up of such a Constituent Assembly in the PIS of J&K. On the other hand, New Delhi had already agreed on the floor of the UN that the question of accession of the state would be settled by a plebiscite. Having taken such a legally untenable stand, New Delhi was forced to be on the defensive, lest it be accused of backing out of its 'pledge' to hold the plebiscite. Accordingly, Benegal N. Rau (India) declared before the UNSC that New Delhi was committed to holding the plebiscite, that the Constituent Assembly of the PIS of J&K 'is not meant to come in the way of the Security Council', and that 'while the constituent assembly might, if it so desires, express an opinion on the question of accession, it could make no decision on the question'.[5] Benegal N. Rau (India) reiterated on 29 March 1951 before the UNSC that 'this opinion [of the constituent assembly] will not bind my Government or prejudice the position of this Council'.[6]

No one bought New Delhi's argument, least of all Pakistan.[7] The UNSC took the view that the matter of the final disposition of the PIS of J&K was an international question, and that it assumed that New Delhi would prevent the Government of the PIS of J&K from taking any action which would interfere with the responsibilities of the UNSC. The UNSC, of course, remained silent about the illegal presence of Pakistan in the PIS of J&K notwithstanding the UNCIP Resolutions, and about its failure to discharge its responsibilities in accordance with principles of international law examined later in the book.

By now it had dawned upon New Delhi that the accession of a princely Indian state to the dominion of India in terms of the Indian Independence Act of 1947, read with the Government of India Act of 1935, as amended, was to be determined by its ruler. Benegal N. Rau (India) declared before the UNSC in the proceedings in 1951:[8]

Under the Constitution which was in force in India between 15 August 1947 and 26 January 1950, which is the material period for this purpose, India was a Dominion under the British Crown. That Constitution was an enactment of the British Parliament. Under that Constitution, often referred to as the Government of India Act, 1935—as amended under the Indian Independence Act, 1947—an Indian State must be deemed to have acceded to the Dominion if the Governor-General has signified his acceptance of an instrument of accession executed by the Ruler. That is all that is required for accession: an instrument executed by the Ruler and accepted by the Governor-General.

On 26 October 1947, in order to get India's help to repel an invasion of the State in which Pakistan was aiding, the Ruler of Kashmir actually executed such an instrument of accession in favour of India, and on 27 October 1947, Lord Mountbatten, then Governor General of India, signified his acceptance of the instrument in the usual formula, 'I do hereby accept this instrument of accession'. The document itself contains no conditions or reservations of any kind; it is in the same form as any other instrument of accession accepted by the Governor-General of India, and it took effect from the moment of acceptance.

Benegal N. Rau (India), however, went on to declare that:[9]

Only, in the case of Kashmir, Lord Mountbatten, after accepting the instrument, wrote a separate letter to the Maharaja or Ruler in which he expressed the wish of the Government of India that 'as soon as law and order have been restored in Kashmir and its soil cleared of the invader, the question of the State's accession should be settled by a reference to the people'. In other words, the acceptance of accession was followed by the expression of a wish to be fulfilled at a future date when certain conditions had been satisfied. Unfortunately, the soil of Kashmir has not yet been cleared of the invader—the Pakistan Army which joined the invader is still there—and so the fulfilment of the wish of the Government of India has been delayed by Pakistan's own act. Meanwhile, the accession to India continues to be effective, and it will inevitably so continue unless and until the people of Kashmir settle the question otherwise.

Not surprisingly, the UK, despite remaining bound by the Indian Independence Act of 1947 and the Government of India Act of 1935, as amended, enacted by its own Parliament, disputed India's reasoning, and drew attention to the 'parallel cases' of Junagadh and Hyderabad. Gladwyn Jebb (UK) contended that:[10]

If the Council were to retrace its steps behind the agreed principles and to take up the legal issues concerning the validity of the Maharaja's accession... how could the Council escape from going on to consider parallel cases in which the question of accession may well at first sight appear to have been decided in accordance with entirely different principles?

He added that:[11]

The proposal is really very simple. All we ask is that both parties to the dispute should give their full assistance to the Council so that—and here I quote the paragraph 1 of the United Nations Commission's resolution of

5 January 1949: 'The question of the accession of the State of Jammu and Kashmir to India or Pakistan will be decided through the democratic method of a free and impartial plebiscite'.

On 30 March 1951, the UNSC passed the Resolution S/2017/Rev.1 submitted by the US and the UK on 21 March 1951. This Resolution declared that the convening of a Constituent Assembly as recommended by the National Conference and any action that Assembly might attempt to take to determine the future shape and affiliation of the PIS of J&K or any part thereof would not constitute a disposition of the state in terms of the principles contained in the UN Resolutions.[12]

On 29 May 1951, Rajeswar Dayal (India) assured the UNSC that 'I reaffirm that so far as the Government of India is concerned the Constituent Assembly for Kashmir is not intended to prejudice the issue before the Security Council or come in its way'.[13]

Proclamation of 1 May 1951

Yuvraj Karan Singh, the then ruler of the PIS of J&K, did not seem too bothered about the UN Resolution of 30 March 1951 or New Delhi's position. The Yuvraj went ahead and issued the Proclamation of 1 May 1951 directing that a state Constituent Assembly, consisting of representatives of the people elected on the basis of adult franchise, shall be constituted forthwith for the purpose of framing the Constitution for Jammu and Kashmir.[14]

Pakistan predictably rushed to the UNSC, which again reiterated its stand. It was the erstwhile Soviet Union that revealed how from the very beginning, the UK and the US aimed to prolong the Kashmir issue and to introduce 'Anglo-American troops into Kashmir so as to convert it into an Anglo-American colony and a military and strategic base' against the Soviet Union.[15] In fact, the original text of the Resolution of 30 March 1951 had contained an open demand that foreign troops be introduced into the PIS of J&K. The Soviet Union pointed out that the plebiscite was sought to be imposed on the people of the PIS of J&K 'ostensibly under the United Nations, but, in reality, under Anglo-American control', notwithstanding the setting up of the state's own Constituent Assembly.

On 29 May 1951, the President of the UNSC sent a cable to the Governments of India and Pakistan, which referred to the steps being taken by the Yuvraj of the PIS of J&K to convene a constituent assembly. The

President declared such action as involving 'procedures which are in conflict with the commitment of the parties to determine the future accession of the State by a fair and impartial plebiscite conducted under United Nations auspices' and expressed trust that:[16]

> [T]he Governments of India and Pakistan will do everything in their power to ensure that the authorities in Kashmir do not disregard the Council or act in a manner which would prejudice the determination of the future accession of the State in accordance with the procedures provided for in the resolutions of the Council and of the United Nations Commission for India and Pakistan.

Again, no such denouncements have ever been made by the UNSC against Pakistan for its consolidation of the occupied territory of the PIS of J&K and its disregard for the obligations imposed by the UNCIP Resolutions.

Furthermore, such a view taken by the UNSC is not only novel, but is also inconsistent with the UN Charter itself. Under the express terms of the Indian Independence Act of 1947, and the Government of India Act of 1935, as amended, the Instrument of Accession of 26 October 1947 and the Constitution of India, the ruler of the PIS of J&K had retained sovereignty over the state. The ruler—that is, the Yuvraj—was the sole authority who could legally decide the polity of the PIS of J&K, and whether and in what manner the transition could be made from monarchy to democracy so as to vest sovereignty in the people of the PIS of J&K who could then express their wish. The PIS of J&K was not a member of the UN and nor was it represented by its sovereign ruler before the UN. Needless to say, the limited powers of the dominion of India over the PIS of J&K did not include the power to question the mode by which sovereignty was to be vested in the people of the state by its ruler. Yet the UNSC deemed it fit to sideline the sovereign ruler of the PIS of J&K, treat him as being irrelevant, and to dictate that if the wishes of the people of his state were to be ascertained, they could be ascertained only in the manner contained in the UN Resolutions.

It may be emphasized that at the time the UN Resolutions in respect of the PIS of J&K were passed, the UNSC was fully aware that the ruler had retained his sovereignty over the state. As noted earlier, the UNCIP Resolutions itself recognize the sovereignty of the ruler over his state and located the powers with respect to the state in the government of the said ruler. The UNCIP Resolution of 5 January 1949 provided that the Plebiscite Administrator 'will be formally appointed to office by the Government of Jammu and Kashmir', that the 'Plebiscite Administrator shall derive from the State of Jammu and Kashmir the powers he considers necessary for organizing and conducting the plebiscite and for ensuring the freedom and impartiality of the plebiscite', and that at 'the conclusion of the Plebiscite, the Plebiscite Administrator shall report the result thereof to the Commission and to the Government of Jammu and Kashmir'. Such provision confirms that the UNSC was all along aware of the fact that the ruler was still the source of power in the PIS of J&K.

It may be argued that the UN had sought to locate in the ruler the power to hold the plebiscite in the PIS of J&K on the premise that it viewed the accession of the state to the dominion of India to be bad as claimed by Pakistan. Assuming this to be correct, the logical consequence would have been as though the ruler had never acceded to the dominion of India, but had remained the absolute sovereign of the PIS of J&K. In such a situation, the state would have had to be treated as a sovereign country. Given that the PIS of J&K was not a member of the UN, the UN would not have been competent, under its own Charter, to take decisions in respect of the state and its people, and, that too, in the absence of its sovereign ruler.

The UNSC and the Plebiscite

Notwithstanding the setting up of the Constituent Assembly in the PIS of J&K, the UNSC, through the UN Representative, continued in its efforts to impose the plebiscite upon the state.

Frank P. Graham, who had been appointed as the UN Representative for India and Pakistan at the 543rd meeting on 30 April 1951, was instructed by the UNSC to proceed to the Indian subcontinent to effect demilitarization of the PIS of J&K on the basis of the UNCIP Resolutions of 13 August 1948 and 5 January 1949.[17] The Yearbook of the United Nations, 1951, discusses the First and Second reports of Graham as also the resolution adopted by the UNSC on 10 November 1951. This Resolution of 10 November 1951 noted 'with gratification the declared agreement of the two parties to those parts of Dr Graham's proposals' which reaffirm 'their acceptance of the principle that the accession of the State of Jammu and Kashmir should be determined by a free and impartial plebiscite under the auspices of the United Nations'.[18]

The Yearbook of the United Nations, 1952, records that the UNSC discussed the Third and Fourth reports of Graham,[19] and adopted the Resolution of 23 December 1951, which, after recalling the UNCIP Resolutions, 'provided that the question of the accession of the State of

Jammu and Kashmir will be decided through the democratic method of a free and impartial plebiscite conducted under the auspices of the United Nations', and urged India and Pakistan to 'enter into immediate negotiations under the auspices of the United Nations Representative for India and Pakistan' on demilitarization.[20]

Pakistan, on its part, continued to reiterate the plea that the PIS of J&K was a 'disputed territory' and that the issue of accession had become 'academic' with the adoption of the UNCIP Resolutions. Mohammed Zafrullah Khan (Pakistan) stated that:[21]

.... The question of [accession] today is really academic. This question of the validity of the accession, of the alleged aggressions by one side or the other—these matters have long been left behind. The crux of the matter, as the representative of India put it the other day, is the implementation of the two resolutions which constitute the agreement between the two Governments on this matter. Since those resolutions were accepted by the two Governments during the last week of December 1948, long after all these matters had happened and had been debated and had been clarified between the Commission and the two Governments, these questions, as I have said, have long been academic.

Constitutional and Political Developments in the PIS of J&K

Yuvraj Karan Singh simply ignored the UN. As detailed earlier, the duly elected Constituent Assembly of the PIS of J&K framed the Constitution of Jammu and Kashmir of 1957, terminated the hereditary office of the ruler and brought about the transition from monarchy to democracy.

Throughout this period, New Delhi officially clung on to the 'pledge' to hold a plebiscite in the PIS of J&K under UN auspices, both domestically and before the international community.[22] Nehru, in his letter dated 4 March 1954 to the then Pakistan President, Mohamad Ali, stated New Delhi's position as under:[23]

Ever since the Constituent Assembly came into being... our position in regard to it has been perfectly clear and has been stated in the Security Council and elsewhere. We said then that the Constituent Assembly was perfectly free to decide, as it liked, in regard to the State's accession or other matters, but, so far as we are concerned, we would abide by our international commitments. There has been at no time any question of our repudiating the decisions of the Constituent Assembly and indeed we have no right to do so. That elected Assembly has every right to express its wishes in any way it chooses. So far as we are concerned, the accession of the Jammu and Kashmir State was legally and constitutionally complete in October, 1947, and no question of confirming or ratifying it arises. Nevertheless, we had said that the people of Kashmir should be given an opportunity to express their wishes about their future, and we had agreed to a plebiscite under proper conditions. We have adhered to that position throughout, subject always to those conditions, which would ensure fair and peaceful plebiscite. It is because those conditions have not been agreed to that delay has occurred.

New Delhi even asked the Constituent Assembly of the PIS of J&K not to pass the resolution confirming the accession to India so that New Delhi was not embarrassed before the UN. Noorani cites Sheikh Abdullah as stating that he had sought to ratify the accession through the state Constituent Assembly, but it was the 'Government of India which contested in the Security Council as well as in Parliament the Assembly's right to do so'.[24] Abdullah is quoted as saying that when at a meeting this was suggested, Nehru angrily told him and Gopalaswami Ayyangar that he would never repudiate his international commitments.[25] Noorani documents Nehru's statement at a press conference in New Delhi on 21 June 1952 as under:[26]

When the Constituent Assembly met in Kashmir for the first time, I might inform you, that it was its intention to pass a resolution forthwith confirming the State's accession to India. We asked it not to do it so as not to be embarrassed before the United Nations... as far as we were concerned we would not be bound by their decision on the question before the Security Council.

B.P. Sharma also records an incident narrated by Sheikh Abdullah that occurred while he, along with Bakshi Ghulam Mohammad, was sitting in Nehru's room in New Delhi. He writes that:[27]

Gopalswami Ayyangar also happened to be there. This was just after the inauguration of the Constituent Assembly. Ayyangar proposed that we should pass a resolution ratifying the accession as final so that the need of holding of a plebiscite may not arise. This enraged Pt. Nehru, who, in an angry tone rebuked Ayyangar by saying that such an action will not be approved by him. India, he said, had made a commitment on an international level as also to the people of Kashmir; that they will get an opportunity to decide about their future affiliations through a plebiscite conducted in a free and fair manner. We cannot go back on this promise.

In fact, Sheikh Abdullah, in his letter dated 4 February 1953 to Shyama Prasad Mukherjee, put it on record that:[28]

.... We are prepared to pass the resolution, but the Government of India in its turn must be in a position to fulfil all the obligations flowing from such a decision. You will perhaps agree that in the event the Government of India declares that the decision of the Constituent Assembly is irrevocable, consideration that would weigh with it would come into conflict with the UNO. It is not in a position to withdraw the case. The alternative for India would be to withdraw from that organization and bear the odium of all other members. The question is whether India is in a position to stand in isolation particularly when all sympathies of foreign powers would be on the side of Pakistan. In this condition of isolation the risk of an armed conflict cannot also be over-ruled. In case the Government of India is prepared to take such steps in order to maintain the validity of the Constituent Assembly's decision, the decision can be taken without loss of much time. But if this cannot be done, may I ask what good will the resolution of the Assembly do if the political uncertainty about the State's future continues even after this? The fulfilment of a mere formality would not satisfy those who are anxious for a permanent settlement of the question.

It, therefore, appears that while Nehru considered accession of the PIS of J&K to India to be complete, he nonetheless wanted to honour an international commitment he was not competent to give. It was the persistent failure of New Delhi to stand by the PIS of J&K that had unconditionally acceded to it, which led to a sense of frustration and disillusionment in the state towards New Delhi. Indeed, the compulsions of New Delhi having to cling onto the promise of a plebiscite took its toll at the domestic level in the state. Even Sheikh Abdullah who, in his speech on 5 February 1948 before the UN General Assembly, had repeatedly and vehemently declared that the question of accession of the PIS of J&K to the dominion of India was not in issue before the UNSC and that he refused to accept 'Pakistan as a party in the affairs of the Jammu and Kashmir',[29] now subscribed to the view that the PIS of J&K still had the option to cede to India, Pakistan or remain independent.[30] Hari Jaisingh records that 'the London Times reported on 12 May 1952 [that] Sheikh [Abdullah] has made it clear that he is as much opposed to domination by India as to subjugation by Pakistan [and] claims sovereign authority for the Kashmir Constituent Assembly without limitation by the Constitution of India'.[31]

Around this time, the US sought to win over Sheikh Abdullah to sell to him the idea of an independent PIS of J&K, which would provide a military base against the erstwhile Soviet Union. Loy Henderson, the then US Ambassador to India, visited Sheikh Abdullah in June 1953. B.P. Sharma opines that such US interest led to the dismissal of the Sheikh Abdullah government by New Delhi on 8 August 1953.[32] Sheikh Abdullah was taken in custody on 9 August 1953 at 8 am, and, except for a few months in 1958, he remained incarcerated in jail till 1964, with an additional case being filed against him on 23 October 1958.[33] Bakshi Ghulam Mohammad was thereafter invited to form the state government.

Less than 10 days after the arrest of Sheikh Abdullah, Nehru held talks with Liaquat Ali Khan in New Delhi from 17 August to 20 August 1953. The Joint Communique, issued on 21 August 1953, yet again reiterated the settlement of the Kashmir issue 'in accordance with the wishes of the people of that State' through 'a fair and impartial plebiscite'.[34]

While New Delhi continued to doggedly reiterate that the accession of the PIS of J&K made by its sovereign ruler to the dominion of India was yet to be settled by holding a plebiscite, the state Constituent Assembly set up by its ruler was, in terms of the Constitution of India, in the process of formulating the constitutional relationship between the state and the Union of India. As discussed earlier, the state Constituent Assembly endorsed on 15 February 1954 the accession of the PIS of J&K to the dominion of India. New Delhi, however, was apologetic about even this decision of the state Constituent Assembly. In his letter dated 5 March 1954 to the Prime Minister of Pakistan, Nehru declared that 'the Constituent Assembly was perfectly free to decide, as it liked, in regard to the State's accession or other matters, but so far as we were concerned, we would abide by our international commitment' of 'a plebiscite under proper conditions'.[35]

The UN and the Developments in the PIS of J&K

Pakistan rushed to the UNSC again. By its letter dated 16 November 1956, Pakistan informed the UNSC that 'according to press reports, a constitution for the State of Jammu and Kashmir, framed by an assembly calling itself a Constituent Assembly and sitting at Srinagar, was due to come into force on 26 January 1957' and that 'that part of the Constitution integrating the State into India would come into force on 17 November 1956'.[36] Pakistan asserted that the move would nullify the UNSC Resolution of 30 March 1951 and would constitute a repudiation of the international agreement that the accession of the PIS of J&K should be decided by a plebiscite under UN auspices. Pakistan asked the UNSC to call upon India to desist from such an action.

Pakistan, by its letter dated 26 November 1956 to the UNSC, confirmed that the action which was to be taken on 17 November 1956, by the 'so called Constituent Assembly at Srinagar' had taken place.[37] By its letter dated 2 January 1957, Pakistan informed the UNSC that India had refused, 'on one pretext or another' to honour its international 'commitments' in terms of the UNCIP Resolutions of 13 August 1948 and 5 January 1949, and that the continuance of direct negotiations between the two Governments held no prospect of settling the issue.[38]

The proceedings at the UN in 1957 recorded a marked shift in New Delhi's stand on the Kashmir issue as discussed below, a stand which it takes till date. The UNSC was not amused by this shift and would have succeeded in sending UN troops into the PIS of J&K to 'assist' in demilitarization, had it not been for the veto by the erstwhile Soviet Union.

In 1957, New Delhi reiterated before the UNSC that Pakistan was an aggressor and sought to make out a case that the UN had already recognized that Pakistan was guilty of aggression. New Delhi did this by relying upon the findings of Owen Dixon who, as UN Representative, had stated '[w]hen the frontier of the State of Jammu and Kashmir was crossed on, I believe, 20 October 1947 by hostile elements, it was contrary to international law' and 'when, in May 1948, as I believe, units of the regular Pakistan forces moved into the territory of the State, that too was inconsistent with international law'.[39] New Delhi also referred to the 'evidence' of Josef Korbel, a member, and later Chairman, of the UNCIP, who had in his book, *Danger in Kashmir*, disclosed that the UNCIP had 'explained to the Pakistanis that the movement of these troops into foreign territory without the invitation of that territory's Government was violation of international law'.[40]

The UNSC disagreed. Tsiang (China) recalled that way back in 1948, the UNSC members 'came to the same conclusion that the charge of aggression should be by-passed', that 'charge was never taken up, never sifted, never even given serious consideration' and that 'I believe it was very wise of the Council to by-pass that charge'.[41] Tsiang (China) happily pointed out that '[i]n fact, before the two parties directly concerned even appeared before the Council, the two parties agreed that the plebiscite should be the answer... [s]o the idea of a plebiscite was not imposed by the Council on the two parties'.[42]

Walker (Australia) asserted that 'the Security Council has never expressed any conclusion on the legal aspects of the original accession of the State of Jammu and Kashmir to India or made any adjudication on the question of aggression' and that 'we have not made any pronouncement at all on this matter, because we do not believe that it would be helpful to do so'.[43] Pierson Dixon (the UK) agreed that he did 'not feel that it would contribute to progress if we were to go over this ground (of aggression) again'[44] and that the question was only 'of carrying out international obligations by which both sides are engaged'.[45] Woodsworth (the US) reaffirmed that those obligations did exist in the UNCIP Resolutions.[46]

Carlos P. Romulo (Phillipines) opined that:[47]

> Although the representative of India has dealt with the question of aggression anew, I do not think that the Council is called upon to make any finding as to whether there has been aggression and by whom it was committed.... In the particular case before us, I incline to the view that the partition of British India between the Dominions of India and Pakistan did not give independence to the princely states but merely gave them the option to accede either to India or to Pakistan. As far as the Security Council is concerned, it took the view—reiterated time and again in resolution after resolution—that the principle of self-determination properly applied to the situation in Jammu and Kashmir merely meant the right of people to be consulted as to whether they decided to accede to India or to Pakistan.

Romulo (Phillipines) categorically stated that '[u]nder the circumstances and pending the holding of a plebiscite, neither India nor Pakistan can claim sovereignty over the State of Jammu and Kashmir'.[48]

Nunez-Portuondo (Cuba) took the view that:[49]

> [T]he very fact that India, on 13 August 1948 and 5 January 1949, accepted agreements to resolve the problem through a free plebiscite in which the people of Jammu and Kashmir would decide their own future, logically and legally bars the Security Council from a decision on the original accusation which subsequent events and situations rendered inoperative. The very procedure proposed by the Commission and accepted by Pakistan and India, we repeat, implicitly resolved the question of the alleged aggression, even if the charge had been fully proved.

Nunez-Portuondo (Cuba) felt that 'the sovereignty of Kashmir rests only with the people of Kashmir' to conclude that '[t]he people of Kashmir should decide of their own free will whether they wish to accede to India or Pakistan'.[50]

Urrutia (Colombia) summarized the stand of the UNSC in the following words: '[w]e are not asking India to agree to submit the legal problem of sovereignty to the Security Council for decision or to a plebiscite for decision' but '[w]hat we are asking India to do is to accept, in accordance with its agreement of 1948, the holding of a plebiscite in Kashmir'.[51]

New Delhi did not mince words in conveying its displeasure to the UNSC regarding the latter's approach to the Kashmir issue. Declaring that it 'would be a sad day' if the UNSC and 'the United Nations as a whole can afford to disregard the legal foundations of a State',[52] Krishna Menon (India) reiterated that:[53]

.... There is only one problem before you—whether you will face it or not, and if you do not face it, I say with great respect it is a matter between yourselves and the instructed judgement of your Governments—and that problem is the problem of aggression.... Any other procedures you may adopt will... aggravate the relations which we are trying very hard to make otherwise...it will also prove to those vast millions of the Indian people... to the masses of them, that the politics of power alignments, religious fanaticisms, personal antagonisms, take precedence over the fundamental principle of the Charter.

Krishna Menon (India) questioned that:[54]

There are people who are likely to ask: has the Security Council no concern about the other principles it affirmed—that there should be no aggressions, there should be no changing of the conditions that existed in the country, of annexations, of affiliations?... Why was not the Security Council concerned about the incorporation of a part of Kashmir into Pakistan by the Pakistan Constitution? Why is the Security Council not equally concerned about the annexation of these territories, about the militarization of them, about the threats of war made in this room?...

These situations do produce some strange spectacles, on which I am entitled to comment because they are political matters. Here we have the representative of Her Britannic Majesty challenging an act of a legislature which has received the royal assent. This is a very unusual procedure. And we are acting in terms of an act of the legislature which received at that time—fortunately for us—the royal assent, and not after the termination of monarchy in India. Therefore, in doing what is being done, those people who are connected with those matters are not only challenging us but challenging their common law—because they have no constitutional law—their statutes, their traditions, and the power of the royal seal on a bill.

Krishna Menon (India) pointed out that when prior to Pakistan moving its regular troops into Kashmir in May 1948, India had demanded that it be allowed to post garrisons in the Northern Areas,[55]

.... The Commission's first truce proposals of 15 April (1948) provided that: 'In the sparsely populated and mountainous region of the territory of Jammu and Kashmir to the north, observers will be stationed....

Now, are not the people of India and their Government entitled to inquire why it is that no observers were stationed and why it is that after the time of the negotiations, after the appointment of the Commission, the advancing of the Pakistan army into this area came about? The Commission had undertaken the responsibility of saying 'observers will be stationed'. It did not say 'observers may be stationed'. There are no observers. Therefore, the effect of the resolutions has been to permit the occupation and annexation of considerable parts of the State soon after the negotiations began.

Krishna Menon (India) stated further that:[56]

.... How is it that no question has been asked by the eleven nations represented round this table—I ask this question only because my people will ask and because the Security Council does not represent only these eleven countries but, as we understand it, all the Member States of the United Nations—about this apparent, gross, obvious, continuous, persistent and flagrant violation of the cease-fire agreement, of international law, of commitments contained in Security Council resolutions and Commission resolutions, and solemn undertakings given by your representatives to our Government, which are in writing and which have been made public?...

My Government is entitled to ask this question: Why is it, when we have committed no violations whatsoever, that there is all this unanimity about impending violations? The Security Council itself—a party to this agreement—is remiss in not drawing the other party's attention to violations; the Security Council is remiss in not asking for the withdrawal of the other party from that area; the Security Council's commissioners make proposals to us which are in gross violation of the commitments. Why is there no unanimity about these violations?

Rebutting the view of the members of the UNSC on the right to self-determination, New Delhi now explained the correct import of such right. Krishna Menon (India) stated that:[57]

What I want to emphasize is that self-determination is a nice word; it is a very nice principle. It ought to be applied to all those countries where, by force of arms, by the vicissitudes of history, people of different culture, different interest and different territories are held under by a colonial Power. If Cuba were under the domination of Spain—which we are glad it is not at present—its demand for self-determination would be quite correct. But without making any irrelevant references to the internal affairs of Cuba, any disturbance, any kind of discontent against the existing authority in Cuba, whether the form of government is one of which any particular member of the Security Council approves or not, we would not think that in terms of the Charter—and we would be the first to resist it—there is a case for self-determination.

This can only be applied to the dependent territories governed by a colonial Power. This expression cannot be used in regard to a constituent unit like Minnesota, which forms part of a federal Union.

It may be noted that in the proceedings before the UNSC in 1957, New Delhi also took the correct view of the sovereignty of the ruler of the PIS of J&K and of the accession of the state to the dominion of India. Krishna Menon (India) explained that:[58]

.... The Ruler is the repository of power. Whether, morally speaking, he is democratic or not is another matter. In an Indian State, however, all power flows from the Ruler - in some cases, this is true only in theory; in many cases, before independence, this was also true in form. There was, therefore, no one else who could have offered the accession.

Krishna Menon pointed out that:[59]

[W]hen the British left India, these [princely Indian] States were to accede to one country or the other, to one Dominion or the other. That was the position. That way was prescribed in the Constitution, and it would be of interest to know that the way of accession was not thought out after the partition. It is contained in the Act of 1935 [Government of India Act] passed by the British Parliament. The way for accession is for the Head of the State to submit an instrument of accession and for the Government of India to accept it or the Government of Pakistan to accept it. So an offer of accession and an acceptance completes accession. That creates a union within the federation....

On 26 October 1947 the Maharaja of Kashmir who was the Head of the State... submitted to the Governor-General of India an instrument of accession.... That instrument was sent over on 26 October and on the 27th, Lord Mountbatten, Governor-General of India, accepted the accession. Lord Mountbatten said: 'I do hereby accept this Instrument of Accession'. The accession is complete....

Therefore, the Government of India... cannot ever accept the idea that accession is anything but an indissoluble bond. When Kashmir acceded, that matter was finished.... Accordingly, any suggestion to us that the accession is provisional or temporary is very wrong.

Having come this far, the logical step would have been for New Delhi to declare that it simply lacked the competence to offer plebiscite to the people of the PIS of J&K. Instead, Krishna Menon (India) stated that:[60]

.... The question was asked to me yesterday, by a very good friend, a person for whom I have a very great regard: If this were so—he used some other words which are not very parliamentary—then why in the world did you suggest a plebiscite?

I want to make this very clear... the accession is complete. But it is possible for any sovereign Government to terminate an accession after the accession and the incorporation in law and in fact of the territory acceded....

With regard to this whole question of a plebiscite, it was not a plebiscite in the beginning; it was what is called a reference to the people, ascertaining their wishes or something of that character; no particular form was given to it.... The accession, it is true, can be terminated by our sovereign will. It is possible for any sovereign State to cede territory. If, as a result of a plebiscite, the people decided that they did not want to stay with India, then our duty at that time would be to adopt those constitutional procedures which would enable us to separate that territory.... I might be the owner of a house, but it may be that for many reasons I may prefer to give it up if certain conditions happen.

Now let us take this question of the plebiscite. I submit that the origin and the family tree of this plebiscite arose from our desire not to take this territory of Kashmir, originally ruled by a rather wrong kind of Maharaja with whom we joined issue, where there was a considerable popular movement, where our national leaders were threatened; and we wanted to settle that....

Krishna Menon (India) argued that the letter of Mountbatten expressing the wish of the Government of India to hold the plebiscite was 'not as part of the law, but as part of a political policy' and that 'whatever we may have said in that way has, first of all, nothing to do with Pakistan and nothing to do with the international community; it is something between the people of Kashmir and ourselves'.[61] The eventual stand taken by New Delhi before the UNSC was that following the accession of the PIS of J&K to the dominion of India, New Delhi's commitment to hold a plebiscite to decide the state's future—after peace was restored and the state was cleared of the invaders—was made only to the people of the state as part of domestic policy. According to New Delhi, such commitment did not constitute an 'international obligation', but was merely an 'engagement' that fell within the domestic jurisdiction of India. Further, since Pakistan had not vacated its occupation and withdrawn its troops, nationals and tribesmen from the Pakistan-held territory of the PIS of J&K in terms of the UNCIP Resolutions, the conditional and contingent 'engagement', if at all, of India to hold a plebiscite in the state did not mature.

Amongst other legal defences taken by New Delhi was the contention that it was released from giving effect to such an 'engagement', due to vital changes in the circumstances, on the principle of *rebus sic stantibus*—the principle being that the passage of time and the change of circumstances must affect the nature of agreements reached.[62] Interestingly, New Delhi listed the annexation of the territory of the PIS of J&K by Pakistan, the policy of subversion, infiltration and sabotage adopted by Pakistan towards the territory of the state with India, and the military alliances entered into by Pakistan as material changes in circumstances releasing New Delhi from its 'wish' to hold a plebiscite.[63] Indeed, New Delhi pleaded that:[64]

.... The continuing process of sabotage, the continuing process of sub-version, the continuing phase of the new war, enjoin upon the Security Council a different action. We have spoken very mildly on this matter, both publicly and privately, in the hope that if there are difficulties they may be smoothed over, or that they will not be aggravated, but we have apparently been fooled in this matter.

The fallout of the improved stand of New Delhi was on the world opinion, which saw New Delhi as trying to wriggle out of its 'pledge' to hold a plebiscite. Few paused to consider the reasons given by India for not hold-ing a plebiscite. Since the refrain was that it was India which was not willing to hold a plebiscite, the violation of the UNCIP Resolutions by Pakistan receded into the background. Thus, Pakistan, the aggressor, strongly backed by the members of the UNSC and comfortably in occupation of a part of the PIS of J&K without any locus standi, effectively made out a case in the public mind for its acts. India has never recovered since.

Pakistan was clearly not impressed by India's views in 1957 either. It referred to the innumerable pledges given by New Delhi to hold a plebiscite under UN auspices[65] and reiterated its stand that there was a 'solemn international agreement' between India and Pakistan to do so.[66] Pakistan reasoned that '[n]o kind of legalistic pretexts on the part of India' can absolve it of its solemn international obligation.[67]

The UNSC expectedly took up the Resolution of 20 February 1957 of Australia, Cuba, the UK and the US, which was based on Pakistan's pro-posal to send a UN force to assist in the demilitarisation of the PIS of J&K.

It was the erstwhile Soviet Union that saved the day for India. Sobolev (USSR) stated that the Kashmir question 'was created nearly nine years ago, by certain Powers which are using every means in their endeavour to foment discord between countries striving for their national freedom and independence' and that these 'Powers were guided primarily by their own interests which were aimed at penetration into this region as one of great strategic importance'.[68] The Soviet Union expressed the view that with the adoption of the state's Constitution 'the Kashmir question has in actual fact already been settled in essence by the people of Kashmir themselves, who consider their territory an integral part of the Republic of India'.[69]

At the 773rd meeting of the UNSC on 20 February 1957, the Soviet Union vetoed the Resolution submitted that day. In its explanation for the veto, the Soviet Union declared that:[70]

> It should be remembered that the Kashmir question has been on the agenda for almost ten years... no satisfactory solution has yet been found, chiefly because of the position adopted by the Western Powers which have been trying to use the Kashmir question to carry through their own political plans.... The fact that Pakistan was encouraged to carry out military preparations and that it was given large-scale military assistance has exposed the intentions of the Western Powers which have been helping to turn the part of Kashmir occupied by Pakistan into a fortified strategic outpost....

Eventually, the UNSC adopted a resolution on 2 December 1957 again calling upon India and Pakistan to comply with the UNCIP Resolutions of 13 August 1948 and 5 January 1949. The *India–Pakistan Question* remained on the agenda of the UNSC and was marked by acrimonious debates. In April–May 1962, the UNSC considered the resolution moved by Ireland on 22 June 1962, asking India and Pakistan to solve the Kashmir problem by negotiations, mediation, arbitration or any other mode of choice. The Soviet Union vetoed the said resolution.[71] While Pakistan and India moved the UNSC to report new developments, the basic positions have remained the same till date. Since the UNSC Resolutions remained dormant for decades, the Kashmir issue was sought to be removed from the UN agenda.[72] However, as Pakistan's then Foreign Minister Khurshid Mahmud Kasuri admits:[73]

> Pakistan and other states with similar concerns and interests took umbrage at this proposal and, following protacted efforts spearheaded by Pakistan, the proposal was abandoned.... Despite our realization and disappointment that the UN had failed to resolve the Kashmir issue, we were extremely keen to retain the Kashmir issue on the UN agenda, as it provided the legal basis of our position on Kashmir.

Notwithstanding Pakistan's occupation of the PIS of J&K having been consolidated through the UNSC, New Delhi felt that the UN now had nothing to do with the matter, and stated, by its Note dated 19 October 1970, that issues between India and Pakistan could be settled bilaterally.[74] The Yearbook of the United Nations, 1971 records New Delhi's stand that:[75]

> [S]ince the State has become an integral part of India by virtue of its accession since 1947, the issues raised by Pakistan concerned matters of domestic jurisdiction.... Government [of India] would not discuss such matters with any other country or in the United Nations, though it was prepared to discuss bilaterally with Pakistan the question of Pakistan's illegal occupation of part of the State.

It may be recalled that the UNMOGIP was stationed, at the instance of the UNCIP Military Adviser, in the PIS of J&K since February 1949. New Delhi eventually asked the UNMOGIP on 8 July 2014 to vacate the 7,000 square feet bungalow provided in central Delhi by the government free of charge for decades. The sense in New Delhi was that 'the UNMOGIP has outlived its use' and since 'violations of LOC by Pakistan continued with impunity,' it did not feel the need to continue paying for 'meaningless friendly gestures'.[76] Rather, as the Indian Ministry of External Affairs put it, such step was in 'line with our effort to rationalise UNMOGIP's presence in India'.[77] The UNMOGIP, on its part, expressed its intention to stay in Delhi on rented accommodation to fulfil the mandate of the UN Resolutions.[78]

As regards New Delhi's improved stand before the UNSC in 1957, such stand confirmed that its approach towards the PIS of J&K since 1947 had been legally untenable. New Delhi itself acknowleged that the ruler of the PIS of J&K was sovereign when he offered accession to India, and that the accession by the sovereign ruler was neither provisional nor conditional but was 'complete' on its acceptance by the dominion of India. There cannot be a more explicit admission by New Delhi that it bungled the Kashmir issue.

The improved stand of New Delhi since 1957 is legally correct, except with regard to its competence to offer plebiscite in the PIS of J&K or to cede national territory and its view that the commitment to hold a plebiscite to decide the state's future—after peace was restored and state was cleared of the invaders—did not constitute an 'international obligation', but was merely an 'engagement' that fell within the domestic jurisdiction of India. Having shown that New Delhi was not competent to offer plebiscite or to cede national territory, let us consider whether New Delhi assumed an 'international obligation' or a domestic 'engagement' to hold a plebiscite to decide the state's future.

The PIS of J&K and Domestic Jurisdiction

New Delhi's stand was that since the monarch of the PIS of J&K did execute the Instrument of Accession in favour of India in 1947, all questions relating to the PIS of J&K fell within its domestic jurisdiction. Thus, New Delhi's commitment to hold a referendum or plebiscite in the PIS of J&K for its people to decide their future was an internal matter.

Now, any question regarding the PIS of J&K, having acceded to the dominion of India, should logically fall within the domestic jurisdiction of India and be excluded from discussion at the UN or any other international fora. But then, as I have argued elsewhere,[79] if India itself raises the question of accession of the state before the UNSC and pledges a plebiscite under international auspices to settle the accession, would the Kashmir question, originally within the domestic jurisdiction of India, become an international issue so as to confer standing on the international community (including Pakistan) to require New Delhi to honour its pledge?

New Delhi's keenness to stress before the UNSC that the holding of a plebiscite in the PIS of J&K was a matter of domestic jurisdiction stems from the provisions of Article 2(7) of the UN Charter, which, to the extent it is relevant for this discussion, mandates that '[n]othing contained in the present Charter shall authorize the United Nations to intervene in matters which are essentially within the domestic jurisdiction of any state or shall require the Members to submit such matters to settlement under the present Charter...'.

That brings us to the question of the meaning of the term 'domestic jurisdiction' in international law. Wright notes that domestic jurisdiction is the residuum of sovereignty remaining outside a state's international obligations.[80] The sphere of domestic jurisdiction of a state cannot be determined directly, but only indirectly by ascertaining the international obligations of that state in a given situation.[81]

While the UN cannot make recommendations to a state concerning a matter within the state's domestic jurisdiction, it can certainly make recommendations to a state to fulfil the state's international obligations insofar as these obligations come within the general scope of the UN Charter.[82] By entering into international obligations, states are presumed to have consented to receiving, as members of the UN, such recommendations concerning the fulfilment of their obligations.[83] Consequently, UN resolutions, which relate to a definite international obligation of a particular state, are not considered to constitute intervention in 'a matter within its domestic jurisdiction'.

Article 2(7) of the UN Charter does not, therefore, prevent the UN from passing a resolution on a matter within the domestic jurisdiction of a member state, provided that the resolution is not in a form constituting an 'intervention'; or from passing a resolution in a form constituting an 'intervention', provided it deals with an international obligation of the state involved and thus does not concern its domestic jurisdiction.[84] Consequently, the prohibition of Article 2(7) of the UN Charter applies only to a resolution of the UN, which is both an 'intervention' and on a matter within the domestic jurisdiction of a state—that is, when the UN seeks to intervene in respect of a domestic matter with regard to which the state has made no international commitment or engagement.

Since it is the presence or absence of an international obligation that determines whether a matter is a domestic one, the issue is necessarily one of international law.[85] Further, the very question of whether or not a state has assumed an international obligation is again one of international law. Moreover, the provisions of the UN Charter and of the Statute of the International Court of Justice, which was established by the UN Charter as the principal judicial organ of the UN, support the proposition that only an international authority can finally determine the validity of a state's claim that a matter is essentially within its domestic jurisdiction.[86]

The Permanent Court of International Justice (PCIJ), in its Advisory Opinion in *Tunis Nationality Decrees*, considered whether the 'dispute between France and Great Britain as to the Nationality Decrees issued in Tunis and Morocco (French Zone) on 8 November 1921 and their application to British subjects by international law were solely a matter of domestic jurisdiction'.[87] The PCIJ ruled in the negative, opining that where a state's discretion in dealing with a matter is limited by its obligations either under general international law or its treaties, such matter is not within its domestic jurisdiction.[88]

Reference can also be made in this regard to *Competence of the General Assembly for the Admission of a State to the United Nations*, wherein the ICJ examined the contention that the UN General Assembly could not consider the procedure adopted by Bulgaria, Hungary and Romania to determine their treaty obligations concerning human rights because the matter was essentially within the domestic jurisdiction of these states.[89] The ICJ held that 'the interpretation of the terms of the treaty for this purpose could not be considered as a question essentially within the domestic jurisdiction of a state,' it being a question of international law.[90]

I have examined elsewhere[91] whether New Delhi was correct in contending before the UNSC that its 'wish' that the question of accession of the

PIS of J&K to India be determined by a plebiscite was a matter within its domestic jurisdiction, and that the UNCIP Resolutions, at best, constituted a domestic 'engagement' rather than an 'international obligation' to do so. It is evident that as long as New Delhi had not expressed any such 'wish' before the UNSC or to a foreign state, the question of assuming an international obligation or engagement did not arise, and the matter did indeed fall within the domestic jurisdiction of India. But, the moment New Delhi expressed the 'wish' before the UN (as well as at bilateral and multilateral conventions and fora on numerous occasions) that the question of accession be determined by a plebiscite, which 'wish' was recognized and accepted by the UN and other states (including Pakistan), New Delhi entered into at least an international engagement to hold the plebiscite, thereby taking the matter out of its domestic jurisdiction.[92] This is precisely why the British wanted to get the UN involved somehow, once the PIS of J&K had acceded to the dominion of India. And this is precisely why Pakistan is, in the words of Pakistan's former Foreign Minister Khurshid Mahmud Kasuri, 'extremely keen to retain the Kashmir issue on the UN agenda, as it provided the legal basis of [Pakistan's] position on Kashmir'.[93] Otherwise, Pakistan would have no locus standi with respect to the PIS of J&K.

Now, Pakistan contends that the UNCIP Resolutions contain an 'international obligation' on the parties to hold a plebiscite. India submits that it is merely an 'engagement' falling within its domestic jurisdiction, that is, a domestic engagement. But then, whether the UNCIP Resolutions constitute an international obligation or a domestic engagement is again a matter of international law, which by its very nature takes the Kashmir issue out of the domestic jurisdiction of India. That such an engagement was a conditional and contingent one is an entirely different matter. And so is the contention that it was made in the context of certain circumstances and was subject to certain assurances. That such an engagement is, according to New Delhi, not enforceable is also beside the point. The point is that New Delhi, by its own admission, had accepted before the UNSC at least an engagement, albeit a conditional, contingent and non-enforceable one. That was sufficient to take the Kashmir issue out of the domestic jurisdiction of India and make it an international matter. More importantly, it permitted the international community to at least argue that India is under an international obligation to hold a plebiscite to determine the validity of the accession of the PIS of J&K to India. The determination of whether or not India is under an international obligation to do so is itself a matter of international law.

New Delhi itself was fully aware of the Kashmir issue having become an international one. Nehru himself declared in Parliament on 7 August 1952:[94]

It is an international problem. It would be an international problem anyhow if it concerned any other nation besides India and it does. It became further an international problem because a large number of other countries also took interest and gave advice....

Earlier, Nehru had, when faced with demands of withdrawing the reference from the UN, emphasized on 7 August 1951 in Parliament that 'Kashmir has become an international issue'[95] and that:[96]

.... I do not understand this cry of our withdrawing this matter of Kashmir from the United Nations. It is not the question of withdrawing it from some law court to the other. This matter is not before the United Nations as a forum. It is before the nations of the world, whether they are united or disunited and whether they are a forum or not. It is an international matter. It is a matter in the minds of millions of men. How can you withdraw from the minds of millions of men by some legal withdrawal or otherwise from some forum. The question does not arise....

Release from the UNCIP Resolutions

It may be recalled that the reference of the Kashmir issue to the UN on 1 January 1948 by New Delhi suffered from the obvious legal infirmity that it was irregular tribal raiders who had invaded the PIS of J&K and who, even though sponsored by Pakistan, could not have been treated in law to be a 'state'. There was, therefore, no 'state' that could have been taken by New Delhi to the UN or have been made party to a dispute. The reference to the UN, as also the UNCIP Resolutions passed in such reference, is therefore without jurisdiction and beyond the UN Charter itself. This, by itself, releases India from such Resolutions.

Having said that, the reference was made by New Delhi under Chapter VI of the UN Charter that contemplates 'Pacific Settlement of Disputes'. Resolutions passed under Chapter VI of the UN Charter are generally operative only with the consent of all parties involved. It is under Chapter VII of the UN Charter that the UNSC can impose obligations on states and not depend on the consent of the concerned states. Chapter VII of the UN Charter relates to 'Action with Respect to Threats to the Peace, Breaches of the Peace and Acts of Aggression'. Article 39 provides that the 'Security Council shall determine the existence of any threat to the peace, breach of the peace, or act of aggression and shall make recommendations, or decide what measures shall be taken in accordance with Articles 41 and 42, to maintain or restore international peace and security'. Article 41 refers to measures not involving the use of armed force to give effect to UNSC decisions, while Article 42 provides for action by air, sea or land forces as may be necessary to maintain or restore international peace and security. Since New Delhi made the reference under Chapter VI of the UN Charter, and not Chapter VII, it is even otherwise not open to the UNSC to take recourse to these provisions to ensure compliance with the UNCIP Resolutions on the Kashmir issue.

It may be recalled that Article 25 of the UN Charter provides that the 'Members of the United Nations agree to accept and carry out the decisions of the Security Council in accordance with the present Charter'. The ICJ has, in *Namibia*,[97] taken the view that while Article 25 cannot be said to be inapplicable to resolutions of the UNSC under Chapter VI of the UN Charter, the question of whether or not a particular resolution under Chapter VI is binding would depend on the language of the resolution, the discussions leading to it, the UN Charter provisions invoked and all other circumstances attendant thereto. The ICJ held that:[98]

113. It has been contended that Article 25 of the Charter applies only to enforcement measures adopted under Chapter VII of the Charter. It is not possible to find in the Charter any support for this view. Article 25 is not confined to decisions in regard to enforcement action but applies to 'the decisions of the Security Council' adopted in accordance with the Charter. Moreover, that Article is placed, not in Chapter VII, but immediately after Article 24 in that part of the Charter which deals with the functions and powers of the Security Council. If Article 25 had reference solely to decisions of the Security Council concerning enforcement action under Articles 41 and 42 of the Charter, that is to say, if it were only such decisions which had binding effect, then Article 25 would be superfluous, since this effect is secured by Articles 48 and 49 of the Charter.

114.... The language of a resolution of the Security Council should be carefully analysed before a Conclusion can be made as to its binding effect. In view of the nature of the powers under Article 25, the question whether they have been in fact exercised is to be determined in each case, having regard to the terms of the resolution to be interpreted, the discussions leading to it, the Charter provisions invoked and, in general, all circumstances that might assist in determining the legal consequences of the resolution of the Security Council.

The entire background leading to the Kashmir issue that has been narrated in the preceding chapters makes out a good case for New Delhi to contend that India, having been induced to make the reference to the UN by fraud, is even otherwise not bound by the UNCIP Resolutions.

Repudiation of the 'International Obligation' to Hold a Plebiscite

Even if one proceeds on the plea of Pakistan that the UNCIP Resolutions impose an 'international obligation', as binding as a treaty obligation, upon India to hold a plebiscite in the PIS of J&K, such 'international obligation' can easily be repudiated by New Delhi on three distinct grounds.

First, New Delhi can assert that it was released from giving effect to such an 'international obligation', due to vital changes in the circumstances on the principle of *rebus sic stantibus*, which it did before the UNSC in the 1957 proceedings considered above.[99] John Fischer Williams writes that while there is no doctrine that one state may by unilateral declaration rescind or modify its obligations, it can assert that the obligations in a treaty which still remain to be executed have lost their force if the essential conditions in which such treaty was concluded have changed.[100]

As far as the Kashmir issue is concerned, the preceding chapters have referred to the change in the vital circumstances surrounding the assumption by New Delhi of the 'international obligation' to hold a plebiscite. Gunnar Jarring, the UN Representative sent to the PIS of J&K to seek demilitarization in 1957, recognized the changing 'political, economic and strategic factors surrounding the whole of the Kashmir question, together with the changing pattern of the power relations in West and South Asia' and pointed out that 'the implementation of international agreements of an 'ad hoc' character, which has not been achieved fairly speedily, may become progressively more difficult because the situation with which they were to cope has tended to change'.[101]

Further, the framing of the Constitution of Jammu and Kashmir of 1957 by the Constituent Assembly of the PIS of J&K, subsequent bilateral agreements between India and Pakistan such as the Tashkent Declaration of 1966, Simla Agreement of 1972 and the Lahore Declaration of 1999, the Kargil conflict, the use of cross-border terrorism by Pakistan to wage a proxy war against India, camouflaged as an indigenous jihad, have also changed essential conditions under which the 'international obligation' to hold a plebiscite was made. Hence, there does exist such a material change in circumstances that New Delhi is well within its right to reconsider its 'obligations' under the UNCIP Resolutions, particularly since no progress has been made on such 'obligations' for almost 70 years now. The then Indian Prime Minister Atal Bihari Vajpayee declared, in an interview to Jeddah based *Malayalam News*, published on 19 December 2000, that the UNCIP Resolutions have lost their relevance as they have become time-barred.[102] Noting that the PIS of J&K with India had participated in local elections and general elections in India, thereby acknowledging its status as one of the states within the Indian Union, the Prime Minister asserted that:[103]

> Five decades ago, India was willing to implement the UN resolutions, but Pakistan had at that time refused to withdraw from occupied Kashmir as the first step to implement the resolutions.... Pakistan's aggression against India in 1965 and 1971, support to terrorism in different parts of India, cross-border violence against India as well as changes in the population profile of Jammu and Kashmir had further made the UN resolutions redundant.

The second ground available to New Delhi to repudiate an 'international obligation' to hold a plebiscite in the PIS of J&K is the patent violations by Pakistan of the UNCIP Resolutions. New Delhi has detailed before the UNSC these violations, as a result of which the 'bottom' of the UNCIP Resolutions has 'been knocked out' by the conduct of Pakistan itself.[104] According to Charles Fenwick, international law provides that the violation of a treaty by one of the contracting states makes it voidable or subject to cancellation by the other party.[105] The principle that a breach, which is material to the main object, liberates the other party from its obligations,[106] has been approved by the ICJ in *Namibia*.[107] The ICJ, in fact, reiterated in *Nicaragua* that:[108]

> [I]n a legal dispute affecting two states, one of them may argue that the applicability of a treaty rule to its own conduct depends on the other State's conduct in respect of the application of other rules, on other subjects, also included in the same treaty. For example, if a State exercises its right to terminate or suspend the operation of a treaty on the ground of the violation by the other party of a 'provision essential to the accomplishment of the object or purpose of the treaty' (in the words of Art. 60, para 3 (b) of the Vienna Convention on the Law of Treaties), it is exempted vis-a-vis the other State, from a rule of treaty-law, because of the breach by that other State of a different rule of treaty-law....

New Delhi would, therefore, be justified in declaring that the non-compliance by Pakistan of the UNCIP Resolutions itself liberates India from an 'international obligation' to hold a plebiscite in the PIS of J&K.

The third ground for repudiating such 'international obligation' to hold a plebiscite is that New Delhi lacked the competence to assume such 'obligation' in the first place and is incapable of its fulfilment. It may be recalled that New Delhi, under the Indian Independence Act of 1947, the Government of India Act of 1935, as amended, and the Instrument of Accession, was not competent to wish that the question of the accession of the PIS of J&K be settled by a reference to the people nor to offer a plebiscite in the state under UN auspices.

It will, therefore, be worthwhile to consider whether India, or for that matter, any sovereign state is bound by an 'international obligation' made on its behalf though the same is inconsistent with the constitution of that state?

As a point of departure, let us set out Pakistan's argument on the constitutional limitations on India to assume such 'international obligation' as under :[109]

.... We have heard from the representative of India long dissertations on the federal nature of the constitution of his country and how its provisions prevent India from carrying out its international obligation to permit the people of Kashmir to exercise their right of self-determination.

Let me quote to you, in this connection, a rule of international law of a binding character, which has a direct bearing on this point:

'Every State has the duty to carry out in good faith its obligations arising from treaties and other sources of international law, and it may not invoke provisions in its constitution or its laws as an excuse for failure to perform this duty'.(General Assembly resolution 375 (IV), annex, article 13)

This rule appears as article 13 of the Draft Declaration on Rights and Duties of States adopted unanimously on 6 December 1949 by the General Assembly of the United Nations at its fourth session....

The latter part of the article, which I quote again: '... it may not invoke provisions in its constitution or its laws as an excuse for failure to perform this duty' is based on the advisory opinion of the Permanent Court of International Justice delivered on 4 February 1932 in the well-known case of the 'treatment of Polish nationals and other persons of Polish origin or speech in the Danzig territory'. The Permanent Court held as follows:

'It should however be observed that, while on the one hand, according to generally accepted principles, a State cannot rely, as against another State, on the provisions of the latter's Constitution, but only on international law and international obligations duly accepted on the other hand and conversely, a State cannot adduce as against another State its own Constitution with a view of evading obligations incumbent upon it under international law or treaties in force'.

No kind of legalistic pretexts on the part of India, based on the Indian Constitution, can absolve it of its solemn international obligation assumed under the two resolutions of the Commission for India and Pakistan....

Pakistan failed to appreciate that the constitutional law applicable (at the time that New Delhi was said to have assumed an 'international obligation' to hold a plebiscite) was contained, not in the Constitution of India, but in the Indian Independence Act of 1947 and the Government of India Act of 1935, as amended—Acts to which both the dominions of India and Pakistan owe their existence and which both accepted. At that time, there was no Constitution of India. The Indian Supreme Court observed, in *In re Delhi Laws Act, 1912*, that although by the Indian Independence Act of 1947 'the control of British Parliament over the Government of India and the Central Legislature was removed, the powers of the Central Legislature were still as those found in the Government of India Act, 1935...'.[110]

It has already been noted that neither of the dominions, in terms of the said British statutes, had paramountcy over the princely Indian states and that both dominions lacked competence to hold a plebiscite to determine the accession of a princely Indian state. The legal position that subsequently the Constitution of India also did not confer upon New Delhi the power to cede national territory is independent of the limitations on the power of New Delhi under the said British statutes in relation to the princely Indian states.

The position, thus, is not that New Delhi can seek to use the protective shield of the Constitution of India to avoid an 'international obligation', but that New Delhi lacked the power to assume the 'international obligation' due to constitutional restrictions contained in the Indian Independence Act of 1947, and the Government of India Act of 1935, as amended. The real question, consequently, is whether India is bound by an 'international obligation' made on its behalf, which is inconsistent with the constitutional law embodied in the Indian Independence Act of 1947, and the Government of India Act of 1935, as amended? Further, should the capacity of New Delhi to contract be limited by the said Acts, are other states held to have notice of any restrictions that the Acts may impose?

The answer to these questions may be borrowed from the legal position in the US, whose Constitution assigns a wide field of reserved powers to the member states of the Union. Charles Fenwick refers to other American commentators to take the view that 'it would seem reasonable that foreign states, contracting with the United States, should be held a knowledge of any express prohibition in the Constitution against the adoption of the provisions in question'.[111]

Oppenheim writes that if the representatives of a State conclude a treaty by exceeding their powers, 'the treaty is not a real treaty, and is not binding on the State they represent',[112] and that:[113]

> [A]lthough the Heads of State are regularly, according to International Law, the organs that exercise the treaty-making power of the State, such treaties concluded on behalf of the State, as violate constitutional restrictions, do not bind the State concerned. This is so for the reason that the representatives have exceeded their powers in concluding the treaties.

Thus, while international law authorizes a sovereign state to negotiate treaties and assume international rights and obligations, other states are presumed to know the internal constitutional limitations on that power, and such international obligations do not bind the state concerned if they violate these constitutional limitations.

As far as the Kashmir issue is concerned, the UN, at least the UK, and certainly Pakistan, were aware of the provisions of the Indian Independence Act of 1947, and the Government of India Act of 1935, as amended, both being Acts of the British Parliament. At least the UK and Pakistan had, as detailed in the preceding chapters, publicly enunciated its statutory provisions, which prescribed the mode by which a legally sovereign princely Indian state could accede to either of the dominions; that is, through its sovereign ruler alone. It may further be recalled that the UNCIP Resolutions indicate that the UN was also conversant with the legal position that the PIS of J&K, notwithstanding its accession, had retained its sovereignty. Thus, it would seem reasonable to contend that the UN, and every state, including Pakistan, 'contracting' with India should be held to a knowledge that the representatives of India 'exceeded their powers' under these Acts, as well as the Instrument of Accession executed thereunder, by wishing or pledging to hold a plebiscite in the state to settle the question of accession, and that too, in the absence of its sovereign ruler.

Again, it has already been discussed that the provisions of a treaty do not invariably bind the subjects of the contracting party unless made binding by Parliamentary action.[114] This rule prevails throughout the British Commonwealth. Charles Fenwick opines that as formal ratification has now become an accepted part of the procedure of treaty making, international law clearly recognizes that there is no legal ground for complaint by one party if the other should subsequently repudiate the agreement signed on its behalf.[115] He states that the majority of writers:[116]

> [M]aintain that foreign governments should be held to a knowledge of the constitutional prerequisites of ratification of each country with which they are

dealing; and they insist that a treaty which has been ratified without the proper observance of these requirements is ipso facto invalid, whatever the proclamation of the head of the state may assert in that respect.

Given that the capacity of New Delhi to deal with the PIS of J&K or its territory was limited by the provisions of the Indian Independence Act of 1947, and the Government of India Act of 1935, as amended, as also the Instrument of Accession executed thereunder, legislative action to give effect to the 'international obligation' to hold a plebiscite in the state, or to cede territory of the state, can be confidently ruled out. The UN and the international community are, in international law, held to have knowledge of the provisions of the said Acts, and any 'international obligation' in contravention of these provisions is ipso facto invalid.

There is nothing much that the UN or the international community can do to enforce the UNCIP Resolutions passed in the proceedings under Chapter VI of the UN Charter; more so, when the commitment made by New Delhi was without jurisdiction. However, the significance of the Kashmir issue being taken out of the domestic jurisdiction and becoming an international matter lies in the fact that it confers standing on the UN and its member states, including Pakistan, to discuss the happenings in the PIS of J&K—which they could not have done, had the matter remained within the domestic jurisdiction of India. It enabled commentators to blur the aggression committed by Pakistan with the standing conferred by New Delhi upon it by taking the Kashmir issue out of India's domestic jurisdiction. Witness the views of Snedden:[117]

> Pakistan became involved with J&K when Jammuites fought to ensure that the princely state joined Pakistan, and when a large number of Muslims fled Jammu Province for Pakistan. In October 1947, Pakistanis became physically involved in J&K when Pakistani Pukhtoons invaded Kashmir Province. Similarly, in November 1947, Muslims in Gilgit removed the Maharaja's governor, asked to join Pakistan, and soon afterwards welcomed a Pakistani administrator. In May 1948 the Pakistan Army officially entered J&K, chiefly to support pro-Pakistan forces. Its presence in Azad Kashmir and the Northern Areas meant that Pakistan quickly became the predominant power in the areas of J&K not under Indian control. Finally, Pakistan became involved with J&K via the United Nations after India involved the UN Security Council on 1 January 1948, hoping to have Pakistani aggression in J&K condemned. This did not happen. Instead, the UN sought to conduct a 'free and fair plebiscite' so that the people of J&K could decide whether to unite J&K, in its entirety, to India or Pakistan. No other options were offered. Pakistan is still involved in J&K because of UN Security Council resolutions, although its involvement is based on more than UN resolutions.

Having noted how it was New Delhi that conferred the 'disputed territory' status on the PIS of J&K, introduced the 'wishes of the people' as a relevant factor to 'settle' the accession of the state to India, took the Kashmir issue to the UN, internationalized the Kashmir problem, and how, after altering the entire international political discourse on Kashmir, aimed for territorial status quo, it will be useful to examine the various proposals that have been made in the past to resolve the Kashmir issue.

Notes and References

1. Anand, Mulk Raj. 1992. *V K Krishna Menon's Marathon Speech on Kashmir at U.N. Security Council*, p. 197. Allahabad: Wheeler Publishing.
2. *Supra* Note 41, Chapter VII, pp. 304, 312–313.
3. Ibid., p. 313.
4. Ibid.
5. S/PV 533 at pp. 6–12, Benegal N. Rau (India), 1 March 1951.
6. *Supra* Note 12, Chapter IV, p. 21.
7. S/PV 534 at pp. 30–32, Mohammed Zafrullah Khan (Pakistan), 6 March 1951.
8. S/PV 538 at pp. 1–7, Benegal N. Rau (India), 29 March 1951.
9. Ibid.
10. S/PV 539 at p. 13, Gladwyn Jebb (UK), 30 March 1951.
11. Ibid.
12. *Yearbook of the United Nations*, 1951. The India–Pakistan Question, pp. 340, 343.
13. *Supra* Note 12, Chapter IV, p. 22.
14. *Jammu and Kashmir Government Gazette* No. 22 dated 1 May 1951.
15. For detailed discussion, see *Yearbook of the United Nations*, 1952. The India-Pakistan Question, p. 232.
16. Extracted in S/PV 1087 at pp. 16–17, Z.A. Bhutto (Pakistan), 3 February 1964.
17. *Supra* Note 12, pp. 340, 344.
18. Ibid., p. 348.
19. *Supra* Note 15, p. 232.
20. Ibid., p. 241. The *Yearbook of the United Nations, 1953*, records that the UN Representative had concluded that 'agreement was not possible at that time between the two governments on the truce agreement based solely on Part II of the 13 August 1948 resolution...' (ibid., The India–Pakistan Question, at pp. 178, 179).
21. S/PV 609 at p. 17, Mohammed Zafrullah Khan (Pakistan), 16 December 1952.
22. *Supra* Note 28, Chapter IV, pp. 219, 222, 261, 265–266.
23. *White Paper: Kashmir – Meetings and Correspondence between Prime Ministers of India and Pakistan (July 1953–October 1954)*, Government of India, p. 71 at 73.
24. *Supra* Note 12, Chapter IV, p. 23.
25. Ibid.
26. Ibid.
27. Also see *Supra* Note 36, Chapter IV, p. 100.

28. For text see Qasim, Mir. 1992. *My Life and Times*, pp. 206–207. New Delhi: Allied Publishers Ltd.

29. See Vashishth, Satish. 1968. *Sheikh Abdullah: Then and Now*, p. 210. Delhi: Maulik Sahitya Prakashan.

30. Ibid., p. 217. Also see Sharma, B P. 1996. 'The Third Alternative - Independent Kashmir', in *Supra* Note 34, Chapter IV, pp. 179, 183.

31. *Supra* Note 35, Chapter IV, p 85.

32. See Sharma, B.P. 1996. The Third Alternative - Independent Kashmir', in *Supra* Note 34, Chapter IV, p. 183.

33. *Supra* Note 104, Chapter IV, p. 142.

34. *Kashmir: White Paper*, Ministry of External Affairs, Government of India, p. 7, July 1953–October 1954.

35. Ibid., p. 73.

36. *Yearbook of the United Nations*, 1957. The India-Pakistan Question, p. 80.

37. Ibid.

38. Ibid.

39. S/PV 799 at pp. 54–56, Krishna Menon (India), 5 November 1957.

40. Ibid.

41. S/PV 765 at pp. 12–15, Tsiang (China), 24 January 1957.

42. Ibid.

43. S/PV 798 at pp. 2–3, Walker (Australia), 29 October 1957.

44. S/PV 797 at p. 6, Pierson Dixon (UK), 25 October 1957.

45. Ibid., p. 11.

46. S/PV 797 at pp. 17–18, Woodsworth (the U.S.), 25 October 1947.

47. S/PV 768 at pp. 53–58, Carlos P. Romulo (Philippines), 15 February 1957.

48. S/PV 773 at p. 10, Carlos P. Romulo (Philippines), 20 February 1957.

49. S/PV 768 at p. 6, Nunez-Portuondo (Cuba), 15 February 1957.

50. Ibid., p. 46.

51. S/PV 768 at pp. 34–37, Urrutia (Colombia), 15 February 1957.

52. *Supra* Note 88, Chapter VIII, p. 6.

53. *Supra* Note 85, Chapter VIII, p. 46.

54. S/PV 765 at pp. 24–25, Krishna Menon (India), 24 January 1957.

55. *Supra* Note 88, Chapter VIII, pp. 5–6.

56. *Supra* Note 50, Chapter VII, pp. 36–41, 82.

57. *Supra* Note 88, Chapter VIII, p. 3.

58. *Supra* Note 32, Chapter VII, p. 31.

59. Ibid., pp. 22–27.

60. S/PV 767 at pp. 19–26, Krishna Menon (India), 8 February 1957.

61. Ibid., pp. 22–27.

62. *Supra* Note 85, Chapter VIII, pp. 26–34.

63. Ibid., pp. 40–41.

64. S/PV 803 at p. 5, Krishna Menon (India), 18 November 1957.

65. S/PV 766 at pp. 10–12, Firoz Khan Noon (Pakistan), 30 January 1957.

66. Ibid., p. 5.

67. S/PV 802 at pp. 8–15, Firoz Khan Noon (Pakistan), 15 November 1957.

68. S/PV 765 at p. 16, Sobolev (USSR), 24 January 1957.

69. Ibid. Also see S/PV 770 at pp. 38–39, Sobolev (USSR), 18 February 1957.

70. S/PV 805 at pp. 16–17, Sobolev (USSR), 21 November 1957.

71. *Supra* Note 12, Chapter IV, p. 37.
72. *Supra* Note 89, Chapter I, p. 293.
73. Ibid.
74. *Yearbook of the United Nations*, 1970. Communications regarding the India-Pakistan Question, pp. 220–221.
75. *Yearbook of the United Nations*, 1971. The situation in the Indian subcontinent, pp. 137, 144.
76. 'Delhi evicts UN's Kashmir observors'. Available online at http://transasianews.com/top-news/2465-delhi-evicts-un-s-kashmir-observers (downloaded on 30 August 2015); 'India asks UN group to vacate rent free office'. Available online at http://news.yahoo.com/india-asks-un-group-vacate-rent-free-office-075936026.html (downloaded on 30 August 2015).
77. 'Vacate official accommodation', India tells UNMOGIP. Available online at http://www.newswala.com/India-National-News/Vacate-official-accommodation-India-tells-UNMOGI-67133.html (downloaded on 30 August 2015).
78. Ibid.
79. *Supra* Note 1, Introduction.
80. *Supra* Note 28, Chapter VI, p. 67.
81. See ibid.
82. Lauterpacht, Hersh. 1950. *International Law and Human Rights*, p. 177. London: Stevens.
83. *Supra* Note 28, Chapter VI, p. 68.
84. Ibid., p. 62.
85. Ibid., p. 65.
86. Ibid., pp. 58, 67–68.
87. *Tunis Nationality Decrees*: PCIJ, 1923, Series B. p. 4.
88. Ibid., p. 24.
89. *Competence of the General Assembly for the Admission of a State to the United Nations:* ICJ Reports, 1950, p. 4
90. Ibid., pp. 70–71.
91. *Supra* Note 1, Introduction.
92. Ibid.
93. *Supra* Note 89, Chapter I, p. 293.
94. Extracted in *Supra* Note 12, Chapter IV, p. 24.
95. *Supra* Note 28, Chapter IV, pp. 286, 294.
96. Ibid., p. 289.
97. *Supra* Note 35, Chapter VI.
98. Ibid., pp. 52–53.
99. *Supra* Note 85, Chapter VIII, pp. 26–34.
100. See Williams, J. F. 1928. 'The Permanence of Treaties", *American Journal of International Law*, Vol 22, p. 89 at 103.
101. Editorial. 2001. 'Kashmir realities', *The Times of India*, New Delhi, 13 March.
102. *Hindustan Times*. 2000. 'UN resolutions on J&K have lost relevance: Vajpayee', New Delhi, 20 December.
103. Ibid.
104. S/PV 1090 at pp. 17–18, M. C. Chagla (India) 10 February 1964.
105. *Supra* Note 4, Chapter VIII, p. 452.

106. Hall, W. E. 1924. *A Treatise on International Law*, 8th Edition by A.P. Higgins, Section 116. Oxford: Clarendon Press.
107. *Supra* Note 35, Chapter VI, p. 47.
108. *Military and Paramilitary Activities in and against Nicaragua (Nicaragua v United States of America)*, Merits Judgement, ICJ Reports 1986, p. 14 at 95.
109. *Supra* Note 67, pp. 10–11.
110. *Supra* Note 4, Chapter V, pp. 803–804.
111. *Supra* Note 4, Chapter VIII, p. 433.
112. *Supra* Note 13, Chapter VII, p. 884.
113. Ibid., p. 887.
114. See *Supra* Note 3, Chapter VIII.
115. *Supra* Note 4, Chapter VIII, p. 435.
116. Ibid., p. 436.
117. *Supra* Note 81, Chapter IV, pp. 83–84.

X

Inadequacies of the Current Proposals to Resolve the Kashmir Issue

The Kashmir issue has engaged the attention of innumerable scholars, analysts, experts, institutions and authorities for almost seven decades now. Most commentators on the Kashmir problem subscribe, though for quite different reasons, to the view that the Kashmir problem is confined to the happenings in the Kashmir Valley with India, and discount the remaining territory of the state that is under the occupation of Pakistan and China. Proposals based on such a stand, due to the very parameters within which they have been formulated, cannot comprehensively resolve the Kashmir issue.

This chapter examines the inadequacies of the few solutions currently suggested to resolve the Kashmir problem. The purpose of doing so is to emphasize that there is perhaps no viable solution to the Kashmir issue other than the one suggested in this book.

Diplomatic Solution

Let us first consider Pakistan's stand on the PIS of J&K. Having consolidated its occupation over about 35 per cent of the territory of the state, which New Delhi has so willingly disowned, Pakistan has staked its claim to even that portion of state which is with India. The successive governments of Pakistan have enjoyed popular domestic support at least on this account—for, there is a genuine belief in Pakistan that New Delhi has cheated the Kashmiri populace of its promised right to choose the future of the state. Pakistan's former Foreign Minister Khurshid Mahmud Kasuri writes that

Pakistan is 'in no position to compromise on the aspirations of the people of Kashmir' and that the 'people of Pakistan would' reject 'any solution if it gave the impression of bartering away Kashmiri sentiments on the issue'.[1] Accordingly, he opines that the solution to the Kashmir issue must be 'in accordance with the aspirations of the people of Kashmir and be acceptable to Pakistan and India'. [2]

It is quite clear that the foreign policy of Pakistan revolves around the Kashmir issue. Indeed, Pakistan loses no opportunity to stake its claim to the entire PIS of J&K before international fora and ably presents its case regarding the urgency for the resolution of the issue. The persistent and somewhat successful efforts of Pakistan to keep the Kashmir problem alive at the international level have sustained its character as an international question threatening world peace, with successive Indo-Pakistan wars bearing testimony to this reality. Pakistan, therefore, has had no hesitation in unabashedly declaring that it would provide 'all out support' to the 'struggling people of Kashmir' for their 'struggle for self-determination'.[3] Those in India are well aware that Pakistan's 'all out support' includes export of terrorism, though most Indians have yet to gauge the intensity with which Pakistan is waging its covert war against India.

The policy of subversion adopted by Pakistan to wrestle the PIS of J&K from India finds mention in the UNSC reports way back in 1948 and in various UN documents recording, for instance, the 1965 Indo-Pakistan war.[4] By way of background, it may be noted that this war was preceded by a clash between India and Pakistan over the Rann of Kutch. Sheikh Abdullah had been arrested again in March 1965 by New Delhi for having met the Chinese premier, Chou-en-Lai, in Algiers where Abdullah had a stopover on his return to India from Mecca. Ramchandra Guha documents the unfolding of events as under:[5]

> Abdullah's arrest and the clash in Kutch had put an idea into the head of the Pakistani president, Ayub Khan. This was to foment an insurrection in the Indian part of Kashmir, leading to either a war ending with the state being annexed by Pakistan, or in international arbitration with the same result. In the late summer of 1965 the Pakistan army started planning 'Operation Gibraltar', named for a famous Moorish military victory in medieval Spain. Kashmiri militants were trained in the use of small arms, with their units named after legendary warriors of the Islamic past—Sulaiman, Salahuddin, and so on.
>
> In the first week of August, groups of irregulars crossed the ceasefire line into Kashmir. They proceeded to blow up bridges and fire-bomb government installations. The intention was to create confusion, and also to spark unrest.

Radio Pakistan announced that a popular uprising had broken out in the Valley. In fact, the local population was most apathetic—some intruders were even handed over to the police.

When the hoped-for rebellion did not materialise, Pakistan launched its reserve plan, codenamed 'Operation Grand Slam'. Troops crossed the ceasefire line in the Jammu sector and using, heavy artillery and mortar, made swift progress. The Indians fought back and, in the Uri sector, succeeded in capturing the pass of Haji Pir, a strategic point from where they could look out for infiltrators.

On 1 September the Pakistan army launched a major offensive in Chhamb... The escalation of hostilities alarmed the superpowers, and on 6 September the United Nations Security Council met to discuss the matter. The UN secretary general, U Thant, flew to the subcontinent, and after meeting the leaders in both capitals got them to agree to a ceasefire.... On 22 September hostilities were finally called off....

The battles took place principally in two sectors in the north-west—Kashmir and the Punjab.... As is common in such cases, both sides claimed victory, exaggerating the enemy's losses and understating their own. In truth, the war must be declared a draw....

The 1965 Indo-Pakistan war was followed by the 1971 Indo-Pakistan war. The humiliating defeat suffered by Pakistan in the 1971 war, and its dismemberment into modern-day Pakistan and Bangladesh, made Pakistan enhance its proxy war against India.

According to Ramesh Khazanchi,[6] General Zia-ul-Haq's 'seminal strategy' to incite locals into militancy was aimed at provoking mass insurrection through the propagation of 'brotherhood of Islam', as against the prevailing notion of 'Kashmiriat'—the centuries-old Sufi thesis of 'brotherhood of mankind'. The 1977 Topac policy was a three-pronged strategy to initiate low-level insurgency and to subvert the police, financial institutions, and the communications network. This was to be followed by direct pressure along the LOC, large-scale sabotage, and the infiltration of mercenaries and special forces to attack vital targets. Religion was to be used at the appropriate time to drive out the (Hindu) Kashmiri Pandits from the Kashmir Valley, and to create a communal divide between Hindus and Muslims to give effect to the principle underlying the two-nation theory.[7] Following the policy of subversion from within, Pakistan was said to have unabashedly recruited, trained, and armed mercenaries to wage the proxy war who, upon infiltrating into the territory of the PIS of J&K with India, caused havoc and destruction. It was reported that thousands of militants recruited from around the world and trained in Pakistan's ISI- sponsored camps were actually retained to do a stint in the state.[8] Militancy makes for a good career, with local militants getting a monthly 'salary' and the deceased militant's kin a 'pension'.[9] Fighting the jihad in the state, along with local militants and foreign mercenaries, were said to be the new breed of highly educated and high-tech militants, such as pilots, doctors and teachers.[10] That it was the Pakistan Army which dictated the 'advances and withdrawals' in the PIS of J&K with India was confirmed by the Islamic State in November 2015; the disclosure being made in the context of the Islamic State running down Al Qaida for allying with an 'apostate' Pakistan Army.[11]

The Topac 2 policy formulated by Pakistan reportedly aimed to set up several bases or modules throughout India, to pump in more sophisticated arms and ammunition, counterfeit currency and drugs into India, and to change the routes of the infiltrators.[12] Pakistan has, over the decades, reportedly overseen the establishment of the narco–terrorist–smuggler nexus, canalization of counterfeit Indian currency, *hawala* transactions to fund fundamentalist bodies in India for the purpose of indoctrination, and the creation of bases all over India to network and to co-ordinate its subversive policy.[13] Simultaneously, Pakistan has ensured that the LOC remains volatile. Indeed, the Indian Army Chief acknowledged on 1 September 2015 the possibility of 'swift, short wars' in future with Pakistan along the LOC, since the 'borders remain alive and active due to frequency of cease-fire violations and infiltration bids'.[14] Pakistan, in turn, warned India that it would pay a heavy price in the event of such wars. Reports in 2015 quote Pakistan's Foreign Secretary Aizaz Chaudhury as disclosing that Pakistan was building tactical battlefield nuclear weapons to deter any possible Indian attack, and suggest that these weapons had already been deployed in areas along the border with India.[15] Pakistan's short-range nuclear-capable missiles with a range of only 60 kilometres could be used should New Delhi attempt to strike at Pakistani terror camps or if there is a 'low-intensity' conflict.[16] The Editorial in the *New York Times* of 9 November 2015 pointed out that due to Pakistan's obsession with India, its nuclear arsenal was growing faster than any other country, and that Pakistan could in a decade become the world's third-ranked nuclear power, behind the US and Russia, but ahead of China, France and Britain.[17] Frightening as it may sound, nuclear weapons, so far being built to deter a war, are now intended to be used for actually fighting a war!

Pakistan has no intention of letting go of the territories of the state under its occupation, that is, the Northern Areas and 'Azad Kashmir', as is evident from the manner in which these regions have been dealt with by Pakistan. Pakistan is not particularly concerned with the Jammu and Ladakh regions of the PIS of J&K, where it would not win a referendum or plebiscite if one was held. Pakistan is, therefore, keen to limit the referendum or plebiscite to the Kashmir Valley in the hope that the Valley would accede to Pakistan or, in case it chooses independence, could be subsequently subsumed into Pakistan. The causes for the discontentment and alienation of the Kashmiri populace from the Indian establishment will be discussed at a later stage. It will suffice to note here that Pakistan from 1989 onwards made a deliberate attempt to portray such discontentment and alienation as a pan-Islamic jihad for liberation. Pakistan—who views Kashmir as an 'article of faith' and, like the British, realizes the importance of the Northern Areas for strategic depth, avenues to China and an alternative route to Afghanistan and the Central Asian republics[18]—projected the expression of resentment in the state as part of a global Islamic pattern linked to the uprisings in Israel and the Islamic Central Asian Republics.[19] The disturbance in the PIS of J&K was, therefore, sought to be identified with the general unrest in the strategic 'Islamic crescent of conflict', from Israel, to the Intifida in Palestine, the struggle in Lebanon and Afghanistan and the stirring in Azerbaijan.[20] Girilal Jain observes that Islamabad sought to cash in on the ascendancy of Islamic sentiment in Muslim countries, which made it difficult for their governments to be seen to oppose Muslim 'causes'.[21] He notes that since the *Ummah* (an Islamic world without frontiers) does not recognize the twin concepts of national sovereignty and non-interference in the internal affairs of countries, it looks upon the Kashmir issue as a Muslim 'cause'. Hence, Pakistan consistently raises the Kashmir issue in Islamic fora and ensures that India is censured for its 'occupation' of the PIS of J&K.

I believe that for any diplomatic strategy to resolve the Kashmir issue in India's interests, it must have two objectives. First, the strategy must make Pakistan, and China, vacate all areas which formed part of the PIS of J&K in 1947. Second, it must make Pakistan accept as valid the accession of the PIS of J&K to the dominion of India, revise its state policy of exporting terrorism, and compel it to cease giving even 'moral or political support' to the supposed jihad in the state.

As far as the first objective is concerned, neither Pakistan nor China could care less about polite requests by India to vacate the territory of the PIS of J&K. It will be recalled that it was New Delhi itself who had, in contravention of the provisions of the Indian Independence Act of 1947 and the Government of India Act of 1935, as amended, introduced 'the wishes of the people' as a criterion to determine the accession of the state. It was New Delhi who referred the Kashmir issue to the UN and voluntarily assumed the 'engagement', if not 'obligation', to 'settle' the question of accession of the state through a UN-supervised plebiscite. It was New Delhi who, thereafter, reiterated this stand on every conceivable occasion and in every conceivable forum, thereby emphasizing that the ultimate decision lay with the people. The current stand of New Delhi is premised on the same principle, namely, that it is the people of the state who will decide. The only difference is that, according to New Delhi, the people have, through the Constitution of Jammu and Kashmir of 1957, decided that their future lies with India. Further, given that New Delhi subscribes to territorial status quo and is willing to disown the territories of the PIS of J&K occupied by Pakistan and China, it is not particularly concerned about the fate of the population residing in those territories of the state. Since New Delhi itself took the erroneous stand that it was for the people of the PIS of J&K to decide their future and that the solution to the Kashmir problem lay in converting the LOC into the international border, even the few countries who are favourably inclined towards India merely endorse this stand in varying degrees. Hence, New Delhi itself does not expect the international community, as a whole, to exert diplomatic pressure on Pakistan and China to vacate the occupied territories of the PIS of J&K.

Coming to the second objective, it is evident that the international community must first share the perception that the accession of the PIS of J&K to the dominion of India in 1947 was valid, legal, final, complete and binding in view of the provisions of the Indian Independence Act of 1947 and the Government of India Act of 1935, as amended, and that there exists no rationale for a reference to the people or a plebiscite to 'settle' such accession. It is only then that the international community, as a whole, could exert pressure upon Pakistan to revise its state policy of exporting terrorism. However, the international community has no such perception. Indeed, one cannot expect the international community to have such perception when New Delhi itself has remained confused. The words '[t]he final status of Jammu and Kashmir has not yet been agreed upon by the parties' in all UN maps[22] over the decades highlight the stand of the international community that the PIS of J&K is a disputed territory between India and Pakistan. A reference to the view of the international community in this regard would be useful.

United States

The American policy towards the PIS of J&K over the years has been dictated by the geopolitical, strategic and business interests of the US with Pakistan. After all, the US had to secure Pakistan and the crucial air base at Peshawar to safeguard Western interests in the Middle East, and later, for the containment of the erstwhile Soviet Union. The US needed Pakistan to create and nurture the Taliban in its madrassas during the Soviet-Afghan war, to be used to evict the Soviets from Afghanistan.[23] The US needed the good offices of Pakistan to build relations with communist China and make allies in the Islamic world. Moreover, the US was, and remains, a major supplier of arms and ammunition to Pakistan, which, for the major period of its existence, remained under military rule. It was, thus, not surprising that the US joined the UK in the UNSC to 'by pass' the question of Pakistan's aggression.[24] The US in fact flirted with the idea of an independent PIS of J&K in 1953, and unsuccessfully tried to win over Sheikh Abdullah.[25] In 1954, the US forged a military alliance with Pakistan and gave it military aid to bring about an Indo-Pakistan military balance. From 1963 to 1965, the US floated the idea of joint control of India and Pakistan over the Kashmir Valley or of partitioning it to give Pakistan access to it.[26] During the Bangladesh war in December 1971, the US warned that Indian troops must respect both the ceasefire line in the PIS of J&K and the international border in Punjab.[27]

The aforesaid US policy has also meant that it would simply ignore the role of Pakistan in instigating, breeding, nurturing, sponsoring and exporting terrorism, not only in India but also in other countries like Afghanistan. Despite Pakistan's brazenly adopting cross-border terrorism as an instrument of state policy, the US opined that there was 'insufficient evidence' of Islamabad's involvement in the bloodshed in the Kashmir Valley.[28] Confronted with burgeoning evidence by its own State Department, Senators and Congressmen about Pakistan's involvement in sponsoring international terrorism,[29] the US then sought to justify its handling of Pakistan with the novel argument that, should the US take action against Pakistan, it would become a rogue state. The Clinton administration declared that 'it will be last nail in the coffin, it could become a failed state and fall off the brink into full-fledged fundamentalism *a la* Afghanistan'.[30] Hence, even during the 1999 Kargil conflict, while the US was warning Pakistan of possible sanctions if it did not pull out of Kargil, its administration made no effort to halt the multilateral aid to Pakistan. The International Monetary Fund gave Pakistan US$51 million in May 1999 with US approval, followed by a further disbursement of US$100 million. Ironically, at the time that Pakistan was engaged in the costly Kargil experiment, the World Bank approved a credit of US$90 million to Pakistan on 18 June 1999 to support its 'Poverty Alleviation Fund'.[31]

It may be recalled that New Delhi had, through the Simla Agreement, sought to bind Pakistan to resolve their differences bilaterally and to respect the LOC. However, by attempting to contain the Kashmir issue to a 'bilateral' level, India unwittingly gave Pakistan the standing in the matter, which it had been desperately seeking—a standing which got renewed each time India reiterated that the Kashmir problem was a bilateral one—and which got further institutionalized with the Lahore Declaration of 1999. The Americans were quick to realize the implications of such a policy. First, Pakistan could now at least argue that the PIS of J&K was a 'disputed territory' and Pakistan could do so as a party to the Kashmir issue, rather than as an aggressor. Second, if there was a settlement, Pakistan would necessarily gain. Alternatively, if there was no settlement, the international community would get its justification to move in to resolve the Kashmir issue in the interests of world peace. Witness the infamous declaration of the US President Bill Clinton referring to Kashmir as 'a nuclear flashpoint'. The US, along with the rest of the Western world, emphasized that in view of the nuclear arms race, the level of tension between India and Pakistan remained a cause for international concern. Moreover, the widespread human rights abuses in the PIS of J&K, too, could be the pretext for the US to intervene. After all, the US has long justified its invasion of Iraq and Afghanistan on the specious plea that the principle of national sovereignty would not protect countries from international intervention to stop flagrant human rights abuses.[32]

Such reasoning, coupled with the realization that a UN-supervised plebiscite would also mean that Pakistan and China would have to vacate the territories of the PIS of J&K under their occupation as a precondition to the plebiscite, apparently prompted the US to simply adopt the stand that with the Simla Agreement, Pakistan and India should resolve the issue bilaterally.[33] The US declared that it no longer supported the plebiscite option in the PIS of J&K, since it had been 'over-taken by history'.[34] The way out was to emphasize that the 'wishes of the Kashmiri people' must be an element in the resolution of the Kashmir issue. Hence, the US asserted that though the Kashmir issue was to be resolved bilaterally between India and Pakistan, and a plebiscite in the PIS of J&K in terms of the UN Resolutions was no longer feasible, the solution should be 'home-grown' taking into 'account the desires of the Kashmiri people'[35]—that is, a plebiscite by the back door, which was moreover confined to that part of the state which was still with India, and did not encompass the full territory of the PIS of J&K. The entire world saw the back door except New Delhi. Further, the mere fact that the US presently does not support a plebiscite under the UN Resolutions does not mean that it is willing to endorse the legal status of the PIS of J&K as an integral part of India. On the contrary, the US has repeatedly declared that it views the PIS of J&K as a disputed territory and that the elections in the state are 'not going to resolve the underlying question of Kashmir as a disputed territory'.[36]

The US has sought to exploit the Kashmir problem to exert leverage on New Delhi on other issues. The US warned that its disaffection over human rights violations in the state could spill over to other aspects of the Indo-US relationship, such as trade, investment, aid, World Bank and International Monetary Fund loans.[37] It was reasoned that making foreign aid dependent on a country's human rights record weakens the security apparatus of a repressive state.[38] The US also sought to link the Kashmir issue to its endeavour to get India to sign the inequitable Non-Proliferation Treaty; the US has openly professed that the road to compel India to sign the Treaty runs through Kashmir.[39] The US has, in the past, sought to block India's claim for membership of the UNSC on the pretext that it has not complied with the UN Resolutions on the Kashmir question.[40]

In such circumstances, it is hardly likely that the US will endorse any diplomatic initiative by New Delhi, should it take one, to ask Pakistan, and China, to vacate the occupied territory of the PIS of J&K, or regard the accession of the state to India as being final and irrevocable.

Europe

The UK has taken a similar stand even after the end of the Cold War, notwithstanding the fact that the Indian Independence Act of 1947 and the Government of India Act of 1935, as amended, are British statutes and bind the British government. The UK, while doubting the viability of a plebiscite today in the territories of the PIS of J&K, continues to subscribe to the view that the 'wishes of the Kashmiri people' form an essential element of any solution to the Kashmir problem. Further, the approach of the British government towards the Kashmir issue has another aspect to it. Given British reliance on the Northern Areas of the state to protect its interests, the UK permitted militants to raise funds, spread propaganda, recruit persons and plot terrorist acts on British soil for export to India. The House of Lords was reportedly told on 11 April 2000 that the then British terrorist laws would not apply to the Kashmiri militant organizations, as in the words of John Steven Bassam, the Parliamentary Under Secretary of State in the British Home Office, the 'intention is not to catch a later day Mandela, a Green activist, a G.M. crop protester or peace protester or indeed, those in support of the Kashmiri cause'.[41] It has been reported that the UK continues to permit radical preachers to influence British Muslims, some of whom have relocated to the Islamic State-held territory in Syria.[42] Individual European countries, as well as the European Union as a whole, have also taken the view that the PIS of J&K is a disputed territory. Indeed, the European Parliament passed a resolution on 12 March 1992, urging India and Pakistan to work for a solution 'which takes account of the views of a large number of Kashmiris who seek the right to self-determination'.[43]

China

China itself holds about 20 per cent of the territory of the PIS of J&K. Moreover, as regards Aksai Chin, Beijing has serious differences with New Delhi on whether Aksai Chin forms part of the PIS of J&K at all. The western portion of the Sino-Indian boundary is said to have originated in 1834, with Raja Gulab Singh's conquest of Ladakh. With Raja Gulab Singh eventually owing allegiance to the British Crown, it was the British who proposed in 1865 the 'Johnson Line', which placed Aksai Chin in the PIS of J&K. Beijing did not accept this boundary and viewed Aksai Chin as forming part of its Xinjiang province. During the Great Game, Britain is believed to have handed over Aksai Chin to China as a buffer against possible Soviet invasion. The newly created border was known as the MacCartney–MacDonald Line. Subsequently, the border was redrawn along the original Johnson Line on British maps and became India's official western boundary in 1947. On the ground, though, the new border was believed to have been left unmanned and undemarcated due to the mountainous terrain. However, China, which enjoyed geographical advantage, had, and continues to have, easy access to Aksai Chin. In fact, it was only through Chinese maps that New Delhi is said to have learnt in 1957 about the road constructed in the 1950s by Beijing through Aksai Chin connecting Xinjiang and Tibet, which ran south of the Johnson Line in many places.

The Chinese policy on the PIS of J&K is further dictated by its boundary dispute with India on the eastern border of India. China and India had gone to war in 1962 over the boundary disputes. After the war, India claimed that China was occupying about 33,000 square kilometres of its territory in the Aksai Chin region of the PIS of J&K.[44] China claimed that India was occupying 90,000 square kilometres on the eastern front, which it views as its territory.[45] Further, Beijing and New Delhi have had serious differences on several other issues. Beijing is sore with New Delhi for its hospitality to the Dalai Lama, the spiritual Tibetan leader, and the Tibetan government-in-exile, while New Delhi accuses Beijing of arming Pakistan and emerging as its largest and most reliable weapons supplier.

Pakistan and China, on the other hand, describe their relationship as 'higher than the Himalayas, deeper than the oceans, sweeter than honey, and stronger than steel', as pointed out by Pakistan's former Foreign Minister Khurshid Mahmud Kasuri.[46] He has detailed Pakistan's closeness to China and their commonality of interest on various fronts,[47] and notes:[48]

> Both Pakistan and China continue to have unsettled borders with India. In a nutshell, the respective relationships of Pakistan and China towards India provided the strategic underpinnings to their relationships with one another.

It may be recalled that Pakistan negotiated the Sino-Pakistan Boundary Agreement of 2 March 1963, by which Pakistan gifted to China the northern frontier of the PIS of J&K by settling for a more southerly boundary along the Karakoram Range, said to coincide with the MacCartney–Macdonald Line. Kasuri, while disclosing that 'the liberation of a part of Kashmir and the Northern Areas became the basis of Pakistan's strategic relationship of China',[49] writes that the Sino-Pakistan Boundary Agreement of 2 March 1963 was of great political significance to both countries' and 'an expression of the overall strengthening of relations between Pakistan and China', as it 'meant that, in the Chinese assessment, Kashmir did not belong to India'.[50]

China has maintained extensive military and strategic ties with Pakistan, and concluded trade, commercial and barter treaties. Beijing has throughout supported Pakistan on the Kashmir issue and has, in fact, joined Pakistan in raising an anti-India campaign. Sarila notes that from 'the 1980s, China has helped Pakistan neutralize the larger Indian conventional force, by supplying it directly, and through North Korea, nuclear weaponry and missiles'.[51]

Beijing stood by Pakistan even during the indefensible invasion by Pakistan of Kargil in India in 1999. Rajesh Ramchandran writes that the Kargil conflict actually suited China. If Pakistan had succeeded in cutting off the Srinagar–Leh highway in the PIS of J&K with India, it would have created operational problems for India not only in Siachen but also in the deployment of forces along the Line of Actual Control in the Aksai Chin region.[52] It would have meant a more secure western flank for China. The Karakoram highway from Kashgar in China to Pakistan, through the territory of the PIS of J&K occupied by Pakistan, would have been free of any Indian threat.[53] It has been reported that in the first week of July 1999, 7 heavy vehicles carrying 4 Chinese officials and 102 Chinese soldiers even crossed into the eastern

Ladakh sector in India.[54] The objective was to divert Indian attention to eastern Ladakh in order to relieve the pressure on Pakistani intruders in the Kargil sector. The Chinese Premier was also said to have pleaded Pakistan's case with the US during the Kargil conflict, and spoke of a face-saving solution for Pakistan, suggesting that at least the retreating Pakistan forces should not be fired upon by the advancing Indian Army.[55] It was China again that came to Pakistan's rescue in March 2016, when China blocked India's bid to ban the chief of the Pakistan-based Jaish-e-Mohammad for the Indian Air Force Base terror attack in Pathankot, and earlier in June 2015, when the UN sanctions committee sought a clarification from Pakistan over the release of Mumbai 26/11 attack mastermind and Laskar-e-Toiba commander Zaki-ur-Rehman Lakhvi, which release, according to India, was in violation of the UN Resolution 1267 dealing with designated entities and individuals.[56] China blocked the latter move on the flimsy pretext that India had not provided sufficient information. Reports disclose further that senior officers of the People's Liberation Army and diplomats attended the function organized by the Pakistan embassy in Beijing in September 2015 to commemorate the '50th Defence Day of India's aggression' on Pakistan in 1965.[57]

With Pakistan having consolidated its control over the occupied territory of the PIS of J&K, Beijing has, over the years, built a massive presence in this territory. According to Harrison, Pakistan has handed over de facto control of the Gilgit–Baltistan region of the PIS of J&K to China.[58] Such territory, which is in close proximity to Afghanistan, Tajikistan and Tibet, has given Beijing strategic, logistical, diplomatic and political advantage and has enabled China to compete with the US and Russia in the battle for oil in Central Asia. Raja Mohan notes that Beijing has made huge investments to expand the Karakoram corridor as a strategic pathway and to construct a parallel railway line as also oil and gas pipelines in order to give China rapid connectivity to Pakistani ports lying in the gateway to the Strait of Hormuz and the Suez Canal.[59] By linking the Karakoram highway to Pakistani ports like Gwadar and Ormara, Beijing gains not just a strategic footprint and unfettered road and rail access to Afghanistan and the Persian Gulf, but becomes in a position to also significantly influence geopolitics and trade in the Indian Ocean region alongside Central Asia.[60] Pramit Pal Chaudhuri and Imitiaz Ahmad detail how the US$46 billion China–Pakistan Economic Corridor (CPEC), which runs through the territory of the PIS of J&K occupied by Pakistan, envisages more than 40 projects that are designed to revive Pakistan's economy and boost Beijing's standing at home and abroad.[61] It is the territory of the PIS of J&K under Pakistan's occupation that is being used to connect China and Pakistan, without which the CPEC could not have been conceived. Pakistan's former Foreign Minister Khurshid Mahmud Kasuri affirms that the CPEC:[62]

> [E]nvisages a road, railway, fibre-optic communication, and pipeline linkages between Gwadar in Pakistan and Xianjiang in Western China. This has great potential for Pakistan and it can become a major economic corridor linking South Asia to China and Central and West Asia.... Once completed, the CPEC will link China directly to the Persian Gulf and the Arabian Sea....

Indeed, China aggressively defended its investments in the occupied territory of the PIS of J&K, which investments the Indian Prime Minister Narendra Modi had strongly objected to during his 2015 China visit. China termed the CPEC project through such territory as a 'livelihood project' for the people there.[63] Unfazed by New Delhi's protests, Pakistan's Prime Minister Nawaz Sharif inaugurated five 'Pakistan–China Friendship Tunnels' on 14 September 2015, built at a cost of about US$275 million, to provide a strategic road link to China via the Gilgit–Baltistan region.[64] These tunnels, built by Pakistan's National Highway Authority in collaboration with the China Road and Bridge Corporation, comprise the network of seven-kilometre-long five tunnels, which restored the Karakoram highway near Attabad Lake in Hunza Valley of the Gilgit–Baltistan region and are said to be linked with the CPEC project.[65] Pakistan reportedly signed a deal with China on 12 November 2015, in terms of which Beijing acquired the usage rights to over 2,000 acres of land in Balochistan in order to develop the Gwadar port, which, as Kasuri stated, will get linked to China's Kashgar city in Xinjiang.[66] Reports in January 2016 disclosed that China even 'sought a legal cover to protect its massive investment' in the Pakistan-occupied territory of PIS of J&K, and that it was at China's insistence that moves were 'afoot in Islamabad to formally incorporate' such territory into Pakistan.[67]

Other reports further suggest the presence of regular Chinese military troops in the Pakistan-occupied territory of the PIS of J&K, ostensibly to provide security to Chinese workers engaged in building the railroads.[68] It has been speculated that the Chinese military activity in the Pakistan-occupied territory of the PIS of J&K was aimed at building tunnels, which would be of immense use as missile shelters. K. Subrahmanyam asserts that China's policy with respect to the PIS of J&K was consistent with a global strategy to challenge the US, as is evident from China's policy towards Iran, the sale of solid-fuel missiles to Saudi Arabia, an agreement to supply Pakistan with nuclear reactors, the gas pipeline from Turkmenistan to China bypassing Russian territory, the expansion of the Chinese navy and the stepping up of Chinese activities in the Western Pacific.[69] Robert Kaplan agrees that

China was, by building ports at Chittagong in Bangladesh, Hambantota in Sri Lanka and Kyaukpyu in Burma, trying to extend its presence so as to establish its supremacy in the Indian Ocean.[70] China's national interest, thus, lies in supporting Pakistan, wherever possible, and continuing to highlight that the PIS of J&K is a 'disputed territory'. The grant of stapled visa by Beijing to people from the territory of the PIS of J&K with India (and significantly, not to persons from Pakistan-occupied territories of the PIS of J&K) subtly makes this point.[71] Beijing apparently intends to use its physical control of about 20 per cent of the territory of the PIS of J&K not only as a bargaining tool for settling the India-China boundary disputes but also for strategic, economic, logistical, diplomatic and political gains. In such circumstances, no diplomatic initiative by India is likely to make China vacate its presence in the PIS of J&K or make it accept the accession of the PIS of J&K to India as final and irrevocable.

Islamic Countries

Pan-Islamic sentiment is believed to be a bonding factor between many Islamic nations and a major determinant of their foreign policy. For instance, Iran has in the past supported the 'right of self-determination' of the Muslim residents of the PIS of J&K, while Afghanistan has declared that supporting liberation struggles does not amount to supporting terrorist movements.[72] The Organisation of Islamic Cooperation (OIC) has 'recommended' sanctions against India.[73] While countries like Burkino Faso urged India and Pakistan to resolve the Kashmir issue through bilateral dialogue,[74] the OIC called upon its members to persuade India to cease her violations in the PIS of J&K, adding 'that any political process or elections held under foreign occupation cannot be a substitute to the exercise of the right of self-determination by the people of Kashmir as is provided in the relevant Security Council resolutions'.[75] The Teheran Federation has reiterated the member-states' support to the people of the PIS of J&K in the 'realisation of their right of self-determination in accordance with the UN Resolution'.[76]

Russia

Russia, who has traditionally supported India on the Kashmir problem, merely endorses New Delhi's legally untenable 'solution' to the Kashmir issue, namely, the conversion of the LOC into the international border.

The international opinion, therefore, seems to be that while it may not be feasible to hold a plebiscite in the PIS of J&K in terms of the UN Resolutions, the state remains a 'disputed territory' between India and Pakistan. Further, fears of escalation of tension and instability, coupled with the newly acquired nuclear power status of India and Pakistan, as also the reported human rights abuses in the PIS of J&K may be used by the international community to justify an interventionist role in resolving the Kashmir issue. The attempt by India to make the Kashmir issue a 'bilateral' one does not help this situation. Rather, it reiterates the standing of Pakistan as a party to the issue, other than as an aggressor. The international community opines that this bilateral issue must be resolved through dialogue, keeping in view the wishes of the Kashmiri people. The earlier demand of a plebiscite or the right to self-determination has thus merely been replaced by the international community with the criterion that 'the wishes of the Kashmiri people be respected while resolving the Kashmiri issue'. This requirement has taken different forms with some countries insisting that the solution must 'take into account' the wishes of the people, which is not quite the same thing as the solution being 'in accordance' with the wishes of the people.

Further, the perceived 'disputed status' of the PIS of J&K itself provides justification for states to term the turmoil in the part of the state with India as a 'freedom struggle' or jihad. Hence, it is hardly likely that the international community will aggressively lean on Pakistan to revise its state policy of exporting terrorism to the PIS of J&K with India or compel it to cease giving even 'moral or political support' to the 'Kashmiri struggle'.

As far as Pakistan is concerned, a diplomatic solution to the Kashmir issue remains elusive. The rationale for the proxy war waged by Pakistan against India is to make New Delhi share its view that the PIS of J&K is a 'disputed territory' and to agree for a referendum or plebiscite in the state under international auspices. Any diplomatic solution to which Pakistan would agree must necessarily achieve this objective. India has withstood international pressure and censure in this regard since 1948 and is not likely to succumb now, given its increasing international clout. On the other hand, the growing reputation of Pakistan as becoming the 'melting pot' of international terrorism has made the international community hesitant about putting its weight behind Pakistan. While Pakistan may, and does, use diplomacy to keep the Kashmir issue alive in international circles, it is doubtful that the international community will play a concrete role in resolving the Kashmir issue in Pakistan's interests.

International mediation has been suggested in the past to resolve the Kashmir issue. However, both India and Pakistan are well aware that international mediation, like any political or diplomatic initiative, is likely to be coloured by the national expediency of the mediating states. New Delhi at least has been quite categorical about ruling out mediation to resolve the Kashmir issue. Thus, no diplomatic strategy will, by itself, provide a solution to the Kashmir problem.

Military Solution

Given the role of Pakistan in fomenting violence in the territory of the PIS of J&K with India, and its policy of waging a proxy war against India, does India have the military option to recover the occupied territories of the PIS of J&K from Pakistan or China, or to even check cross-border terrorism? The obvious answer is no, not least because of China's clout, Pakistan's increasing nuclear capability and the condemnation of the world community that would follow. The international community has consistently stated that there is no military solution to the Kashmir issue, and New Delhi has been equally consistent in subscribing to that view. Incidentally, it is in this context that the international community reiterates the sanctity of the LOC. This approach has been misread by New Delhi to be an endorsement of its view that the Kashmir solution lies in converting the LOC into the international border.

It may be recalled that New Delhi implicitly ruled out the military option by agreeing to the UN-supervised ceasefire line in Karachi in 1949, and explicitly in the Tashkent Declaration of 1966 and the Simla Agreement of 1972. In the Simla Agreement, New Delhi expressly declared inter alia that the LOC 'shall be respected by both sides without prejudice to the recognised position of either side', that '[n]either side shall seek to alter it unilaterally irrespective of mutual differences and legal interpretations' and that '[b]oth sides further undertake to refrain from the threat or the use of force in violation of this line'.

Even otherwise, war is a costly affair and India is simply not in a position to go to war with Pakistan or, for that matter, with China, to have the occupied territories of the PIS of J&K vacated. India is not even in a position to adopt the policy of 'hot pursuit' and the 'right of reprisal', in order to attack and destroy the training camps and bases in Pakistan and in the territory of the PIS of J&K that it has occupied.[77] The statements of Indian politicians warning Pakistan of 'hot pursuit' have, in the past, invited prompt rebuke by the US, which required 'both parties to respect the line of control and refrain from provocative actions, including support for militant forces or cross border pursuit of militant forces'.[78] This is notwithstanding the fact that the US itself exercised the right of 'hot pursuit' to apprehend and kill Osama bin Laden and the right to use military force in 'self-defence' to flatten Afghanistan and Iraq.

Then there is the further question about India's capability of winning the war, if there was one. Indian foot soldiers may be amongst the best in the world, defending the borders in immensely stressful conditions without proper arms, equipment, clothing and pay. There can be no doubt as to their bravery, patriotism and sense of duty. But just how professionally are the departments of defence and intelligence of the country being managed? The strength of a nation is best tested at the time of war. Reports confirm the complete failure of Indian intelligence as also poor leadership from top to bottom and the lack of any strategic plan whenever India has been engaged in war.[79]

The manner in which New Delhi has responded to national security challenges serves as an index of how competent it is to wage war. Much has been written about India being a soft state and a soft target. The primary reason for this is that New Delhi's approach to national security threats continues to remain casual.

Witness New Delhi's response to the abduction by the Jammu Kashmir Liberation Front (JKLF) of 23-year-old Rubaiya, daughter of the then Indian Home Minister Mufti Sayeed on 8 December 1989. The incident has been viewed as a watershed for militancy in the territory of the PIS of J&K with India, with five JKLF leaders released from prison in exchange for her freedom on 13 December 1989.[80] Aditya Sinha details how New Delhi simply caved in to the demands of the JKLF, who were anyway about to release Rubaiya, with the *Kashmir Times* describing the abduction of 'an innocent Muslim girl' as a 'blatant act of cowardice'.[81] It was New Delhi that reportedly put pressure on the then state Chief Minister Farooq Abdullah to prematurely give in, which Abdullah himself cited on 22 July 2015 as an instance of how New Delhi had compromised national interest.[82]

The 1993 Hazratbal incident was no better. For months, the state government in the part of the PIS of J&K with India was said to have failed to act when militants occupied the Hazratbal Shrine. The militants even held a blood donation camp and an exhibition of sophisticated weapons inside the Shrine.[83] By the time the Indian security forces laid siege to the Shrine, it was too late. A large number of civilians had been taken hostage by the militants. The security forces put into effect a strategy of starving the militants into surrender. However, the innocent persons taken as hostages would also then starve. In an extraordinary order, the Indian Supreme Court directed that 'authorities will permit food packages prepared under their supervision comprising rice, dal, chapatti /paratha or nan and one vegetarian or non-vegetarian item fit for consumption with chapati etc. in the Shrine' for 'small groups of inmates whose number may be of 5 to 10 (or more if the authorities so approve) at the Iron Bar Fencing of the Shrine'.[84] The Supreme Court did not, however, deem it fit to clarify how it could be possible for anyone to ensure that the 'small groups of inmates whose number may be of 5 to 10' would not include the militants. On the other hand, if the Supreme Court had intended to include the militants within the term 'inmates', it would amount to sustaining the militants whom the security forces were trying to flush out. Be that as it may, the stand-off continued till 16 November 1993, when the militants quietly vacated the Shrine, presumably after striking a secret deal with the Army.[85] The restraint and patience shown by the Indian soldiers manning the cordon at Hazratbal for 32 days in sub-zero temperatures, while watching the 'inmates' enjoy their 'rice, dal, chapati/paratha or nan and one vegetarian or non-vegetarian item' was commendable. However, it was the month of heightened national and international media attention that did more damage to India's position than all the agencies of Pakistan together could do. The lesson to be learnt was that timely action could often pre-empt a delicate and volatile situation.

New Delhi simply did not learn that lesson as was evidenced by the Chrar-e-Sharief tragedy. State inaction to pre-empt the 50 to 200 foreign militants from occupying since December 1994 the Shrine Sheikh Nooriddin in Chrar-e-Sharief in the part of the PIS of J&K with India was said to have enabled the militants to fortify their positions, build bunkers and mine the area around the Shrine with improvised explosive devices and booby-traps rigged with liquid petroleum gas cylinders. On 17 March 1995, Chrar-e-Sharief was cut off from the rest of the state by the Indian security forces. The entire population (of 8,000) was said to have already left. This was followed by a stand-off for 66 days, with multiple authorities issuing orders. As security forces advanced on 11 May 1995, the Shrine itself went up in flames. Ramesh Vinayak[86] found it incomprehensible that media was kept away from the crisis—could militants have set fire to the Shrine, if they knew that besides the Army's guns, cameras, too, were trained on them? Anjan Mitra[87] describes how the media, including Pakistan TV and Radio, Azad Kashmir Radio, BBC, CNN, Radio Germany and the Voice of America, gave skewed versions of the incident blaming the Indian security forces for burning down the Shrine, while India feebly pleaded that it was Pakistan's ISI that had directed the militants to do so.

The 1999 Kargil conflict highlighted the failure of the Indian intelligence agencies and security mechanisms, as also the confused state of the Indian leadership. Reports[88] point out that the Indian Army had permanent all-weather posts for patrolling the infiltration routes in Mushkoh, Drass, Kaksar, Kargil, Batalik and Chorbat La areas. These company-strength posts (eighty men) were located close to the LOC, with commandos required to send out regular patrols to reconnoitre the area. Also, a helicopter patrol carried out surveillance flights in the glaciated and remote areas of Kargil every fortnight during the winter months, in what was known as 'Winter Air Surveillance Operations'. The purpose of this patrol was to give senior Army officials—such as the Battalion, Brigade and Division Commanders—ground information about the activity in the area. Such a surveillance grid was reinforced by the artillery reconnaissance carried out by separate helicopter-borne observation officers. Yet, a brigade strength of Pakistani intruders simply walked across the LOC and captured the heights in Indian territory, and as early as September 1998, if Brigadier Rashid Qureshi, the Director General of Pakistan's Inter-Services Public Relations, is to be believed.[89]

The first information about the infiltration came not from Indian intelligence but from two local shepherds, Tashi Namgyal and Tsereng Norphel, on 6 May 1999.[90] Till then, the Indian Army had no clue that soldiers from Pakistan had already breached the LOC and had occupied large portions of Indian territory in the Kargil sector. Even a month after the operations, it had no idea of how many Pakistani soldiers were occupying Indian territory. Not only had the intruders crept across the LOC, but they had even constructed their own bunkers using Indian cement bags![91] Tololing complex virtually sits on the Srinagar–Drass–Kargil–Leh Highway and one can reportedly note any movement there with a simple pair of binoculars.[92] Yet the intelligence agencies could not observe the purchase of cement bags and the casting of slabs by the intruders to fortify their bunkers in the Tololing complex. The Pakistan Army 'outpasses', which were recovered by the Indian security forces, confirmed that the intruders, after taking 'clearance' from their superiors, even took local buses to Srinagar unnoticed.[93]

It has been reported that while the Indian Research and Analysis Wing has a Rs 20,000 million secret fund to cultivate moles to provide information, there was simply no collection, let alone collation or dissemination, of information by the intelligence agencies.[94] Reports[95] also disclose that during the period that Operation Vijay was underway by the Indian forces to recover the territory occupied by the intruders, the Indian Defence Ministry approached European firms to buy snow shoes for the Indian soldiers. The European firms told the Ministry that they were unable to sell it snow shoes, since the Pakistan Army had bought 50,000 pairs of snow shoes. Enquiries revealed that Pakistan had also purchased large quantities of other specialized mountaineering equipment from Western European firms several months ago. The Defence Ministry admitted that had the 'intelligence operatives abroad been alert, they would have immediately picked up the signals since most of the armies purchase their equipment from these few firms and only large orders normally trigger alarm bells in defence circles'.[96] The entire system had failed.

Praveen Swami refers to the minutes of the meeting held on 19 May 1999 at Srinagar of the Unified Headquarters, the apex body of organizations managing security in the PIS of J&K with India, to conclude that the Army knew next to nothing about the scale or the character of the intrusion, and even less about the structure of the war that was about to follow.[97]

The then Indian Defence Minister's utterances on the full-scale invasion in Kargil reflected New Delhi's confusion. On 14 May 1999, he declared that the Pakistani shelling in Kargil was 'sporadic' and that the Indian Army was well prepared.[98] On 15 May 1999, he assured the nation that the intruders would be flushed out within 48 hours.[99] On 16 May 1999, he reiterated that the Army had cordoned off the area and that the Indian 'objectives' would be realized within the next two days.[100] On 20 May 1999, he asserted that the situation was 'well under control'.[101] On 28 May 1999, he even absolved Nawaz Sharif, the then Pakistan Prime Minister, and the ISI of having a role in Kargil—an assertion which evoked amazement throughout the world.[102] Patrick French responded by writing in the *Independent* that 'there has been consistent support, infiltration and training of terrorists by successive [Pakistan] governments, especially over the past 10 years'.[103] It has since been confirmed that it was Nawaz Sharif who had given the go-ahead to the Kargil plan, before signing the Lahore Declaration in February 1999.[104] A diary recovered from a Pakistani officer of the 12 Northern Light Infantry of Pakistan revealed that the intruders had crossed the LOC on 2 February 1999, that is, 18 days before Indian Prime Minister Vajpayee's Lahore bus trip on 20 February 1999.[105] Hence, while Nawaz Sharif and Vajpayee were busy exchanging *jhappies* (hugs) at Lahore on 21 February 1999, the Pakistani soldiers were capturing the heights in Kargil.[106]

On 29 May 1999, the then Indian Defence Minister stated that the Indian troops had flushed out the intruders from the Drass sector and had restored the sanctity of the LOC.[107] On 1 June 1999, he made the infamous offer of 'safe passage' to the intruders—a statement that stunned Indian field commanders and troops and left them doubting the political determination of New Delhi to see the battle to its logical conclusion.[108] The then Indian Defence Minister was not the only one who had bungled. A member of the Indian National Security Advisory Board reportedly declared that Pakistan had not even done anything illegal by crossing the LOC as '[t]he L.O.C. is an elastic concept' and that '[u]nless it is converted into an international border, international law allows either side to change it to their advantage'.[109]

At the time that the then Indian Defence Minister was busy assuring the country that the Indian Army had restored the sanctity of the LOC, the Additional Director General of Military Operations was showing slides to journalists to indicate the areas in the Drass sector, where the intruders continued to occupy territory on the Indian side.[110] Indian leaders seemed unaware that it did not help when the politician does not speak in the same voice as the bureaucracy which does not say the same thing as the Army.

It reportedly[111] took the Kargil conflict to get the members of the National Security Council to even meet for the first time, months after it was established. The meeting, which should have been a high strategy affair, took place under an embarrassingly public *shamiana* (marquee) at the Hyderabad House in New Delhi, in a sort of *Apna Utsav* (festival) with lunch on the house, catered by a five-star kitchen.[112]

In contrast, the intruders acted professionally. The militant-engineered killings followed a set pattern, which was designed to clear a specific belt of population along the LOC, in order to create a 'free zone' for the intruders/militants.[113] Pakistan would build up the arms stock in these 'free zones' for eventual use in a camouflaged aggression in the state.[114] Further, they enrolled the services of local youth to gather information from the Army's porters; the consequent accurate shelling caused more than 80 per cent of the casualties in the Kargil conflict.[115] The intruders spoke in Pushto, Afghanistan's language, knowing that the Indian Army did not have many officers fluent in Pushto, and thus would be unable to intercept their communications.[116] So confident were they of achieving their aim that when the then Indian Defence Minister offered them safe passage, the Harkat-ul-Mujahideen cheekily said from Islamabad that they would give the Indians safe passage if they withdrew.[117] Pakistan used the media skilfully to spread its propaganda during the Kargil conflict. Pakistan upgraded its transmitters of Radio Skardu situated across the border, to enable it to broadcast its propaganda in Kargil around the clock. India's Doordarshan, with its low-powered transmitter in Kargil, could do little to check such propaganda.[118]

Despite the Kargil fiasco, New Delhi did not seem to have learnt a lesson. Reports[119] in November 1999 revealed that Indian Border Security Force (BSF) had stumbled across a 200-metre long tunnel, which had been dug from 30 metres inside the Pakistan territory and had penetrated more than 170 metres into Indian territory in the Rampur Sector of the Gurdaspur district between Chandigarh and Kamalpur. The height of the tunnel was about five feet, and there were a number of holes in the roof to let in fresh air and facilitate breathing. The motive was obvious—to enable infiltration and the smuggling of narcotics and explosives. The BSF denied any security failure, alleging that the tunnel was dug at night and that it was virtually impossible to detect a tunnel constructed across the border in this area, since it was densely covered by elephant grass. What the BSF failed to explain, however, was how the digging, which went on for three months, remained undetected when the border is said to be lit at night by floodlights and there is round-the-clock patrolling.[120]

The IC-814 hijack drama in December 1999 was no different. The hijacking of the Indian Airlines plane, IC-814, en route from Kathmandu to New Delhi, by Pakistan-sponsored armed militants on 24 December 1999, exposed the lack of preparedness on the part of the authorities to deal with an emergency situation. The plane touched down at Amritsar airport for a brief halt, before it was forced to fly to Lahore, then to Dubai and finally to Kandahar in Afghanistan.[121]

While there is a crisis management group in New Delhi, it was reportedly unable to meet for the first one and a half hours of the hijacking.[122] The Air Traffic Controllers' Watch Supervisor Officer and the anti-hijacking control room could not immediately contact the dozen odd designated officials in the Civil Aviation, Home, and Defence Ministries, simply because they did not have their updated telephone numbers. Worse, those who were contacted did not know what they were supposed to do. The Delhi airport reportedly did not have telephone numbers of linguists who play a key role in negotiations, or even a time zone map.[123] The then Indian Foreign Secretary reportedly tried to call 'the police and airport decision-makers in Amritsar', only to discover that even those numbers had changed.[124] The pilot of the hijacked plane, Devi Saran, in an article written on 24 December 2000, describes how he tried his best to persuade the hijackers to land in Amritsar, so as to give enough time to the authorities to act.[125] However, Amritsar did not even have a contingency plan. The pilot recalled that '[b]etween notifying Varanasi of the hijack and taking off at Amritsar, there were nearly three hours' and that 'it is nothing less than amazing that in this period, no one could come to a decision on how to handle the crisis'.[126] And, of course, once the plane landed at Kandahar, there was not much India could do.

It is widely believed that the hijack was a joint operation of Pakistan's ISI and the Taliban. Christophe Jaffrelot recorded that when the plane landed in Kandahar, 'the hijackers were welcomed by the Taliban' and that according to Mullah Wakil Ahmed Muttawakil, the then Foreign Affairs Minister in Kabul, 'the hijackers were taking instructions from Pakistani officials present at the airport'.[127] It was, therefore, not surprising that the Taliban immediately ruled out its storming the hijacked plane to rescue the passengers, or permitting any one else to do so. Safe passage of the hijackers was not negotiated, it was taken for granted. The hijackers reportedly even got more arms at Kandahar, with Taliban authorities telling Indian negotiators that they were sending 'toilet paper' to the aircraft.[128]

Commodore Bhaskar writes that the IC-814 hijack was a classic case of how the media can influence the unfolding and management of terrorism.[129] The first reports of the hijack were breathless and narrative and kept altering depending on who was at the end of the phone.[130] Reports of four passengers being killed at Amritsar proved incorrect, the description of the arms with the hijackers kept changing, their identity was incessantly speculated upon and Osama Bin Laden suddenly loomed larger than life.[131] Such a volatile situation was created that the relatives of the hostages recommended that 'terrorists should not even be kept in jail after they are arrested', and that they 'should be killed in encounters'[132]—a perfect prescription for state terrorism. New Delhi eventually buckled under the pressure of the demands of the hijackers, and three jailed terrorists were released. However, the last thing that India needed was the ignominy of the country's Foreign Minister accompanying the terrorists to Kandahar and handing them over to victorious hijackers. Rajesh Ramchandran points out that there is simply no explanation as to why the then Indian Foreign Minister deemed it fit to accompany the terrorists to Kandahar.[133]

It was reported[134] that when the terrorists landed at Kandahar airport, the Taliban Minister of Civil Aviation waited at the foot of the ladder near the special Alliance Air aircraft to warmly hug them and to escort them to a motorcade. The Indian Foreign Minister then alighted from the aircraft and found that there was nobody to receive him on behalf of the Taliban—he reportedly had to wait for 15 minutes on the tarmac.[135] It strains credulity to understand why the Minister was so eager to hold hands with Taliban leaders for the television cameras or to thank them so effusively. On returning to New Delhi on 31 December 1999, he again 'conveyed' India's 'gratitude' to the Taliban and authorities in Afghanistan for their 'constructive' cooperation.[136]

Such new-found Indian affection for the regime that allowed the militants and hijackers to drive off into the sunset was incomprehensible. But did they drive off into the sunset? Reports[137] disclosed that the officials of the Indian Airlines, who remained on the scene to bring back the hijacked plane after the hostages and negotiators flew home, stated that the show had been completely stage-managed by these smooth operators. The world watched as the hijackers drove off in a cloud of dust. The media speculated about the road taken by them, some said Quetta and others felt Herat. But little did they realize that the road actually led to the end of the tarmac. When the Indian Airlines officials asked the Taliban to refuel the plane so that they too could leave, it stalled, reportedly saying that there was no fuel, no pressure in the fuel tank, and that 'a gift' was in the plane.[138] The hijackers drove back at about 9.30 PM, since they wanted to remove some baggage containing explosives. Completely conversant with the layout of the plane, they first searched the front hold and then the rear one, where they found it. Thereafter, they drove off towards the exit, leaving the Indian Airlines officials looking at each other in shock.[139]

It was after the departure of the hijackers that the Taliban agreed to let the plane take off. However, due to foggy weather in Delhi, the Indian Airlines officials decided to leave the next morning. They asked the Taliban to put them up in the accommodation vacated by the Indian negotiators, but were stunned to learn that it was occupied by the hijackers.[140] This was confirmed by a West European diplomat, who told New Delhi that the hijackers spent the night of 31 December 1999 in Kandahar in the same barracks that had been used by the Indian negotiators.[141]

Brahma Chellaney[142] records that the Taliban later sent India a bill of $112,000 for 'services' rendered at Kandahar and that while the then Indian Foreign Minister insisted that New Delhi pay it, the then Indian Prime Minister refused to do so. Be that as it may, New Delhi could not have done much about the Taliban angle, after the Indian Foreign Minister's pointless trip to Kandahar. His having held hands with the Afghan Foreign Minister and having publicly thanked the Taliban for its help would have made India a laughing stock of the world, if India had subsequently castigated the Taliban for its connivance with Pakistan-sponsored militants.[143]

The Red Fort attack in Delhi by militants on 22 December 2000 was a psychological blow and challenge to New Delhi—that the militants could strike wherever and whenever they wanted with impunity. It was initially reported on 23 December 2000, that on 22 December 2000, two armed intruders had been shot dead and an army jawan injured in a shootout inside the Red Fort, following a gun battle that lasted for over 30 minutes.[144] It was then disclosed on 24 December 2000, that on 22 December 2000, at about 9 PM, two militants entered the Lahore Gate of the Red Fort, went on a shooting spree through the prohibited area of the Fort and escaped unhurt by means of a rope which was tied to a pillar near the eastern wall of the Fort.[145] A suitably embarrassed Indian Army was groping for an answer as to how the two armed militants could run amuck in a supposedly high-security area for as long as an estimated 15 minutes, amble across the entire width of the Red Fort, kill three persons and escape, unchallenged.[146]

That was not the end of the goof-up though. It transpired that the militants escaped through a breach in the wall of the Fort, dumped their AK-47s near an electricity pole, crossed the road to the side where a police van was stationed 200 metres away according to the rule book and merrily walked on foot towards the nearby Inter State Bus Terminal.[147] The Indian Army officials claimed that immediately after the shootout, it had sent a message at 9.23 PM to the police and specifically identified the location of the militants. The police asserted that the call was relayed to all police vans in the area. However, the police combed the wrong side of the road.[148] Further lapses and loopholes came to light on 26 December 2000. Notwithstanding the 'combing operation' on 22 December 2000, during which the Red Fort complex and neighbouring areas were searched for clues, the police did not come across the AK-47s dumped by the militants near the electricity pole; rather, they were found by sanitation workers.[149] Neither did the police detect the AK-56 or the hand grenades, which had been buried by the militants a few metres behind the Fort—these were later recovered on 26 December 2000.[150]

Pakistan is well aware that India is a soft state and a soft target. Arun Joshi[151] reports that the Pakistan Rangers, at their quarterly meeting at Wagah with the BSF officials, had enquired whether the border fencing was going on, as had been reported in the Indian media. The BSF officials had stated that the fencing was not going on. So Pakistan thought that it would check out India's claim. It was for this 'aerial espionage' that two Pakistani jets audaciously sauntered into Indian airspace on 19 February 2001. What was even more shocking was that the intrusion was not detected by the Indian Air Force, but by the Indian Army ground troops, as the IAF simply did not have the low-level transportable radars it had been requisitioning since the Ninth Plan Period.[152]

The random listing of cases can be endless. Take, for instance, the audacious attack on the Indian Parliament in 2001 or the deadly 26/11 Mumbai strikes in 2008 by Pakistan-sponsored militants, both highlighting the complete failure of the Indian intelligence. The January 2016 attack on the Indian Air Force Base at Pathankot marked another watershed. This was a case where New Delhi had prior actionable intelligence about the impending attack and yet could not foil it. As per press reports,[153] heavily armed terrorists on a suicide mission evaded an oblivious BSF to cross the international border from Pakistan into India, stole the official vehicle of a Punjab police superintendent to drive to the Base under the nose of the Punjab police, entered the guarded and sanitized Base undetected, found a disused shed inside the Base to rest for about 20 hours, shifted the furniture around to make themselves comfortable, ate meals, talked on the phone to their handlers in Pakistan and bid farewell to their families, before storming out on 2 January 2016 at 3.30 am to inflict casualties. This, despite New Delhi having reportedly received specific information a day earlier around 7.30 am from the Punjab government about the armed terrorists being spotted in Pathankot.[154] What could be more telling about the security lapses than the fact that during the entire period when the terrorists, said to be as many as six in number, were already camping inside the Base, the clueless Indian security forces were engaged in securing the perimeter and the gates in order to avert the entry of the terrorists into the Base.

Such incompetence by New Delhi is compounded by its utter indifference to security threats. To illustrate, New Delhi has done little to check provocative incursions by China into the Ladakh region of the PIS of J&K with India, which have been reported consistently over the last few years.[155] It transpires that Beijing routinely stations troops of the People's Liberation Army in Ladakh. It was reported in April 2013 that Chinese troops had reinforced their positions 19 kilometres into Ladakh and were seeking to control the route leading onto the strategically vital Karakoram Pass. While such incursion could have resulted in India losing access to about 750 square kilometres area, New Delhi dismissed the Chinese action as being as insignificant as 'acne'.[156] It did not help matters when, instead of taking a firm stand with China, the then Indian Foreign Minister, during his visit to China in May 2013, inexplicably expressed his desire to live in Beijing.[157] The Indian Chief of Air Staff went on to advise on 28 November 2015 that India should not even look at China as an adversary.[158]

Indian security forces complain about New Delhi's unresponsiveness to technological upgradation of their equipment. Reports[159] in July 1999 disclosed that the Indian Defence Ministry had, for the past one year, been sitting on the request of the Indian Army for electronic surveillance sensors to monitor the movement across the LOC. The Srinagar-based Commander of the Indian Army's 15 Corps, which supervised the Kargil operations, revealed on 16 July 1999 that 82 per cent of the Indian Army's casualties in the Kargil conflict had been caused by Pakistani artillery shelling, and not in hand-to-hand battles to capture the hill tops.[160] He asserted that 'these casualties could have been minimized if we had gun-locating radar and better surveillance equipment'.[161]

D.D. Sharma[162] opines that the Indian armed forces have been neglected for far too long, such that the primitive equipment seriously impairs their operational capabilities. In the Kargil conflict, the enemy had the advantage of being at a height, which, however, disappeared at night. Indian soldiers needed thermal imaging equipment, which detects body heat from a distance, to locate enemy formations, and laser technology to blast them.[163] They required both ground and underground sensors and alarm systems to detect the movement of soldiers.[164] Instead, they had to do with obsolete, inferior, heavier and bulkier weapons as compared to those of the intruders; even their snow tents and shoes were larger, heavier and bulkier.[165] The quality of woollen socks and trousers was poor—as they bit through into the skin—and there was a shortage of weapons, bullet-proof jackets and woollen vests.[166]

Such mindless approach by New Delhi towards national security gets aggravated by allegations of corruption in awarding the lucrative defence contracts. On 13 March 2001, *Tehelka*, a dotcom company, released several videotapes that recorded, through spy cameras, the shady deals being struck to procure defence contracts; such deals allegedly involved the bribing of important government and Army officials.[167] Shishir Gupta[168] wrote about how the state-of-art Russian Krasponol laser-guided ammunition worth millions of dollars went haywire during the Kargil conflict, when the Army decided to test the same on Pakistani Army positions across the LOC. This contract was procured despite the ammunition failing in five of the six trial tests. Fresh allegations of corruption in procuring defence contracts continue to surface from time to time.

These reports of New Delhi's institutional failure make the loss of human life even more tragic. A Pakistani soldier, who spent 77 days in Indian territory on a height in Kargil waiting for Indian soldiers to come up, was quoted in the *Time* as saying:[169]

These Indians were crazy—They came like ants. First you see four. Then there are 10, then 50, then 100, and then 400. Our fingers got tired of shooting at them. We felt sorry for them. Sometimes they came in such large numbers we were afraid of using up all our ammunition.

Those who were captured by the intruders were tortured to death. Reports disclosed[170] that Lieutenant Kalia, Mula Ram, Banwar Lal, Chet Ram, Argon Baswana and Naresh Singh formed a patrol party which went missing on 14 May 1999, whereas the Indian Air Force's Squadron Leader Ajay Ahuja became captive after his MIG-21 plane was shot down on 27 May 1999 by a stinger missile over the Montho Dhalo area.[171] The body of Squadron Leader Ajay Ahuja was handed over to India by the Pakistani Army on 28 May 1999, while the bodies of the six soldiers were given on 9 June 1999. The bodies were in mutilated conditions and showed signs of inhuman treatment and torture. The eyes of some of the soldiers had been gouged out, and their ears, nose and genitals had been chopped off.[172] Post-mortem reports of the soldiers indicated penetration of the left eye with objects, compound fracture of the skull leading to severe loss of brain tissue, multiple gunshot wounds, severe compound fractures, injuries with penetrating objects and death after being shot in the mouth.[173] In a poignant article, which captures the trauma that families of the tens of thousands of soldiers tortured or killed over the years must have gone through, Alka Ahuja, the wife of Squadron Leader Ajay Ahuja, wrote about how she was told on 27 May 1999 that his plane had been shot down.[174] She learnt on 28 May 1999 that 'Ajay was tortured for six hours to death'. The post-mortem report showed that he had been repeatedly stabbed in stomach and shot through the ear. She writes that:[175]

> I developed a strange fascination for the post-mortem report. I would read it repeatedly, recreate the scenes and match these with the details of May 27 the way I spent it. And so, when I was enjoying my lunch, Ajay had just fallen to the clutches of the intruders. And when I was surfing the TV Channels, the intruder had begun working on Ajay's legs. And when I dozed off, Ajay breathed his last.

It is in the context of such lackadaisical attitude with which New Delhi treats national security, and the lives of its soldiers, that the broader question arises as to whether India can really afford to go to war to recover the occupied territories of the PIS of J&K from Pakistan or China, or to even adopt the policy of 'hot pursuit' and the 'right of reprisal' in order to check cross-border terrorism. If not, New Delhi clearly does not have the military option to resolve the Kashmir issue.

Peacefully Engaging Pakistan

Several commentators suggest that once New Delhi engages Pakistan peacefully, New Delhi should have no problem in resolving the Kashmir issue. Assuming that this is true, how does one engage Pakistan? A few commentators contend that an unstable Pakistan will threaten the existence of India. They feel that Pakistan is being reshaped by the radical Islamic order and that it should be freed from extremist Islamic influences. Pakistan may then view the Kashmir issue in a more positive light. Accordingly, it is opined that instead of isolating Pakistan, it is necessary to organize an 'international aid Pakistan consortium' to give it economic aid, which would lead to democratic rule and help check fundamentalism.[176]

Other proposals to handle Pakistan are less kind. For instance, K. Subrahmanyam[177] recommends the Chinese Sun Tsu doctrine: 'the perfect subjugation of the adversary without going to battle'. He reasons that 'if India raises its defence expenditure to 3% of G.D.P. from the present 2.3%, Pakistan will try to match it and go broke. This was how the U.S. under Reagan precipitated the Soviet collapse'.[178]

G.M. Telang[179] feels that the focus should be on exposing Pakistan's role in the violence in the state, since a realistic assessment of the rhetoric of the Kashmir issue will be possible only if the enormity of the problem facing Indian security forces is fully appreciated. He opines that it is nobody's case that in the midst of insurgency, fuelled by vast quantities of sophisticated arms generously shipped across the border by Pakistan, the Indian security forces need not be overly worried about human rights. However, the violations should be seen as aberrations, whose correction is best left to India's democratic procedures.

Others suggest that the wealth of data that India has on Pakistan-sponsored terrorism and ISI links with various insurgent groups across South Asia should be put on the internet to identify Pakistan for what New Delhi claims it is—a terrorist state. After all, in the new theatres of war, top secret information can be less useful than information that is intelligently deployed.[180] Such option, however, has limited value in resolving the Kashmir issue. The international community is well aware of Pakistan's subversive policy in the PIS of J&K with India, though it was only in the mid-1990s that it even acknowledged that Pakistan gave 'support' to the militants, and it took the Kargil conflict to compel the world to accept the fact that such support was not merely 'moral'. Following the end of the Cold War and the containment of the erstwhile Soviet Union, the diminishing need of Pakistan's good offices to engage China and the Islamic countries and the increasing economic clout of India, the international community has not found any difficulty in now recognizing that Pakistan has become a breeding ground for terrorism.[181]

Proposals to engage the Pakistani establishment bilaterally to resolve the Kashmir issue are not likely to be successful either, as is illustrated by the conduct of successive Pakistani governments. K. Subrahmanyam[182] points out that while Indian and Pakistani envoys were signing the agreement to submit the Rann of Kutch dispute for arbitration in June 1965,

General Ayub Khan was preparing for the infiltration of terrorists into the part of the PIS of J&K with India through Operation Gibraltar. Zulfikar Ali Bhutto wheedled the Simla Agreement out of Indira Gandhi and, at the same time, ensured that New Delhi did not protest too loudly about the annexation of the territory of the PIS of J&K occupied by Pakistan. General Zia-ul-Haq talked of a no-war pact, at a time when he was supporting the Khalistani terrorists in Punjab and pushing ahead with his nuclear war programme. Benazir Bhutto spoke to Rajiv Gandhi about greater understanding between the post-partition generations, even as her ISI was promoting insurgency in the Kashmir Valley and her Army was toying with the idea of nuclear blackmail in 1990. Atal Bihari Vajpayee took the bus to Lahore in 1999, while the Pakistani Army was on its way to Kargil. Past experience, therefore, refutes the possibility of bilateral talks with Pakistan paving the way for a solution to the Kashmir problem.

Noorani agrees. He notes that bilateral talks after 1950 were:[183]

[A]ll doomed to fail: two in 1953 at Karachi and New Delhi, at Murree in 1960; the Swaran Singh-Bhutto talks 1962-63; at Tashkent in 1966 and its follow up that year; at Simla in 1972, at Islamabad between Foreign Secretaries in January 1994, their Joint Statement at Islamabad on 23 June 1997; the Lahore Summit in February 1999; and the Agra Summit in July 2001. The process was interspersed with summits in 1985, 1997 and continued after 2001 notably in Islamabad in January 2004 and New York in September 2004. Since 1972, the effort was to 'evolve a mechanism for solution rather than settle the dispute itself at the meetings'.

Confederation of India and Pakistan

Given the irreconcilable standpoints of India and Pakistan on the Kashmir issue, several commentators have taken the view that it might be simpler to consider reunifying both 'Kashmirs' as a prelude to formation of a Confederation, in one form or the other. It is reasoned that if two Vietnams, two Germanys can get reunited, why not India and Pakistan.[184] K.F. Rustamji,[185] a retired Member of the National Police Commission, proposed the name 'Pakindia' for such confederation. Acharya Vinoba Bhave, too, had suggested a confederation between India, Pakistan and Kashmir.[186]

The proposal of a confederation was considered by Nehru, but nothing came out of it. Nehru, in his letter to V.K.T. Chari, Advocate General of Madras, had written:[187]

[I]f there is to be Confederation and there can be a Confederation, we need
not do anything which would look like an annulment of the partition of
India. Pakistan and India must remain separate Sovereign States and Kashmir
must be brought into the Confederation. The question is: Must Kashmir be
by itself a separate sovereign entity. The Confederation, ordinarily, would,
probably, involve the Sovereign States of India and Pakistan, having uni-
form laws and policies on certain subjects, e.g. Defence, External Affairs
and Communications at least. The question is: What other subjects can be
brought into this? These might be—control and movement of population
and passport and visas: A customs union with common trade policies: some
attempt at financial integration might also be necessary and worthwhile.
Protection of minorities would be a very important issue.

Those propounding the idea of a confederation, or a variant of it, suggest
that if the borders within the PIS of J&K cannot be redrawn, they could be
made irrelevant. Benazir Bhutto, the former Prime Minister of Pakistan, had
reportedly proposed that the borders could be 'open and porous'; both 'sections' of Kashmir could be 'demilitarized' and 'patrolled' by an 'international
peace keeping force' or a 'joint Indian–Pakistani peace keeping force'; both
legislative councils could meet 'separately' and on occasions 'jointly'; people
on both sides of the borders could meet and interact 'freely' and 'infor-
mally'. Borders could be opened for unrestricted trade, cultural cooperation
and exchange, and tariffs and quotas could be eliminated.[188] There could
be educational and technological exchange at the academic level as well as
expansion of a South Asian Free Market Zone, to be modelled after the
European Commission and the North American Free Trade Agreement.[189]
Ishwar Sharma[190] suggested that the common heritage, history and civiliza-
tion could be given a constructive direction. An institutional framework
could be devised to enable both India and Pakistan to have common perspectives with regard to defence and economic development, without,
however, losing their sovereign and independent status.[191] Further, such a
framework would gradually lead to a Commonwealth of the South Asian
Association for Regional Cooperation (SAARC) countries, similar to the
European Union.[192]

Though Ayub Khan, the then Pakistan President, had expressly told
Sheikh Abdullah that a confederation was no remedy,[193] Khurshid Mahmud
Kasuri, former Pakistan Foreign Minister, has detailed the 'contours
of agreement' on the Kashmir issue said to have been arrived at during
back-channel discussions, which envisages a 'Joint Mechanism' of Indian,
Pakistani and Kashmiri representatives to govern the state.[194] The proposed
agreement provided for major, though gradual, reduction of armed forces

in the region 'in consonance with the improvement of the situation on the ground',[195] de-radicalization, disengagement and rehabilitation of the militants,[196] grant of 'maximum self-governance' in 'legislative, executive and judicial areas' to each side of the LOC[197] and 'some form of Joint Mechanism' so that the Kashmiris do not get separated permanently from their brethren across the LOC.[198] Through such Joint Mechanism, 'Kashmiris on both sides could co-operate in specified areas of mutual interest and where the Indians and Pakistanis would also be present in one form or the other'.[199] The Joint Mechanism contemplated that New Delhi and Islamabad would nominate a specified number of members and 'would be entrusted with the responsibility of increasing the number of crossing points, and encourage travel, trade, and tourism'[200] and of encouraging 'the promotion of common policies towards the development of infrastructure, hydroelectricity, and exploitation of water resources'.[201] The LOC 'can and should be made "irrelevant"' so that 'the border would cease to exist between the Kashmiris, and they would require no visas or passports to travel across the LOC'.[202]

In September 2015, Raj Chengappa confirmed that not only had New Delhi and Islamabad arrived at such agreement during their back-channel dialogue but also that:[203]

> Pakistan did not push its maximalist demand of referring the dispute to the UN for a plebiscite or third-party intervention. Both sides also tacitly agreed that there would be no redrawing of borders and any future agreement should ensure that the LOC acted as a border between the two countries.

Since Pakistan, under its own Constitution, does not view the PIS of J&K as part of Pakistan, there is no constitutional prohibition on Islamabad to assume such role in the PIS of J&K. But there do exist constitutional prohibitions on New Delhi under its Constitution to do so, or to permit Pakistan to do so.

Constitutional permissibility apart, the formation of a confederation of India and Pakistan seems a bit far-fetched, at least in the near future, given the acrimonious relations between the countries. Pakistan is said to have adopted a policy for decades of distorting historical events aimed at instilling in the people of Pakistan a hatred for 'Hindu' India. K.K. Aziz, in his book, *The Murder of History*, cites scores of examples from text books in Pakistan of patent falsehoods designed purely for this purpose—after all, history taught from childhood irreversibly colours the perception of the students.[204] The national daily, *The Times of India*,[205] carried the article, *Two Nation Theory*, by Irfan Husain published in the Pakistani paper, *Dawn*, who wrote:[206]

Defenders of so-called ideology of Pakistan have tried to establish the geographically untenable position that we are part of West Asia and not South Asia. To sustain this fiction, they have done their wicked worst to purge our culture of subcontinental influences.... Students are taught Arabic (badly) at an early age and indoctrinated to despise anything Indian....

Akbar Zaidi, Pakistan's historian and political economist, asserted in 2015 that history is taught in Pakistan 'from an ideological viewpoint' and cites Pakistan student textbooks, in which it is incredulously claimed that Pakistan 'came into being in 712 AD when the Arabs came to Sind and Multan'.[207] He refers to the 'victory myth' prevalent in Pakistan that it had won, and not lost, the 1965 Indo-Pak war.[208] Another instance is the common belief in Pakistan that India was solely responsible for the creation of Bangladesh and that the 1971 Indo-Pak war was merely a manifestation of India's intention to dismember Pakistan. This, despite the reports that the Inquiry Commission set up by the then Pakistan Prime Minister Zulfikar Ali Bhutto—which comprised Hamoodur Rahman, the then Chief Justice of Pakistan, S. Anwarul Haq, the then Judge of the Pakistan Supreme Court, and Tufail Ali Abdur Rahman, the then Chief Justice of Sind and Baluchistan—recorded that the widespread atrocities, faulty military planning, lack of political insight, abuse of power by Pakistani Generals, 'immoral character' of military leadership indulging in making money, piling up properties, grabbing lands, womanizing and drinking and the complete failure of the civilian and military leadership, were responsible for the loss of East Pakistan.[209] Successive Pakistani governments suppressed the findings of the Inquiry Commission, and those indicted by the Commission were, in fact, rewarded with military and political sinecures.[210] It was only on 30 December 2000 that the Inquiry Commission report was said to have been made public by Pakistan.[211]

Pakistan's former Foreign Minister Khurshid Mahmud Kasuri discloses in his book published in late 2015:[212]

History as a subject receives very low priority in Pakistan. Either very little is taught to Pakistani children about the early history of the sub-continent or it is grossly misrepresented....not many know that Quaid-i-Azam Muhammad Ali Jinnah was a very important leader of the Indian National Congress.... Historical distortions, especially in the Pakistani narrative, must be highlighted and addressed since the current state of intolerance in Pakistani society is deeply linked to this narrative. The problem in Pakistan is further aggravated by the fact that not only have conscious efforts been made to tamper with history but also to infuse ideology in the curriculum. This has halted the process of critical thinking.... [Gandhiji] is ubiquitously painted as a scheming Hindu nationalist leader who said one thing and meant another.... Hardly anyone in Pakistan is aware that he was assassinated by an extremist Hindu, Nathuram Godse, who admitted in court that he killed Gandhiji because he thought Gandhiji was sympathetic towards the Muslims and towards Pakistan. Hardly any prescribed textbook in Pakistan mentions the fact that at one stage, according to some historians, Gandhiji had proposed that [Jinnah] be made the Prime Minister of United India.

Again, *The Times of India* published a report entitled *Pakistan plagued by 'death of collective vision'*, which quoted an article by Yvette Claire Rosser that reiterated that '[t]extbooks have been used to manufacture a siege mentality—a culture of mistrust and fear to counter the threat from Dar-al-Harb India and decadent Western values, all the while containing fissiparous provincial ethnicities'.[213]

Nothing can be more telling of the stranglehold of the Pakistan's establishment on the information reaching the common person in Pakistan than the ban on Indian movies. Ludicrous as it may seem, it was 'at the behest of 26/11 mastermind Hafiz Saeed, [that] the Lahore High Court placed a ban on the anti-terrorism film', Phantom, which supposedly portrayed him in bad light.[214] Pakistan imposed the ban in August 2015 when the movie had not even been released in India. Hafiz Saeed, who according to New Delhi had orchestrated the 26/11 Mumbai attacks and for whom the US had announced a reward of US$20 million, was apparently apprehensive about 'Phantom's invasion of Pakistan and influencing the Pakistani mind'.[215]

Many in India, too, oppose the idea of a confederation, or a variant of it, which contemplates any form of reunification. Ashutosh, the spokesperson for the Aam Aadmi Party, for instance, holds the view that 'the battle for Pakistan was not merely political but civilizational' and that 'territorial boundaries have been drawn on this subcontinent for eternity'. In his opinion, any attempt at reunification of a divided India 'can be likened to Hitler's policy of Anschluss'.[216]

Post-partition generations in both India and Pakistan have been conditioned to treat each other as rivals, having been fed with gory details of the religious frenzy, violence and destruction accompanying the partition of the Indian subcontinent, with distorted versions of what actually led to the partition and with propaganda to demonise each other's view point. In these circumstances, the possibility of a national consensus within India and Pakistan for a confederation seems unlikely.

Given such bleak prospects for a resolution of the Kashmir issue, a few commentators urge that New Delhi should give up its stand that the PIS of J&K was an integral part of India, call upon Pakistan to comply with the UN Resolutions by withdrawing its troops from the territory of the state it has occupied and hold a plebiscite, which would be likely to reinforce the existing division of the state. The onus would then be on Pakistan in giving effect to such solution to the Kashmir problem.[217]

Snedden offers a 'rudimentary framework' for an extended process of dialogue by which the people of the PIS of J&K would determine a solution to the Kashmir dispute and the international status of the region.[218] He acknowledges that the challenge is to get India and Pakistan to accept the possible international status of the PIS of J&K or part of it; and to get the people of the state desirous of independence to be able to successfully 'sell' this option to India and Pakistan.[219] Snedden suggests that India and Pakistan should recognize and accept this option if 'some, or a majority, of the people' of the state 'after exhaustive discussion, suitable consideration and deep reflection on the significant ramifications of independence decide that it was the preferred option'.[220] Interestingly, he writes that neither India nor Pakistan have become 'emotionally reconciled of Partition' and that a 'deep and genuine process of acknowledgement, grieving and reconciliation needs to occur before India and Pakistan can move forward positively and resolve their differences'.[221] According to him, the Governments of India and Pakistan lack sufficient incentive or will to resolve the Kashmir dispute, and have not been compelled by their respective populations either.[222] Snedden opines that in light of 'competing and irreconcilable ideas of nationhood, respectively based around the predominance of secularism or religion; opportunistic, suspicious and unbending national and individual egos expounding paternalistic and nationalistic rhetoric; and entrenched strategic, military and political rivalry and culture not prepared "to give an inch" to the other side on any issue at any time', both countries 'should step aside' and 'let the people decide'.[223]

While there is nothing to support the view that there are 'competing and irreconcilable ideas of nationhood' between India and Pakistan, which had more or less existed as one unit for centuries before the British decided to partition the Indian subcontinent to satisfy their requirements for the Great Game, such an approach would simply perpetuate the legally flawed policy adopted by New Delhi in respect of the PIS of J&K. Further, any political settlement by New Delhi with Pakistan or the Kashmiri people or the militants in terms of above-mentioned strategies, to the extent they involve an alienation or the cession of territory by India, cannot even be considered by New Delhi as the Constitution of India forbids it to do so. Nor is New Delhi competent to amend the Constitution to permit it to do so.

Having noted the inadequacies of the current solutions suggested to unravel the Kashmir knot, let us now examine the solution offered by this book.

Notes and References

1. *Supra* Note 89, Chapter I, p. 348.
2. Ibid., p. 227.
3. *The Times of India.* 1998. 'Pakistan to extend all out support to Kashmir: Sharif', New Delhi, 31 December.
4. See The *Yearbook of the United Nations, 1965.* The India-Pakistan Question, pp. 159–162.
5. *Supra* Note 28, Chapter I, pp. 397–399.
6. Khazanchi, Ramesh. 1998. 'Kashmir: soft Sufi to radical Islam', *The Times of India*, New Delhi, 19 December.
7. *Hindustan Times.* 1999. 'Mercenaries from 14 nations involved in proxy war in J&K', New Delhi, 23 August; *Hindustan Times.* 1999. 'ISI's new policy code named Topac 2', New Delhi, 27 August; Marwah, Ved. 1998. 'Hostage to misuse', *Hindustan Times*, New Delhi, 15 July.
8. *The Times of India.* 1999. 'Pak recruits mercenaries in Central Asia', New Delhi, 28 August.
9. *The Times of India.* 2000. 'Chronology of major killings in J&K since 1997', New Delhi, 3 August; *The Times of India.* 1998. 'Pak fuelling terrorism in J&K: UK reports', New Delhi, 17 September.
10. Chaudhuri, Pramit Pal. 2001. 'Naked truth about e-jihadis', *Hindustan Times*, New Delhi, 19 February; Chhabra, Rahul. 2001. 'Satellite-based transactions funding militants', *Times of India*, New Delhi, 4 January; *The Indian Express.* 1999. 'Death of pilot-turned militant throws up alarming questions', New Delhi, 21 September.
11. Baruah, Sanjib. Kr. 2015. 'IS, Lashkar trade barbs on Kashmir', *Hindustan Times*, New Delhi, 22 November.
12. *Hindustan Times.* 1999. 'ISI's new policy code named Topac 2', New Delhi, 27 August.
13. Rajeshwar, T. V. 1999. 'War by other means', *Hindustan Times*, New Delhi, 10 July; Thapar, Vishal. 2001. 'Ammo fires: not quite accidental', *Hindustan Times*, New Delhi, 5 August; Thakurata, Pranjoy Guha. 2001. 'Hi-tech terrorists worry officials', *Hindustan Times*, New Delhi, 31 May; *The Times of India.* 2000. 'ISI minting Indian currency', New Delhi, 10 January; *Hindustan Times.* 1998. 'Trains from Pak a conduit for ultras', New Delhi, 12 January; *Hindustan Times.* 2001. 'ISI pumps in fake notes every day', New Delhi, 26 March; *The Indian Express.* 1996. 'Commerce body blames Pak for pumping fake currency into J&K', New Delhi, 9 September; *The Indian Express.* 1995. 'Drug lords savour a new high in Jammu', New Delhi, 11 December; *Hindustan Times.* 2000. 'Pak peps up narco assault', New Delhi, 9 November; *The Times of India.* 2000. 'Heroin is new weapon of militancy in J&K', New Delhi, 23 May.
14. Pandit, Rajat. 2015. 'Army Chief says India needs to be ready for short wars', *The Times of India*, New Delhi, 2 September.
15. Variyar, Mughda. 2015. 'Indian strike on Pakistani terror camps could lead to nuclear war, say experts'. 22 October. Available online at http://www.ibtimes.co.in/indian-strike-pakistani-terror-camps-could-lead-to-nuclear-war-say-experts-651505 (downloaded on 5 November 2015).
16. Ibid.
17. *New York Times.* 2015. 'The Pakistan Nuclear Nightmare: Editorial'. 9 November. Available online at http://www.ndtv.com/world-news/the-pakistan-nuclear-nightmare-new-york-times-editorial-1241866 (downloaded on 10 November 2015).

18. *Hindustan Times.* 2000. 'The K factor', New Delhi, 28 March.

19. Ahmed, Akbar S. 1996. 'Kashmir 1990: Islamic revolt or Kashmir Nationalism' in *Supra* Note 34, Chapter IV, p. 51.

20. *Supra* Note 34, Chapter IV, p. 10.

21. Jain, Girilal. 1996. *Waxing of the Crescent: OIC trains its guns on Kashmir,* in *Supra* Note 34, Chapter IV, p. 222.

22. See *Supra* Note 3, Chapter V, p. 133.

23. *Hindustan Times.* 1999. 'Focus on terrorism', New Delhi, 15 September; *Hindustan Times.* 1999. 'The Afghan cauldron', New Delhi, 15 September.

24. Rasgotra, Maharaja Krishana. 1993. 'America meddles in Kashmir again', *Hindustan Times,* New Delhi, 3 June.

25. Jha, Prem Shankar. 2000. 'Cost of terrorism', *Hindustan Times,* New Delhi, 14 January; *The Indian Express.* 1994. 'US reviving Dixon Plan in bid to end Kashmir row', New Delhi, 19 December.

26. *Supra* Note 23.

27. Ibid.

28. Haniffa, Aziz. 1995. 'USA rules out possibility of mediating in Kashmir', *The Statesman,* New Delhi, 24 May.

29. *Hindustan Times.* 2000. 'Put Pak on terrorist list, but waive some sanctions', New Delhi, 12 February; *Hindustan Times.* 1998. 'US 'consistent' on Kashmir issue', New Delhi, 4 March.

30. Rajghatta, Chidanand. 2001. 'Sattar blames US curbs for Pak extremism', *The Times of India,* New Delhi, 20 June; Rajgopalan, S. 2001. 'US explains position on Pakistan terrorism', *Hindustan Times,* New Delhi, 3 May; *Hindustan Times.* 2000. 'US has "reasons" why Pak can't be dubbed terrorist', New Delhi, 15 January.

31. *The Times of India.* 1999. 'Pakistan gets fresh funds even as US mulls sanctions', New Delhi, 19 June.

32. *The Times of India.* 1999. 'Clinton seeks right to bypass UN in trouble spots', New Delhi, 23 September.

33. Nayar, K. P. 1995. 'India should beware of even-handedness', *The Indian Express,* New Delhi, 12 December; *Hindustan Times.* 1999. 'US rejects Pak plea for plebiscite in Kashmir', New Delhi, 25 September; *The Times of India.* 2000. 'Take steps for talks with India: US to Pakistan', New Delhi, 8 May.

34. *Supra* Note 34, Chapter IV, pp. 12–13.

35. *The Times of India.* 1998. 'Polls do not resolve Kashmir issue', New Delhi, 28 November; *Hindustan Times.* 1997. 'US will not accept Kashmir as an integral part of India', New Delhi, 11 August.

36. Ibid.

37. *Supra* Note 34, Chapter IV, p. 13.

38. Ibid., p. 8.

39. Ibid., p. 13.

40. *Hindustan Times.* 2000. 'India rebuffs bid to link UN Seat with the Kashmir issue', New Delhi, 8 March.

41. *Hindustan Times.* 2000. 'Brand UK terrorist state, Lanka tells US', New Delhi, 14 April.

42. *The Times of India.* 2015. 'Dad-in-law of PIO recruit blames UK', New Delhi, 7 September.

43. *Supra* Note 12, Chapter IV, p. 674.

44. Hongwei, Wang. 2002. 'Remembering a war: The 1962 Indo-China conflict'. Available online at http://www.rediff.com/news/2002/dec/26chin.htm (downloaded on 30 August 2015).

45. Ibid.

46. *Supra* Note 89, Chapter I, p. 677.
47. Ibid., pp. 100–103,675.
48. Ibid., pp. 675–676.
49. Ibid., p. 409.
50. Ibid., p. 676.
51. *Supra* Note 6, Chapter I, p. 403.
52. Ramchandran, Rajesh. 1999. 'The China Syndrome, *Hindustan Times*, New Delhi, 20 June.
53. Ibid.
54. *Hindustan Times*. 1999. 'Chinese soldiers crossed LAC during Kargil conflict: India', New Delhi, 8 September.
55. *Hindustan Times*. 1999. 'Bill spoke to Jiang frequently during the Kargil conflict', New Delhi, 7 September.
56. See *The Indian Express*. 2016. 'At UN, China blocks India bid to ban Jaish chief', New Delhi, 1 April; *The Times of India*. 2015. 'China blocks India's move in UN seeking action against Pakistan on Lakhvi'. Available online at http://timesofindia.indiatimes.com/india/China-blocks-Indias-move-in-UN-seeking-action-against-Pakistan-on-Lakhvi/articleshow/47781771.cms (downloaded on 30 August 2015).
57. *The Times of India*. 2015. 'PLA brass 'endorse' Pak's narrative of 1965 war', New Delhi, 17 September.
58. Harrison, Selig S. 2010. 'The other Kashmir problem', *The Indian Express*, New Delhi, 28 August.
59. Mohan, Raja C. 2010. 'A new challenge', *The Indian Express*, New Delhi, 31 August.
60. Ibid.
61. Chaudhuri, Pramit Pal & Imitiaz Ahmad. 2015. 'China's 3,000-km lifeline for Pakistan', *Hindustan Times*, New Delhi, 30 August.
62. *Supra* Note 89, Chapter I, p. 682.
63. *NDTV*. 2015. 'China defends projects in Pakistan-occupied-Kashmir, Objects to India's oil exploration in south China'. Available online at http://www.ndtv.com/india-news/china-defends-projects-in-pakistan-occupied-kashmir-objects-to-indias-oil-exploration-in-south-china-768667 (downloaded on 30 August 2015).
64. *The Times of India*. 2015. 'Sharif inaugurates Pakistan-China friendship tunnels', New Delhi, 15 September.
65. Ibid.
66. *The Times of India*. 2015. 'China gets 2,000 acres in Pak port city', New Delhi, 13 November.
67. Padgaonkar, Dileep. 2016. 'Vindicating Mufti'. *The Times of India*. New Delhi, 9 January.
68. Gupta, Shishir. 2010. 'Army passes intel to Govt. PLA men at pass linking POK to China', *The Indian Express*, New Delhi, 31 August.
69. Subrahmanyam, K. 2010. 'Pakistan: China's other North Korea', *The Indian Express*, New Delhi, 3 September.
70. *The Times of India*. 2010. 'China for supremacy in Indian ocean', New Delhi, 31 August.
71. *Supra* Note 69.
72. *Supra* Note 34, Chapter IV, p. 11. Srinagar: Valley Book House.
73. Dhar O. N. 1993. 'Police revolt and after: intriguing coincidences point to Pakistani design', *The Indian Express*, New Delhi, 27 May.
74. *The Indian Express*. 1995. 'Burkino Faso supports India on Kashmir', New Delhi, 6 November; Gupta, Shishir. 2001. 'Jehadi outfits hold secret meet in Jeddah', *Hindustan Times*, New Delhi, 20 January.

75. *The Indian Express.* 1996. 'OIC meet terms J&K Poll process a sham', New Delhi, 15 August.

76. *Hindustan Times.* 1999. 'The OIC's new odyssey', New Delhi, 26 December.

77. Dixit, J. N. 2000, 'Dilemmas of a dialogue', *Hindustan Times,* New Delhi, 30 August.

78. *Hindustan Times.* 1998. 'US takes strong exception of Advani's warning on J-K', New Delhi, 2 May.

79. Vardarajan, Siddharth. 2000. 'The government cult of secrecy', *The Times of India,* New Delhi, 6 September; Subrahmanyam, K. 2000. 'Its official now', *The Times of India,* New Delhi, 7 September; Joshi, Manoj. 2000. 'How we won the east and nearly lost the west', *The Times of India,* New Delhi, 1 December; *The Times of India.* 2000. 'Revealed: Official history of 1965 war', New Delhi Edition, 6 September.

80. *Hindustan Times.* 2000. 'The rise of the Harkat', New Delhi, 2 January.

81. Sinha, Aditya. 1996. *Farooq Abdullah, Kashmir's prodigal son: A biography,* pp. 217–223. New Delhi: UBS Publishers' Distributors Ltd.

82. *Hindustan Times.* 2008. 'We planned to release Rubaiya anyway'. Available online at JKLF http://www.hindustantimes.com/india-news/we-planned-to-release-rubaiya-any-way-jklf/article1-318863.aspx (downloaded on 30 August 2015); 'Release of terrorists for Mufti's daughter was a mistake: Farooq Abdullah'. Available online at http://time-sofindia.indiatimes.com/india/Release-of-terrorists-for-Muftis-daughter-was-a-mistake-Farooq-Abdullah/articleshow/48181733.cms (downloaded on 30 August 2015).

83. Sinha, S. K. 1993. 'Hazratbal episode, lessons for future', *Hindustan Times,* New Delhi, 29 November.

84. *State of Jammu and Kashmir v Jammu and Kashmir High Court Bar Association & Ors.:* (1994) Supp (3) SCC 708 at pp. 710–711.

85. Karim, Asfir. 1994. *Kashmir: The Troubled Frontiers,* p 116. New Delhi: Lancer Publishers Ltd.

86. Vinayak, Ramesh. 1995. 'A shocking setback', *India Today,* p. 59. Delhi: Living Media Ltd., 11 May.

87. Mitra, Anjan. 1995. 'While Doordarshan dithered', *Hindustan Times,* New Delhi, 28 May.

88. *Hindustan Times.* 1999. 'Patrolling with eyes wide shut', New Delhi, 6 August.

89. *Hindustan Times.* 1999. 'Intrusions began in September says Qureshi', New Delhi Edition, 27 July.

90. *The Times of India.* 1999. 'Defence Ministry officials concede intelligence lapses', New Delhi, 12 June.

91. Ibid.

92. *Hindustan Times.* 1999. 'Army seizures dent Govt. Kargil theory', New Delhi, 5 August.

93. Ibid.

94. *Hindustan Times.* 1999. 'The lessons from Kargil: no more Panipats, please', New Delhi, 11 July.

95. *The Times of India.* 1999. 'Shopping spree preceded intrusion', New Delhi, 24 June.

96. Ibid.

97. Swami, Praveen. 1999. 'An Army caught napping', *Frontline,* p. 33, Chennai, 10 September. Chennai: Kasturi & Sons Ltd.

98. *Hindustan Times.* 1999. 'The lessons from Kargil: no more Panipats, please', New Delhi, 11 July.

99. Ibid.

100. Ibid.

101. Ibid.
102. Ibid.
103. *Hindustan Times*. 1999. 'Sardonic response to George's clean chit to Sharif, ISI', New Delhi, 31 May.
104. *The Times of India*. 1999. 'Kargil invasion was scripted in 1987', New Delhi, 13 September; *Hindustan Times*. 1999. 'Sharif approved Kargil incursions in January: Beg', New Delhi, 15 July.
105. *Hindustan Times*. 1999. 'Intrusions began a week before Lahore', New Delhi, 30 November.
106. Ibid.
107. See *Hindustan Times*. 1999. 'Vajpayee government does U-turn on Kargil', New Delhi, 3 June.
108. Ibid.
109. *The Indian Express*. 1999. 'Pakistan not done anything illegal says Bharat Karnad', New Delhi, 19 June.
110. *Hindustan Times*. 1999. 'Army, Fernandes differ over Kargil gains', New Delhi, 30 May.
111. *The Indian Express*. 1999. 'High Insecurity', New Delhi, 19 June.
112. Ibid.
113. *Hindustan Times*. 1999. 'India ignored all signs of Pak's design on Kargil', New Delhi, 25 September.
114. Ibid.
115. *The Indian Express*. 1999. 'Twenty Kargil locals behind Pakistani artillery's marksmanship', New Delhi, 2 June.
116. *Hindustan Times*. 1999. 'Language of enemy foxed Army', New Delhi, 27 July.
117. *The Times of India*. 1999. 'Militants reject Indian offer', New Delhi, 3 June.
118. *The Indian Express*. 1999. 'Pakistan has edge in war of the waves', New Delhi, 4 June.
119. *Hindustan Times*. 1999. 'India protests over tunnel near border', New Delhi, 24 November; *Times of India*. 1999. 'Smugglers and terrorist dug tunnel: BSF', New Delhi, 25 November.
120. Ibid.
121. *Hindustan Times*. 1999. 'The hijacking that should not have been', New Delhi, 26 December.
122. *Hindustan Times*. 2000. 'Many committees but no decisions', New Delhi, 2 January.
123. Ibid. Also see *Hindustan Times*. 2000. 'But for a few files, nothing has changed since hijack', New Delhi, 24 December.
124. Ibid. *The Indian Express*. 2016. 'How wires got crossed in Delhi'. New Delhi, 9 January.
125. Saran, Devi. 2000. 'I still have nightmares', *Hindustan Times*, New Delhi, 24 December.
126. Ibid.
127. Jaffrelot, Christophe. 2016. 'Decoding Rawalpindi', *The Indian Express*, New Delhi, 29 January.
128. *Hindustan Times*. 2000. 'Gang got arms at Kandahar', New Delhi, 1 January.
129. Bhaskar. 1999. 'IC-814 will be known for media hijack', *Hindustan Times*, New Delhi, 27 December.
130. Ibid.
131. Ibid.
132. *Hindustan Times*. 2000. 'No love lost for terrorists', New Delhi, 1 January.
133. Ramchandran, Rajesh. 2000. 'Photo-ops and slaps on the wrist', *Hindustan Times*, New Delhi, 9 January.

134. *Hindustan Times*. 2000. 'Taliban rolled out red carpet for Azhar Masood', New Delhi, 24 January.
135. Ibid.
136. *Hindustan Times*. 2000. 'India lauds Taliban role', New Delhi, 1 January.
137. *Sunday Times of India*. 2000. 'Taliban, hijackers had last laugh', New Delhi, 9 January.
138. Ibid.
139. Ibid.
140. Ibid.
141. Ibid.
142. Chellaney, Brahma. 2000. 'Anniversary of Shame', *Hindustan Times*, New Delhi, 26 December.
143. *Hindustan Times*. 2000. 'Probing the bungling', New Delhi, 11 January.
144. Chabbra, Rahul. 2000. 'Shootout raises questions about security to Red Fort', *The Times of India*, New Delhi, 23 October; Cherian, John. 2001. 'Raid on the Red Fort', *Frontline*, 19 January, p 22. Chennai: Kasturi & Sons Ltd.; *Times of India*. 2000. 'Two militants killed in Red Fort Shootout', New Delhi, 23 December.
145. Menon, Vinay & Chetan Chauhan. 2000. 'Red Fort raid: It was all over in 15 minutes', *Hindustan Times*, New Delhi, 24 December.
146. Thapar, Vishal. 2000. 'Wake up call', *Hindustan Times*, New Delhi, 24 December.
147. Ibid.
148. *Hindustan Times*. 2000. 'PCR van was merely 200 m away from the escape point', New Delhi, 25 December.
149. *The Times of India*. 2000. 'Lapses and loopholes in the shootout and after', New Delhi, 27 December; Chhabra, Rahul. 2000. 'Many twists and turns in official police version', *The Times of India*, New Delhi, 27 December.
150. Ibid.
151. Joshi, Arun. 2001. 'Pak jets violated airspace to gauge border fencing', *Hindustan Times*, New Delhi, 26 February.
152. Gupta, Shishir. 2001. 'Airspace violation was spotted by army not by the Air Force', *Hindustan Times*, New Delhi, 23 February.
153. Tiwary, Deeptiman. 2016. 'For 20 hrs, terrorists hid in elephant grass', *The Sunday Express*, New Delhi, 10 January; Baweja, Harinder & Chitleen K. Sethi. 2016. 'When terror checked in', *Sunday Hindustan Times*, New Delhi, 10 January; Swami, Praveen. 2016. 'Terrorists hid overnight in airbase shed', *The Indian Express*, New Delhi, 12 January.
154. Jain, Bharti. 2016. 'Warned Centre 20 hrs before attack', *The Times of India*, New Delhi, 9 January.
155. Gupta, Shishir. 2010. 'Army passes intel to Govt. PLA men at pass linking POK to China', *The Indian Express*, New Delhi, 31 August.
156. Pandit, Rajat & Sanjay Dutta. 2013. 'Chinese incursion 19 km, but 750 sq km at stake for India', *The Times of India*, New Delhi, 2 May.
157. Ibid.
158. *The Sunday Express*. 2015. 'Stop seeing China as an adversary', New Delhi, 29 November.
159. *The Times of India*. 1999. 'Bureaucratic delays short change the Army', New Delhi, 20 July.
160. Ibid.
161. Ibid.
162. Sharma, D. D. 1999. 'After the victory', *Hindustan Times*, New Delhi, 2 September.
163. Ibid.

164. *The Times of India*. 2000. 'Sneak raids mark post-Kargil period', New Delhi, 6 November.
165. *The Times of India*. 1999. 'Vintage weapons clog Army wheels', New Delhi, 11 June.
166. Ibid.
167. Gupta, Shishir. 2001. 'Krasnopol shells failed even the Kargil test', *Hindustan Times*, New Delhi, 17 March.
168. Ibid.
169. *Time*. 1999. 'In enemy territory: A soldier's story', New York/Hong Kong, p. 37, 12 July.
170. *Hindustan Times*. 1999. 'Prosecute torturers, India tells Pakistan', New Delhi, 17 June.
171. Ibid.
172. *The Times of India*. 1999. 'Outrage at Pak barbarism with captured soldiers', New Delhi, 11 June.
173. *Hindustan Times*. 1999. 'Inhuman torture confirmed', New Delhi, 12 June; *The Indian Express*. 1999. 'India slams Pakistan on torture', New Delhi, 17 June.
174. Ahuja, Alka. 2000. 'Hope and sorrow', *Hindustan Times*, New Delhi, 21 May.
175. Ibid.
176. *The Times of India*. 2000. 'Engaging Pakistan', New Delhi, 15 August.
177. *Hindustan Times*. 1999. 'What should we do with Pakistan', New Delhi, 11 July.
178. Ibid.
179. Telang, G. M. 1993. 'Issue in Kashmir: protecting human rights from arsenal sent by Pakistan', *The Indian Express*, New Delhi, 14 June.
180. *The Indian Express*. 1999. 'The digital battlefield', New Delhi, 14 June.
181. *The Times of India*. 2000. 'CIA terms Pakistan breeding ground of extremists', New Delhi, 4 February; *The Times of India*. 1999. 'Pakistan base of terrorist attacks on India: says US', New Delhi, 4 November; *The Times of India*. 2000. 'US warns Pak on support to militant groups', New Delhi, 29 January; *The Times of India*. 2000. 'US wants Pakistan action on terrorism', New Delhi, 18 February; *Hindustan Times*. 2000. 'US 'convinced' of Pak complicity in hijack', New Delhi, 26 January; *Hindustan Times*. 2000. 'Elements within Pak Govt. backing violence in J&K: Bill Clinton', New Delhi, 23 March; *Hindustan Times*. 1999. 'US may go public with the evidence against Pakistan', New Delhi, 19 June; *The Times of India*. 2000. 'US tells Pakistan to get cracking on terrorism', New Delhi, 22 January; *Sunday Times of India*. 2000. 'Recapture Lahore spirit: European MPs', New Delhi, 13 March; *Hindustan Times*. 2000. 'France for Pak to use influence on militants', New Delhi, 4 June; *Hindustan Times*. 2000. 'Pak responsible for instability in Kashmir: UK', New Delhi, 22 January.
182. Subrahmanyam, K. 1999. 'Advice for Mr. Aziz', *The Times of India*, New Delhi, 7 June.
183. *Supra* Note 12, Chapter IV, pp. 51–52.
184. *The Times of India*. 1996. 'Kashmir: the great illusion', New Delhi, 22 September.
185. Rustamji, K. F. 1991. 'Blueprint for a Kashmir settlement', *The Telegraph*, New Delhi, 2 October.
186. *Supra* Note 12, Chapter IV, p. 84.
187. Extracted in ibid.
188. *The Times of India*. 1999 'Bhutto rues her Kashmir policy', New Delhi, 10 June.
189. Ibid.
190. See Sharma, Ishwar. 1996. 'Jammu and Kashmir Crises – II Nature, Scope of Political Initiative', in *Supra* Note 34, Chapter IV, p. 385.
191. Ibid.
192. Ibid.

193. *Supra* Note 104, Chapter IV, p. 154.
194. *Supra* Note 89, Chapter I, pp. 323–348.
195. Ibid., p. 325.
196. Ibid., p. 328.
197. Ibid., p. 337.
198. Ibid., p. 341.
199. Ibid., p. 342.
200. Ibid., pp. 342–343.
201. Ibid., p. 344.
202. Ibid., pp. 347–348.
203. Chengappa, Raj. 2015. 'The secret Indo-Pak talks', *India Today*, 21 September, p. 24. New Delhi: Living Media India Ltd.
204. See *Sunday Times of India*. 2000. 'When hatred feeds on hate', New Delhi, 9 July.
205. *The Times of India*. 2000. 'Two nation theory', New Delhi, 7 November.
206. Ibid.
207. *Sunday Times of India*. 2015. 'We lost in 1965 war', says Pak historian, 6 September.
208. Ibid.
209. Ibid.
210. See *India Today*. 2000. 'Behind Pakistan's defeat', p. 30, 1 August. Delhi: Living Media Ltd.; *Hindustan Times*. 2000. 'Suppressed Pak report blames Yahya, Niazi for Dhaka defeat', New Delhi, 12 August.
211. *Hindustan Times*. 2000. '1971 war report', New Delhi, 31 December; *Hindustan Times*. 2001. 'Moral lapses, poor leadership caused Pak debacle in 1971', New Delhi, 1 January.
212. *Supra* Note 89, Chapter I, pp. 124–128.
213. *The Times of India*. 2001. 'Pakistan plagued by 'death of collective vision', New Delhi, 20 March.
214. Bhattacharya, Ananya. 2015. 'Phantom ban in Pakistan: Why is Hafiz Saeed so threatened by a film?', *India Today*, 24 August Available online at http://indiatoday.intoday.in/story/phantom-ban-in-pakistan-why-is-hafiz-saeed-so-threatened-by-a-film-saif-ali-khan-katrina-kaif-kabir-khan-terrorist-26-11-mumbai-attacks/1/460663.html (downloaded on 30 August 2015).
215. Ibid.
216. Ashutosh. 2016. 'A Dangerous Worldview', *The Indian Express*, New Delhi, 4 January.
217. Sandhu, Kanwar. 2001. 'Why are we tongue-tied?', *Hindustan Times*, New Delhi, 31 July.
218. *Supra* Note 81, Chapter IV, pp. 225–227.
219. Ibid., pp. 226–277.
220. Ibid., p. 227.
221. Ibid., p. 222.
222. Ibid., p. 221.
223. Ibid., pp. 221–222, 227.

XI

The Way Forward

The way forward on the Kashmir issue must necessarily begin by undoing the mistakes committed in the past. It would, therefore, be useful to begin by listing a few factors that must be kept in mind while formulating any solution to the Kashmir problem.

First, the legal status of a princely Indian state under the Indian Independence Act of 1947, and the Government of India Act of 1935, as amended, must be appreciated. Upon the lapse of the British paramountcy on 15 August 1947, the princely Indian states became sovereign, in the full sense of the term, with their rulers being the sole repositories of power who could choose to remain independent. New Delhi did not possess any sovereignty over the states. Rather, New Delhi's powers with respect to the states were to be strictly circumscribed by the instruments that could be executed under the said Acts.

As regards the PIS of J&K, the Instrument of Accession of 26 October 1947, executed by Raja Hari Singh, its sovereign ruler, itself specified the limited purposes for which the state was acceding to the dominion of India, and further authorized the dominion Indian legislature to make laws for the state only with respect to defence, external affairs, communications and certain ancillary matters—none of which empowered New Delhi to reopen the question of the accession itself of the PIS of J&K to the dominion of India, it being an Act of State. Further, the Raja had expressly declared that nothing in the Instrument of Accession affected the continuance of his sovereignty in and over the state, or the exercise of any power, authority and right then enjoyed by him as ruler of the state.

Second, New Delhi was, never, at any point of time, given the power to declare that the accession of the PIS of J&K to the dominion of India by its sovereign ruler be further 'settled' in accordance with 'the wishes of the people' to be ascertained by a reference to the people. Rather, such a proposal negates the very premise underlying the said British statutes—namely, that it was the sovereign ruler of a princely Indian state who was to decide the future of that state. In other words, New Delhi was not constitutionally or legally competent to require that the accession of the PIS of J&K be 'settled' by a reference to the people or a UN-supervised plebiscite.

Though New Delhi had no power to introduce, in derogation of the aforesaid British statutes that gave birth to both India and Pakistan and were accepted by both India and Pakistan, the 'wishes of the people' as being the deciding factor for the question of accession of a princely Indian state, all parties concerned with the Kashmir issue today subscribe to the view that the 'wishes of people' are a relevant, if not sole, factor to 'settle' the accession. Since it was New Delhi itself that had made the 'wishes of the people' relevant to the question of accession of the PIS of J&K, and subsequently assumed the 'engagement', if not an 'obligation', to hold the plebiscite in the territory of the PIS of J&K under UN auspices, it simply had no answer when confronted with such an 'engagement' and was compelled to take recourse to legal defences noted earlier in order to repudiate it.

Thus, the second point that must be noted while formulating a solution to the Kashmir issue is that the people of the PIS of J&K, and New Delhi itself, must be made to realize that in terms of the Indian Independence Act of 1947, read with the Government of India Act of 1935, as amended, the 'wishes of the people' were completely irrelevant to the question of accession, and therefore, it was not for the people to decide the future of the state. It must be recognized that the people of the PIS of J&K, like the people of other princely Indian states, were not given a 'birth right' to self-determination by these Acts, nor did the Instrument of Accession promise or confer any such right. The international community must be made aware that its insistence on taking into account the will of the Kashmiri people to resolve the Kashmir issue is legally unfounded.

Third, it must be remembered that it was New Delhi's repeated 'pledges' from 1947 onwards to hold the UN-supervised plebiscite to determine the question of the accession of the PIS of J&K that has enabled the international community and Pakistan to view the state as a 'disputed territory'. By doing so, New Delhi assumed, though without jurisdiction, at least an 'engagement', if not 'obligation', to hold a plebiscite under UN auspices, which took the matter out of the domestic jurisdiction of India. That India has repudiated such an 'engagement' is an entirely different matter. The point is that the assumption of such 'engagement' on the floor of the UN itself confers standing on the UN and its member states, including Pakistan, to comment on the happenings in the territory comprising the PIS of J&K.[1] The legally misconceived stand of New Delhi on the PIS of J&K since

1947 has permitted Islamabad to project what is a form of 'terrorism' or 'secessionist movement' for New Delhi to be a jihad or 'freedom struggle', with national, geo-strategic and political interests of several other countries compelling them to endorse Pakistan's view in varying degrees. Thus, New Delhi, by entering into at least an 'engagement' to hold a plebiscite in the PIS of J&K under UN auspices, provided legitimacy to the jihad or 'freedom struggle' said to be underway in Kashmir.

Fourth, the constitutional limitations on the power of New Delhi to cede national territory, including the territory of the PIS of J&K held by Pakistan, may be emphasized. These rule out the possibility of New Delhi disowning such territory and its people. Rather, New Delhi is under a constitutional obligation to have the aggression by Pakistan and China, vacated, and to extend to its citizens living under such foreign rule the guarantees contained in the Constitution of India, and, indeed, the Constitution of Jammu and Kashmir of 1957. New Delhi's policy, from 1948 till date, of maintaining territorial status quo and aiming to convert the LOC into the international border is constitutionally impermissible, and has to be excluded from consideration as a possible solution to the Kashmir problem.

Fifth, it must be noted that while New Delhi is under a constitutional obligation to retrieve the territory of the PIS of J&K under the occupation of Pakistan and China, neither Pakistan nor China are likely to indulge India by willingly vacating such territory. India does not have the military option to reclaim its territory. Nor would any diplomatic offensive requiring Pakistan and China to vacate the occupied territory of the PIS of J&K succeed; more so, when New Delhi itself has, from 1948 onwards, been following the policy of maintaining territorial status quo.

The international community wants India and Pakistan to engage in a dialogue to find a solution acceptable to both New Delhi and Islamabad. It is highly improbable that any dialogue between India and Pakistan will result in Pakistan accepting that the PIS of J&K had legally acceded to the dominion of India or that Pakistan's presence in the state continues to be in violation of international law.

India, however, needs the international community to get Pakistan (and China) to vacate the occupied territory of the PIS of J&K, and to restrain Pakistan from cross-border terrorism. It is only if the international community, as a whole, pressurizes Pakistan to do so, and warns it of isolation and international sanctions if it fails to respond, that Pakistan may be compelled to comply—a case in point is the international condemnation of Pakistan for its Kargil invasion forcing Pakistan to withdraw.

But then, it has been noted that the international community does not quite agree, at least publicly, that Pakistan has committed aggression in the PIS of J&K or that Pakistan is, as a matter of state policy, sponsoring terrorism in the PIS of J&K with India. Nor will the international community ever do so at the cost of its members' own national, geo-strategic and political interests. The only way the international community can be pressed to further pressurize Pakistan to vacate aggression and check cross-border terrorism is if an international authority, whose decision is binding on the world community, including Pakistan, confirms the following propositions:

1. That the dominion of India, under the Indian Independence Act of 1947, and the Government of India Act of 1935, as amended, possessed no sovereignty over the princely Indian states on the lapse of British paramountcy on 15 August 1947.

2. That the sovereign rulers of the princely Indian states were the sole repositories of power to offer accession to either of the dominions of India or Pakistan.

3. That 'the wishes of the people' of a princely Indian state were alien to the question of accession of such princely Indian state to either of the dominions of India or Pakistan.

4. That the accession by the sovereign ruler of the PIS of J&K to the dominion of India in 1947 was legally valid, final, complete and irrevocable.

5. That the Government of India was not competent to propound or accept, whether in the UN or outside, that the accession of the PIS of J&K to the dominion of India by its sovereign ruler be further determined by the 'wishes of the people' ascertained by a plebiscite or referendum.

6. That the UN, and every state, including Pakistan, 'contracting' with India are held to have had the knowledge that representatives of the dominion of India exceeded their powers under the said Acts, as well as the Instrument of Accession of 26 October 1947 executed thereunder, by wishing or pledging to hold a plebiscite in the PIS of J&K to settle the question of accession, and, that too, in the absence of its sovereign ruler. The UN and the international community are, in international law, held to have had knowledge of the provisions of the said Acts, and cannot compel the giving of effect to an 'international obligation' contained in UN Resolutions on PIS of J&K, which is inconsistent with these provisions.

7. That the dominion of Pakistan had no locus standi to impugn the accession made by the sovereign ruler of the PIS of J&K to the dominion of India in 1947.

8. That Pakistan and China have no legal right to be in the possession and control of the territory of the PIS of J&K presently occupied by them, and nor was Pakistan competent to negotiate and give away a part of such territory, being Indian territory, to China.

The only body in existence today, which can confirm these purely legal propositions, is the judicial organ of the UN, that is, the ICJ. If the

ICJ decides in favour of India, such finding will not be without the legal consequences. In *Namibia*,[2] the ICJ observed that once it was found that the annexation of Namibia by South Africa was an act of aggression, a 'binding determination made by a competent organ of the United Nations to the effect that the situation is illegal cannot remain without consequence' and that when 'the Court is faced with such a situation, it would be failing in the discharge of its judicial functions if it did not declare that there is an obligation, especially upon the Members of the United Nations, to bring that situation to an end'.[3] The ICJ held that by 'maintaining the present illegal situation, and occupying the Territory of Namibia without title, South Africa incurs international responsibilities arising from a continuing violation of an international obligation', and that 'South Africa is under an obligation to withdraw its administration from Namibia immediately and thus put an end to its occupation of the Territory'.[4] The ICJ took the view that the member states of the UN were 'under obligation to recognise the illegality of South Africa's presence in Namibia and the invalidity of its acts on behalf of or concerning Namibia, and to refrain from any acts and in particular any dealings with the Government of South Africa implying recognition of the legality of, or lending support or assistance to, such presence and administration'.[5] Ammoun J., in his separate opinion, specified the military and economic prohibitions on the member states of the UN in dealing with South Africa. States were prohibited from providing any sort of military assistance, nuclear or conventional arms and ammunition, spare parts, technology, personnel, oil supply, transportation facilities as also economic, industrial or financial assistance, in the form of gifts, loans, credit, advances or guarantees, or in any other form. This prohibition was not confined to states but also applied to institutions in which states have voting rights, such as the International Bank for Reconstruction and Development, the International Development Association and the International Finance Corporation.[6] As far as non-member states were concerned, the ICJ declared that no state that entered into relations with South Africa concerning Namibia could expect the UN or its members to recognize the validity or effects of such relationship, or of its consequences.[7]

Thus, should the ICJ confirm the eight propositions formulated above, the very presence of Pakistan and China in the territory of the PIS of J&K would constitute 'aggression' under the principles of international law, which will be considered shortly, and the international community would have no option but to put an end to that illegal situation. It follows that Pakistan and China would suffer the legal consequences outlined by the ICJ in *Namibia*; that is, Pakistan and China would be held to be under an obligation to withdraw from the territory of the PIS of J&K occupied by them; the member states of the UN would be under an obligation to recognize the illegality of the presence of Pakistan and China in the said territories, and to refrain from any acts and dealings with Pakistan or China implying recognition of the legality of, or lending support or assistance to, such presence; and the non-member states would also be obliged to give assistance in such action. The UN Charter, the international treaties and agreements and the mechanisms evolved thereunder, which are detailed in the next chapter, would automatically come into play to compel Pakistan and China to withdraw from the territory of the PIS of J&K under their respective occupation, and also to require Pakistan to check terrorism. The failure to do so would invite isolation from the world community as also sanctions—political, diplomatic, military as well as economic. It would no longer be possible for Pakistan or any foreign state or the UNSC or for even the people of the PIS of J&K to contend that the Kashmiri people have a 'right to self-determination' or that it is a jihad or 'freedom struggle' that is underway in the territory of the PIS of J&K with India. No longer would the international community be able to plead that if it acts against such jihadis or 'freedom fighters', it would be doing so at the risk of arresting a later day Mandela.

Further, should the ICJ decide, in contravention of settled international legal principles and the UN Charter, any or all of the aforesaid propositions against India, it does not follow that the territories that comprise the PIS of J&K would cede to Pakistan; rather one would simply fall back on the existing stands of both countries. New Delhi could still maintain its official position that the people of the state, including the Kashmiris, have already expressed their wish, through the state Constituent Assembly, in favour of the accession of the PIS of J&K to India. In fact, Jammu and Ladakh are clamouring to merge into the Union of India. Further, it may be recalled that New Delhi, by insisting on converting the LOC into the international border, has been quite willing to let go of the occupied territory of the PIS of J&K held by Pakistan and China. Thus, even in the unlikely event of the ICJ opining that the 'wishes of the people' were relevant for the issue of accession, India would retain the territory of the PIS of J&K with India through the device of the state Constituent Assembly having expressed the 'wishes of the people' on the question of accession, and does not stand to lose more than what it already appears to be happy to lose.

Interestingly, should the 'wishes of the people' be taken into account, Pakistan does not stand to gain anything. It can only hope to retain the territory of the PIS of J&K occupied by it, where an uprising against Pakistan rule is picking up momentum. The repressive state action in Pakistan revealed by citizens of Pakistan, like the Muttahida Quami Movement

(MQM) leaders who came to India to educate the Indians, especially the 'Indian Muslims' on the 'dangers of Talibisation', would help dissuade even devout pro-Pakistan Kashmiri Muslims from opting for Pakistan.[8]

The reference of the Kashmir issue to the ICJ by New Delhi would thus be the first step in unravelling the Kashmir knot. It may be pointed out that Article 36(3) of the UN Charter itself indicates that the UNSC, when seized of a matter under Chapter VI of the Charter, should, in making recommendations, 'take into consideration that legal disputes should as a general rule be referred by the parties to the International Court of Justice'. Indeed, the failure of the UNSC to recommend that the Kashmir issue be referred to the ICJ is yet another indication of it having abdicated its responsibility under the UN Charter.

Should New Delhi move the ICJ as suggested and obtain a favourable result, it would still need to generate the international and national political will to give effect to it. After all, law alone cannot resolve the Kashmir problem. New Delhi must recognize that opinion has as much, if not more, power than law. The world opinion today on the Kashmir issue is certainly not favourable towards India, not least because of the general impression that it has backed out of its 'international obligation' to hold a plebiscite. A finding by the ICJ that India is legally in the right would provide New Delhi with a good basis to change world opinion.

New Delhi must accept that there is a feeling amongst the Kashmiri populace of having been wronged by New Delhi that has sustained the turmoil in the territory of the PIS of J&K with India. A successful reference to the ICJ will help New Delhi put forward a cogent case 'before the Kashmiri people' that in terms of the Indian Independence Act of 1947, read with the Government of India Act of 1935, as amended, the 'wishes of the people' were completely irrelevant for the question of accession, and, therefore, it was not for them to decide the future of the state in the first place. It is crucial for New Delhi to explain to the Kashmiri people that, by failing to hold a plebiscite in the state, no injustice has been meted out to them. After all, as Thomas Hobbes put it, the source of every crime is some defect in the understanding, some error in reasoning or some sudden force of passions. New Delhi must aim to correct that defect, error or force. New Delhi will never be able to stem the unrest in the part of the state with it nor check the indigenous element of the terrorist activity, unless it is able to address this feeling of injustice.

For the Kashmiri populace to take New Delhi seriously, New Delhi must endeavour to undo past mistakes so as to regain some credibility and legitimacy in the state. The later chapters of the book detail how New Delhi slowly and systematically eroded the autonomy of the state, which had been contemplated by the Instrument of Accession and is reflected in Article 370 of the Constitution of India. Popular resentment in the state was met with a policy of 'area clearance' by New Delhi, that is, the ruthless killing of militants in the disturbed areas while brutally suppressing the civilian population into submission. Such policy was facilitated by draconian penal laws. The unrest in the PIS of J&K with India has assumed its present dimensions reportedly due to blatant rigging of elections; misuse of state machinery to quell the legitimate grievances of the people; links of the militants with government employees, legislators, politicians as also with elements in the police, administration and bureaucracy; rampant corruption in the state; collapse of state institutions; and destruction of the fabric of civil society. These are a few of the ground realities, as will be discussed shortly, that New Delhi must aim to change, for which some semblance of accountability and governance, respect for human rights and the rule of law, and a clear, directed policy conforming to the principles of civilized society are imperative. New Delhi must appreciate that bad laws are the worst kind of tyranny and a state with defective laws will have defective morals. On the same footing, humane and just laws would be the highest testimony to any government. As with forms of law, so with forms of government, it is the national character which is decisive.

Thus, the second step to unravel the Kashmir knot is for New Delhi to start the process of regaining moral authority in the state, its success depending largely on the character of the Indian State.

Let us consider both these steps to resolve the Kashmir issue in some depth now.

Notes and References

1. *Supra* Note 1, Introduction.
2. *Supra* Note 35, Chapter VI.
3. Ibid., pp. 54–56.
4. Ibid. Also see ibid., p. 58.
5. Ibid.
6. Ibid., pp. 92–95.
7. Ibid.
8. *The Times of India*. 2000. 'Let Pakistan be a federation: MQM', New Delhi, 6 October.

XII

Approaching the International Court of Justice

This chapter discusses the first step to unravel the Kashmir knot—namely, a legal reference of the Kashmir issue by New Delhi to the ICJ. The chapter begins with a summary of the stand eventually taken by India before the UNSC in 1964—the last time there were extensive debates on the *India–Pakistan Question*—to demonstrate that New Delhi had by then itself realized that its stand on the PIS of J&K in 1947 was legally untenable. The chapter then details how India could make the suggested reference to the ICJ and the principles on which the ICJ would have to decide the limited reference as discussed in the previous chapter. It finally considers the legal question as to whether Pakistan can refuse to be party to such a limited reference, should India make one to the ICJ.

Eventual Stand of India in the UN

It appears that by 1964, New Delhi had become much wiser. Though it had still not occurred to New Delhi that it lacked competence to introduce the 'wishes of the people' as the deciding factor for the question of accession of a princely Indian state, it did realize that there was no provision in the Indian Independence Act of 1947, or the Government of India Act of 1935, as amended, for consulting the people of the acceding state or requiring that the accession be ratified by ascertaining the wishes of the people of that state.

M.C. Chagla (India) declared before the UNSC on 5 February 1964 that:[1]

.... It was also provided that it was open to every princely State to accede to either India or Pakistan. The law did not provide that the Instrument of Accession could be conditional. Once the accession was accepted either by the Governor-General of India or of Pakistan, the particular princely State became an integral part of one or more of the two Dominions. It is significant to note that there was no provision for consulting the people of the princely State concerned. Nor was there any provision that accession had to be ratified by ascertaining the wishes of the people of the acceding State....

It has also to be remembered that the partition of India was confined to British India and that in drawing the lines of the frontier, questions of Muslim majority provinces were taken into consideration only with regard to British India. There was no question whatsoever with regard to the religious complexion of the population of the princely States. The question whether one princely State should accede to India or Pakistan was left to the determination of the Ruler of the State.... The British Government had made it quite clear that the partition was only of British India and that this principle (of the two nation theory) did not apply to those States, such as Kashmir and several hundred others, which were ruled by Indian princes....

It was entirely for the Ruler of Jammu and Kashmir to decide taking all factors into consideration.... The question of religion did not come into play at all.

Therefore, there is no substance in the suggestion that the accession of Jammu and Kashmir was not complete and absolute because the people of that State had not been consulted nor been given opportunity to express their choice....

Jammu and Kashmir became an integral part of India when the Instrument of Accession was signed and accepted, and from that date till today it continues to occupy the same position vis-a-vis the Indian Union, and no further question can possibly arise of annexing Kashmir or further integrating it into the Indian Union. You cannot make more complete what is already complete....

Similarly, while it had still not dawned upon New Delhi that the UN Resolutions on holding a plebiscite in the PIS of J&K were beyond the competence of India, Pakistan and indeed, the UN itself, New Delhi did reiterate its repudiation of the 'conditional', 'contingent' and 'obsolete' UN Resolutions. M.C. Chagla (India) pointed out that:[2]

The two resolutions of the Security Council dealing with the plebiscite were conditional and contingent on Pakistan vacating its aggression, and that condition has not been complied with. It is really more than a condition. It was the basis on which these two resolutions were founded, and the condition not having been complied with and the basis having disappeared, these resolutions are no longer binding on us. In any case, by the passage of time and various factors intervening...they have become obsolete.... I wish to make it clear on behalf of my Government that under no circumstances can we agree to the holding of a plebiscite in Kashmir....

Pakistan mockingly contrasted each declaration made by New Delhi at the time with its earlier contrary stand taken in its own White Paper as also before the international community and the UNSC. Pakistan happily drew parallels with the cases of Hyderabad and Junagadh to highlight New Delhi's own policy of making the wishes of the people a relevant factor to settle the accession of a princely Indian state. Pakistan's reasoning was impeccable, but for the crucial fact that New Delhi was not legally competent to add to the Instrument of Accession executed under the Indian Independence Act of 1947, and the Government of India Act of 1935, as amended, a requirement that the people of the princely India state would settle the question of such accession. New Delhi's policy of requiring a reference to the people to settle the question of accession of a princely Indian state, be it the PIS of J&K, Hyderabad or Junagadh, was itself ultra vires the said British statutes—statutes that bind both India and Pakistan and, indeed, the UK.

Pakistan's response raises a further question: should there be a reference to the ICJ as suggested, could Pakistan seek to reopen the accession of the princely Indian state of Hyderabad and the princely Indian state of Junagadh to India? If one was to locate the answer in law, without getting into the broader consideration of what would be the equitable thing to do, the answer would be no. While Hyderabad and Junagadh were legally sovereign states on the lapse of the British paramountcy in 1947, they lost their identity as such upon their merger into the Union of India. Thus, there is no princely Indian state of Hyderabad or of Junagadh in existence today. The territories that comprised those states have also not maintained their distinctiveness. The PIS of J&K, on the other hand, did not execute an instrument of merger at all.

Moreover, the ICJ gets the jurisdiction to hear a matter only with the consent of the parties. Pakistan has, as will be discussed shortly, unreservedly accepted the compulsory jurisdiction of the ICJ, while India has accepted it with reservations that enable it, in effect, to submit only what it chooses to place before the ICJ qua Pakistan. New Delhi can, therefore, make the suggested reference in relation to the Kashmir problem and, at the same time, refuse to submit to the jurisdiction of the ICJ the accessions of Hyderabad and Junagadh.

New Delhi can, nonetheless, use Pakistan's stand on Hyderabad and Junagadh to substantiate the proposition that upon the lapse of the British paramountcy, the PIS of J&K became fully sovereign. New Delhi could rely heavily on Pakistan's admissions; for instance, its assertion in the *Hyderabad Question* that 'the result of the Indian Independence Act was that the States were independent' and 'could thereafter choose to accede to one or the other of the two Dominions, or they could remain independent'.[3] Given that the Indian Independence Act of 1947, and the Government of India Act of 1935, as amended, do not contemplate a conditional accession or an accession which was to be ratified by ascertaining the wishes of the people of that state, this admission by Pakistan itself will suffice to confirm that the accession by the sovereign ruler of the PIS of J&K was legal, final and irrevocable, being an Act of State; that Pakistan had no locus standi to impugn the accession; that the 'wishes of the people' were irrelevant for the question of accession; that Pakistan had the knowledge that representatives of the dominion of India had exceeded their powers under the said Acts, as well as the Instrument of Accession executed thereunder, by wishing or pledging to hold a plebiscite in the PIS of J&K to settle the question of accession and that the very presence of Pakistan and China in the territories of the PIS of J&K constituted aggression.

It may be pointed out here that the question of a reference to the ICJ for an advisory opinion had been suggested by the Swedish government in 1957 on 'certain legal aspects',[4] which were contained in two questions formulated by the Swedish government.[5] The UNSC, however, was in no mood to involve the ICJ at all. As Colombia pointed out, 'the position of the United Nations was quite different'; that '[w]hat we advocated' was that 'we are going to forget about, to waive, this inquiry into the law' and proceed on the footing that 'Mr. Nehru has volunteered the statement that, whether or not Kashmir belongs to India, if the result of the plebiscite is not favourable to India it would cede Kashmir'.[6] Colombia emphasized that '[w]hat we wanted to say is that Kashmir's accession to, or incorporation in, India does not concern us' and nor does it 'change the position of the Council'.[7]

Pakistan's response was understandable since the last thing it wanted was a legal scrutiny of its claim to the PIS of J&K. Firoz Khan Noon (Pakistan) stated that '[i]n our view, the issues involved in the Kashmir dispute are of a political, rather than a juridical, nature' and that '[a]ny reference to the International Court of Justice will merely delay the settlement of a long-standing dispute and such delay, I beg to submit, might endanger peace'.[8]

New Delhi's reaction was, to say the least, evasive and calculated to have the suggestion of a reference to the ICJ dismissed. Cryptically declaring that the Government of India did not reject these ideas 'because if we did we should be doing wrong',[9] and that it had 'not said that an advisory opinion may not be sought',[10] New Delhi now took refuge behind the ruler's sovereignty in the PIS of J&K to plead its 'difficult position'. Krishna Menon stated that '[t]here are the parties to the accession, the Head of the State of Jammu and Kashmir and the Head of the then State of India, in 1947, the Governor General' and that the 'ruler, not us, may vary the terms of the accession'.[11]

Interestingly, New Delhi declared that 'this question of referring the legality of the accession to the International Court would only arise, if we were prepared to have this matter referred, in the case of 560 states' and 'if the Pakistan Government were willing to subscribe to it and have it applied to those States that have acceded to Pakistan'.[12] New Delhi also sought to make out a case that such legal reference on the validity of the accession was unnecessary as, in its view, the UNSC had already pronounced itself on the 'question of sovereignty' of India over the PIS of J&K and that such question was 'out of the debate'.[13] Unfortunately, only New Delhi seemed to be of that view, with the rest of the world, as discussed earlier, opining that the future of the PIS of J&K was yet to be decided.

Simply put, New Delhi was not inclined to refer the questions formulated by the Swedish government to the ICJ. Perhaps it is fortunate that New Delhi took such a view, as the questions as formulated were not directed at the crux of the matter, namely, the competence of New Delhi to offer and accept that the question of the accession of the PIS of J&K be settled by a plebiscite or a reference to the people. Rather, the questions were aimed at inviting a finding in respect of the assumption of an 'international obligation' by India to hold a plebiscite.

Pakistan sought to emphasize that the Kashmir problem was more 'political' than 'juridical' in nature. It lies in India's interest to view the Kashmir issue as a juridical one rather than a political one; more so, because the current ground realities indicate that the less New Delhi talks of a political solution, the better it is for India. In other words, given the bungling by New Delhi from 1947 onwards, it has become imperative to depoliticize the Kashmir problem, and litigation is certainly a convenient way to do so. Nor is it open to Pakistan to plead that the Kashmir problem is not amenable to a legal resolution on the pretext that it is a political issue. All international issues are political by nature. At times, the parties are able to separate the legal from the political aspect of the issue, and thereby resolve the issue by themselves. In other cases, as in the Kashmir problem, a legal tribunal is required to do that job as also to decide the limited legal issues raised before it without going into its wider context. After all, as Merills points out that:[14]

The cases in which the Court's competence to handle politically charged disputes has been questioned have all been referred unilaterally and involved a basic disagreement as to how the dispute should be characterised. For the applicant the legal aspect was paramount and the intention in taking the case to the Court was to vindicate a claim based on legal rights. For the respondent, on the other hand, the core of the issue was political, and so, though legal issues may be involved, the case was unsuitable for adjudication. Faced with this incomplete depoliticisation, the Court has taken the only position open to a legal tribunal and, having established that it has the right to decide the issue of characterisation, has ruled that whatever the politics of the dispute maybe, the applicant has the right to a decision, provided only that the case presents a legal issue....

Given that India is in law entitled to the entire territory that comprises the PIS of J&K, it lies in India's interest to make the reference to the ICJ, though limited to the eight propositions on the Kashmir problem formulated earlier. Should the ICJ find in favour of India, the UN and the international community will have no option but to condemn Pakistan as the aggressor, to require Pakistan to vacate the aggression and to refrain from cross-border terrorism. The role of China in the entire matter is dependent upon Pakistan's claim to the PIS of J&K, and in case of a favourable decision by the ICJ, China will have no option but to vacate the territories of the PIS of J&K occupied by it. Let us, therefore, consider how New Delhi could propose such a reference to the ICJ and the principles applicable for a legal resolution of the Kashmir problem as the first step to unravel the Kashmir knot.

The Proposed Reference to the ICJ

The UN has, in the past, categorically ruled out intervention to enforce the UN Resolutions on the PIS of J&K.[15] The international community today also does not support the holding of a plebiscite in the state, though for reasons not entirely founded in law. India has a legal basis for denouncing its 'engagement' to hold a plebiscite in the PIS of J&K, as noted earlier. New Delhi would be likely to get away with not holding such plebiscite, given the disinclination of the UN and the international community to press for a plebiscite in a territory held by three sovereign countries—India, Pakistan and China. The stand taken by New Delhi in 1948 before the UNSC will not, therefore, preclude it from now seeking alternatives to resolve the Kashmir issue.

India, Pakistan and the international community continue to subscribe to the Simla Agreement, which mandates that India and Pakistan settle their differences by peaceful means through bilateral negotiations or by any other peaceful means mutually agreed upon between them. In fact, India has informed the UN General Assembly that the Simla Agreement is the 'only' viable framework, mutually agreed upon, under which the Kashmir issue can be resolved through dialogue.[16] While 'bilateral negotiations', as envisaged by the Simla Agreement, would necessarily imply that India has to lose something to win something and that 'something' in the context of the Kashmir problem necessarily means loss of territory, and quite likely, territories already occupied by Pakistan and China, bilateral negotiations will be to the prejudice of India, apart from the questionable legality of such negotiations. The alternative provided under the Simla Agreement is that the differences may be settled by India and Pakistan through 'any other peaceful means mutually agreed upon between them'. There is nothing to prevent New Delhi from suggesting to Pakistan that as one of such 'other peaceful means', the limited reference, as suggested, be made to the ICJ. And should Pakistan not agree to such limited reference to the ICJ under the Simla Agreement, there is nothing in law to prevent New Delhi from making the reference unilaterally to the ICJ, as will be examined later in this chapter.

In the event of a reference being made to the ICJ, limited to the eight propositions on the Kashmir problem formulated earlier, it will be useful to consider how the ICJ would treat the matter.

In *Fisheries*,[17] the ICJ held that the Court, as an international judicial organ, 'is deemed to take judicial notice of international law, and is therefore, required to consider on its own initiative all rules of international law which may be relevant to the settlement of the dispute'.[18] Article 38 of the Statute of the International Court of Justice provides that the ICJ, whose function is to decide in accordance with international law such disputes as are submitted to it, shall apply international conventions establishing rules expressly recognized by the contesting states; international customary law; the general principles of law recognized by civilized nations; as also judicial decisions and the teachings of the most highly qualified publicists of the various nations, as subsidiary means for the determination of rules of law.

The ICJ is, therefore, bound to construe the provisions of the Indian Independence Act of 1947, and the Government of India Act of 1935, as amended—being Acts enacted by the British Parliament that created India and Pakistan and were accepted by India and Pakistan. It is bound to take into account the lack of competence of New Delhi under these

Acts to offer and accept that the accession of a princely Indian state by its sovereign ruler to the dominion of India be further determined by the 'wishes of the people' ascertained by a plebiscite or referendum. It is bound to examine the lack of power of New Delhi to introduce the 'wishes of the people' as a criterion to settle accession of a princely Indian state to the dominion of India. The ICJ is bound to hold that it was the sovereign ruler who alone was competent under these Acts to decide the future of his state. The ICJ is bound to decide that the accession by the sovereign ruler to the dominion of India in terms of the said Acts was legally valid, final, complete and irrevocable. The ICJ is bound to find that the UN and every state, including Pakistan, 'contracting' with India are held to have had the knowledge that representatives of the dominion of India exceeded their powers under the said Acts, by wishing or pledging to hold a plebiscite in the PIS of J&K to settle the question of accession, and, that too, in the absence of its sovereign ruler. The ICJ is bound to note that the UN and the international community cannot compel the giving of effect to an 'international obligation' contained in UN Resolutions on the PIS of J&K, which is inconsistent with the provisions of the said Acts or the Instrument of Accession executed under the said Acts. The ICJ is bound to determine that Pakistan had no locus standi to impugn the accession or to be in the territory that comprises the PIS of J&K or to cede such territory to a third country. The ICJ is bound to conform to all the constitutional and statutory provisions, judicial decisions and authoritative pronouncements cited in the preceding chapters in support of such legal propositions.

The ICJ is bound to rule on the proposition that insofar as the PIS of J&K became part and parcel of Indian territory, the very presence of troops of Pakistan and China in the territory of the state must be considered as an act of aggression. Indeed, Article 2(4) of the UN Charter itself mandates that '[a]ll Members shall refrain in their international relations from the threat or use of force against the territorial integrity or political independence of any state'. The ICJ is bound to take into account its own decisions and international conventions on what constitutes 'aggression', so as to invite the sanction by the international community against Pakistan (and China). A precedent in point is *Namibia*.[19]

In *Namibia*, the ICJ found that the annexation of Namibia by South Africa was an act of aggression.[20] It recorded that South Africa throughout, and even before the Court, sought to justify its continued occupation by claiming the right of conquest or the effect of acquisitive prescription. The ICJ took the view that while the law of former times—as in the Berlin Act of 1885 and the Treaties of Bardo and Algeciras and numerous other treaties—tolerated conquest and annexation, modern law, that is, that of the UN Charter, the Pact of Bogota and the Charter of Addis Ababa, condemns conquest and annexation.[21] The ICJ dismissed the claim of South Africa, holding that the most categorical rebuttal of such claim is that conquest and acquisitive prescription have totally disappeared from the new law, and that the new law 'damns' war and proclaims the inalienability of sovereignty.[22] The ICJ reasoned that 'occupation and annexation achieve the ultimate aims of aggression bringing about the destruction of the entity which was the... target',[23] and relied on the Moscow Declaration of 30 October 1943 to hold that the annexation of a territory by the mere movement of troops or by the presence of foreign troops constitutes 'aggression'.[24]

Should the suggested reference be determined by the ICJ in India's favour, the ICJ is bound to find that the mere presence of troops of Pakistan and China in the territories of the PIS of J&K occupied by them is an act of aggression. The ICJ is bound to rule that Pakistan and China will suffer the legal consequences of such finding, which have been discussed in the previous chapter. The ICJ is bound to direct the member states of the UN to recognize the illegality of the presence of Pakistan and China in the said territories and to refrain from any acts and dealings with Pakistan or China implying recognition of the legality of, or lending support or assistance to, such presence. The ICJ is bound to call upon the non-member states to assist in such action. The ICJ is bound to require Pakistan and China to withdraw from the territories of the PIS of J&K occupied by them. This is, perhaps, the only means to compel Pakistan, and China, to restore the territories of the PIS of J&K to India.

In addition to the overt aggression committed by Pakistan, New Delhi can also point out the sustained efforts of Pakistan over the years in recruiting, training, arming, equipping, financing, supplying and otherwise encouraging, aiding and directing mercenaries and jihadis to fan terrorism in the part of the PIS of J&K with India and beyond. These acts would, under international law, constitute covert aggression against India. The Definition of Aggression, annexed to the General Assembly Resolution 3314 (XXIX), was approved by the UN General Assembly on 14 December 1974, and includes in Article 3 as 'aggression', 'the sending by or on behalf of a state of armed bands, groups, irregulars or mercenaries, which carry out acts of armed force against another state'.

In *Nicaragua*, the ICJ ruled 'that an armed attack must be understood as including not merely action by regular armed forces across an international border, but also "the sending by or on behalf of a State of armed bands, groups, irregulars or mercenaries, which carry out acts of armed force against another State of such gravity as to amount to" (inter alia) an actual armed attack conducted by regular forces, "or its substantial involvement therein".[25] The ICJ held that the description contained in Article 3, paragraph (g) of the Definition of Aggression annexed to the General Assembly Resolution 3314 (XXIX) 'may be taken to reflect customary international law'.[26]

In the said case, the ICJ considered the complaint of Nicaragua that the US was rendering logistic, financial and other assistance to the contra forces, which were trying to overthrow the Government of Nicaragua. Nicaragua contended that the US by 'recruiting, training, arming, equipping, financing, supplying and otherwise encouraging, supporting, aiding and directing military and paramilitary actions in and against Nicaragua, has violated and is violating' the UN Charter and its treaty obligations.[27] The ICJ made findings that the 'contra force ha[d], at least at one period, been so dependent on the United States that it could not conduct its crucial or most significant military or paramilitary activities without the multifaceted support of the United States',[28] that the 'United States Government was providing funds for military and paramilitary activities by contras in Nicaragua',[29] that there had been intermittent flow of arms,[30] that an agency of the US government supplied to the *Fuerza Democratica Nicaraguense* a manual of psychological guerrilla warfare, whose text advised the use of professional criminals to perform unspecified 'jobs', and the use of provocation at mass demonstrations so that the resulting police violence would make them 'martyrs'.[31]

The ICJ ruled that the principle of respect for state sovereignty in international law is closely linked with the principles of prohibition against the use of force and of non-intervention, which forbid all states or groups of states to intervene, directly or indirectly, in the internal or external affairs of other states.[32] The ICJ found that the aforesaid support given by the US constituted a clear breach of the principle of non-intervention.[33]

The ICJ also considered 'whether there might be indications of a practice illustrative of a belief in a kind of a general right for States to intervene, directly or indirectly, with or without armed force, in support of an internal opposition in another State, whose cause appeared particularly worthy by reason of the political and moral value with which it was identified'.[34] It held 'that no such general right of intervention, in support of an opposition within another State, exists in contemporary international law'.[35] On a parity of reasoning, it was not legally permissible for Pakistan to extend even its moral or political support to the alleged 'uprising' in the PIS of J&K in 1947, nor to the supposed jihad today.

Nicaragua lays down another principle relevant for the purpose of the Kashmir problem. It appears that the Nicaraguan Junta of National

Reconstruction had, following the recommendation of the XVIIth Meeting of the Consultation of Foreign Ministers of the Organization of American States, made a pledge to the Organization of American States and to the people of Nicaragua to hold free elections. The question arose as to whether the US could assume the task of compelling Nicaragua to honour the pledge. The ICJ held that the pledge was 'essentially a political pledge' and that 'even supposing that such a political pledge had had the force of a legal commitment, it could not have justified the United States insisting on the fulfilment of a commitment not made directly towards the United States, but towards the Organisation, the latter being alone empowered to monitor its implementation'.[36] Further, 'even supposing the United States were entitled to act in lieu of the Organisation, it could hardly make use of the purpose of methods which the Organisation could not use itself' and that 'in particular, it could not be authorised to use force in that event' since '[o]f its nature, a commitment like this is one of a category which, if violated, cannot justify the use of force against a sovereign State'.[37]

Thus, it is, even otherwise, not open to Pakistan to cite the non-compliance by India of the UN Resolutions for a plebiscite as a justification for overt conflicts, like in Kargil, or for its subversive activities to provide 'all out support' for the supposed jihad in the PIS of J&K.

The ICJ is also bound to take into consideration the stand of the international community with reference to East Pakistan, now Bangladesh, which in the words of Jamil Baroody (Saudi Arabia) was that '[r]ebellion inside a State, even if it gathers momentum to become a civil war or a bloody conflict—call it revolution—should never be exploited by outside forces'.[38] The ICJ will have to consider Pakistan's own stand before the UNSC on India's alleged interference in East Pakistan. Pakistan minced no words in asserting that it wants 'peace with justice and our only demand is that our country should be spared from invasion, that foreign interference should stop, that an internal struggle should not be interpreted as giving rise to an external obligation'.[39]

Terrorism and Subversive Activities

Given that the internationally accepted definition of aggression includes covert war through terrorism and subversive activities, India would do well to use the concrete and substantive evidence it has of Pakistan's political, military and financial support to the carrying out of terrorist activities in the territory of the PIS of J&K with India and beyond, including the abduction and murder of foreign tourists and prominent Indian citizens, the attacks on military and sensitive installations in the state, the Hazratbal episode, the Chrar-e-Sharief incident, the Kargil conflict, the hijacking of the Indian Airlines plane, the Red Fort shootout, the attack on the Indian Parliament, the 26/11 Mumbai attack, the Pathankot Air Force Base attack, innumerable bomb blasts and so on so forth. It is well documented that Pakistan openly houses individuals wanted by India for terrorist activities. It is equally well recorded that terrorist training camps operate on Pakistan's soil. It expressly permits terrorists to run offices, indulge in provocative anti-India propaganda and collect funds to wage a jihad in India. It, in fact, assists them in crossing the LOC into the Kashmir Valley, along with arms, drugs and counterfeit currency. Should there be a reference to the ICJ as suggested, India can, in addition to the said decisions of the ICJ, draw upon the international obligations of Pakistan to refrain from terrorism and subversive activities. These obligations are contained in the Tashkent Declaration of 1966, the Simla Agreement of 1972 and, of course, numerous international conventions.

It is well settled that states must not engage in or support terrorism or subversive activities. Oppenheim notes that customary international law imposes an obligation on each state to prevent hostile expeditions from its territory, and itself to refrain, directly or indirectly through organizations receiving from it financial or other assistance or closely associated with it by virtue of the state's constitution, from engaging in or actively supporting subversive activities against another state.[40] This rule forms the basis of the anti-terrorism instruments formulated over the decades. For instance, the UN, in its General Assembly Resolution 2131 (XX) (1965), declared that '[n]o State has the right to intervene, directly or indirectly, for any reason whatever, in the internal or external affairs of any State' and that 'no State shall organize, assist, foment, finance, incite or tolerate subversive, terrorist or armed activities directed towards the violent overthrow of the regime of another State or interfere in civil strife in another State'. This rule was reiterated in the Declaration on Principles of International Law Concerning Friendly Relations and Co-operation among States, adopted by the UN General Assembly on 24 October 1970, while also emphasizing that every state has the duty to refrain from acquiescing in organized activities within its territory directed towards the commission of such acts.

Again, the UN General Assembly, by its Resolution 48/122 (1993) on *Human Rights and Terrorism*, unequivocally condemned 'all acts, methods and practices of terrorism in all its forms and manifestations, wherever and by whomever committed,' and has reiterated this principle in subsequent Resolutions. Then there are multilateral conventions on the suppression of international terrorism, some of which are aimed at preventing specific acts of terrorism, such as the hijacking and sabotage of aircraft.

There is, thus, relative clarity of international law on what constitutes aggression and the international obligations of states to check terrorism and subversive activities. In view of the aforesaid precedents and well-settled principles of law, the legal reference of the Kashmir problem to the ICJ is, perhaps, the best starting point to unravel the Kashmir knot. But then, can Pakistan refuse to be party to a reference to the ICJ, limited to the questions on the Kashmir problem that India chooses to refer?

Pakistan and the Proposed Reference to the ICJ

Given that the jurisdiction of the ICJ 'only exists within the limits within which it has been accepted',[41] what if Pakistan refuses to submit to the jurisdiction of the ICJ?

Now, the consent of a state to submit to the compulsory jurisdiction of the ICJ can be given in a number of ways. Merills states that the consent can 'be given before the dispute arises by means of a compromisory clause in a treaty, or a declaration under Article 36 (2) of the Court's Statute', or alternatively, 'consent can be given after a dispute has arisen by means of a special agreement between the parties, or in response to the unilateral reference to the Court'.[42] However, as Merills points out, 'once the legal act indicating consent has been offered, jurisdiction may be established, even if the State is unwilling to litigate when the actual case arises'.[43] The question, therefore, is whether Pakistan has already given its consent in any of the said ways.

If one goes through the maze of international treaties and conventions pertaining to the ICJ and its precursor, the Permanent Court of International Justice (PCIJ), it will become evident that while India is not bound to refer any issue or dispute with Pakistan to the ICJ and can choose to refer to the ICJ what it wishes, Pakistan has no choice in the matter. Rather, Pakistan has accepted the compulsory jurisdiction of the ICJ without making any reservations, thereby giving its unconditional consent to submit to the jurisdiction of the ICJ, should India unilaterally make the limited reference to the ICJ as suggested.

British India and the PCIJ

As a point of departure, it will be instructive to note the provisions of the Statute of the Permanent Court of International Justice approved by the League of Nations on 13 December 1920, and which entered into force on 2 September 1921, after the Protocol of Signature of the Statute of the Court had been ratified by a majority of the members of the League of Nations.

Article 36(2) of the Statute provided for a declaration by the states that they recognize as compulsory ipso facto and without special agreement, in relation to any other member of the League of Nations or state accepting the same obligation, the jurisdiction of the Court in all or any of the classes of legal disputes concerning the interpretation of a treaty; any question of international law; the existence of any fact which, if established, would constitute a breach of an international obligation; and the nature or extent of the reparation to be made for the breach of an international obligation.

The states that were parties to the Statute of the Permanent Court of International Justice could, therefore, make declarations under Article 36(2) of the Statute in respect of the compulsory jurisdiction of the PCIJ. These declarations could be made with or without special agreements, which included reservations or exceptions. At that point of time, there was a concept of Commonwealth reservation, that is, British India or other Commonwealth states could make a reservation that they accept the compulsory jurisdiction of the PCIJ, except with regard to 'disputes with the government of any other Member of the League which is a member of the British Commonwealth of Nations, all of which disputes shall be settled in such manner as the Parties have agreed or shall agree'.[44]

The Government of India, on behalf of British India, made such a declaration under Article 36(2) of the Statute of the Permanent Court of International Justice, on 19 September 1929, to the effect that the Government of India accepts 'as compulsory ipso facto and without special convention on condition of reciprocity the jurisdiction of the Court', but subject to the Commonwealth reservation.[45]

The declarations given by India and Pakistan after attaining independence in 1947 with regard to the jurisdiction of the ICJ were, however, different.

India, Pakistan and the ICJ

As regards the ICJ, Article 36(1) of the Statute of the International Court of Justice states that the jurisdiction of the Court comprises all cases that the parties refer to it and all matters specially provided for in UN Charter or in treaties and conventions in force. Article 36(2) of this Statute enables the state parties to declare that they recognize as compulsory ipso facto and without special agreement, in relation to any other state accepting the same obligation, the jurisdiction of the Court in all legal disputes concerning the interpretation of a treaty; any question of international law; the existence of any fact which, if established, would constitute a breach of an international obligation; and the nature or extent of the reparation to be made for the breach of an international obligation. The declaration may be made unconditionally or on condition of reciprocity on the part of several or certain states, or for a certain time.

India's declaration under Article 36(2) of the Statute of the International Court of Justice was filed on 18 September 1974, which accepted the compulsory ipso facto jurisdiction of the ICJ over all disputes, other than (i) disputes with the government of any state which is or has been a member of the Commonwealth of Nations, and (ii) disputes concerning the interpretation or application of a multilateral treaty, unless all the parties to the treaty are also parties to the case before the Court or Government of India specially agrees to submit to the jurisdiction.[46] Thus, India has accepted the compulsory jurisdiction of the ICJ, subject to the said reservations. Pakistan's declaration under Article 36(2) of the Statute of the International Court of Justice, accepting the ICJ's compulsory jurisdiction was filed on 13 June 1960, but does not contain the reservations made by India.[47]

India, Pakistan and the General Act of 1928

Reference may also be made to the General Act for Pacific Settlement of International Disputes, which was signed at Geneva on 26 September 1928, and which provided for judicial settlement of international legal disputes by resort to the PCIJ.

Article 17 of this General Act of 1928 provided that all disputes (including those referred to in Article 36(2) of the Statute of the Permanent Court of International Justice) with regard to which the parties are in conflict as to their respective rights shall, subject to any reservations that may be made under Article 39 of the General Act of 1928, be submitted for decision to the PCIJ. Article 39 of the General Act of 1928 enabled a party acceding to the General Act to make its acceptance conditional upon certain reservations to be indicated at the time of accession.

British India, which had already made the aforesaid declaration in terms of Article 36(2) of the Statute of the Permanent Court of International Justice, had acceded to the General Act of 1928 on 21 May 1931, but with reservations, including the Commonwealth reservation.[48]

As far as India was concerned, the Minister of External Affairs, by his communication dated 18 September 1974 to the then UN Secretary General, declared that the 'Government of India never regarded themselves as bound by the General Act of 1928 since her Independence in 1947, whether by succession or otherwise' and that 'India has never been and is not a party to the General Act of 1928 ever since her Independence'.[49]

However, Pakistan, by its Declaration of 30 May 1974, stated that 'it continues to be bound by the accession of British India to the General Act of 1928' and that it 'does not, however, affirm to the reservations made by British India'.[50]

The legal position that emerges is that India has made reservations while accepting the compulsory jurisdiction of the ICJ. Where the dispute is with a Commonwealth state, India is not bound to submit to the jurisdiction of the ICJ. Pakistan is a Commonwealth state. India is not bound by the General Act of 1928 either. India is, therefore, entitled to refer to the ICJ only what it chooses to refer qua Pakistan.

Pakistan, on the other hand, remains bound by the General Act of 1928 and has accepted the compulsory jurisdiction of the ICJ without reservations. Pakistan's declarations constitute its unconditional consent to submit to the jurisdiction of the ICJ, should India unilaterally make the limited reference to the ICJ as suggested.

In this regard, New Delhi could rely on the decision of 21 June 2000 of the ICJ in the *Case concerning the Aerial Incident of 10 August 1999 (Pakistan v India)*.[51]

The Atlantique Case

Pakistan, in its application of 21 September 1999 to the ICJ, claimed that India had fired upon, with air-to-air missiles, an unarmed Atlantique aircraft of the Pakistan navy which, according to Pakistan, was flying over Pakistan air space.[52] Pakistan demanded that India should pay an amount of US$60.2 million as compensation for the loss of the Pakistani aircraft and for the loss of the personnel on board.[53]

India responded before the ICJ by stating that the Pakistani plane was shot down in the Kutch region of Gujarat as it was a spying mission and had violated the April 1991 bilateral agreement, which specified that combat aircraft, including bombers, fighter jets, military trainers, assault helicopters, as well as reconnaissance planes, would not fly within 10 kilometres of each other's territory.[54] Hence, India denied all allegations made by Pakistan with respect to the said incident and declared that 'Pakistan is solely responsible for the incident and must bear the consequences of its own acts'.[55]

India, by its letter dated 2 November 1999, raised preliminary objections regarding the jurisdiction of the ICJ to entertain Pakistan's application. It is these preliminary objections that are important for our purpose.

India's stand was that there was no treaty or convention in force between India and Pakistan which conferred jurisdiction upon the ICJ under Article 36(1) of the Statute of the International Court of Justice. India argued further that its Commonwealth reservation in its Declaration of 18 September 1974, filed under Article 36(2) of the Statute, disentitled Pakistan, being a Commonwealth country, from invoking the jurisdiction of the ICJ against India. Again, India's Declaration of 18 September 1974, stating that it was not a party to the General Act of 1928 also barred Pakistan from invoking the jurisdiction of the ICJ against India.

The ICJ dismissed Pakistan's application for want of jurisdiction with two of the sixteen judges giving separate dissenting opinions.

The majority opinion delivered by Gilbert Guillume, the President of the ICJ, took the view that India cannot be regarded as a party to the General Act of 1928 in view of its communication of 18 September 1974. The majority opinion held that the reservations made by India in its declaration under Article 36(2) cannot be termed as extra-statutory or obsolete. Given that India had made its intention clear to limit in this manner the scope of its acceptance of the ICJ's jurisdiction, the ICJ was bound to apply it.[56]

Al-Khasawneh J (Jordan) gave a dissenting opinion on the ground that the reservations made by India under Article 36(2) did not bar the ICJ's jurisdiction, particularly since these were aimed to exclude only Pakistan, and such arbitrary exclusion puts the reservation outside the purview of permissibility. Finally, Pirzada J (Pakistan) also gave a dissenting opinion, taking the view that both Pakistan and India were successor states to British India; that the General Act of 1928 devolved upon and continues to apply to both Pakistan and India and that India's reservations did not bar the jurisdiction of the Court.

It will at once be noticed that Pakistan, by having moved the ICJ in the *Case concerning the Aerial Incident of 10 August 1999 (Pakistan v India)*, invited a finding from the ICJ that India was not bound to refer any issue or dispute with Pakistan to the ICJ, whether under the General Act of 1928 or under Article 36(2) of the Statute of the International Court of Justice read with India's declaration, as qualified by valid reservations. More importantly, Pakistan has reiterated before the ICJ that it has accepted the compulsory jurisdiction of the Court without the reservations that India had claimed, whether it be under Article 36(2) of the said Statute or under the General Act of 1928. Thus, while India can choose to refer to the ICJ what it wishes qua Pakistan, Pakistan has no choice in the matter. Rather, Pakistan would be precluded on the principle of *estoppel* from resisting such a limited reference.

New Delhi, and its legal advisers, are, however, oblivious to the fact that it could lie in India's national interest to make a reference to the ICJ. On the contrary, the then Indian Attorney General proudly declared at a public function in New Delhi on 25 June 2000 that the ICJ's decision of 21 June 2000, in the *Case concerning the Aerial Incident on 10 August 1999 (Pakistan v India)*, was crucial for India since it checked Pakistan from referring the Kashmir issue to the ICJ.[57] The then Attorney General insisted that '[t]he Atlantique downing case was the precursor for Pakistan to raise the Kashmir dispute before the International Court',[58] unmindful of the fact that that might be precisely what India should work towards, though, of course, on its terms.

It seems that New Delhi and its legal advisers remain unaware of the legal implications of the decision of the ICJ in the *Case concerning the Aerial Incident on 10 August 1999 (Pakistan v India)*. The Indian Solicitor General cited the ICJ decision before the Indian Supreme Court on 1 September 2015 to erroneously argue that India was 'forbidden' from raising before the ICJ the issue of Pakistan illegally holding 54 Indian armed forces personnel as prisoners of war since the two wars in 1965 and 1971, as 'the I.C.J. had rejected Pakistan's case and upheld India's argument that the countries had agreed under the Simla Agreement of 1972 and reiterated in the Lahore Agreement in 1999 to resolve all outstanding disputes bilaterally'.[59] New Delhi failed to appreciate that the said ICJ decision is an authority for the proposition that while Pakistan has accepted the compulsory jurisdiction of the Court without the reservations that India had claimed, India is not bound to refer any issue or dispute with Pakistan to the ICJ in light of such reservations. It does not follow that India cannot at all choose to refer an issue or dispute with Pakistan to the ICJ. Rather, the majority opinion in the ICJ decision, while dismissing Pakistan's application for want of jurisdiction, found that such dismissal did not relieve India and Pakistan from the obligation under Article 33 of the UN Charter that requires parties to seek a solution through any of the mechanisms specified in the said Article or other peaceful means of their own choice. The ICJ held that this obligation has merely been 'restated' in the Simla Agreement and the Lahore Declaration, and reminded India and Pakistan that they remain under such obligation flowing from the UN Charter.[60]

In any case, the Simla Agreement and the Lahore Declaration cannot be construed to preclude India from discharging its own obligation under the UN Charter to seek the resolution of the Kashmir issue through any peaceful means of its choice. And should they do, Article 103 of the UN Charter provides that '[i]n the event of a conflict between the obligations of the Members of the United Nations under the present Charter and their obligations under any other international agreement, their obligations under the present Charter shall prevail'. India would be well within its rights to make a unilateral reference of the Kashmir issue to the ICJ, limited to the propositions set out earlier.

To conclude, the first step towards unravelling the Kashmir knot is for New Delhi to make the reference to the ICJ as formulated above, with the hope that the findings of the ICJ will help change the national and international political discourse on the Kashmir issue. However, that is not enough to unravel the Kashmir knot. New Delhi still has to win the faith and confidence of the people of the PIS of J&K so that it can legitimately claim moral authority to be in the state. This second step to resolve the Kashmir issue will perhaps be more trying than the first, in light of how New Delhi has so far dealt with the part of the state with it, as discussed in the next three chapters.

Notes and References

1. S/PV 1088, pp. 5–7, M.C. Chagla (India), 5 February 1964.
2. Ibid., p 7.
3. S/PV 425, pp. 9–12, Mohammed Zafrullah Khan (Pakistan), 19 May 1949.
4. See S/PV 798, p. 10, Gunnar Jarring (Sweden), 29 October 1957.
5. See S/PV 801, p 34, Gunnar Jarring (Sweden), 13 November 1957.
6. S/PV 771, pp. 3–4, Urrutia (Colombia), 18 February 1957.
7. Ibid.
8. *Supra* Note 67, Chapter IX, pp. 7–8.
9. S/PV 769, p. 62, Krishna Menon (India), 15 February 1957.
10. *Supra* Note 87, Chapter VIII, p. 36.
11. S/PV 800, pp. 11–14, Krishna Menon (India), 11 November 1957.
12. Ibid.
13. Ibid.
14. Merills, J G. 1998. *International Dispute Settlement*, p. 158. Cambridge: Cambridge University Press.
15. Zaidi, Mubashir & Udayan Namboodiri. 2001. 'Way to peace is through Lahore, not UN: Annan', *Hindustan Times*, New Delhi, 12 March.
16. *Sunday Statesman*. 1994. 'Pakistan told to eschew terrorism', New Delhi, 30 October.
17. *Fisheries Jurisdiction (Federal Republic of Germany v Iceland)*, Merits Judgement, ICJ Reports 1974, 175.
18. Ibid., p. 181.
19. *Supra* Note 35, Chapter VI.
20. Ibid., p. 91.

21. Ibid.
22. Ibid., pp. 91–92. The UN has reiterated that acquisition of a territory may not be effected by the use or the threat of force. In its Resolution 2628 (XXX) of 4 November 1970, the UN General Assembly 're-affirm(ed) that the acquisition of territories by force is inadmissible', and that consequently, the occupied territories must be restored.
23. Ibid.
24. Ibid.
25. *Supra* Note 108, Chapter IX, p. 103.
26. Ibid.
27. Ibid., p. 18.
28. Ibid., p. 63.
29. Ibid., pp. 58, 61.
30. Ibid., p. 86.
31. Ibid., pp. 68–69.
32. Ibid., p. 111.
33. Ibid., p. 124.
34. Ibid., p. 108.
35. Ibid., pp. 108–110.
36. Ibid., pp. 132–133.
37. Ibid.
38. S/PV 1616, pp. 2–3, Jamil Baroody (Saudi Arabia), 16 December 1971.
39. S/PV 1611, pp. 18–19, Z.A. Bhutto (Pakistan), 12 December 1971. Also see S/PV 1613, p. 28, Z.A. Bhutto (Pakistan), 13 December 1971.
40. Oppenheim, L. 1992. *International Law*, 9th Ed. by Sir Robert Jenning and Sir Arthur Watts, pp. 393, 396. London: Longman Group UK Ltd.
41. *Phosphates in Morocco*: PCIJ, 1938, Series A/B, No. 74, 23.
42. *Supra* Note 14, p. 122.
43. Ibid.
44. See *Case concerning the Aerial incident of August 10, 1999 (Pakistan v India)*, Jurisdiction of the Court Judgement of June 21, 2000: ICJ Reports, 2000, p. 12 at 23.
45. See ibid., p. 40.
46. Ibid., p. 25.
47. Ibid.
48. Ibid., p. 23.
49. Ibid., pp. 20, 24.
50. Ibid., p. 21.
51. Ibid., p. 12.
52. Ibid., p. 61.
53. Ibid., p. 63.
54. *The Times of India*. 1999. 'Pakistan to blame, says India', New Delhi, 11 August.
55. See *Supra* Note 44, p. 63.
56. Ibid., pp. 29–33.
57. *Hindustan Times*. 2000. 'Sorabjee: Pak plan to globalise Kashmir issue nipped in bud', New Delhi, 26 June.
58. Ibid.
59. *The Times of India*. 2015. 'Indian can't move ICJ for 1965, 1971 POWs: Govt to SC', New Delhi, 2 September.
60. *Supra* Note 44, pp. 34–34.

XIII

The Article 370 Debate

It may be recalled that notwithstanding the accession of the PIS of J&K to the dominion of India, the ruler of the state had retained his sovereign powers over the state. The constitutional relationship between the state and the Union of India was still to be governed by the Instrument of Accession of 26 October 1947, in contrast to the relationship of all other princely Indian states with the dominion of India. It appears that, initially, New Delhi did honour this relationship. The state was, more or less, autonomous. Then started a process by which New Delhi effectively eroded the autonomy of the state and sought to rule the state reportedly with the aid of pliable, and often corrupt, regimes which was compounded by poor governance. In order to check Pakistan's proxy war, New Delhi complemented the coercive state laws with even more drastic penal legislation—laws which not only gave the security forces a licence to kill, but also provided a legal cover to shield them from prosecution. Few paused to consider the impact such laws would have if used by authorities to check popular resentment against the political vacuum, denial of basic needs and lack of administration. It is this process which was, to a large extent, responsible for the disillusionment of the Kashmiri populace and for its alienation from the world's largest democracy, and which created a fertile ground for militancy in the state. Let us examine this process in some detail.

Erosion of Article 370 of the Constitution of India

Article 370 of the Constitution of India permitted the state to have its own constitution as formulated by its own constituent assembly, which was to decide the constitutional relationship between the state and the Union of India. Indeed, the Constitution Bench decision of the Indian Supreme Court in *Prem Nath Kaul* held that the purpose of Article 370 was to limit the accession of the state to the dominion of India to the terms of the Instrument of Accession until the state Constituent Assembly determined the constitutional relationship between the two.[1]

On 20 March 1952, Mirza Mohammad Afzal Beig, the chairman of the Basic Principles Committee of the state Constituent Assembly, described the proposed constitutional relationship of the state with the Union of India as being 'an Autonomous Republic within the Indian Union'.[2] This relationship was later crystallized in the Delhi Agreement of 24 July 1952 between Sheikh Abdullah and Nehru. The Delhi Agreement gave the state a special status as compared with other states that had acceded to the Union of India. The preferential treatment primarily comprised the vesting of residuary powers of legislation in the state legislature, and not in the Union Parliament as in the case of the other states; permitting the state legislature to make laws conferring special rights and privileges upon the state subjects and allowing the state to have its own flag in addition to the Union flag.[3] Further, the Sadar-i-Riyasat, equivalent to the Governor in other states, was to be elected by the state legislature itself, rather than being appointed by the President of India on the advice of the Government of India. Again, Article 352 of the Constitution of India, which empowers the President of India to proclaim a general emergency, would apply to the state with the modification that it would apply 'in regard to internal disturbance at the request or with the concurrence of the Government of the State'.[4]

The Delhi Agreement was released by Nehru at a press conference in Delhi on 26 July 1952.[5] The Indian Parliament ratified the Delhi Agreement on 7 August 1952 while the state Constituent Assembly ratified the Delhi Agreement on 21 August 1952.[6]

It may be recalled that it was the persistent failure of New Delhi to stand by the PIS of J&K that had unconditionally acceded to it, which led to a sense of frustration and disillusionment in the state towards New Delhi, with Sheikh Abdullah eventually expressing the view that the state still had the option to cede to India, Pakistan or remain independent. It was following the arrest of Sheikh Abdullah on 8 August 1953 in the circumstances referred to earlier that New Delhi began to encroach upon the autonomy of the state.

Broadly speaking, Article 370 of the Constitution of India mandates that the Indian Parliament will not have the power to make laws for the PIS of J&K on a matter beyond the subjects specified in the Instrument of Accession, unless and until the President of India (the formal head of the executive) obtained the 'concurrence' of the state government to permit the

Indian Parliament to legislate on such matter. The idea was to restrain New Delhi from dealing with matters of the state not ceded to the dominion of India and to enable the state to be governed by its own constitution. New Delhi, however, used this very provision to pass a series of Presidential orders and thereby to apply through successive executive action almost the entire Constitution of India to the state. New Delhi's defence that such application was with the 'concurrence' of the regimes in the state, though technically correct, misses the point, particularly in light of an unenviable history of rigged elections in the state.[7] B.K. Nehru, who was sworn in as the Governor of the state on 26 February 1981, writes that:[8]

> From 1953 to 1977, Chief Ministers of that State had been nominees of Delhi. Their appointment to that post was legitimatised by holding of farcical and totally rigged elections in which the Congress Party led Delhi's nominee was elected by huge majorities.

Article 370 was meant to preserve the autonomy of the state, whose sovereign ruler had chosen not to adopt the Constitution of India in its entirety, and had instead expressly sought to retain his sovereignty over the state. The effect of the Presidential orders issued by New Delhi under Article 370(1) of the Constitution of India was exactly the opposite.

Interestingly, the framers of the Constitution of India might not have even contemplated that New Delhi (through the President of India) could issue successive executive orders under Article 370(1) of the Constitution of India. At least, the then President of India, Rajendra Prasad, who had presided over the Constituent Assembly of India, and Gopalaswami Ayyangar, who had drafted Article 370 (draft Article 306A), did not think that the President of India could.

Rajendra Prasad questioned, in his Note of 6 September 1952, 'the competence of the President to have repeated recourse to the extraordinary powers conferred on him by Article 370' and noted that 'any provision authorizing the executive government to make amendments in the Constitution' was an incongruity.[9] After all, it is a legislative function to amend a constitution, and, for the rest of the country, the Constitution of India vests such power in Parliament and not in the executive. Prasad, while agreeing with Ayyangar, stated that he had 'little doubt' that 'the intention is that the power [under Article 370(1)] is to be exercised only once, for then alone would it be possible to determine with precision which particular provisions should be excepted and which modified'.[10]

The issue as to whether the President of India could exercise his power under Article 370(1) of the Constitution of India from time to time was considered by the Constitution Bench of the Indian Supreme Court in *Sampat Prakash*.[11] Part III of the Constitution of India guarantees certain fundamental rights to the people of India, with Article 13 mandating that any law inconsistent with, or in contravention of, such fundamental rights will be void to the extent of such inconsistency or contravention. This case related to the immunity granted to the preventive laws in the PIS of J&K with India from being challenged on the ground of their being inconsistent with the guaranteed fundamental rights. The President of India, by successive executive orders under Article 370(1), had extended the period of such immunity from 'five years' under the Constitution (Application to Jammu and Kashmir) Order of 1954 to 'ten years' under the Constitution (Application to Jammu and Kashmir) Second Amendment Order of 1959 to 'fifteen years' under the Constitution (Application to Jammu and Kashmir) Amendment Order of 1964. The question arose as to whether the President could take repeated recourse to Article 370(1) to make such modifications. Regrettably, the Supreme Court said he could. The Court opined that the 'legislative history' of this article indicated that the Constituent Assembly framing the Constitution of India 'preferred' to confer on the President the power to apply the various provisions of the Constitution with exceptions and modifications, in view of the special circumstances prevailing in the state.[12] The Court reasoned that 'the President would have to take into account the situation existing in the State when applying a provision of the Constitution and such situations could arise from time to time' and that there 'was clearly the possibility that, when applying a particular provision, the situation might demand an exception or modification of the provision applied; but subsequent changes in the situation might justify the rescinding of those modifications or exceptions'.[13] This, the Court concluded, 'could only be brought about by conferring on the President the power of making orders from time to time under Art. 370'.[14]

The above reasoning of the Indian Supreme Court in *Sampat Prakash* is totally inconsistent with the purpose for which Article 370 was framed by the Constitution-makers, as noted by the earlier Constitution Bench decision of the Supreme Court itself in *Prem Nath Kaul*—namely, to limit the accession of the state to the dominion of India to the terms of the Instrument of Accession until the state Constituent Assembly determined the constitutional relationship between the state and the Union of India.[15] Indeed, the Supreme Court failed to appreciate that its interpretation of the powers of the President of India under clause (1) of Article 370 of the Constitution of India nullifies the protection accorded to the state under clause (3) of Article 370 against encroachment upon its autonomy by New Delhi. Surprisingly,

Sampat Prakash was decided by the Supreme Court without reference to its earlier decision in *Prem Nath Kaul*, though one of the judges was common in both the cases.

Not only did New Delhi take repeated recourse to Article 370(1) of the Constitution of India to apply to the PIS of J&K almost the entire Constitution of India, but it also chose to apply to the state certain provisions of the Constitution of India with substantial modifications. What made matters worse was that these substantial modifications were made by New Delhi in exercise of its executive power, with the concurrence of reportedly pliant regimes in the state. In other words, New Delhi bypassed its own Parliament in applying drastically amended laws to the state. An earlier decision of the Indian Supreme Court in 1961 in *Puranlal Lakhanpal*,[16] which had ruled that the widest interpretation be given to the term 'modification' in Article 370(1), came in handy in emasculating the constitutional protection granted to the PIS of J&K.

As a result, the state did get a 'special status', though certainly not of an 'autonomous republic' within the Union of India. Rather, it found itself at the other end of the spectrum, with mere executive directions by New Delhi deciding its fate.

Mohd. Maqbool Damnoo[17] illustrates this position. It may be recalled that under the Delhi Agreement, the Sadar-i-Riyasat was to be the head of state and was to be elected by the state legislature itself, instead of a Governor appointed by the President of India on the advice of the Government of India. Pursuant to the state Constituent Assembly resolution, New Delhi issued an order under Article 370 of the Constitution of India on 15 November 1952 to reflect this position. However, through the Constitution (Application to Jammu and Kashmir) Sixth Amendment Order of 1965, New Delhi used its executive powers to replace the Sadar-i-Riyasat of the state with a Governor who was to be appointed by the President of India on the advice of the Government of India. This action of New Delhi was questioned before the Indian Supreme Court in *Mohd. Maqbool Damnoo*. The Constitution Bench of the Supreme Court had an answer that defied comprehension. The Court held that it 'is true that the Governor is not elected as was the Sadar-i-Riyasat, but the mode of appointment would not make him any the less a successor to Sadar-i-Riyasat' as both are 'heads of State', and that since the Governor was the 'successor' of the Sadar-i-Riyasat, he was entitled to exercise all the powers of the Sadar-i-Riyasat.[18]

Given that Article 370 of the Constitution of India was intended as a device to continue the constitutional relationship between the state and the dominion of India till the state Constituent Assembly, and not New Delhi, further defined that relationship, it is regrettable that the Supreme Court did not feel that there was anything illegal or improper about New Delhi replacing the elected head of the state by its own appointee. The Supreme Court overlooked its own ruling in *Madhav Rao* wherein it had emphasized the general proposition that 'the negotiations, the assurances given by leading statesmen, and the terms of the covenants and agreements were certainly not intended to be an exercise in futility'.[19] The Court had held that the executive power vested in the President of India was 'plainly coupled with a duty—a duty to maintain the constitutional scheme and the sanctity of the solemn agreements entered into by the predecessor of the Union of India, which are accepted, recognised and incorporated in the Constitution'.[20] Interestingly, a single judge of the Jammu and Kashmir High Court took the view in December 2015 that the replacement of an elected Sadar-i-Riyasat with New Delhi's appointed Governor was unconstitutional, inasmuch as 'the "elective" status of the head of state was an important attribute of the constitutional autonomy enjoyed by the state, a part of the "Basic Framework" of the state constitution'.[21] It is another matter that within days, the Division Bench of the same High Court stayed this judgement on 1 January 2016.[22]

Futility of Article 370 of the Constitution of India

The judicial sanction accorded to the dilution of Article 370 of the Constitution of India rendered it toothless to check extension of New Delhi's jurisdiction over the state on matters not covered either by the Instrument of Accession or otherwise ceded by the state, even after the state Constituent Assembly had been convened and dispersed.

Article 368 of the Constitution of India mandates that a constitutional amendment in relation to states in India would require a two-thirds vote of both Houses of Parliament, along with ratification by one half of the states. For the PIS of J&K, executive orders under Article 370 have sufficed to bring about constitutional amendments till date. Sukumar Muralidharan[23] points out that as many as 42 orders were issued by the President of India under Article 370(1) of the Constitution of India, between 1954 and 1986, applying central legislation to the state. Jagmohan quotes M.C. Chagla, the then Indian Education Minister, as having observed in December 1964 that '[t]hrough Article 370, the whole of the Indian Constitution can be applied to Jammu and Kashmir'.[24] Noorani asserts that '[e]ventually 94 of the 97 entries in the Union List were extended to Kashmir, as were 260 of the 395 Articles of the Constitution of India—in each case with the "concurrence" of the state government, which had no authority to accord the concurrence in the absence of the constituent assembly'.[25]

K.R. Malkhani records that the provisions of Articles 356 and 357 of the Constitution of India were applied to the state in 1964, without even a reference to the state government, in contravention of Article 370.[26] Article 356 provides for the dismissal of the state government by New Delhi and imposition of President's rule upon proclamation of an Emergency under Article 352 of the Constitution of India, while Article 357 enables Parliament and the President to exercise state legislative power during such Emergency. Further, since the Sadar-i-Riyasat has been replaced as the head of state by New Delhi's appointed Governor, the state can be ruled directly by New Delhi also through Section 92 of the Constitution of Jammu and Kashmir of 1957 which provides for Governor's rule, with the concurrence of the President of India on the aid and advice of the Union Cabinet, and not Parliamentary ratification.[27] Such Central rule could last for six months, while conferring full legislative powers on the Governor.

Noorani further records that Article 370 was used freely not only to amend the Constitution of India in its application to the state, but also the state Constitution—on 23 July 1975 'an Order was made debarring the state legislature from amending the state Constitution on matters in respect of the Governor, the Election Commission and even "the composition" of the Upper House, the Legislative Council'.[28]

A.C. Bose agrees that 'Article 370 has never stood in the way of the Government of India behaving with or in this State as it liked'.[29] Indeed, G.L. Nanda, the then Indian Home Minister, stated in the Lok Sabha on 4 December 1964 that Article 370 was 'not a wall or a mountain but a tunnel'[30] and that[31] 'it is through this tunnel that a good deal of traffic has already passed and more will. Article 370, whether you keep it or not, has been completely emptied of its contents. Nothing has been left in it'.

The emasculated Delhi Agreement of 1952 was followed by the Sheikh Abdullah–Indira Gandhi Accord of 1975 to restore a semblance of autonomy to the state. This Accord, too, was not honoured by New Delhi. The consistent demand in Kashmir has, accordingly, been the restoration of the sanctity of Article 370 of the Constitution of India and relegation of the state to its pre-1953 status.

Interestingly, commentators on the Kashmir issue are divided on whether the sanctity of Article 370 of the Constitution of India ought to be restored or whether Article 370 should be abrogated.

At one end of the spectrum are commentators who share the view that there is nothing sinister about Article 370. Several commentators, like Wajahat Habibullah[32] and Ajit Bhattacharjea,[33] moot the grant of autonomy to the state to the degree it enjoyed at the time of accession. B.G. Verghese agrees that such dispensations and exceptions are perfectly normal in a pluralist society.[34] Further, the Jammu and Kashmir High Court took the view in October 2015 that Article 370, though titled as 'Temporary Provision' in the Constitution of India, has assumed a place of permanence in the Constitution, reasoning that[35] '[i]t is beyond amendment, repeal or abrogation in as much as the Constituent Assembly of the state before its dissolution did not recommend its amendment or repeal'.

Jagmohan, former Governor of the state, however, asserts that Article 370 has become 'an instrument of exploitation in the hands of the ruling political elites and other vested interests in bureaucracy, business, the judiciary and bar' and that 'the politicians, the richer class have found it convenient to amass wealth and not allow healthy financial legislation to come to the State'.[36] Jagmohan opines that quite a few of the current problems in the state are 'due to the insufficiency, and not the surfeit, of powers in the Central Government'.[37] He further points out that the Union of India provides the entire funds for the state's Five-Year Plans, and also for a substantial part of the non-plan expenditure, and that if New Delhi was to restrict itself to external affairs, defence and communications, the state would not be able to survive. Tavleen Singh agrees that the state's special category status makes it India's 'most pampered state', being 'entitled to more Central assistance than other states and gets ninety per cent of it as grants whereas other states are not entitled to more than thirty per cent as grants'.[38] She contends that there 'is no poverty in Kashmir and this is something other Indians notice'.[39]

Then there are Kashmiri Pandits who advocate the abrogation of Article 370. The Hindu right-wing BJP hardliners, as also some strategic analysts, share this view, reasoning that the special status of the state merely serves to keep alive the historical dispute. The Rashtriya Swayamsevak Sangh (RSS) has consistently demanded that Article 370 be scrapped, contending that it was 'temporarily intended', and that it has served its purpose.[40] Indeed, in 1996, the then Indian Prime Minister and BJP leader, Atal Bihari Vajpayee, had himself reportedly sought the abrogation of Article 370, stating that it had outlived its utility and lost its relevance.[41] However, post the state assembly elections in 2015, the BJP entered into a political alliance with the state's People's Democratic Party (PDP) to form the state government, with a promise to maintain the present constitutional status of the state.[42]

Further, there is no consensus even within the state with regard to the restoration of the sanctity of Article 370 of the Constitution by returning to the pre-1953 status. Keeping aside the territory of the PIS of J&K under Pakistan's occupation, it may be recalled that the state has three ethnic–geographical regions: a Dogra Hindu-majority Jammu, a Muslim-majority Kashmir and a Buddhist-majority Ladakh. In contrast to the Kashmir Valley, where Hindus are less than one-fourth of the population, Jammu's population consists of nearly two-third Hindus, with the Muslims roughly constituting the other third.[43] Hari Om notes that while the demands of the Kashmir Valley range from azadi to the pre-1953 political set-up, Jammu and Ladakh clamour for 'full integration with India' and 'application of the Indian Constitution *in toto*'.[44] Balraj Puri points out that while Kashmiris begrudge the lack of human rights, and resent the farcical holding of elections that do not allow them to elect their true representatives, the people of Jammu complain that political power is concentrated in the hands of the Kashmiri leadership, while the Dogris rue the fact that their language is not recognized.[45] Each of the three regions, thus, has a varying demographic composition, with strong regional identities. Commentators plead that the demand in Jammu for statehood[46] and the movement in Ladakh for Union Territory status[47] have to be viewed in the context of the uneven development of the three regions in the state, and particularly of the rough treatment that Jammu and Ladakh have received at the hands of successive state governments.[48]

The Farooq Abdullah government, soon after assuming office in the state in 1996, set up a committee on 29 November 1996, under the chairmanship of Karan Singh, the former Yuvraj of the state, to 'examine and recommend measures for the restoration of autonomy to the State of Jammu & Kashmir consistent with the Instrument of Accession, the Constitution Application Order, 1950 and the Delhi Agreement of 1952' and to 'examine and recommend safeguards that be regarded necessary for incorporation in the Union/State Constitution to ensure that the Constitutional arrangement that is finally evolved in pursuance of the recommendations of this Committee is inviolable'.[49]

Abdullah declared that the State Autonomy Committee (SAC) would prepare the report on autonomy for the state on the premise that the accession of the state to India was final and irrevocable, and that the report would form the basis for negotiations between his government and New Delhi.[50] He asserted that 'the autonomy we want is between the parameters, between the time of accession in 1950 and the Sheikh Abdullah–Indira Gandhi accord in 1975'.[51]

The SAC report, which dealt with the Centre–state relations, sought to retain autonomy for the state as envisaged by Article 370 of the Constitution of India.[52] As the state Constituent Assembly had ceased to exist without recommending the abrogation of Article 370, the SAC report sought to accord permanence to Article 370 by proposing that the term 'temporary' be deleted from the title of Part XXI and the heading of Article 370 of the Constitution of India.[53] The SAC report asserted that the state should return to its pre-1953 status, and all orders made by the President of India, which were not in conformity with the Constitution (Application to Jammu and Kashmir) Order of 1950, and the terms of the Delhi Agreement of 1952, be repealed; that is, all matters except for defence, external affairs and communications were to go.[54]

The SAC report found opposition within the state itself, leading to widespread agitation in Jammu and Ladakh.[55] The BJP members in the state legislative assembly reportedly termed the SAC report as 'secessionist'.[56] The National Conference members, on their part, were peeved with New Delhi for failing to honour its commitments and threatened that if New Delhi did not heed to their demands, the country 'could face disintegration like the Soviet Union'.[57] Given the two-third majority of the National Conference in the state legislative assembly, it was inevitable that the recommendations of the SAC report were adopted on 26 June 2000.[58] However, the Indian Home Ministry promptly discounted the state resolution on the SAC report on 26 June 2000 itself.[59] Four days later, the then Indian Prime Minister Atal Bihari Vajpayee declared that the issue of granting autonomy to the state would be considered in accordance with the Constitution of India, while at the same time reassuring the country that the state did not want to secede from India.[60]

On 4 July 2000, the Indian Cabinet dismissed the state resolution endorsing the SAC report, stating that it would set the clock back,[61] and that the restoration of the pre-1953 status 'would reverse the natural process of harmonising the aspirations of the people with the integrity of the nation'.[62] The Union Cabinet declared that there was, nevertheless, a clear case for the devolution of more financial and administrative powers to the state, and that steps would be taken to harmonize relations with the state in light of the report of the Sarkaria Commission, which had been constituted in 1983 by New Delhi to examine the balance of power between the Government of India and the state governments under a quasi-federal Constitution of India.[63]

Since then, Srinagar and New Delhi have been talking in terms of 'devolution' of more financial and administrative powers to the state rather than 'autonomy'.[64] Notably, New Delhi again indicated after the 2001 Agra Summit between India and Pakistan that while the autonomy resolution could not be accepted, it was 'willing to consider according special powers to the State if there was a necessity as part of the process of devolution of power to the States'.[65]

The Hurriyat, too, was quick to dismiss the autonomy proposal. Syed Ali Shah Geelani reportedly declared that no autonomy package proposed by the state government would work without involving Pakistan, and that 'Pakistan can't be ignored' as it 'is a party to the dispute as it holds one-third territory of Kashmir'[66]—a stand that it takes till date.

The state government had, along with the constitution of the SAC in 1996, constituted another committee, known as the Regional Autonomy Committee (RAC), which, as the name suggests, was to study the issue of autonomy within the state. The RAC aimed to tackle the concerns of Jammu and Ladakh, noted above, regarding the 'hegemony' of the Kashmir Valley. The RAC report released in April 1999 sought to decentralize political and economic power by reconstituting the state's existing three divisions of Kashmir, Jammu and Ladakh into eight new administrative provinces, on the ground that the present divisions were hampering democratic participation at the grass-roots level.[67] The RAC report was criticized for dividing the state along communal lines. Balraj Puri asserted that under the guise of a common ethno-linguistic character, all Muslim-majority areas in Jammu were being sought to be detached from Jammu.[68] Puri argued that the RAC report overlooked the far greater variation within each of the proposed regions, thereby threatening the 5,000-year-old 'Kashmiriat'—the syncretic fusion of Islam, Hinduism and Sikhism in a composite culture. This, he contended, undermined the secular nature of the state and would make India susceptible to a more fundamentalist brand of Islam.[69] The former Yuvraj, Karan Singh, too, criticized the RAC report as a 'disingenuous attempt' to divide Jammu into three regions along religious lines and communal considerations.[70]

Yet other commentators suggest cantonization and sub-cantonization, along the lines of the Swiss model, in accordance with the composition of the population in different areas. M.P. Khosla reasons that such structural changes would improve the political environment and decentralize administration, through a network of effective local authorities with funds for developmental schemes administered by directly elected leaders.[71]

Closely linked to the issue of such division of the state is the demand for the trifurcation of the state.[72] Jammu Mukti Morcha (JMM), which raised the demand for trifurcation on 2 March 1990, opined that the 'union of Jammu, Kashmir and Ladakh is an unnatural wedlock'.[73] The JMM argued

that from the very beginning Jammu had been denied its due share in the
state legislature, had less representatives than Kashmir in the Lok Sabha and
was poorly represented in the state secretariat. This was despite Jammu having
equal, if not more, population than Kashmir and contributing 70 per cent of
the state's revenue. JMM alleged discrimination against Jammu in the selec-
tion of students for professional colleges, in recruitment to government jobs
and in the establishment of new institutions. JMM claimed that the 'grant
of autonomy will not solve the problem' and will instead 'lead to greater discontent and deepen the resentment of Jammuites and Ladakhis towards the
Kashmiri hegemony'.[74] Reports state that the RSS also demanded the trifurcation of the state, asserting that at least Jammu and Ladakh, which wished to
integrate fully into the Union of India, should be allowed to do so.[75]

In response, the editorial of the national daily *Hindustan Times* dismissed
the claim of trifurcation as being 'no different from the argument which
the pre-Partition Muslim League had offered in support of its demand of
Partition'.[76] Balraj Puri opined that the proposal of the trifurcation of the
state 'ignores the reality of regional, ethnic and cultural identities which
cuts across religious identities'.[77] Prem Shankar Jha took the view that the
trifurcation of the state would undermine 'Kashmiriat', which linked the
state to a secular India.[78] Amitabh Mattoo reasoned that trifurcation 'could
lead to violent social disruptions in the state and create a communal polari-
sation that would not just irretrievably destroy the cultural and social fabric
of the state' but would 'have dire consequences for communal relations in
the rest of India'.[79]

The then Indian Home Minister L.K. Advani stated in Parliament on
25 June 2000 that New Delhi was opposed to the division of the state and,
that too, along religious lines,[80] and reiterated this on 22 October 2000
in Srinagar.[81] On 20 November 2000, Advani dismissed the RSS-backed
proposal of the trifurcation of the state along ethnic lines, saying that it
was 'a remedy worse than the disease'.[82] On 27 February 2001, the then
Parliamentary Affairs Minister Pramod Mahajan ruled out trifurcation while
stating in Parliament that 'Jammu and Ladakh are inseparable parts of the
Jammu and Kashmir state'.[83] The state has not been trifurcated till date.

Too Little, Too Late

In the acrimonious debate for and against autonomy, it has been overlooked
that while the denial of autonomy may have been the main cause for the
alienation of the people of the state prior to 1989, it hardly seems to be

their priority now. Reports[84] reveal that people would rather talk about their dry fields, the lack of water to irrigate them, young boys being picked up by the security forces, and custody deaths. The common Kashmiri was quoted as asking whether autonomy meant that 'we can walk home in night without being stopped by security forces or we will get more jobs or will militancy end'.[85] In such circumstances, the autonomy proposal is too little, too late to reverse by itself the alienation of the people; rather, it merely serves as an index of New Delhi's bona fides. The outright rejection by the Indian Cabinet of the state resolution on autonomy merely reinforced the 'I told you so' syndrome in the Kashmir Valley.[86]

I believe that while the return of the state to the pre-1953 status may be constitutionally warranted, New Delhi simply cannot afford such a situation today, unless it first makes the legal reference to the ICJ to confirm, as it were, its title deed to the state and creates a suitable political climate for restoration of autonomy. The reason for this is the reported large-scale subversion from within, as discussed in the next chapter. The reported infiltration of militants in the institutions of the state will simply lead to an 'autonomous' state being taken over by Pakistan-sponsored jihadis. A case in point is that of East Pakistan, now Bangladesh. As Zulfikar Ali Bhutto (Pakistan) himself stated before the UNSC on 12 December 1971, the demand of the Awami League in the December 1970 elections was for autonomy and not secession, but suddenly, after winning the election, this demand for autonomy was converted into a demand for secession.[87] Bhutto wryly pointed out that 'the line between maximum autonomy and secession can be a thin one' and that through 'international manipulation and other factors, a struggle for autonomy was converted into a struggle for secession'.[88]

India cannot even think of taking the risk, particularly since it has not brought about a change in the demographic profile of the Kashmir Valley, unlike what Israel reportedly did in Arab-dominated territory and what Pakistan has reportedly done in the territory of the PIS of J&K it occupies.[89] As a result, irrespective of the role of New Delhi in creating the current mess in the state, New Delhi today is not in a position to confer upon the state the autonomy promised in terms of the Instrument of Accession of 26 October 1947, or in Article 370 of the Constitution of India, or in the Delhi Agreement of 1952, or even in the Sheikh Abdullah-Indira Gandhi Accord of 1975—the ground realities in the state being completely different from what they were when the promises were made. Let us now examine these ground realities in the territory of the PIS of J&K with India, which New Delhi would have to grapple with before it is even in a position to claim moral authority in the state.

Notes and References

1. *Supra* Note 8, Chapter IV.
2. Cited in *Supra* Note 36, Chapter IV, p. 144.
3. See *The Times of India*. 2000. 'The J-K pact facts', New Delhi, 22 June.
4. Ibid.
5. *Supra* Note 36, Chapter IV, p. 145.
6. Ibid.
7. See Maheshwari, Anil. 1996. 'A new beginning', *Hindustan Times*, New Delhi, 26 May.
8. Nehru, B.K. 1997. *Nice Guys Finish Second*, pp. 614–615.New Delhi: Viking/Penguin Books.
9. *Supra* Note 16, Chapter IV, p. 122.
10. Ibid. Also see *Supra* Note 12, Chapter IV, p. 509.
11. *Sampat Prakash v Jammu and Kashmir State:* (1969) 2 SCR 365.
12. Ibid., p. 375.
13. Ibid.
14. Ibid., p. 376.
15. See *Supra* Note 8, Chapter IV.
16. *Puranlal Lakhanpal v. President of India:* AIR 1961 SC 1519 at 1521.
17. *Mohd. Maqbool Damnoo v State of Jammu and Kashmir:* AIR 1972 SC 963.
18. Ibid., p. 969.
19. *Supra* Note 5, Chapter I, p. 81.
20. Ibid., p. 82.
21. *The Indian Express*, 2015. 'Changing Sadr-e-Riyasat to Governor goes against J&K constitution : HC', New Delhi, 29 December.
22. Sharma, Arun. 2016. 'J&K High Court stays order to hoist state flag on buildings', *The Indian Express*, New Delhi, 2 January.
23. Muralidharan, Sukumar. 2000. 'From demand to dialogue', *Frontline*, 4 August, p. 23. Chennai: Kasturi & Sons, Ltd.
24. Jagmohan. 1993. *My Frozen Turbulence in Kashmir*, p. 252. New Delhi: Allied Publishers.
25. *Supra* Note 3, Chapter V, p. 61.
26. Malkani, K. R. 1989. 'Why Article 370 must go?', *The Indian Express*, New Delhi, 10 June.
27. *Supra* Note 12, Chapter IV, p. 624.
28. Noorani, A. G. 2000. 'Article 370: Law and politics', *Frontline*, 29 September, p. 92. Chennai: Kasturi & Sons, Ltd.
29. Bose, A.C. 1996. 'Fragmentation of J&K and Article 370', in *Supra* Note 34, Chapter IV, p. 128.
30. Extracted in *Supra* Note 3, Chapter V, p. 61.
31. Ibid.
32. *Hindustan Times*. 2000. 'Autonomy is the only way to resolve the Kashmir crisis', New Delhi, 28 August.
33. Bhattacharjea, Ajit. 1991. 'Kashmir policy: The case for reconsideration', *The Indian Express*, New Delhi, 6 August.
34. Verghese, B. G. 1992. 'Ekta Yatra and Mistaken notion on Article 370', *The Indian Express*, New Delhi, 17 June; Verghese, B. G. 1995. 'Form and content', *The Indian Express*, New Delhi, 28 May.

35. *The Times of India*. 2015. '"Article 370 is permanent", rules J&K HC', New Delhi, 13 October.

36. *Supra* Note 24, pp. 230–231.

37. Jagmohan. 1996. 'Kashmir's autonomy bogey', *The Indian Express*, New Delhi, 8 October.

38. *Supra* Note 31, Chapter IV, p. 236.

39. Ibid.

40. Kaul, Sumer. 1998. 'A people disowned', *Hindustan Times*, New Delhi 19 February.

41. *The Indian Express*. 1996. 'Art 370 has lost relevance: BJP', New Delhi, 1 July.

42. 'Jammu and Kashmir Government Formation: BJP and PDP Reach Consensus on Article 370, AFSPA, Say Sources'. Available online at http://www.ndtv.com/india-news/jammu-and-kashmir-government-formation-bjp-and-pdp-reach-consensus-on-article-370-afspa-say-sources-741324 (downloaded on 30 August 2015); 'Article 370 cannot be touched, says Mehbooba Mufti'. Available online at http://www.livemint.com/Politics/DgeF86M3X7mxxJ7VEZpHoM/Jammu-and-Kashmir-Article-370-cannot-be-touched-says-Mehbo.html (downloaded on 30 August 2015).

43. Panda, Jaya Ram. 1995. 'Ethnicity and Terrorism', in B P Singh Sehgal, *Global Terrorism: Socio-Politico and Legal Dimensions*, p. 170. New Delhi: Deep & Deep Publications.

44. Om, Hari. 1992. 'Getting back to Delhi agreement', *Hindustan Times*, New Delhi, 15 June.

45. *The Times of India*. 1997. 'Intra-regional dialogue is needed in J&K: Balraj Puri', New Delhi, 4 May.

46. See *Supra* Note 43, p. 175.

47. Hazra, Indrajit. 2001. 'Those with guns are heard, we aren't, Ladakhis tell Pant', *Hindustan Times*, New Delhi, 31 May.

48. *The Indian Express*. 1999. 'The regional riddle', New Delhi, 14 April.

49. *The Times of India*. 1997. 'Jammu & Kashmir State Autonomy Committee Notification', New Delhi, 1 January.

50. *The Indian Express*. 1996. 'Karan Singh to head panel on J&K autonomy', New Delhi, 14 October.

51. Ibid.

52. *Hindustan Times*. 2000. 'Proposals set alarm bells ringing', New Delhi, 11 February; *The Times of India*. 2000. 'Temporary, yes but only to preserve J&K's autonomy', New Delhi, 12 July.

53. Ibid.

54. Singh, Karan. 2000. 'Time to regain Paradise', *Hindustan Times*, New Delhi, 31 July; *The Indian Express*. 1999. 'Give J-K more powers, revamp links with Centre: Farooq Panel', New Delhi, 16 April.

55. *Hindustan Times*. 2000. 'Centre urged not to accept J&K Govt.'s report on autonomy', New Delhi, 4 February; *Hindustan Times*. 2000. 'BJP, NC on collision course over autonomy', New Delhi, 8 February; *Hindustan Times*. 2000. 'Jammu bandh', New Delhi, 7 November.

56. *Hindustan Times*. 2000. 'War of words at the autonomy debate', New Delhi, 28 February.

57. Ibid.

58. *The Times of India*. 2000. 'J&K thumps nose at Centre', New Delhi, 27 June.

59. *The Times of India*. 2000. 'Home Ministry discounts passing of J-K autonomy Bill', New Delhi, 27 June.

60. *The Times of India*. 2000. 'Don't think J&K is going to secede – PM', New Delhi, 1 July.

61. *The Times of India.* 2000. 'Cabinet spikes J&K autonomy proposal', New Delhi, 5 July; *Hindustan Times.* 2000. 'Cabinet stresses devolution', New Delhi, 5 July.

62. *Hindustan Times.* 2000. 'Cabinet rejects autonomy, says no setting clock back', New Delhi, 5 July.

63. *Supra* Note 61.

64. *The Times of India.* 2000. 'Devolution, not autonomy, is the mantra now', New Delhi, 13 July.

65. *Hindustan Times.* 2001. 'Advani willing to consider special powers for Kashmir', New Delhi, 26 July.

66. *Hindustan Times.* 2000. 'Hurriyat leader denies deal with Govt.', New Delhi, 6 April.

67. *The Indian Express.* 1999. 'Slice J-K into 8 provinces—says panel', New Delhi, 19 April.

68. Puri, Balraj. 2000. 'Regional autonomy', *The Times of India,* New Delhi, 8 May.

69. Ibid.

70. Singh, Karan. 2000. 'J&K—The way forward', *Hindustan Times,* New Delhi, 9 February.

71. Khosla, M. P. 1993. 'Kashmir problem: Winning people back', *Hindustan Times,* New Delhi, 26 April.

72. Joshi, Arun. 2001. 'Move to put J&K trifurcation on peace talks agenda', *Hindustan Times,* New Delhi, 9 May.

73. *The Times of India.* 2000. 'The Kashmir triangle', New Delhi, 7 October.

74. Ibid.

75. *The Times of India.* 2000. 'RSS floats idea of trifurcation', New Delhi, 10 August.

76. *Hindustan Times.* 2000. 'Pernicious plan', New Delhi, 9 October.

77. Puri, Balraj. 2001. 'A state divided', *The Times of India,* New Delhi, 30 January.

78. Jha, Prem Shankar. 2000. 'Secularism betrayal', *Hindustan Times,* New Delhi, 14 July.

79. Mattoo, Amitabh. 2000. 'Divide and rule', *The Times of India,* New Delhi, 6 October.

80. *Hindustan Times.* 2000. 'Advani rules out trifurcation of J&K', New Delhi, 26 June.

81. *The Times of India.* 2000. 'When Advani says no to RSS', New Delhi, 23 October.

82. *Hindustan Times.* 2000. 'Home Ministry concerned over security implications', New Delhi, 21 November.

83. *The Times of India.* 2001. 'No plan to split up J&K, says Mahajan', New Delhi, 28 February.

84. *Hindustan Times.* 2000. 'Autonomy not priority of Valley residents', New Delhi, 19 July.

85. Ibid.

86. *Hindustan Times.* 2000. 'Farooq sitting pretty', New Delhi, 6 December.

87. S/PV 1611 at p. 20, Z.A. Bhutto (Pakistan), 12 December 1971.

88. Ibid.

89. Ramchandran, Rajesh. 2000. 'Hobson's choice', *Hindustan Times,* New Delhi, 26 March.

XIV

Grappling with the Ground Realities

The political vacuum in the PIS of J&K with India over the years has been well documented. With the arrest of Sheikh Abdullah in 1953, New Delhi reportedly installed pliant regimes in the state, which succeeded in alienating the idealistic youth and in creating an extremely corrupt and spineless political elite.[1] Prolonged incarceration in jail from 8 August 1953 to 8 April 1964, and India's decisive victory in the 1971 Indo-Pakistan war are believed to have made Sheikh Abdullah realize the virtues of making peace with New Delhi. As a prelude to his being restored to office in 1975, he, however, sought a review of the erosion of autonomy of the state. Thus, the Sheikh Abdullah–Indira Gandhi Accord of 1975.

Elections were held in the PIS of J&K with India in 1977. The people voted enthusiastically for Sheikh Abdullah. Such vote was viewed as a popular mandate for the Sheikh Abdullah–Indira Gandhi Accord of 1975, and rendered the demand for a plebiscite irrelevant.[2] Zafar Mehraj notes that after the Accord, the separatist movement in the state declined, and only gained momentum with the death of Sheikh Abdullah on 7 September 1982.[3]

March 1987 Elections

Almost all commentators refer to the March 1987 state assembly elections as being responsible for the heightened militancy in the state. Few elections in India are said to have been so blatantly and shamelessly rigged as the March 1987 elections in the state, which broke the faith of even the staunchest pro-India Kashmiris in the institution of Indian democracy. In fact, several militant leaders active in the state were candidates in the 1987 elections and were said to have been arbitrarily arrested and tortured upon 'defeat'.[4] Noorani records that '[a]ll those who later spearheaded the insurgency had participated in the electoral process in some capacity or the other'.[5]

The backlash of the rigged elections of 1987 saw militants occupying the centre stage in the state. New Delhi simply did not bother to formulate a policy to address the legitimate grievances of the local populace, which at that time were, as listed by Inder Mohan, the erosion of the right to autonomy, unemployment of the educated youth, lack of industrial development despite local potential, incompetent and corrupt administration, non-remunerative agricultural economy, and the growing political awareness sharpened by the state lawlessness.[6] Hence, when the JKLF gave a call for azadi (in contradistinction to merger with Pakistan) in 1989, many more people in the state endorsed it than in the past. This was the moment that Pakistan had been waiting for; it happily encouraged the JKLF, which was then the major militant group in the state.

Then came the abduction by the JKLF of 23-year-old Rubaiya, daughter of the then Indian Home Minister Mufti Sayeed, on 8 December 1989—the first incident to bring New Delhi to its knees with five JKLF leaders being released from prison in exchange for her freedom on 13 December 1989.[7] Militants skilfully used the local press to give prominence to their activities and 'successes' and to promote their 'struggle' through their writings.[8] It was reported that crowds went wild in the Kashmir Valley, singing and dancing in the streets and chanting anti-India slogans.[9] Such was the scale of eruption that even Pakistan was taken by surprise; and readily cashed in on what it termed as a jihad.[10]

Hijacking Popular Discontentment

It may be recalled that Pakistan had engaged the services of pan-Islamic terrorist outfits and had sponsored numerous fundamentalist schools, madrassas and bodies in the state to wage a jihad. Pakistan's former Foreign Minister Khurshid Mahmud Kasuri admits that:[11]

> In order to defeat the Soviet invasion of Afghanistan, Pakistan and the US decided to support the Mujahideen. For this purpose, young men from all over the Islamic world were invited to fight the 'Godless Soviets'.... The Islamic freedom fighters, who had succeeded in driving out the Soviets from Afghanistan in 1989, were emboldened to replicate the same techniques in Kashmir with the support of Pakistan's intelligence agencies, in resentment over manipulated elections and human rights violations in Indian Kashmir

and of Pakistan's grievance of India not taking serious steps to resolve the issue of J&K through negotiations.

Given the total negation of the rule of law and the sustained political vacuum in the state, Pakistan did not find it difficult to use religious propaganda, through these outfits and bodies, to preach a jihad. Tavleen Singh observes that even then, instead of acting to check the deteriorating situation, New Delhi found it convenient to blame everything on Pakistan and the ISI.[12] Nobody was prepared to admit that Pakistan had merely jumped onto a bandwagon that had already begun to roll in the streets of Srinagar.[13] This deliberate decision to evade reality did not bring the government any closer to addressing the grievances of the people, particularly when the behaviour of the Indian troops and paramilitary forces detracted from, rather than added to, the moral authority of the Indian State.[14]

This was the perfect time for Pakistan and its outfits to put into play its strategy of ethnic cleansing by forcing Kashmiri Pandits to flee from the state; a deliberate attempt to destroy the 'Kashmiriat'. Jagmohan has detailed the horrifying plight of the Kashmiri Pandits, many of whom he writes were tortured to death.[15] It is believed that 95 per cent of the migration took place between 20 January 1990 and 23 January 1990, when mosques blared anti-India slogans and several Kashmiri Pandits received threatening letters from militants, warning them to vacate their houses as they were to be used as hideouts.[16] Even more terrifying was the rumour that some militant organizations had demanded that the Kashmiri Pandit men move out leaving their daughters and wives behind.[17] This provoked the largest exodus, with the Pandits leaving in trucks in the dead of the night.[18] Since curfew had been imposed, they could not even withdraw money.[19]

New Delhi's Response

Rather than doing something about the trauma and misery in the PIS of J&K with India, New Delhi used the situation to claim that the turmoil in the state was 'only' the handiwork of Pakistan-sponsored terrorists, who were targeting innocent Kashmiri Pandits, 'misguiding' the local youth and inciting violence. Few bothered to reason that when a whole population took to the streets in protest—and, that too, without a political leader—there was something much more to the problem. Even the fact that old men, women and children formed part of the protest processions, and openly assisted the militants, did not seem to strike anyone as being odd.

In the absence of a coherent policy, the Kashmir Valley was simply handed over to the Indian security forces, which, empowered by the coercive penal laws and aided by legal cover for their acts, did whatever they deemed necessary to maintain 'law and order'. New Delhi apparently ignored the popular discontentment in the state. Rather, its approach was that 'Pakistan' must not be allowed to happen at any cost, and for that, it simply took recourse to 'area clearance'. The persistent failure of New Delhi to formulate a policy to control the situation created the cycle of violence which continues till date. Militancy provoked state violence, which led to the killing of innocent people, thereby rationalizing militancy.

Indian security forces in the PIS of J&K with India were, accordingly, left to grapple with faceless and nameless enemies enjoying popular support. The stress of the proxy war took its toll on the Indian security forces and the state police, with the uncertainty and insecurity stemming from the sudden attacks by militants reported to have had an adverse psychological effect on them.[20] It was, therefore, not surprising to read reports[21] of the growing tendency amongst the security personnel to overreact to the slightest provocation, which has been termed 'decompensation' by pyschoanalysts. The Indian Minister of State for Defence stated in Parliament on 11 December 2015 that since 2012 there had been eight cases of 'fragging' (that is, killing a fellow soldier or a superior) and as many as 413 suicides by military personnel.[22] The causes were said to include prolonged deployment of the security forces in the PIS of J&K with India.[23] The common refrain of the security forces has been that '[w]e are unwilling, led by the unqualified, doing the unnecessary for the ungrateful'.[24] Needless to say, this has led to increased human rights abuses by the security forces and the state police, ranging from large scale fake encounters to people simply disappearing. Noorani has detailed the terrible torture and inhuman treatment said to have been meted out by the Indian security forces in the state.[25]

Political Role of the Indian Army

The reported political role of the Indian Army in the PIS of J&K with India may be mentioned here. Reports[26] disclosed that on 15 August 1995, the then Indian Home Ministry, in consultation with the state government, deemed it fit to recruit surrendered or renegade militants in the security forces, as part of an overall strategy to restore normalcy in the state.[27] The role of renegade militants, also known as counter-insurgents, in the state was always dubious. Although the Indian Army used these renegade militants in its counter-insurgency operations, and reportedly with some success,[28] there was said to be widespread bitterness against the renegade militants who, with the patronage of the security forces, acted as local bullies.[29] Renegade militants also demanded political power. And this led to the security forces having a political role in the state.

For instance, it is believed that the Indian Army unofficially 'sponsored' renegade militants to stand as candidates in the 1996 elections in the state. Rahul Bedi writes that the Indian Army actively supported a handful of such candidates, and was keen that they win and become their captive 'pressure groups' within the state legislative assembly once the new government assumed office.[30] These candidates, the Indian Army hoped, would check investigations into Army excesses since 1989. During the Parliamentary elections in May 1996, the supporters of the renegade militants were the only people who reportedly carried arms openly across the Kashmir Valley, despite Indian Army patrols.[31] Moreover, the Army and the renegade militants were said to have worked together to ensure that people came to vote.[32] It was for these reasons that the security forces reportedly often turned a blind eye to the increased extortion, rape and mindless killings alleged to have been done by renegade militants.[33] Rahul Bedi cites the intelligence agencies as cautioning that the Indian Army had ceased to be apolitical and had been overstepping its brief by meddling in affairs about which it understood little or nothing. Intelligence officers warned that a complex, dangerous and shadowy game was being played in the state with none of the players knowing what moves the others were on the verge of executing.[34]

Even more disturbing are the reports[35] that in 1998, the Army Training Command in Simla prepared a 'Concept Paper', *Management of Internal Conflict*, which argued that in situations of full-blown insurgencies, all other security organizations and civil apparatus must be placed under the exclusive operational command of the Indian Army. Praveen Swami notes that the Concept Paper inter alia demanded special legal protection for the Army in all counter-insurgency operations where it was deployed.[36] The Paper contended that it was imperative 'from the point of view of morale as well as operational efficiency to protect the rights of soldiers', thereby implying that an engagement with terrorism could not be attempted without a general abrogation of human rights.[37] Swami, quite correctly, opined that the Concept Paper served to illustrate the profound poverty of doctrinal thought in India's internal security establishment. Instead of debating new methods to engage with nuclear Pakistan and the well-armed jihadis, the Army took the retrograde step of getting into an authoritarian mode.[38]

Such an authoritarian stand by the Army fitted in with the coercive penal laws analysed in the next chapter, which gave the security forces full freedom to do whatever they wished with impunity in the name of crushing militancy in the state.

Environment of Fear

The overwhelming fear and gnawing uncertainty in the violence-ravaged Kashmir Valley took its toll on the mental health of its citizens, with a manifold increase in psychiatric disorders.[39] Ramesh Vinayak described how parents were in perpetual dread that their daughter may become a victim of the lust of militants, or their son may be arrested on suspicion of being a militant or an accomplice.[40] The minds got scarred in Kashmir, with people not knowing whether they would still be alive in the evening, young girls being taken to the police station against the law, and graveyards springing up.[41] Quraishi recorded that the common man in Kashmir was scared of both the militants and the Indian security forces; with the refrain being "'[b]eware of American mind, Chinese arms, Pakistan army officers and Indian security men", a combination driving people mad with apprehension for the future'.[42] Moreover, with thousands of men dying in the protracted conflict, female-led single parent families emerged in a big way. At the same time, large numbers of children were rendered orphans since 1990. Violence became endemic to Kashmiri society, with recurrent phases of violence led by each new generation in the state. It is precisely this kind of trauma and terror that is afflicting the state's civil society today, which in turn, breeds terrorism. It matters little whether such trauma and terror is the result of state violence or militant violence. Any government today would need to address the consequences of such trans-generational misery and violence.

Subversion from Within

Other aspects that New Delhi and the state government would have to consider include the large scale subversion over the years from within. Jagmohan, who was appointed by New Delhi in 1990 as the Governor of the territory of the PIS of J&K with India, recorded that 'due to total inaction, unbelievable incompetence, widespread corruption and passive connivance, the administrative machinery and all other levers of power structure had been taken over by the subversives and their collaborators', and that the instrumentalities of the state readily assist the militants.[43] Jagmohan, who was New Delhi's appointee, squarely blamed New Delhi for its policy of appeasement towards Kashmiri politicians,[44] and wrote that 'it aided and abetted the Topac plan [of Pakistan], albeit unwittingly' by not intervening but allowing 'subversion to penetrate all components of the power structure'.[45] Jagmohan described the 'non-existent' state government and the 'deaf' New Delhi,[46] as also the subversion in the services with the 'police, the general services, the hospital administration, the press, the Bar and the Bench' being affected.[47] He recorded that government servants were involved in subversive activities, with some of them even acting as organizers and group leaders; they were often 'area commanders' of militant organizations.[48]

The links of militants with elements in the police have been reported. The infiltration of fundamentalists in the state police force was said to be the result of the flawed policy of recruitment of police officers.[49] Vishal Thapar and Rashid Ahmed documented that at the height of militancy, several personnel deserted the state police and joined the jihadi groups, resulting in the police as a force remaining suspect.[50]

Reports have consistently suggested a nexus between militants and state politicians, too, with politicians paying *hafta* (protection money) to militants.[51] The reports alleged that some ministers, legislators and bureaucrats were in league with the ISI agents responsible for exporting militancy to the state,[52] and that the homes of the ministers and legislators were 'not only hideouts for militants, but strategy planning centres'.[53]

In 1995, the then Governor of the state General Krishna Rao reportedly accused a section of the state government employees of working hand in glove with militants.[54] Reports[55] disclosed that in the said year, the state government's efforts to weed out militants and militant-linked employees from the administration failed when faced with the prospect of state paralysis. The then Chief Minister Farooq Abdullah reportedly admitted in the state legislative assembly in 1997 that some employees of the administration had militant links.[56]

Even elements in the Indian security forces were accused of having links with militants. Farooq Abdullah reportedly alleged in 1995 that there was a nexus between the militants and the paramilitary forces, who along with the bureaucracy, aimed to delay the process of normalization.[57] Mustafa Kamal, Farooq Abdullah's younger brother and the then state Health Minister, was reported in 1997 as reiterating that 'a section of the security forces and bureaucracy have developed a vested interest in the continuation of militant activities'.[58]

Gunbir Singh recorded that elements in the Indian security forces considered the Kashmir Valley to be a prize posting and paid hefty sums for getting transferred there.[59] Innocents arrested were said to be subsequently released by these elements for a price. Even militants were believed to be released, but for a king's ransom.[60] Lalita Panicker wrote how the militants and the security forces had, over the years, learned to coexist. She disclosed that it was not unknown for a militant to slide into a Central Reserve Police Force or BSF bunker at night to effect a swift exchange of money for ration rum.[61] Given such camaraderie, it was not surprising to read reports[62] that when the Hizbul Mujahideen declared a unilateral ceasefire on 24 July 2000, the Indian Army deemed it fit to hold a 'friendly cricket match' on 3 August 2000 in Handwara, Kupwara between the Hizbul Mujahideen and the Army's 4 Rashtriya Rifles. The Army lost by 24 runs, adding to the heroic image of the militants.

Siddharth Vardarajan noted that the Indian Army, in turn, was critical of the police-run Special Task Force (STF) comprising surrendered militants.[63] It was pointed out that since the STF personnel were paid a meagre monthly salary, and got 'an opportunity' to earn cash rewards based on the number of militants killed and arms recovered, this was 'an invitation for corruption'.[64] Reports[65] also suggested links between the police, petroleum dealers and trans-border narcotic smugglers to smuggle heroin-purifying chemicals from Pakistan into the state.

Lack of Governance

Other commentators have pointed out that corruption has been the bane of the state, with the state being dogged by a number of scams. The then Chief Minister Farooq Abdullah reportedly acknowledged that the state administration had become synonymous with corruption.[66]

Nazir Masoodi asserted that the police, revenue and BSF officials siphoned off large sums of money in fake relief cases in the state.[67] As per migrant Kashmiri Pandits, some government agencies misappropriated relief funds meant for their rehabilitation.[68] There were said to be widespread irregularities in appointments in the state. T.V. Rajeshwar wrote about hundreds of state employees who were appointed surreptitiously at various levels, with every unfair appointment provoking a huge outburst of resentment.[69]

Then, there has been the question of the government losing its grip in the state. That it was the militants' writ that ran in the state in the 1990s has been well documented. Since 1990, the militants persistently sought to *talibanise* the Kashmiri society, and routinely issued diktats to the local population.[70] The writ of the militants was not confined to requiring Kashmiri Muslims to follow the strict Islamic code. Rather, the militant outfits openly challenged the authority of the state. To take an example, while no census could be held in 1991 due to militancy, the state government was not in a position to conduct a census in the state even in the year 2000, with the militant outfits warning government employees against participating in the census exercise.[71] The then Director of Census Operations acknowledged that neither the people nor the enumerators were cooperating with the government to conduct the census. He was reduced to 'appealing' to the militants to withdraw the boycott call and to offering that he was willing to discuss their apprehensions.[72] The stark ground reality can perhaps be gauged from the press statement made by Mufti Sayeed on 1 March 2015, one day after assuming office as the state Chief Minister, in which he expressed his gratitude to Pakistan, the Hurriyat and the militants 'for their generosity' in 'allowing' the 'democratic process in the state' during the 2015 state assembly elections.[73] Reports in 2016, in fact, record the growing support for militants in the PIS of J&K with India, highlighting how the local youth risk their lives to help trapped militants escape by assembling at the encounter sites and flinging stones at the Indian security forces and how residents of different villages clash over 'the right to bury' Pakistani militants slain by Indian security forces with thousands of mourners in attendance at their funerals.[74]

There was reportedly a complete breakdown of the judicial system as well. The state judiciary could do little about the human rights violations, in view of the legal cover provided by the coercive provisions of the laws. Even more alarming were the reports that security forces were flouting court orders with impunity in the state.[75] While the judiciary has been said to be helpless in protecting the human rights of innocent civilians, it was reportedly not in a position to even try the apprehended militants, due to militants' threats against judges, police and state officers.[76]

Several commentators acknowledge the complex ground realities in the state, some of which have been listed above by way of illustration.

Harish Khare asserted that it was the decades of anti-people attitude of Kashmir's malignant and parasitic political elite—with New Delhi deliberately looking the other way—which produced dissatisfaction on such a large scale that it was surprising that insurgency took so long to break out, with or without prompting from Pakistan.[77] The problem, he contended, was not minoritism, but the outright contempt for democracy in the state shown by all popular and secular leaders of every political hue.[78]

According to Praful Bidwai, the factors responsible for the alienation of the Kashmiri people included the rigging of election after election; the imposition of unpopular leaders; extension of over 200 Central laws and 42 amendments to the Constitution of Jammu and Kashmir of 1957, many without legal warrant or propriety, and the routine violation of human rights by security forces.[79]

Akbar Ahmad recorded that a feeling of social, economic and political frustration existed in the state; the denial of basic needs, rampant corruption, absence of industry and the stagnant economy were related to the feeling of being deliberately neglected—or discriminated against—by New Delhi.[80] Indeed, Ashok Mitra pointed out that '[b]ehind the façade of the constitutional apparatus rests the nitty-gritty of rude fact: the Valley is an occupied territory; remove for a day India's Army and security forces and it is impossible to gauge what might transpire at the next instant… they certainly do not want to be any part of India'.[81]

Suggestions of Commentators

Commentators have accordingly suggested ways of re-establishing New Delhi's moral authority in the state. Amitabh Mattoo emphasizes the importance of winning the trust of the Kashmiri people, preserving 'Kashmiriat', refraining from viewing ordinary Kashmiris as militants or separatists or even pro-Pakistan, discussing autonomy, encouraging a dialogue between the people and New Delhi, and admitting the mistakes, such as the rigging of elections, the installation of puppet governments, and the harassment by security forces.[82]

Ishwar Sharma writes that New Delhi should admit to the alienation of the Kashmiri people from the mainstream.[83] He opines that it is the responsibility of the elite, academics, teachers, lawyers, social workers and political activists to persuade alienated youth to return to the mainstream. Such persons must also interact with the state government in a determined manner to create the conditions necessary to convince the people about the sincerity of the government. The state should then hold a dialogue, dismantle the security apparatus and provide for the safe return of migrants. Sharma feels that the administrative structure needs to be substantially overhauled, and that the deployment of local administrators of proven merit and integrity would create the necessary goodwill.

Balraj Puri argues that human rights should form the basis of any policy in the state, and that the human rights movement in the state should, therefore, be encouraged, instead of allowing it to lapse into a secessionist movement.[84] Mohan Guruswamy adds that all such political, psychological, economic, social and military action, which is required to win the population back, should be taken.[85]

Noorani suggests that:[86]

> First and foremost, a Human Rights Commission must be set up in the state consisting of people who enjoy the confidence of the people. Secondly, if in 1974, Britain could ask a committee headed by a former Lord Chancellor, Lord Hardinar, to consider measures to deal with terrorism in Northern Ireland which were 'consistent to the maximum extent practicable in the circumstances with the preservation of civil liberties and human rights', there is no reason why India cannot emulate the example in Kashmir urgently. Thirdly, a high level inquiry into the outrages since January 1990 is called for, preferably by a Commission of Inquiry set up under the law or an unofficial body to which the State pledges its full cooperation. The people of the State sorely need some impartial, independent authority to whom they can pour out their woes. The importance of this step cannot be exaggerated. It must consist of persons with manifest integrity. Fourthly, the people of India must be told the truth as well…. Fifthly, India must encourage the leaders of the three regions of the state to meet and, particularly, those of the Valley to meet amongst themselves….

N.C. Menon argues that the hearts and minds of Kashmiris be won back—not with guns or heroics, but with new ideas and programmes, improved implementation and better communication.[87] The steps that should be taken include initiating programmes, such as providing Kashmiri children in camps outside the state with educational facilities in fields such as medicine and engineering in other Indian cities, which will also promote assimilation; directly administering the schemes in the state from New Delhi to avoid local middlemen; enhancing the security environment by improving police intelligence, and both providing and appearing to provide protection; and undertaking counter propaganda imaginatively and with fanfare. Menon insists that counter strategies should be used. To take an example, in case a bridge is blown up by terrorists, local persons should be involved rather than bringing in outsiders, so that future destructive activity of the terrorists would anger the local people.

Few would dispute the proposition that the absence of good governance in the state has nourished the militancy. I believe that New Delhi must take the steps suggested and more. However, the real question is whether it is in a position to do so. As Rajmohan Gandhi points out, 'when the Government of India is unable to ensure good governance in the Capital, which overflows with lawmakers and law-enforcers', the 'hard fact is that New Delhi is not capable of providing better governance in Kashmir'.[88]

The issue, therefore, is not whether there should be good governance and imaginative measures to win back the trust of the people. Clearly, the Kashmir turmoil has assumed its present dimensions due to the lack of good governance and such imaginative measures. When the Indian polity stands accused of failing the Indian people, would not such a polity, coupled with state repression and a dead administration, lead even the most pro-India Kashmiri to conclude that the sovereign ruler has been replaced by a despotic Indian State. Surely, New Delhi must have been aware that the blatant rigging of elections would merely give rise to public resentment, particularly against the background of the already prevalent popular disillusionment with New Delhi over the plebiscite issue and the dilution of the state's autonomy, as also the persistent efforts of Pakistan to rake up trouble in the state. Surely, it must have known that the misuse of state machinery to quell the legitimate grievances of the people would result in the loss of legitimacy of the state and its institutions. Surely, it must have realized that governmental lawlessness would create a conducive environment for Pakistan to impress upon Kashmiri Muslims the virtues of waging a jihad against India. Surely, it must have known that the consequent excesses by the Indian security forces would further alienate the people, given that the avowed policy of security forces is to mindlessly use coercive measures to contain secessionist tendencies anywhere in the country. Surely, New Delhi must have appreciated the fact that it is an unjust society that causes and defines terrorism, and an unjust social structure that creates aggressive social disturbances. If New Delhi could not do much about this disturbing state of affairs before the Kashmir issue assumed its current dimensions, it faces a greater challenge now—when the rejection by the Kashmiri people of anything Indian, the absence of the rule of law, the reported emergence of 'vested interests' in keeping the militancy alive, the reported links between militants and elements in the police–administration–bureaucracy, the reported nexus of politicians and legislators with militants and of the security forces with renegade militants, the reported rampant corruption in the state, the reported collapse of institutions in the state, and the destruction of the fabric of civil society, raises grave doubts about the ability of any government at present to govern the state.

I believe that the deeper question really is about the nature and attitude of the Indian State. Those familiar with the Indian State will readily agree that the rot is deep-rooted. India may have the best of talent. The people may be highly qualified, illustrious and hardworking. But generally speaking, the working of the Indian system, plagued by criminality, corruption, nepotism and lawlessness, ensures mediocrity in all branches of the Indian State. The men and women who man the various branches of government are more often than not occupying high offices for reasons other than merit. The failings of the Indian State rule out the ability of New Delhi to formulate, and give effect to, a cohesive policy towards the PIS of J&K. In no other area is this more evident than, perhaps, in New Delhi's methods of containing and handling terrorism. It would, therefore, be helpful to now examine the underpinnings of New Delhi's approach to conflict resolution.

Notes and References

1. *The Indian Express*. 1998. 'In J&K guns have changed hands, little else', New Delhi, 25 May.
2. *Supra* Note 89, Chapter XIII.
3. Mehraj, Zafar. 1996. 'Rise of Militancy in Kashmir—A Perspective', in *Supra* Note 34, Chapter IV, p. 62.
4. See *Hindustan Times*. 2000. 'Who's Salauddin?', New Delhi, 21 August.
5. *Supra* Note 12, Chapter IV, p. 191.
6. Mohan, Inder. 1989. 'Root of the problem', *Hindustan Times*, New Delhi, 4 October.
7. *Hindustan Times*. 2000. 'The rise of the Harkat', New Delhi, 2 January.
8. Sahni, Sat Paul. 1995. 'Media and Spread of Terrorism' in B. P. Singh Sehgal, *Global Terrorism: Socio-Politico and Legal Dimensions*, pp. 131–132. New Delhi: Deep & Deep Publications.
9. *Supra* Note 31, Chapter IV, p. 137.
10. Ibid.
11. *Supra* Note 89, Chapter I, pp. 134–135.
12. *Supra* Note 31, Chapter IV, p. 138.
13. Ibid., p. 206.
14. Ibid., p. 138.
15. *Supra* Note 24, Chapter XIII, pp. 231–254.
16. *Sunday Times of India*. 1996. 'Refugees from paradise', New Delhi, 1 January; *Sunday Times of India*. 1996. 'Is it time to go home?', New Delhi, 24 November.
17. Ibid.
18. Ibid.
19. Ibid.
20. *The Times of India*. 1999. 'Tough action to contain Valley militancy urged', New Delhi, 6 November.
21. *Hindustan Times*. 1999. 'The unwilling versus the ungrateful', New Delhi, 26 September.
22. *The Times of India*. 2015. 'Armed forces still record at least 100 suicides every year', New Delhi, 12 December.
23. Ibid.
24. *Hindustan Times*. 1999. 'The unwilling versus the ungrateful', New Delhi, 26 September.
25. *Supra* Note 12, Chapter IV, pp. 532–536.

26. *The Times of India.* 2000. 'Recruiting ex-militants in police criticized', New Delhi, 6 January.
27. *The Indian Express.* 1995. 'As victims train guns on tormentors', New Delhi, 25 June.
28. *The Indian Express.* 1996. 'In J&K guns have changed hands, little else', New Delhi, 25 May.
29. *Hindustan Times.* 2000. 'Iron in Kashmir's soul', New Delhi, 16 April.
30. Bedi, Rahul. 1996. 'The Army's insurance policy', *The Indian Express*, New Delhi, 29 June.
31. Ibid.
32. Baweja, Harinder. 1996. 'Voting under coercion', *India Today*, 15 June, p. 68. Delhi: Living Media Ltd.
33. See *Supra* Note 28.
34. Ibid.
35. Swami, Praveen. 1999. 'Changing Strategies', *Frontline*, 10 September, p. 36. Chennai: Kasturi & Sons Ltd.; Swami, Praveen. 2000. 'A dubious document', *Frontline*, 8 December, p. 23. Chennai: Kasturi & Sons Ltd.
36. Ibid.
37. Ibid.
38. Ibid.
39. Bhatia, Ashima Kaul. 2000. 'Circle of unreason', *Hindustan Times*, New Delhi, 5 September; Joshi, Arun. 2001. 'They can escape guns but not nightmares', *Hindustan Times*, New Delhi, 12 March; *The Indian Express*. 1999. 'Violence scarred Valley suffers mental trauma: VHAI report', New Delhi, 1 March.
40. Vinayak, Ramesh. 1994. 'The scarred psyche', *India Today*, 15 April, p. 130. New Delhi: Living Media Ltd.
41. *Hindustan Times.* 2000. 'Women's group report on J&K an account of scarred minds', New Delhi, 21 August.
42. Quraishi, Humra. 2001. 'Living in a war zone', *Sunday Times of India*, New Delhi, 22 July.
43. *Supra* Note 24, Chapter XIII, p. 31.
44. Ibid., p. 92.
45. Ibid., p. 14.
46. Ibid., p. 321.
47. Ibid., p. 375.
48. Ibid., p. 380.
49. Dhar, O.N. 1993. 'Police revolt and after: Intriguing coincidences point to Pakistan', *The Indian Express*, New Delhi, 27 July; Swami, Praveen. 1999. 'An Army caught napping', *Frontline*, 10 September, p. 33. Chennai: Kasturi & Sons, Ltd.; *The Indian Express*. 1997. 'Kashmiris join CRPF and BSF in large numbers', New Delhi, 15 March.
50. Thapar, Vishal & Rashid Ahmed. 2001. 'Kashmir's dirty Harrys', *Hindustan Times*, New Delhi, 25 February.
51. *The Indian Express.* 1997. 'Counter-insurgents warn J-K against raw deal', New Delhi, 17 June.
52. *The Indian Express.* 1997. 'Parrey repeats his charge against NC', New Delhi, 21 April; *The Indian Express*. 1996. 'Ex-ultras to be nominated as MLC's', New Delhi, 29 December.
53. *The Times of India.* 1996. 'Kuka Parrey's charge leads to war of words', New Delhi, 27 December.
54. *The Indian Express.* 1995. 'Gen Krishna Rao losing on friends, gaining on foes', New Delhi, 12 April.
55. *The Indian Express.* 1995. 'J&K Govt. agrees to review employees dismissal', New Delhi, 9 June.

56. *The Indian Express*. 1997. 'Parrey repeats his charge against NC', New Delhi, 21 April; *The Indian Express*. 1996. 'Ex-ultras to be nominated as MLC's', New Delhi, 29 December.

57. *The Times of India*. 1995. 'Farooq opposes talks with separatists', New Delhi, 28 March.

58. *The Indian Express*. 1997. 'Security forces stoking militancy: Farooq's brother', New Delhi, 17 March.

59. Singh, Gunbir. 1997. 'Is peace returning to happy Valley, a businessman wonders', *The Times of India*, New Delhi, 20 January.

60. Ibid.

61. Panicker, Lalita. 2000. 'Enchanted Valley', *The Times of India*, New Delhi, 16 May.

62. *Hindustan Times*. 2000. 'Army team bites dust', New Delhi, 6 August.

63. Vardarajan, Siddharth. 2000. 'No hot pursuit, we'll wait in ambush', *The Times of India*, New Delhi, 18 August.

64. Ibid.

65. *The Indian Express*. 1997. 'S-I death reveals police hand in narco smuggling', New Delhi, 16 January.

66. *The Times of India*. 1995. 'Farooq opposes talks with separatists', New Delhi, 28 March.

67. Masoodi, Nazir. 1999. 'Govt gives away relief package for 'dead' families living in PoK', *The Indian Express*, New Delhi, 1 May.

68. *The Times of India*. 1998. 'Give white paper on relief for Kashmiri migrants', New Delhi, 28 December.

69. Rajeshwar, T.V. 1997. 'Distortions of democracy', *Hindustan Times*, New Delhi, 17 September.

70. *Supra* Note 8, p. 131; *The Indian Express*. 1995. 'Kashmir media buckles under severe pressure, New Delhi, 29 December; *The Indian Express*. 1995. 'Kashmir dailies forced to lay off staff', New Delhi, 26 July.

71. *The Times of India*. 2000. 'Stop census in J&K or else…', New Delhi, 4 September.

72. *Sunday Times of India*. 2000. 'Militants' threat holds up census in J&K', New Delhi, 17 September.

73. *The Indian Express*. 2015. 'CM Mufti Sayeed credits Pakistan, militant outfits for peaceful polls in J&K, Opposition hits out at PM Modi', New Delhi, 2 March.

74. Editorial. 2016. 'Pathankot, Pampore', *The Indian Express*, New Delhi, 24 February; Masood, Bashaarat. 2016. 'New headache in Valley: Crowds swelling at militant funerals, *The Indian Express*, New Delhi, 9 March. *The Indian Express*. 2015. 'CM Mufti Sayeed credits Pakistan, militant outfits for peaceful polls in J&K, Opposition hits out at PM Modi', New Delhi, 2 March.

75. Sachar, Rajinder. 1999. 'Uneasy times in Kashmir', *Hindustan Times*, New Delhi, 23 December; Nayar, Kuldip. 1994. 'The image trap', *The Indian Express*, New Delhi, 31 December; Pandit, M Saleem. 2001. 'Girl languishes in jail despite release orders', *The Times of India*, New Delhi, 13 February; Amnesty International. 1999. *India: "If they are dead, tell us" "Disappearances" in Jammu and Kashmir*, February. AI Index ASA 20/02/99 at p. 31.

76. *The Times of India*. 2000. 'CM proposes SP disposes', New Delhi, 2 November; *The Times of India*. 2000. 'J&K may withdraw 800 TADA cases against militants', New Delhi, 9 December; Rajagopalan, S. 2001. 'US reports attack India for rights abuses in J&K', *Hindustan Times*, New Delhi, 27 February; Amnesty International, *India: 'If they are dead, tell us'*, pp. 29–34.

77. Khare, Harish. 1991. 'Answering BJP on Kashmir: Need to recognise the Farooq legacy', *The Times of India*, New Delhi, 20 December.

78. Ibid.

79. Bidwai, Praful. 2000. 'New Opening in J-K', *The Times of India*, New Delhi, 29 July.

80. Ahmed, Akbar S. 1996. 'Kashmir 1990: Islamic revolt or Kashmir Nationalism' in *Supra* Note 34, Chapter IV, p. 62. Also see *The Indian Express*. 1996. "Azad' call fades as basic issues grip Kashmiri minds', New Delhi, 16 September.

81. Extracted in *Supra* Note 3, Chapter V, p. 137.

82. Mattoo, Amitabh. 2000. 'A fine balance – Commandments for a Kashmir policy', *Hindustan Times*, New Delhi, 13 June.

83. *Supra* Note 190, Chapter X, p. 385.

84. Puri, Balraj. 1992. 'Human rights key to Kashmir policy', *The Times of India*, New Delhi, 11 February.

85. Guruswamy, Mohan. 1993. 'Kashmir: Eating soup with knife', *Hindustan Times*, New Delhi, 12 April.

86. *Supra* Note 12, Chapter IV, pp. 521–522.

87. Menon, N.C. 1992. 'Hearts and minds of men', *Hindustan Times*, New Delhi, 4 June.

88. *Supra* Note 71, Chapter VIII.

XV

Doctrinal Bankruptcy towards Conflict Resolution

As a point of departure, let us draw parallels with how other states have successfully quelled an insurgency. Ashok Malik gives the instance of China, which used force to break the back of insurgency in Xinjiang, China's most porous zone having borders with Mongolia, Russia, Kazakhstan, Krygzstan, Tajikistan, Afghanistan, India, Tibet and the territory of the PIS of J&K occupied by Pakistan.[1] He writes that in the early 1990s, the separatist impulses of the Uyghurs, backed by newly freed Central Asian neighbours and groups in Pakistan and Afghanistan, took Beijing by surprise. Beijing's response was three-phased. First was the brutal military tactics, which broke the militancy's back by 1998. Second was frenetic diplomacy with neighbouring states and insurgent groups. The final weapon was trade. China offered its neighbours lucrative deals, and reopened ancient border posts. Substantial exports from Xinjiang were to neighbouring countries. Malik notes that China was evidently of the view that its neighbours were unlikely to ever back Uyghur terrorism if they had a stake in the stability of the area.

Citing the Chinese policy, it has often been argued that before China could use diplomacy and trade as a means to check the militancy, it had broken the back of militancy by 'brutal military tactics'. An essential component of such a strategy is 'area clearance'; that is, the elimination of the militants and the ruthless suppression of the civilian population.[2]

New Delhi seems to be following this strategy in the PIS of J&K with India, facilitated by laws conferring extraordinary powers on security forces to do whatever is necessary in the interests of the security of India. There has been a consistent demand from the people of the state that the coercive penal laws in operation in the state be repealed and that New Delhi should desist from its policy of holding the state by force. Such demand has been echoed by several commentators pleading for respect for human rights and the rule of law in the state. New Delhi, however, cites the proxy war being waged by Pakistan and cross-border terrorism, to complement the strict state laws with equally coercive Parliamentary penal laws.

It is here that the fallacy in New Delhi's approach lies. Regardless of the violence and havoc spread by terrorists, the state cannot imitate the criminal by endorsing state terrorism. When the state terrorises its own people, it commits an offence more intolerable than terrorism itself.[3] In *D.K. Basu*,[4] the Indian Supreme Court explained that 'State terrorism would provide legitimacy to "terrorism"', and further that the fact that 'the terrorist has violated the human rights of innocent citizens may render him liable for punishment but it cannot justify the violation of his human rights except in the manner permitted by law'.[5] In any case, New Delhi lacks the competence to make laws, which have the effect of sanctioning state terrorism. It is settled law that abduction or elimination of suspects, torture or custodial violence to extract information is impermissible under the Constitution of India.[6]

Coercive Laws

An analysis of the coercive laws in force in the PIS of J&K with India would reveal that such laws facilitate state violence and lawlessness, without the authorities having to be bothered about accountability. Regrettably, the Indian Supreme Court has, more or less, upheld the constitutional validity of several of these laws. Given such judicial sanction, New Delhi has tried to break the back of the militancy in the state by sheer force—a strategy that has not only been counterproductive but which has also detracted from the legitimacy and credibility of New Delhi in the eyes of the common person in the state.

It is, therefore, useful to first analyse a few of the objectionable features of such coercive laws as also the patent infirmities in the decisions of the Indian Supreme Court upholding their constitutional validity. It is imperative that such laws be brought in line with the norms of a civilized society subscribing to the rule of law. After all, nations are not ruled primarily by law, much less by violence. It is the justness of the law that is crucial for the common person to respect it. Subjecting popular discontentment to draconian laws is a recipe for disaster, as discussed later in this chapter.

Let us start with the constitutional provisions. It may be recalled that Part III of the Constitution of India guarantees certain fundamental rights to the people of India, with Article 13 mandating that any law inconsistent with, or in contravention of, such fundamental rights will be void to the extent of such inconsistency or contravention. In *Mian Bashir Ahmad*,[7] the Full Bench of the Jammu and Kashmir High Court, while considering the constitutional validity of provisions of the State Representation of the People Act of 1957 containing the anti-defection law, noted that the Constitution of the state is contained not only in the Constitution of Jammu and Kashmir of 1957, but also in the Constitution of India, insofar as it is applicable to the state, and that since 'the residents of the State are citizens of India, they have been guaranteed the fundamental rights contained in Part III of the Indian Constitution with the exceptions provided therein'.[8]

In *Master Sewanath*,[9] the Full Bench of the Jammu and Kashmir High Court held that in light of Article 13(1) of the Constitution of India, all laws that were prevalent before the Constitution of India came into force in the state on 14 May 1954, which were in any way in conflict with or inconsistent with the provisions of the Constitution of India, shall be deemed to be void and ineffective.

The fundamental rights guaranteed by the Constitution of India constitute the core values of the Constitution and one of the essential pillars of the vibrant Indian democracy. New Delhi, however, selectively denied such rights to the state; something which could not have been done in the rest of the country. The Constitution (Application to Jammu and Kashmir) Order of 1954, issued by New Delhi under Article 370(1) of the Constitution of India, had inserted in the Constitution, as applicable to the state, clause (c) in Article 35. This provision granted absolute immunity to the preventive laws made by the state legislature for a period of five years.[10] Further, the Indian Supreme Court had upheld such provision as also the extension of the life of the provision by New Delhi to 10 years, and then to 15 years, by the Constitution (Application to Jammu and Kashmir) Second Amendment Order of 1959 and the Constitution (Application to Jammu and Kashmir) Amendment Order of 1964, respectively.[11] It was the protection to coercive state laws given by Article 35(c) of the Constitution of India that deprived the residents of the state of constitutional guarantees available to other citizens of India.[12] The Full Bench of the Jammu and Kashmir High Court chipped in by holding in *Mohamad Subhan*[13] that in view of the provisions of Article 35(c) of the Constitution of India, as applied to the state, New Delhi could even omit the 'application' of fundamental rights to the citizens of the state.

State Coercive Laws

The preventive detention law enacted by the state legislature contained several offending provisions, notably Section 8 of the successive Jammu and Kashmir Preventive Detention Acts that enabled the authorities to simply cite public interest for detaining any person, without having to disclose the grounds on which the detention order had been made. The authorities were given further protection from disclosing the facts, which they considered to be against the public interest to disclose. Such a draconian provision was contrary to the express mandate of Article 22(5) of the Constitution of India, which provides that '[w]hen any person is detained in pursuance of an order made under any law providing for preventive detention, the authority making the order shall, as soon as may be, communicate to such person the grounds on which the order has been made and shall afford him the earliest opportunity of making a representation against the order'. Given the strict preventive detention provisions, it is not surprising that over the years, thousands of people in the state have been detained under the preventive detention laws, and often under orders passed mechanically without application of mind,[14] or for vague reasons.[15]

While the Jammu and Kashmir Public Safety Act of 1978 also permitted preventive detention anywhere and in such conditions as the government may specify, without having to disclose to the detenu the grounds of his detention, the Jammu and Kashmir Disturbed Areas Act permitted police officers of a certain rank to 'fire upon' any person, who was indulging in any act which may result in serious breach of public order, or who was acting in contravention of a law or order prohibiting the assembly of five or more persons or the carrying of weapons, firearms, ammunition or explosive substances.

Parliamentary Coercive Laws

The state laws were complemented by even more stringent Parliamentary laws. The Armed Force (Jammu And Kashmir) Special Powers Act of 1990 was modelled on the Armed Forces (Special Powers) Act of 1958 (AFSPA), the latter having been enacted by the Indian Parliament to contain the turmoil in the states of Assam, Manipur, Meghalaya, Nagaland and Tripura and the Union Territories of Arunachal Pradesh and Mizoram in the north-east region of India. The 1990 Act enabled the security forces to take overall control of the areas declared to be 'disturbed' and to arrest in such areas, without warrant, any person against whom even a 'reasonable suspicion' existed that he had committed or was about to commit a cognizable offence, and to use such force as was necessary to effect the arrest, including the power to kill. And the security forces could do this without having to worry about being prosecuted for their actions.

Then, there were the dreaded Terrorism and Disruptive Activities (Prevention) Acts (TADA), succeeded by the Prevention of Terrorism Act of 2002 (POTA). The TADA permitted arrest and detention on vaguely defined grounds of 'terrorist' and 'disruptive activities'. Section 4 defined 'disruptive activities' to mean 'any action taken, whether by act or speech or through media or in any manner whatsoever', which questions, disrupts or is intended to disrupt, whether directly or indirectly, the sovereignty or integrity of India, or which is intended to bring about or supports any claim, whether directly or indirectly, for the cession of any part of India or the secession of any part of India from the Union. By this yardstick, anyone who calls for the conversion of the LOC into the international border would be liable to be booked under the TADA! Significantly, even if a person does not advocate violence, he could still be booked under the TADA, should he fall within the vaguely defined term 'disruptive activity'.

Abetment and possession of unauthorized arms were made punishable offences in vague and wide terms. Section 2(1)(a) defined the term 'abet' to include 'the communication or association with any person or class of persons who is engaged or assisting in any manner terrorists or disruptionists'. The Indian Supreme Court itself held in *Kartar Singh*[16] that this definition is so 'blissfully and impermissibly vague and imprecise' that:[17]

> [E]ven an innocent person who ingenuously and undefiledly communicates or associates without any knowledge or having no reason to believe or suspect that the person or class of persons with whom he has communicated or associated is engaged in assisting in any manner terrorists or disruptionist, can be arrested and prosecuted by abusing or misusing or misapplying this definition.

Section 5 of the TADA made the mere unauthorized possession of specified arms and ammunition in a notified area a substantive offence. The person could, therefore, be held under the TADA, irrespective of his association or communication with terrorist activity. Section 21 of the TADA shifted the burden of proof onto the accused to prove his innocence. People could be arrested on mere suspicion and remanded to custody without charge for 180 days, which could be extended up to one year—in other words, given the stringent bail provisions, the TADA in effect enabled six months to one year detention without charge or trial. Trial was to be conducted in special courts, which could sit in camera or in jail. Section 15(1) of the TADA made confession to a senior police officer admissible in evidence, though such confession is inadmissible under the general criminal law. Section 16(2) of the TADA enabled the identity of a witness to be kept a secret. The TADA excluded the right of appeal to the High Court; the convict had only one right of appeal, which could be preferred within 30 days to the Supreme Court. The TADA also provided for preventive detention in Section 7, which enabled the Central Government to confer powers of a police officer, including the powers of arrest and investigation, upon any officer of the Central Government for the purpose of preventing terrorist and disruptive acts as defined by Sections 3 and 4 of the Act.

Having listed some of the stringent provisions of the state law and of the central legislation applied to the state, it would be relevant to note their constitutional validity.

Constitutional Validity

As far as the aforesaid state enactments are concerned, it has been noted earlier that New Delhi took repeated recourse to Article 370(1) of the Constitution of India in order to grant immunity to the coercive state laws from being challenged as being inconsistent with the guaranteed fundamental rights contained in the Constitution of India. Indeed, New Delhi deliberately emasculated Article 370 of the Constitution to enable it to confer protection upon such coercive laws so that they could remain on the statute-book. It has been examined how it was constitutionally impermissible for New Delhi to do so, as also the infirmities in the decisions of the Indian Supreme Court endorsing New Delhi's actions. Should it be found that New Delhi was not competent to take repeated recourse to Article 370(1) of the Constitution so as to protect the state enactments referred to above, the constitutionality of same would be dubious on this ground alone.

The constitutional validity of the central legislation applied to the state may now be discussed with reference to the decisions of the Indian Supreme Court upholding the constitutional validity of the AFSPA as well as of the TADA. These decisions of the Indian Supreme Court are being discussed here at some length with a view to analyse their fallacies, as also to highlight the existence of a general trend to give judicial sanction to draconian laws considered necessary by New Delhi to crush terrorism—an approach that would need to be revised before New Delhi can even hope to regain its moral authority in the state.

Constitutional Validity of the AFSPA and the TADA

The Constitution of India provides that it is the state legislatures, and not Parliament, that have the legislative competence to enact laws in respect of the legislative entry of 'public order' in the State List contained in the Seventh Schedule of the Constitution. Both the AFSPA and the TADA were, therefore, challenged in the Indian Supreme Court on the ground of lack of legislative competence of Parliament to make such laws in *Naga People's Movement of Human Rights*[18] and *Kartar Singh*, respectively. In both cases, the Indian Supreme Court took the view that the enactments did not fall under 'public order' under the state's domain. The Supreme Court opined that 'the ambit of the field of legislation with respect to "public order" in Entry 1 of the State List has to be confined to disorders of lesser gravity having an impact within the boundaries of the State' and that the 'activities of the terrorists and disruptionists pose a serious challenge to the very existence and sovereignty as well as to the security of India notwithstanding the fact whether such threats or challenges come by way of external aggression or internal disturbance'.[19] According to the Court, terrorism 'cannot be classified as the mere disturbance of "public order"' and that 'it is much more, rather a grave emergent situation created either by external forces particularly at the frontiers of this country or by anti-nationals throwing a challenge to the very existence and sovereignty of the country in its democratic polity'.[20]

The Court reasoned further that should the subject matter of the enactments not be covered by an entry in the State List contained in the Seventh Schedule of the Constitution of India, it would follow that Parliament would have legislative competence under its residuary powers under Article 248 read with Entry 97 of the Union List contained in the said Schedule.[21] The Court held that it would therefore be unnecessary to go into the question of whether it falls under any entry in the Union List or the Concurrent List contained in the said Schedule.[22]

The approach of the Supreme Court in both *Naga People's Movement of Human Rights* and *Kartar Singh* is, in my opinion, fallacious.

The larger 13-judge bench decision of the Supreme Court in *Keshavananda Bharati*[23] construed the provisions of Articles 245, 246 and 248 of the Constitution of India to hold that the power of Parliament and state legislatures 'to make laws does not extend to making a law which contravenes or is inconsistent with any provision of the Constitution' and that a 'law is inconsistent with the provisions of the Constitution when, being given effect to, it impairs or nullifies the provision of the Constitution'.[24]

In construing the subject matter of the AFSPA, or the TADA, one has therefore to look at the entire constitutional scheme. Though Parliament has plenary powers within its legislative sphere, these are subject to the express or implied limitations imposed by the Constitution of India and the constitutional scheme. Parliament lacks the competence to enact a law, which has the effect of impairing or nullifying other provisions of the Constitution. Even otherwise, the Constitution Bench of the Supreme Court in *Indira Gandhi*[25] held that *expressio unius est exclusio alterius* is a well-recognized rule of construction that applies to the Constitution of India, and that, therefore, 'an expressly laid down mode of doing something necessarily prohibits the doing of that thing in any other manner'.[26] In other words, every positive direction in the Constitution of India contains an implication against anything contrary to it, or which would frustrate or disappoint the purpose of that provision. This limitation upon Parliament is as strong as though a negative direction has been expressed. Simply put, when a power is given under the Constitution to do a certain thing in a certain way, the thing must be done in that way alone or not at all.

The Constitution of India, in the event of a grave emergent situation where the security of India or any part thereof is threatened, empowers the Union Cabinet to advise the President to make a Proclamation to that effect under Article 352 of the Constitution. Parliament may then step in under Article 250 of the Constitution to enact necessary laws to tackle the grave emergent situation in the whole country or any part thereof. Article 355 specifically imposes a constitutional duty upon the Union to protect every state from external aggression and internal disturbance. Hence, when there exist specific provisions in the Constitution directly touching upon the subject matter and rationale of the AFSPA and the TADA, and which are meant to counter a grave emergent situation threatening the security of India or any part of the territory thereof, Parliament was not competent to ignore these provisions, especially its power under Article 250, and instead seek to rely on its legislative power with reference to the Union List or its residuary power under Article 248 read with Entry 97 of the Union List to enact the said Acts.

The significance of not taking recourse to Articles 352 and 250 of the Constitution is that New Delhi, by enacting such laws, nullified and circumvented the express constitutional limitations and safeguards contained in the said Articles upon the exercise of power by it. The Presidential Proclamation declaring Emergency has to be laid every six months before Parliament for approval, as mandated by Article 352(4) and (5) of the Constitution. The President is required to revoke the Proclamation declaring Emergency, as required by Article 352(7), if the Lok Sabha passes a resolution disapproving the Proclamation or its continuance in force. Similarly, Article 250(2) of the Constitution provides that the law enacted by Parliament under Article 250(1) shall cease to have effect after six months of the expiry of the Proclamation. The decisions of the Supreme Court in both *Naga People's Movement of Human Rights* and *Kartar Singh* have the effect of wiping out such constitutional limitations upon the exercise of power by New Delhi. It is beyond the competence of any of the organs of the Indian State, being creatures of the Constitution, to do so.

Again, the view of the Supreme Court noted above in *Kartar Singh*[27] that 'the ambit of the field of legislation with respect to "public order" under Entry 1 of the State List has to be confined to disorders of lesser gravity having an impact within the boundaries of the State' is quite surprising. Surely, the lack of public order in a state, which has an impact outside the boundaries of that state, does not result in the lack of legislative competence of such state to enact laws in respect of 'public order' within the state. On the contrary, the constitutional scheme makes it clear that if state laws enacted to maintain public order are ineffective, or fail to contain the threat to the security and sovereignty of such part of India, then Parliament may step in under Article 250 of the Constitution of India, complete with the aforesaid safeguards, to enact the necessary legislation, but only after the President has proclaimed Emergency on the ground of the security of India, or any part thereof, being threatened.[28]

Indeed, the entire approach of the Supreme Court in *Naga People's Movement of Human Rights* and in *Kartar Singh* conflicts with another principle of law enunciated by the 13-judge bench of the Supreme Court in *Keshavananda Bharati*,[29] referred to earlier in the book while discussing the issue of whether the power of Parliament to amend the Constitution could be located in its residuary power. This principle asserted that where the Constitution-makers were keenly conscious of the importance of a matter and made a provision in respect of that matter in the Constitution, the power to legislate on that matter cannot then be read into the residuary power of Parliament under Article 248 of the Constitution or Entry 97 of the Union

List.[30] The Supreme Court in *Keshavnanda Bharti* relied on the legislative history of the residuary provisions in the Government of India Act of 1935, and the scheme of distribution of powers under the Constitution, to reason that the very fact that the provision for amendment of the Constitution was given a special setting in Part XX of the Constitution confirms that the power of amendment was not to be located either in Article 248 or in Entry 97 of the Union List.[31]

On the same footing, the danger of a grave emergent situation threatening the security of the country and the need for protecting every state against internal disturbance was prominently present in the minds of the framers of the Constitution of India. This is evident from the casting of the duty referred to earlier on the Government of India under Article 355 of the Constitution, and from the special setting of provisions in this regard in Part XVIII of the Constitution (Emergency Provisions). Accordingly, the power to enact legislation in respect of internal disturbance could not have been put in the residuary powers of Parliament. Rather, the constitutional scheme confirms that such power to legislate has been expressly granted to Parliament under Article 250 of the Constitution of India, which it may exercise on the invocation of the emergency provisions, but with the safeguards provided therein.

Further, as regards the PIS of J&K with India, the Constitution Bench of the Indian Supreme Court categorically held in *Farooqui*[32] that since Articles 248 and 249 of the Constitution of India had not been applied to the state and Entry 97 of the Union List had been omitted, all residuary powers vested with the state. The Constitution (Application to Jammu and Kashmir) Amendment Order of 1985, issued by the President on 4 June 1985 under Article 370(1) of the Constitution of India, applied Article 248 and Entry 97 of the Union List to the state. In other words, Parliament assumed the residuary power of legislation, which till then, had vested in the state legislature. Since the legality of the repeated recourse to Article 370(1) of the Constitution of India by New Delhi is itself debatable, so would be the applicability to the state of the central legislation, even if one proceeds on the footing that the Supreme Court was correct in locating the power of Parliament to enact such legislation in Article 248 read with Entry 97 of the Union List.

The AFSPA and the TADA were, therefore, patently unconstitutional for the reasons discussed above. The POTA, enacted by the Indian Parliament, suffered from the same infirmities. Further, not only were these draconian enactments ultra vires the Constitution of India, their provisions marked a retrograde departure from civilized criminal jurisprudence. For instance,

Section 4 of the AFSPA empowered any officer of rank, if he was of the opinion that it was necessary to do so for the maintenance of public order, after giving such warning as he considered necessary, to fire upon or otherwise use force even to causing of death, against any person who was acting in contravention of any law or order for the time being in force in the disturbed area, prohibiting the assembly of five or more persons or the carrying of weapons, firearms, ammunition or explosive substances. While granting such licence to kill, it was left to the officer to subjectively opine the necessity to fire or use such force causing death, and to decide the nature of the warning he may choose to give. The minimum requirement of reasonableness or proportionality of use of force was conspicuous by its absence. Dicey writes that officers, magistrates, soldiers and policemen occupy the same position in the eyes of law as ordinary citizens.[33] While the soldier or the policeman is bound to put down breaches of peace, he is authorized to employ only such force as may be necessary for such purpose.[34] The soldier or policeman cannot, as such, be exempted from being made liable under law for his conduct in restoring order, and must be called to account for use of excessive or unnecessary force.[35]

Furthermore, there was an obvious reason for striking down Section 4 of the AFSPA as being unconstitutional. The reason is that Parliament, in enacting Section 4, sought to usurp judicial functions. Surely, the reasonableness, proportionality and quantum of force used in any given circumstance for the purpose of preventing an offence are always questions for the court to decide. It is a judicial function to assess the legality of the action of the officer in question, should he be accused of having acted illegally. If the legislature takes away this function, it would amount to legislative adjudication.

Cooley illustrates the principle of legislative adjudication by pointing out that Parliament lacks the competence to require the courts to sit on trial over the rights of parties without determining the legal sufficiency of evidence, or to prescribe conclusive rules of evidence, as each of these would merely be an indirect method of disposing of controversies.[36] He lists the judicial authorities for the proposition that whether or not the evidence is sufficient to overcome the presumption of innocence of an accused, and to establish his guilt beyond reasonable doubt, is for the determination of the court and not Parliament.[37] It is the job of the courts, and not of Parliament, to determine a controversy on the basis of existing facts, or to dispose of matters affecting the life, liberty or property of citizens.

In *Jiti*,[38] I had the occasion to address the Indian Supreme Court on the implied constitutional limitations imposed upon the Indian Parliament in the exercise of its legislative power. That case related to the constitutional validity of Section 32A of the Narcotic Drugs and Psychotropic Substances Act of 1985 (NDPS Act) which, as construed by the Supreme Court in its decision in *Maktool Singh*,[39] took away the power of the appellate court, pending the appeal of the convict, to suspend the sentence awarded under the NDPS Act, with an exception not relevant to our purpose. The constitutional validity of Section 32A of the NDPS Act was challenged primarily on the ground that Parliament was not competent to take away, by statutory prohibition, the judicial function of the court in the matter of deciding as to whether or not, after the conviction under the NDPS Act, the sentence deserved to be suspended, and also under what circumstances, restrictions or limitations the sentence could be suspended or granted. Given that sentencing was essentially a matter of judicial discretion, and further that, there existed well-settled principles relating to suspension of sentence by the appellate court, it was not open to Parliament to control the action of the appellate court by requiring it not to suspend the sentence under the NDPS Act. Reliance was placed on Cooley's Constitutional Limitations for the proposition that the legislature cannot, directly or indirectly, control the action of the courts or interfere with judicial jurisdiction in such manner so as to take cases out of the settled course of judicial proceedings.[40]

The Supreme Court struck down Section 32A of the NDPS Act as being unconstitutional insofar as it took away the power of the court to suspend the sentence pending the appeal. The Supreme Court held that the 'exercise of judicial discretion on well recognised principle is the safest possible safeguards for the accused which is at the very core of criminal law administered in India' and that the 'Legislature, cannot, therefore, make law to deprive the Courts of their legitimate jurisdiction conferred under procedure established by law'.[41]

The Supreme Court, while upholding the constitutional validity of the AFSPA, failed to appreciate the principle that wherever there is deprivation of life or personal liberty, the cause of such deprivation is required to be inquired into by a judicial officer. The courts cannot, by legislation, be deprived of this power or relieved of this duty.[42] Section 4 of the AFSPA, which deprives the courts of the power to review the reasonableness, proportionality and quantum of force used by security forces in any given circumstance for the purpose of preventing an offence and instead contemplates such power to be exercised subjectively by the security forces, has evidently been enacted without due consideration of the proper boundaries that mark the separation of legislative and judicial duties. After all, it is not legislation, which 'adjudicates in a particular case, prescribes the rule contrary to the general law, and orders it to be enforced'.[43]

As regards the TADA, its stringent provisions had been commented upon and diluted by the Indian Supreme Court itself. Nevertheless, the Supreme Court, in *Kartar Singh* and *Sanjay Dutt*,[44] upheld Section 5 of the TADA, which made the mere unauthorized possession of specified arms and ammunition in a notified area a substantive offence. The person could, therefore, be booked under the TADA, irrespective of his association or communication with terrorist activity. While the majority opinion of the Supreme Court in *Kartar Singh* did not find anything objectionable about Section 5, the minority opinion held that Section 5 may be invoked only if there was some material to show that the person who possessed the arms intended it to be used for terrorist or disruptionist activity, or that it was an arm and ammunition which had, in fact, been used.[45]

The Constitution Bench of the Supreme Court, in *Sanjay Dutt*, took the view that as the Supreme Court had upheld the constitutional validity of the TADA in *Kartar Singh*, it must construe Section 5 to provide that once the prosecution has proved unauthorized conscious possession by the accused of any of the specified arms and ammunition in a notified area, conviction would follow unless the accused rebutted the statutory presumption that the weapon was meant to be used for a terrorist or disruptive act.

This approach of the Supreme Court, in *Kartar Singh* and *Sanjay Dutt*, is again fallacious, since there was nothing for the accused to rebut in Section 5 *at the time* he was arrested by the police under the TADA and put in jail for months, if not years. Mere unauthorized possession of specified arms and ammunition in a notified area was made a substantive offence pertaining to terrorist and disruptionist activity. It may be true that the accused was not justified in possessing the specified arms and ammunitions in a notified area, but then surely, mere unjustified possession did not necessarily mean that a person was a terrorist or a disruptionist. It was simply not possible for an accused to rebut *at the time of arrest* the statutory presumption that the weapon was meant to be used for a terrorist or disruptive act. Any provision of law that deprives the accused of his liberty without giving him, *at the time of such deprivation*, an effective opportunity to defend himself, is on the face of it unconstitutional. This assumes importance when one considers the functioning of the Indian legal system—after all, law cannot be divorced from reality. It is common knowledge that prisoners languish in jails for decades without trial, even under the general law. It is the Indian prisons that make men guilty; they detain them for the commission of one crime, and return them, if returned alive, fitted for the perpetration of thousands. It is also common knowledge that often the police itself implicates innocent persons by planting weapons on them, and that corruption pervades the entire process. How else can one explain reports that indicate that Gujarat, where there had been no terrorist problem in 1994, had the highest number of detenus in 1994 under the TADA—above 19,000.[46]

If the approach of the Supreme Court while examining the constitutional validity of the TADA was surprising, its approach to the subsequent issue of whether the provisions of the TADA would continue to govern pending cases, notwithstanding the lapse of the TADA on 23 May 1995, was incomprehensible.

Application of the TADA after Its Lapse

The Division Bench of the Supreme Court declared in *Abdul Aziz*[47] that the continuation of pending cases under the expired TADA was constitutionally permissible in view of the special saving clause, Section 1(4) of the TADA. That provision inter alia stated that the lapse of the TADA would not affect the previous operation of or anything duly done or suffered under the TADA; any right, privilege, obligation or liability acquired, accrued or incurred under the TADA; any penalty, forfeiture or punishment incurred in respect of any offence under the TADA and any investigation, legal proceeding or remedy in respect of any such right, privilege, obligation, liability, penalty, forfeiture or punishment as aforesaid.

The Supreme Court, in *Abdul Aziz*, held that though it had not specifically considered the constitutional validity of Section 1(4) of the TADA in *Kartar Singh*, it was to be taken as constitutionally valid, since the TADA was in general held to be valid. The Supreme Court rejected the contention that there was discriminatory procedure for trial between persons who had committed the same offence before the expiry of the TADA and those committing it post-TADA. It reasoned that Parliament, by enacting Section 1(4), had made a clear distinction between two classes of offenders—those who had committed offences when the TADA was in force, and those who were not offenders under the TADA as their activities took place after the expiry of the TADA—and that these two classes of persons could not be treated at par.

It is regrettable that the Division Bench of the Supreme Court, in *Abdul Aziz*, overlooked the Constitution Bench decision of the Supreme Court to the contrary in *Lachmandas Kewalram Ahuja*.[48] The Supreme Court, in the latter case, held that there is no vested liability in matters of procedure, and that where there are two procedures prescribed by the law, one of which is harsher or more onerous than the other, the harsher procedure cannot be justified, unless it is based on a reasonable classification having a nexus with the object of the statute.[49] The continuation of the prejudicial and discriminatory procedure, in the absence of any nexus between the basis of the classification and the object of the statute, violates the equality clause of Article 14 of the Constitution of India, and renders the proceedings void under Article 13 thereof. The Supreme Court considered and rejected the classification as 'fanciful' between cases where the offence was being tried under the statute in question before the advent of the Constitution, and cases where the same offence was committed after the advent of the Constitution inasmuch as the same had no reasonable relation to the object sought to be achieved by the statute.[50]

As a result of Section 1(4) of the TADA, there were two procedures relating to the trial of terrorists and disruptionists—one under the onerous and prejudicial lapsed TADA, and another under the ordinary law of the land. The continuation of the TADA provisions with respect to cases pending under the TADA resulted in a classification being made between those who had committed a terrorist or disruptionist act when the TADA was in force, and those who committed a terrorist or disruptionist act after the lapse of the TADA on 23 May 1995. On the application of the ratio of *Lachmandas Kewalram Ahuja*, it becomes evident that such a classification was discriminatory and void under Articles 13 and 14 of the Constitution of India, since it had no nexus with the object of the TADA to prevent and cope with terrorist and disruptionist activities. If terrorist and disruptionist activities required the application of special procedure, there was no obvious reason why it should be applied to persons who had committed a terrorist or disruptionist act before the lapse of the TADA, and not to those who committed such an act after its lapse. The same consideration applies to both categories of cases. Hence, there is no nexus which connected the basis of the supposed classification with the object of the TADA, since the object of the TADA was wide enough to cover both categories of persons.

Moreover, the finding of the Supreme Court in *Abdul Aziz* that the validity of Section 1(4) of the TADA was to be taken as having been upheld in *Kartar Singh* is inconsistent with the elementary proposition of law that a case is an authority only for what it actually decides, and not for what may by implication flow from it. Since the Supreme Court in *Kartar Singh* did not specifically consider the validity of Section 1(4), it is difficult to appreciate how the same could be said to have been upheld by it. In any case, the statutory provisions contained in Section 1(4) of the TADA cannot override the constitutional prohibition of the equality clause contained in Article 14 of the Constitution.

The preceding discussion does point to the existence of a general trend of the Indian Supreme Court to uphold draconian laws empowering New Delhi to crush terrorism. Such a trend, coupled with judicial decisions facilitating the emasculation of Article 370 of the Constitution, indicates a hands-off approach to the Kashmir issue by the otherwise activist court, which does little credit to the Indian Supreme Court as an institution championing the protection of civil liberties and human rights.

Given the judicial sanction accorded to New Delhi to do whatever it deemed fit to contain terrorism, New Delhi has had no qualms in following the policy of 'area clearance'. A few words here about the importance of taking appropriate steps to tackle terrorism would not be out of place.

Addressing Terrorism

Terrorism itself is a controversial term. In *Hitendra Vishnu Thakur*,[51] the Indian Supreme Court noted that while it is not 'possible to give a precise definition of "terrorism" or to lay down what constitutes "terrorism"', it 'may be possible to describe it as use of violence when its most important result is not merely physical and mental damage of the victim but the prolonged psychological effect it produces or has the potential of producing on the society as a whole'.[52]

Terrorism is nothing but an ideology that preaches violence, instead of recourse to legal or other remedies, as a means to realize its ends. More often than not, terrorism gets popular support when the state fails to respond to the basic needs of the people, resulting in deprivations - both real as well as perceived—of political, social and economic rights. Terrorism breeds from a sustained feeling of oppression, injustice and inequality. The magnitude of the crime committed by the terrorist is proportionate to the magnitude of the real or perceived injustice which prompts it.

While it will readily be agreed that the killing of innocent persons by terrorists is an inhuman and dastardly act that deserves condemnation, surely the state is not legally justified in inflicting torture upon persons suspected to be terrorists or harbouring terrorists. Even if the person tortured is in fact a terrorist, a barbaric crime cannot justify a barbaric penalty. Moreover, the terrorist is not wholly a terrorist—he is a terrorist at times. He, too, has his family and loved ones, who relive the trauma and pain inflicted upon him, and they take to terrorism.

It is also important to appreciate that forms of violence triggered by religious, political or ideological considerations have a psychological and sociological aspect attached to them, which makes it impossible to formulate a straitjacket remedy. It is due to this psychological and sociological aspect that it is said that 'wars of subversion are won and lost in the mind'. One man's justice is often another man's injustice. Subjecting religious, political or ideological turmoil to coercive state laws will merely reinforce such violence as well as the conviction that injustice has been, and always will be, meted out.

Indeed, laws do not persuade just because they threaten. If the terrorist views the law as his enemy, he will be an enemy of the law. The terrorist has no hesitation in breaking such law; rather, he reasons that if the law is of such a nature that it requires him to be an agent of 'injustice' to another, then he will happily break the law. Nor will shiny new laws deter the terrorist; he will be just as content to violate the new laws as he was to violate the old ones. After all, the only hope for people crushed by law is to assume power through extra-constitutional means, and those who have much to hope but nothing to lose will readily take recourse to such means. It has been forgotten how important it is for the state to have laws that give the masses a way to express their displeasure, because if this is not provided, the masses will resort to illegal methods, which will produce much worse effects. New Delhi has failed to address these aspects of terrorism in the territory of the PIS of J&K with India, or for that matter, in other parts of the country.

New Delhi's policy of 'area clearance', facilitated by the erosion of Article 370 of the Constitution of India and draconian penal laws, has been a knee-jerk response to the extremely volatile situation in the territory of the PIS of J&K with India. The policy and laws aim at strengthening the hands of the Indian State and its security forces by conferring extraordinary and coercive powers upon them. Militancy in the state has been seen merely as a law and order situation, which must be handled with a stern hand by enacting stricter laws. The roots of disaffection are simply ignored. The Indian security forces, clueless about the roots of the violence in the state, have no option but to carry out the directives of their political masters to contain the violence, resulting in blatant human rights violations. Terrorism is directly linked with human rights at different levels. At one level, it is the human rights of the victims of terrorism that are violated—be they innocent civilians or security personnel. At another level, when the state chooses to imitate the terrorist by responding with state terrorism, the violations are of the human rights of the terrorist and of the innocent persons who are unfortunate enough to get in the way. In other words, inept handling of terrorism by the state gives rise to further serious human rights abuses.

In order to regain moral authority in the state, New Delhi must engage with the Kashmiri populace to explain how it has not acted unfairly by not holding a referendum or plebiscite, and that no 'right to self-determination' was promised or could have been promised in the Instrument of Accession of 26 October 1947 executed by Raja Hari Singh. New Delhi must reach out to the people in the territory of the PIS of J&K occupied by Pakistan and China, to remind them that such territory is very much a part of the Union of India and that the residents of such territory are legally and constitutionally citizens of India.

New Delhi must aim to respect the constitutional autonomy guaranteed to the state and to revoke its encroachment upon the state's jurisdiction. It is imperative for New Delhi to ensure that the governance, policy as also the laws in operation in the state conform to the constitutional and moral values underlying the Constitution of India, both in spirit and in letter. Experience suggests that laws that do not embody public opinion can never be effective; rather, they are counterproductive. New Delhi must accept that laws have to find their roots in the acceptance by the people, and should, accordingly, repeal all laws that have the effect of alienating the people from the Indian State. After all, as Nehru himself pointed out in his speech in the Indian Parliament on 7 August 1952 that:[53]

> We do not want to win people against their will and with the help of armed forces…. Because the strongest bonds that bind will not be bond of your armies or even of your Constitution…but bonds which are stronger than the Constitution and laws and armies—bonds that bind through love and affection and understanding of various peoples….

New Delhi must, therefore, revisit the manner in which it has dealt with the PIS of J&K with India from 1947 onwards. In the ultimate analysis, it is the national character of the Indian State, and of the men and women who run it, which will be decisive of the issue as to whether New Delhi can regain moral authority in the PIS of J&K.

Notes and References

1. Malik, Ashok. 2000. 'Trade Against Terror', *India Today*, 9 October. Delhi: Living Media Ltd.
2. *Supra* Note 34, Chapter IV, p. 6.
3. Singh, Gurcharan. 1995. 'State terrorism and Human Rights', in Sehgal B. P. Singh, *Global Terrorism: Socio-Politico and Legal Dimensions*, p. 178. New Delhi: Deep & Deep Publications.
4. *D.K. Basu v State of West Bengal:* AIR 1997 SC 610.
5. Ibid., p. 622.

6. Ibid., pp. 615, 618, 619.
7. *Mian Bashir Ahmad v State*: AIR 1982 J&K 26.
8. Ibid., p. 86.
9. *Master Sewanath v Faqir Chand*: AIR 1965 J&K 62.
10. Similarly, the 'reasonable restrictions' that could be imposed by the state on the exercise of the fundamental freedoms contained in Article 19 of the *Constitution of India*, as applied to the state by Para 4(d)(iii) of the 1954 Order, were qualified by inserting a clause (7) to Article 19 to the effect that the words 'reasonable restriction' 'shall be construed as meaning such restrictions as the appropriate Legislature deems reasonable'. In other words, it was not open to the citizens to challenge the reasonableness of any restriction imposed by the state, thereby rendering the fundamental rights toothless. In *Galodhu v Nanak Chand* (AIR 1955 J&K 25), the Full Bench of the Jammu and Kashmir High Court held that in view of the provisions of Article 19 (7) as applied to the state, the Court had no power to even examine the restrictions, which were imposed by the *Right to Prior Purchase Act of 1936*, on the right to acquire, hold and dispose of property in the state, to find out whether or not they were reasonable.
11. *P. L. Lakhanpal v State of Jammu and Kashmir*: (1955) 2 SCR 1101; *Abdul Ghani v State of Jammu and Kashmir*: AIR 1971 SC 1217.
12. For instance, see *Mohd. Sabir v State of Jammu and Kashmir*: AIR 1971 SC 1713.
13. *Mohamad Subhan v State*: AIR 1956 J&K 1.
14. For instance, *Avatar Singh v State of Jammu and Kashmir*: AIR 1985 SC 581. In *Jaya Mala v Home Secy, Govt. of Jammu and Kashmir:* AIR 1982 SC 1297.
15. For instance, *Chaju Ram v State of Jammu and Kashmir*: AIR 1971 SC 263.
16. *Kartar Singh v State of Punjab*: (1994) 3 SCC 569.
17. Ibid., pp. 648–649.
18. *Naga People's Movement of Human Rights v Union of India*: AIR 1998 SC 431.
19. *Supra* Note 16, pp. 633–634.
20. Ibid.
21. Ibid., pp. 629–630.
22. Ibid., p. 635.
23. *Supra* Note 27, Chapter IV.
24. Ibid., p. 1782.
25. *Indira Gandhi v Raj Narain*: AIR 1975 SC 2299.
26. Ibid., p. 2446.
27. *Supra* Note 16.
28. Hingorani, Aman. 1995. 'TADA is not constitutional; strike it down', *The Indian Express*, New Delhi, 27 February.
29. *Supra* Note 27, Chapter IV.
30. Ibid., p. 1614.
31. Ibid., p. 1782.
32. *State of Jammu and Kashmir v Farooqui*: AIR 1972 SC 1738.
33. Dicey, A.V. 1914. 'Introduction to the Study of the Law of the Constitution'. Available online at http://www.constitution.org/cmt/avd/law_con.htm (downloaded on 15 November 2015).
34. Ibid.
35. Ibid.
36. See Cooley, T.M. 1931. *The General Principles of Constitutional Law in the United States of America*, pp. 49–50. Boston: Little, Brown, and Company.

37. Ibid.
38. *Jiti v Union of India* (Writ Petition (Criminal) No. 243/1999) tagged to *Dadu v State of Maharashtra* (Writ Petition (Criminal) No. 169/1999): AIR 2000 SC 3203.
39. *Maktool Singh v State of Punjab*: JT 1999 (2) SC 176.
40. Cooley, T.M. 1927. *A Treatise on Constitutional Limitations*, pp. 206-207. Boston: Little, Brown and Company.
41. *Supra* Note 38, p. 3210.
42. *Supra* Note 36, p. 185.
43. Ibid., p. 184.
44. *Sanjay Dutt v State of Maharashtra*: JT 1994 (4) SC 540.
45. *Supra* Note 16, p. 760.
46. See Verma, Neelam. 1994. 'Unlawful law', *Rashtriya Sahara*, October, p. 13, New Delhi.
47. *Abdul Aziz v State of West Bengal*: AIR 1996 SC 3305.
48. *Lachmandas Kewalram Ahuja v State of Bombay*: 1952 SCR 710.
49. Ibid., pp. 731–734.
50. Ibid., pp. 733–734.
51. *Hitendra Vishnu Thakur v State of Maharashtra*: AIR 1994 SC 2623.
52. Ibid., pp. 2629–2630.
53. Extracted in *Supra* Note 12, Chapter IV, p. 25.

Epilogue

This book challenges the current discourse on the Kashmir issue, both nationally and internationally. The partition of the Indian subcontinent and the Kashmir issue were perhaps amongst the earliest manifestations of the Cold War that was soon to begin. The book details how Britain ruthlessly pursued its policy to communalize and then divide the Indian subcontinent in order to create a friendly state in the north-western region of colonial India, 'Pakistan', that would help check the spread of Soviet influence in the oil-rich Middle East and satisfy British political, strategic and defence interests. Since the north-western region of colonial India crucial for Britain's Great Game was predominantly Muslim, the British stoked religious frenzy to portray that the partition was a necessity to accommodate the differences between Hindus and Muslims. Britain, therefore, must shoulder the responsibility for its policies; for the generations of dismembered lives and the innocent blood that flowed in the subcontinent, as also for the new breed of international terrorism that exists today. Indeed, as Sarila points out:[1]

> The successful use of religion by the British in India to gain political and strategic objectives was replicated by the Americans in Afghanistan in the 1980s by building up the Islamic jihadis, all for the same purpose of keeping the Soviet communities at bay. The Muslim League's 'direct action' before partition in India was the forerunner of the jihad in Afghanistan. However, Al Qaida's attacks on the World Trade Center towers in New York and the Pentagon in Washington on 11 September 2001 woke up the West to the dangers of encouraging political Islam.... It was the Pakistan Government that, through the Jamaat-i-Islami, Pakistan, and their intelligence service, the ISI, created the Taliban movement in Afghanistan. The preachings of the Jamaat's founder, Abdul Al Mawdudi, a migrant from India, envisaged a clash of civilization and governments founded *strictly* on the tenets of the Shariat; he counseled jihad against non-believers. These views found an echo in many Muslim lands; they influenced Osama bin Laden. Even after the US-backed jihad in Afghanistan had succeeded, Pakistan continued to

help the Taliban train terrorists to fight non-believers in the name of Allah. Without Pakistan's backing, it is doubtful whether Islamic terror could have spread so far and wide in the world, despite Osama bin Laden, Saudi and Gulf petro dollars and Arab suicide bombers. The Americans are now taking steps to rein in the export of terror from Pakistan. But the genie has escaped the bottle. Some of the roots of the present Islamic terrorism menacing the world surely lie buried in the partition of India.

In the process, it is the people of the subcontinent who have been taken for a ride. The leadership in India and Pakistan cannot escape blame either, for letting Britain get away with its ruthless policies. Unfortunately, New Delhi has had a propensity to act against India's interests right from 1947. When Raja Hari Singh, the sovereign ruler of the PIS of J&K, unconditionally acceded to the dominion of India in the manner prescribed under the British statutes, namely, the Indian Independence Act, 1947, read with the Government of India Act, 1935, as amended, New Delhi 'pledged' to the world that it will regard it to be 'purely provisional' and subject to the 'reference to the people' who would 'settle' the accession. When Pakistan-sponsored tribals invaded the state in 1947, New Delhi invited the UNSC, at the instance of the British, to intervene, thereby ensuring that Pakistan got to retain the areas that it had already occupied before the ceasefire. Such a situation satisfied British interests, but has till date compromised India's geopolitical interests. After all, India lost direct territorial contact with Afghanistan, while Pakistan and China could conceive the China–Pakistan Economic Corridor through what is constitutionally and legally Indian territory.

When the UNSC, then virtually run by the British and the Americans, shifted the focus from aggression to plebiscite in the PIS of J&K, New Delhi ought to have admitted that its stand of introducing the 'wishes of the people' as the deciding factor to settle the accession was legally misconceived. New Delhi ought to have reasoned that in view of the same British law—which was binding on the British and that gave birth to Pakistan and had been accepted by Pakistan—the accession of the state to the dominion of India was valid and complete; and that the very presence of Pakistan in the state constituted aggression. Instead, New Delhi reiterated its 'pledge' on the floor of the UN that the accession of the state to the dominion of India by its sovereign ruler be further determined by holding a UN-supervised plebiscite. New Delhi, thus, facilitated the taking of the Kashmir issue out of the domestic jurisdiction of India and conferring upon each member of the UN a standing in the matter to further its own national, economic and geo-strategic interests. New Delhi itself created doubts about the future of the state, and thereby permitted the UN and its member states, notably Pakistan, to argue that it was 'disputed territory'. New Delhi continued to cling to its 'pledge' of holding a plebiscite in the state; hence, when the state Constituent Assembly was established, as envisaged in Article 370 of India's own Constitution, New Delhi was compelled to distance itself from such an Assembly as also its resolutions to the effect that the state has been and will remain an integral part of India.

New Delhi had, by then, realized the virtues of keeping away from the intervention of the UNSC, but it was too late—the UNSC had tied India's hands from recovering a substantial portion of the state, and its people, who continued to remain under foreign rule. And so, New Delhi took the easy way out—it simply disowned that part of the state and its unfortunate people, who happen to be citizens of India under the Constitution of India. Having been compelled by the UNSC to respect the ceasefire line and to helplessly watch Pakistan consolidate its control over the territory of the state illegally under its occupation, New Delhi now decided that the UNSC had nothing to do with state, and that the Kashmir issue must be resolved bilaterally with Pakistan in terms of the Simla Agreement of 1972 and the Lahore Declaration of 1999, thereby reiterating that at least Pakistan has a standing in the matter other than as an aggressor.

New Delhi kept quiet at the happenings in the part of the state occupied by Pakistan; it simply ignored the territory of the state held by China. New Delhi emphasized the 'inviolability' of the LOC at every conceivable occasion. It aimed at territorial status quo, even though New Delhi lacks competence to cede national territory under the Constitution of India. And when the Indian forces reclaimed part of the territory of the state during the Indo-Pakistan wars, New Delhi actually handed back such territory to Pakistan.

The compulsions of New Delhi's legally misconceived stand made it defensive on the Kashmir issue. New Delhi somehow forgot that it was the one who took the Kashmir issue to the UN. New Delhi first internationalized the Kashmir problem; it then abhorred such internationalization. New Delhi has, over the decades, let Pakistan set the agenda and has been reactive to its arguments. New Delhi has let Pakistan fashion the Kashmir issue in terms of 'the right to self-determination', 'violation of human rights' and 'nuclear flashpoint in South Asia'. New Delhi now jumps with joy at the slightest indication of a country endorsing the Kashmir issue to be a 'bilateral' one; it terms it as a major diplomatic victory. All of New Delhi's energies have been frittered away in seeking to check the 'internationalization' of the Kashmir problem, and at considerable national cost. New Delhi even now does not realize that it is only the international community that can pressurize Pakistan to vacate its aggression and to stop cross-border terrorism.

The book further discloses that if New Delhi's flair for bungling is bad news, the good news is that Pakistan's leaders are even more myopic than those of India. There was no certainty that the PIS of J&K would have acceded to India in 1947. It was the Pakistan-sponsored tribal invasion of the state in 1947 that helped the Raja make up his mind. Having successfully turned the tables on India in the UNSC with the indulgent backing of the West, Pakistan could have legalized its occupation of the areas of the state under its control, which New Delhi seemed more than willing to disown. That way, Pakistan could at least have got a substantial portion of the state, whereas in law it was entitled to nothing. Yet, Pakistan insists till date on the holding of a plebiscite in terms of the UN Resolutions and seeks to internationalize the Kashmir issue. Surely Pakistan cannot be unaware that its attempt to internationalize the Kashmir problem would work to its detriment—since, along with any 'engagement' or 'obligation' of India to hold a plebiscite in the state, Pakistan's failure to vacate the territories of the state under its occupation as required by the UN Resolutions, as well as its illegal cession of territory to China and its role in sponsoring cross-border terrorism, would also be highlighted. Surely, Pakistan cannot but realise that should a plebiscite be held, it is improbable that Jammu and Ladakh would choose Pakistan over India; even Kashmiri Muslims are averse to acceding to Pakistan. Given the inhuman conditions reported in the territory of the state under the occupation of Pakistan and the popular uprising there against Pakistani rule, it is hardly likely that even the people of such territory would want to accede to Pakistan.

By hard bilateral negotiations under the Simla Agreement and the Lahore Declaration, Pakistan could have still wheedled a good deal out of India, not least because New Delhi is still struggling to understand the implications of its actions. Yet, Pakistan insists on calling upon the international community to intervene in the Kashmir issue, forgetting that its own actions, if put under the scrutiny of an international body, particularly of a judicial body like the ICJ, will invite censure for committing aggression and then compounding it by terrorism.

This book has suggested that the solution to the Kashmir problem should, in the first instance, be located in law, and that this is, perhaps, the only option available to comprehensively resolve the issue, more so in light of the ground realities in the state and the inadequacies of other solutions proposed to resolve the Kashmir issue. The mere declaration by New Delhi ad nauseam that the state became an integral part of India in 1947 will not suffice to convince the world, and certainly not Pakistan or the people of the state, about the merits of India's case. If New Delhi wishes to resolve the Kashmir issue, it will have to do something more than to simply disown the territory of the state under occupation of Pakistan and China, and the Indian citizens residing there. And one such measure would be to call upon the ICJ to confirm, and the word confirm is used here deliberately, that on the lapse of British paramountcy on 15 August 1947, the sovereign rulers of the princely Indian states were the sole repositories of power to offer accession to either of the dominions of India or Pakistan under the Indian Independence Act of 1947, and the Government of India Act of 1935, as amended; that 'the wishes of the people' of a princely Indian state were alien to the question of accession of a princely Indian state to either of the dominions of India or Pakistan; that the accession by the sovereign ruler of the PIS of J&K to the dominion of India in 1947 was legally valid, final, complete and irrevocable; that the dominion of India was not competent to propound and accept, whether in the UN or outside, that the accession of the PIS of J&K to the dominion of India by its sovereign ruler be further determined by the 'wishes of the people' ascertained by a plebiscite or referendum; that the UN, and every state, including Pakistan, 'contracting' with India are held to have had the knowledge that representatives of the dominion of India exceeded their powers under the said Acts by wishing or pledging to hold a plebiscite in the PIS of J&K to settle the question of accession, and, that too, in the absence of its sovereign ruler; that the UN and the international community cannot compel the giving of effect to an 'international obligation' contained in the UN Resolutions on the PIS of J&K which is inconsistent with the said Acts or the Instrument of Accession executed under the said Acts; that the dominion of Pakistan had no locus standi to impugn the accession by the sovereign ruler of the PIS of J&K to the dominion of India in 1947; that Pakistan and China have no legal right to be in possession and control of the territory of the PIS of J&K presently occupied by them, and nor is Pakistan competent to negotiate and give away a part of such territory, being Indian territory, to China.

Should India succeed in a reference limited to these propositions, the UN and the world community will have no option but to condemn Pakistan as the aggressor, to put an end to the illegal situation by requiring Pakistan to vacate the aggression in the state and to refrain from cross-border terrorism, and from even professing 'support' to the jihadis in the state. China, too, will have no choice but to vacate the territory of the state occupied by it. Further, should India fail in its reference, it does not follow that the territory which comprises the PIS of J&K with India would automatically go to Pakistan. Rather, New Delhi would simply fall back on its current position, that is, the 'wishes of the people' have already been ascertained through the state Constituent Assembly and reflected in the Constitution of Jammu and Kashmir of 1957.

The legal reference to the ICJ would not, however, by itself suffice to resolve the Kashmir issue. Should New Delhi obtain a favourable result in the reference, it will still need to generate the international and national political will to give effect to it. In order to regain moral authority in the state, New Delhi must be able to put forward a cogent case before the people of the state that the 'wishes of the people' were completely irrelevant to the question of accession; therefore, by failing to hold a plebiscite in the state, New Delhi has not been unjust to them. New Delhi must remind the international community and, more importantly, the people of the state that the residents of the territory of the state held by Pakistan and China are legally and constitutionally citizens of India. New Delhi must realize that the historical, psychological, political and sociological aspects of the militancy in the PIS of J&K set it apart from militancy anywhere else in the world. The obsession of Pakistan with acquiring the state adds an angle unknown to history. New Delhi must re-examine how it has treated the state since 1947, and to make amends, New Delhi must subscribe to the rule of law in the state, aim to restore the sanctity of Article 370 of the Constitution of India and revise its approach towards conflict resolution. It is thus necessary for India to change the international and national political discourse on the Kashmir issue.

A few words here about the UN would be relevant. The role of the UNSC in the Kashmir question raises doubts as to whether the UN can, with credibility, even claim to be an organization committed to world peace. The persistent, unabashed and reckless refusal of the UNSC to act in accordance with the UN Charter and settled principles of international law is as much responsible for the continuance of the Kashmir problem since 1947 as are the acts and omissions of the leadership in Britain, India and Pakistan. Instead of insisting on Pakistan vacating its aggression, it legitimized the illegal occupation by Pakistan and thereafter, by China, of the territory of the PIS of J&K. It even looked the other way when the Pakistan-sponsored tribal invasion in 1947 was followed by the sending of regular Pakistan troops into the state on 8 May 1948. That the UNSC was fully aware of the implication of merely enforcing a ceasefire, without first requiring the aggression to be vacated, can be culled out from the passionate plea made in 1971 by China, on behalf of Pakistan, against India's 'aggression' in East Pakistan, now Bangladesh. This is what Huang Hua (China) had to say:[2]

An argument has been raised to the effect that a request can first be made for a cease-fire by both India and Pakistan, and the cessation of all military actions, although the question of withdrawal of military forces can be deferred to a later date. That is an argument to which we definitely cannot agree, because the present objective situation is that the Indian Government has brazenly carried out subversion and aggression against Pakistan and has flagrantly sent troops to invade [East] Pakistan territory. In these circumstances, the key to the realization of peace and security on the sub-continent is that the Indian Government's subversion and aggression must be immediately stopped. Indian troops must withdraw from Pakistan territory immediately, unconditionally and completely.

The demand for only a cease-fire in place by two sides, without a demand for withdrawal of Indian troops, is in effect tantamount to conniving at and encouraging aggression and to recognizing the Indian aggressor troops remaining in Pakistan territory as legal. To do so would be of no help whatsoever to the settlement of the arms conflict between India and Pakistan or relaxation of tension in that area. On the contrary, it would bring extremely grave and dangerous results… have not the resolutions passed by the United Nations on the question of the Middle East, which failed to demand the immediate withdrawal of the Israeli aggressor troops from Arab territory but only called for a cease-fire in place, resulted in legalizing the fruits of aggression and imposing them on the Arab countries and people and in creating in the Middle East the danger of aggression and war on a still larger scale?

Such enlightened view in the context of East Pakistan, now Bangladesh, indicts the UNSC and the international community in general for conniving in, and encouraging, aggression by Pakistan in the PIS of J&K; for legalizing the fruits of aggression and imposing them upon the people of the state and upon India. The UNSC is just as responsible as Pakistan and Britain for the devastating turmoil on the Indian subcontinent, as also for the rise of international terrorism today.

Ironically, the strongest words against the UNSC have perhaps been used by Pakistan itself in 1971. New Delhi had, by then, secured Soviet support, which vetoed the UNSC Resolutions on India's role in East Pakistan, now Bangladesh. Zulfikar Ali Bhutto accused the UN of having 'betrayed' Pakistan[3] and lamented before the UNSC about 'the farce and the fraud of the United Nations' and 'the impotence and incapacity of the Security Council and the General Assembly'.[4] Having denounced the UNSC for having 'excelled in the art of filibustering' and having 'failed miserably, shamefully', Bhutto declared that he found it 'disgraceful to [his] person and to [his] country to remain [there] a moment longer than [was] necessary'.[5]

The member states seemed to know perfectly well where the problem lay. Jamil Baroody of Saudi Arabia pointed out that:[6]

> The responsibility for such a sad state of affairs may be attributed to the violations of the purposes and principles of the Charter by the permanent members of the Security Council, who cannot divest themselves of the habit of invariably placing their national interests first and foremost, without due regard to whether the position they often assume serves the cause of peace and justice.... Should we therefore amend the Charter and eliminate the Security Council.... it is you here, gentlemen, who are supposed to declare yourselves on questions of peace and security. I have been here for 26 years and with one or two exceptions— when perhaps you were fortunate because circumstances between the parties concerned turned out to be favourable to their coming to an agreement—you have accomplished nothing in the Council. That is the truth....

And these outbursts, perhaps, also reveal the truth about the Kashmir affair at the UN. It is, therefore, the UN and the international community as a whole, along with the leadership in Britain, India, Pakistan, China and the PIS of J&K as also the terrorist outfits, who share the blame for the trans-generational massacres, bloodshed, trauma, misery and pain of innocents in the territory that comprises that state.

This book comes at a crucial juncture when New Delhi is seeking to engage elements in Islamabad, the state's political groups and the militant outfits to resolve the Kashmir issue, and China is seeking to expand its presence in the part of the state held by Pakistan and in the entire region. At such a time, when there seems a real possibility of New Delhi initiating a dialogue to resolve the deadlocked Kashmir issue, this book suggests what that dialogue should be. The proposed way forward to unravel the Kashmir knot is certainly worth a try and, if successful, could bring lasting peace to the Indian subcontinent, and perhaps closure to the trauma of its partition.

Notes and References

1. *Supra* Note 6, Chapter I, p. 415.
2. S/PV 1607, p. 7, Huang Hua (China), 5 December 1971.
3. S/PV 1611, p. 17, Z.A. Bhutto (Pakistan), 12 December 1971.
4. S/PV 1614, pp. 6–10, Z.A. Bhutto (Pakistan), 14/15 December 1971.
5. Ibid.
6. S/PV 1616, pp. 2–3, Jamil Baroody (Saudi Arabia), 16 December 1971.

About the Author

Aman M. Hingorani is a lawyer and mediator in the Supreme Court of India and the High Court of Delhi. Dr Hingorani has also acted as an arbitrator and as adjunct faculty to teach law students and run training courses for young law teachers. He has taught in programmes at various institutions in India (including National Judicial Academy, Bhopal; Campus Law Centre, University of Delhi; Indian Law Institute, New Delhi) and abroad (including Keble College, University of Oxford, UK; Law School, Warwick University, UK; South Asian Institute of Advanced Legal and Human Rights Studies, Dhaka, Bangladesh). He has prepared curriculum for law courses and other activities, such as the modules for the Indo-British Project on Advocacy Skills Training, British Council, New Delhi; the alternative dispute resolution (ADR) preparatory material for the All-India Bar Examination conducted annually by the Bar Council of India; and the ADR Manual for the Federation of Indian Chambers of Commerce and Industry as its National Consultant.